THE TRANSMISSION OF DOUBT

THE TRANSMISSION OF DOUBT

Talks and Essays on the Transcendence of
Scientific Materialism through Radical Understanding

DA FREE JOHN

Compiled and Edited with an Introduction
and Commentary by Georg Feuerstein

THE DAWN HORSE PRESS
CLEARLAKE, CALIFORNIA

12\11

First Edition April 1984
Printed in the United States of America
International Standard Book Number: paper 0-913922-77-3
Library of Congress Catalog Card Number: 83-73638

Produced by The Johannine Daist Communion
in cooperation with The Dawn Horse Press

About the cover: The cover portrays a contemporary version of the Greek Trojan horse. This metallic marvel suggests the appeal of science and technology that lured Man into the trap of materialism. The resulting spiritual decay can be clearly witnessed in any modern Troy as our civilization is besieged by the doubting mood of scientism.

Excerpts from *Mysticism and the New Physics* by Michael Talbot, reprinted by permission of Bantam Books, Inc. Copyright © 1981 by Michael Talbot. All rights reserved.

CONTENTS

EPILOGUE

FOREWORD

by Fred Alan Wolf, Ph.D.

Fred Alan Wolf, author of Taking the Quantum Leap, *is a former professor of physics at San Diego State University*

No doubt about it, we are living in a time of transition. Today, we are beginning to realize that human and therefore inevitably all consciousness is itself capable of undergoing a radical evolution. And thus it is quite timely that *The Transmission of Doubt* appears. The originator of this volume is uniquely qualified to say and write what he does at this time. He has managed to tunnel through (a quantum-physical tunneling-through, not a classical-physical hurdling-over) a barrier that has been erected and strengthened, albeit for the "right" reasons, by the Western-Industrial-Academic-Scientific establishment to "make our lives better." The barrier that Master Da Free John points to, from the vantage point of one who has "quantum-physically" tunneled through and erected a signpost on the other side for all to see and understand, is the human ego.

According to the "dogma" of traditional science the universe is dead. Life arises through the setting in motion of all that has occurred, is occurring, and will occur from some central "point" in spacetime, back in time to the "Big Bang." Evolution is mechanics arising from and out of that impossibly-difficult-to-imagine earlier aeon. Thus, all life is fundamentally dead. When we die, that's it. Science as a tradition studies the physical domain of the universe and claims that all that is is physical and therefore dead.

Yes, psychologists exist. But they too are victims of the establishmentarian viewpoint. So, too, the psyche is physical and dead.

Master Da Free John asks us to consider the universe as a psycho-physical whole. It is simultaneously mechanical and living. From my view of modern science or the "new physics" called quantum mechanics, Master Da Free John's Teaching rings remarkably true. According to this view, the living observer is not passive and dead but active and participatory and always disturbing, in a non-causal manner, the mechanisms of purely physical phenomena. In other words, purely physical phenomena do not exist separate from the observer.

Thus, the ego or the artificial barrier that separates that "internal sense of I-ness" from all the rest of the processes going on in the whole, total, impossibly vast, all-time-pervading, light-like expansive YOU–NIVERSE is, in spite of its overwhelming power of submission, an illusion, which traditional science has managed to maintain erect through its adherence to the falsifiable lie that the universe is rationally dead and mechanical.

Master Da Free John puts down hard traditional science. Yet, this criticism is not to be taken as scientific phobia. It is more a "wake-up call" to those who are on the "edge of our time," able to realize that a transition to God-Realization as the (yours and mine) only true Condition existing both beyond and within the barriers of spacetime is occurring NOW. The simple recognition of this fact of existence alters radically the human condition and allows the mechanics of self-contraction through fear (which is the ego) to be witnessed in each and every one of us by each and every one of us.

Thus, the "wake-up" call is loudest for the rationally trained minds amongst us. The Adept's argument is radical, logical, pervasive, coherent, and certainly consistent with my view of the new physics. It even offers the chance of further scientific enquiry—a new physics of the Spirit is within our grasp now.

Of course, doubt is likely to arise in the rationally inclined reader. It certainly arose in me when I first became acquainted with Master Da Free John's Teaching. Doubt is a universal process which arises naturally through the quantum processes of the Principle of Indeterminism (as first put forward by physicist Werner Heisenberg in 1927), or as it is sometimes called, the Uncertainty Principle. Read on anyway. This is no usual religious espousal. As intellectual as you are you will find Master Da Free John's arguments compelling.

The Adept Da Free John invites us to be as intelligent as we are capable of being. He calls this "supreme intelligence." He points out that the ego and the scientific mind also want to serve humanity by conforming to reality. But the reality that ego and science conform to is a false reality. This illusion of reality is conceived through "self-abstraction and the objectification of existence," which arises from the desire of non-participation (let Johnny do it, I'm too tired) or self-contraction (which makes us all too tired because it takes up so much of our energy and time to maintain our egoic masks).

In chapter 9, "Philosophy Is a Stress-Based Activity," Master Da Free John speaks about control and our lack, or illusion of abundance, of it. This "control" (which arises from the concept of "counter-roll" or stopping the rolling motion of an object by one's devisal means) appears to us as "real." We talk about self-control, will power, body dexterity, etc., and dream of machines that are our willing slaves "under our control." According to quantum physics such control is clearly impossible at the most fundamental level of atomic and subatomic existence. Thus it is that the desire for more and more control must end in unhappiness and further feelings of defeat, fear, and narcissism.

Even the simple realization that we are truly incapable of controlling anything will help us to realize that that desire for control is a trap. This in itself may not awaken us to our true Condition, but it will at least appear to the sleeplike dream we all walk in as a clarion call. The universe demands egos. We have responded to that demand by worshipping them, elevating them to impossible heights of illusion supported by traditional Western thinking and rational thought all over both hemispheres.

Master Da Free John is not on an "ego-trip." Careful consideration will reveal that the ego that may be felt to arise while reading his writings is none other than the reader's. Master Da Free John is inviting us to enter the disposition of God-Realization in the "seventh stage of life," the highest Realization of humankind according to the Way of Radical Understanding as taught by him. It is then, as he puts it, that his "real Work in life begins." For, Enlightenment or God-Realization is only the beginning of the whole spiritual adventure.

I invite you to consider this profound man's wisdom, to awaken with me to his clarion call, to revitalize the enquiry into science which will once and for all end the "transmission of doubt."

Certainty, Doubt, and Ecstasy

Conventional certainty is a selfish pretense, always based on limited experience.

Conventional uncertainty, or chronic doubt, is a selfish presumption, always based on limited understanding.

Ecstasy is the only and selfless absolute, based on the transcendence of limited experience and conventional or limited understanding while yet being itself the basis for unlimited experience and unlimited understanding.

Da Free John
Scientific Proof of the Existence of
God Will Soon Be Announced
by the White House! *p. 25*

SCIENCE AND TRANSCENDENTAL REALIZATION

by Georg Feuerstein

1. The Crisis of Modern Civilization

Human civilization is like a mighty river, composed of countless branches, currents, pools, stagnant waters (the cultural failures), and numerous tributaries. It leisurely meanders through space and time, until it meets with massive resistance—the great natural and man-made crises—then having to force its way through perilous, narrow ravines and cascade down sheer precipices, to gather in wild torrents below, until its path begins to even out and run smoothly once again. It inexorably presses on toward the ocean—the emergent global culture of the twentieth century. But unlike its counterparts in Nature, the river of human civilization, though ocean-bound, does not inevitably merge into the sea. Rather, it is still in the process of shaping its riverbed: The unitary world culture of which peace-lovers and visionaries dream is no predetermined destiny. Its creation is entirely dependent on conscious cooperation, well-grounded in just those sentiments, attitudes, and moral values that are exceedingly rare among today's cultural leaders.

In fact, our civilizational river is currently passing through a particularly difficult and treacherous terrain, which is perhaps best described as a kind of moral or cosmological no-man's-land. This awesome landscape has been vividly portrayed by Radhakamal Mukerjee:

> *Modern man is a chronic victim of conflict, contradiction and frustration of basic urges and satisfactions. The major profound and inescapable discords between his normal, personal, emotional demands and social pressures and expectances now cover all dimensions or orders of human adjustment and wish-fulfillment, so that the face of our entire civilization bears an indelible neurotic stamp.... Everything from food, sex, income and leisure to consumption, recreation and adventure is given a wrong neurotic twist.... There is an inordinate, general striving for power, prestige and possessions, with a premium on appropriative and aggressive drives, as providing security through the fortification of one's viable position and status rather than through love, sharing and affection. ... Civilized man has now lost the spiritual support of the familiar symbols, metaphors, and myths of ancient folk culture that had dealt with his psychic tensions and conflicts and given him emotional poise and security.... A pathological self-image underlies the wholesale distortion and perversion of social behaviour patterns, institutions, morals, values and symbols.... The irrational, disintegrative myths, phantasies and propaganda of mass culture, indeed, give significant expressions to an emergent barbarism. ... Everywhere the outer-directedness, discontinuity and pseudo-personalization produce monotony, indifference and boredom, and prevent authentic experience and swallow up the individuality of genuine personalities. Gregariousness of the ant and bee type becomes an obsession with its high psychological and spiritual costs of the neglect of solitude and contemplation and of autonomous growth and enrichment of personality.*[1]

Mukerjee is by no means alone in his trenchant criticism of our contemporary civilization. His voice is one among a growing chorus whose combined vocalization will, hopefully, prove strong enough to effect incisive changes before it is drowned by the deafening cacophony of civilizational collapse. The cartographic sketch that Mukerjee prepared of our present-day civilization is mainly from the perspective of social philosophy and psychology. It can be rounded out by the

---

1. R. Mukerjee, *The Sickness of Civilization* (Bombay: Allied Publishers, 1964), pp. 82–93.

astute observations and considerations of hundreds of other renowned
scientists, artists, educators, statesmen, and religious leaders.

One of the scholars who perhaps has best understood the real
nature of the present crisis of mankind and its root causes is the Swiss
cultural philosopher Jean Gebser. In the preface to his voluminous
major work *Ursprung und Gegenwart*,[2] he impressed on the reader
that the crisis he was speaking about was not merely a moral,
economic, ideological, political, or religious crisis, but something far
more fundamental: the death throes of the old rational consciousness
and the birth pains of the new integral consciousness—a major
mutation comparable to that which catapulted Homeric Man into the
world of Socrates, Plato, and Aristotle. For Gebser, the "integral" or
"aperspectival" consciousness meant the actualization of the Whole,
by which the Origin is rendered transparent in the present.

Thus, our modern crisis concerns Man's total being in its
relationship to the world but also to the Transcendental Reality, not as
an abstract, other-worldly goal but as the Process of Life in every
moment.

Gebser, who first formulated his ideas in the thirties, shared his
inspired vision with the Indian philosopher-sage Aurobindo Ghose[3]
and the French paleontologist-theologian Pierre Teilhard de Chardin.[4]
The torch that was lit by these three pioneers, simultaneously but
apparently independent of each other, is now burning bright among
the present generation of "new consciousness" thinkers. Even though
Gebser was enthusiastic, even prophetic, about the integral consciousness, he was certainly less naive than some enthusiasts of the
"Aquarian Age" movement. For him, the new consciousness was only
an emergent *possibility* for mankind. The other possibility that he saw
was global destruction. He debunked the nowadays widely believed
millenarian myth of the inevitability of a new, "golden" epoch in
which all wrongs will be righted and humanity will be saved from
itself. He persistently emphasized the fact that for the promise of the
new consciousness to come true, a healthy commitment to personal
transformation is absolutely essential. And he meant not merely

2. See Jean Gebser, *Ursprung und Gegenwart* (Stuttgart, West Germany: Deutscher
Taschenbuch Verlag, 1973). 3 vols.

3. See Sri Aurobindo, *The Life Divine* (Pondicherry, India: Sri Aurobindo Ashram, 1977). 2
vols.

4. See P. T. de Chardin, *The Future of Man* (New York: Harper & Row, 1969).

gestures of self-improvement but the hard labor of genuine self-transcendence.

The same principle is today passionately avowed by the Adept Da Free John, who, however, does not speak as a scholar but with the authority and the undoubted advantage of one in whom the spiritual process has fulfilled itself. Thus, what was for Gebser, de Chardin, and possibly even for Sri Aurobindo principally an inspired vision, a *theoria,* a network of intuitions about Man's evolutionary potential, and what is, I suspect, for many contemporary advocates of the new consciousness only hopeful dogma or gray theory, is for Master Da Free John a present Actuality. Like the other great Adepts before him, he embodies that highest human aspiration of which Faust despaired, failing as he did to associate it with self-transcendence and the disposition of Ignorance[5]: the Realization of the Transcendental Identity of all things, which is not the product of mystical inwardness, but the continuous Condition of all states of consciousness and objective reality.

We would do well to listen to the Wisdom or "God-talk" of such a Realizer! What Master Da has to say about our present-day worldwide difficulties is simple and lucid. In a talk entitled "The Urgency of the Teaching," he places our contemporary situation in the broadest possible frame of reference, which allows one to peep beyond the narrow concerns of specialism and self-interest. His words are directed at the heart:

There is simply no light abroad in the world today. There is nothing but corruption, nothing but the failure to accept the Way of God. There is absolutely no sign of the Way of Truth, except in rare instances of individuals and small groups of people. The Truth is essentially hidden and secondary. There is a long history of corruption in every area of human life, and the entire social structure of the world is devoted to subhuman ends and forms of self-indulgence. There are no signs of an imminent Golden Age in the disposition or condition of humanity at large. Rather, the signs are of the necessity for a great

---

5. Master Da Free John's term "Ignorance," or "Divine Ignorance," is capitalized to convey its transcendental import. It is not lack of knowledge or the absence of intelligence but is synonymous with Transcendental Consciousness or Reality. See pp. 126–29 and p. 224 for an elaboration of the principle of Ignorance.

purification, a great reestablishment of order, a righteous readjustment of the whole world.[6]

Elsewhere he writes:

The Wisdom-Culture of Man at Infinity has been arrested all over the world. Everywhere, individuals are dominated by subhuman powers. The politics of human life has been brought under the control of salt-of-the-earth ideologies and gross scientific or technological machines of State. The truly spiritual understanding of Man is suppressed in every area of common education, and official voices are present everywhere to anathematize the deep visions and urges of the higher material, psychic, and spiritual or Transcendental dimensions of the human gesture in the world. Truly, it is always more or less so in the human world, but it is also clearly so at the present time.

The result of this suppression of Man by Nature and by the State is the appearance of a universal and chronic disease. It is frustration, or depression of Life. Everyone suffers this chronic depression, and everyone must struggle to overcome it. But the effects of the propagandistic subhuman powers of the world tend to minimize the conscious, responsible, and active mode of individual participation in the stream of experiential events. We tend to be passively or helplessly aligned to "what is," because our Force of Life is frustrated, in doubt, crippled by a profound despair, which is always present, even if concealed under an exterior gloss of enthusiasm and competence.

The usual man, who is mechanically and passively, if fitfully or neurotically, associated with the conventions of daily experience, is the subject of profound frustration of the Force and Condition of Life. The Life that appears to move him is inherently moved to Realize its Transcendental Condition of Radiant Bliss, the Freedom of Absolute Consciousness. And that Radiant Life would even Radiate as the world and as the body-mind of Man, except that the Force of that Absolute Radiance is confused with the independent self-position of the mortal individual, and thus it is constantly frustrated by all the petty limitations of functionally and socially organized desire and energy.

6. Da Free John, *Scientific Proof of the Existence of God Will Soon Be Announced by the White House!* pp. 383–84. The subtitle of this major work reveals its scope and content: *Prophetic Wisdom about the Myths and Idols of mass culture and popular religious cultism, the new priesthood of scientific and political materialism, and the secrets of Enlightenment hidden in the body of Man.*

Therefore, the Condition of our Life must be Realized. We must not merely be filled with Life. The self that seeks to be filled must become a sacrifice. The individual must become Ecstatic, or self-released. We must function in the mode of self-transcendence rather than self-indulgence.

In summary, Man is subhuman until he Awakens from mere desire, or self-indulgence, to Love, or self-transcendence, in constant Communion with the Living God and in Lawful or responsible management of all functional and relational conditions of experience. The Awakened or true Man is inherently Free of all the frustrating limitations of Nature and the State. He is Radiant in the world, so that the Transcendental Reality is alive as him. Therefore, a world of human beings so Awakened may create a truly benign and moral Culture, or true State, founded in the Wisdom-Influence of the Radiant Transcendental Consciousness. And only human beings so Awakened and so ordered are free of the inherent and chronic frustrations that produce subhuman societies, subhuman cravings, and subhuman destinies, before and after death.[7]

2. Radical Transcendentalism versus Problem-Solving Approaches

For Buckminster Fuller, who regarded our present crisis primarily as an ecological problem, our salvation lies in "design science," an alternative technology, and conscious, cooperative planning. He proposed to alter our physical environment in order to change our mental universe. But the kind of transformation he wanted to see happen presupposes a level of conversion to the new way of thinking implicit in his policies and programs for survival. Although he did not underestimate the formidable ideological and psychological obstacles that confront his budding design science and philosophy of the "Universal Man," he nevertheless approached our contemporary dilemma primarily from the perspective of the scientist and engineer that he was.

7. Ibid., pp. 83–88.

Fuller, for whom God is "the integrity of the anticipatory intellectual wisdom,"[8] was not oblivious to the spiritual aspect of human existence, but his genius expressed itself in the area of technological innovation rather than individual psychological and spiritual transformation. In other words, he was active as a remarkable thinker and inventor, and not as a spiritual teacher. He proceeded on the basis of knowledge, even though this was, in his case, rooted in deep intellectual intuitions about the nature of existence. Yet, knowledge or intellectual understanding on its own is an insufficient tool for dealing with our present-day crisis, because our cultural dilemma has deep psychological roots. Therefore, another approach is clearly called for—an approach that accounts for the fact that the human being is what the father of general systems theory, Ludwig von Bertalanffy, called an "open system": Man is (potentially) open to *all* dimensions of reality, not least to that "Ultimate General System" which Bertalanffy (like so many other scientists) risked to ponder only in his most private moments.[9] In other words, we must make a *spiritual* response today.

Such an orientation is to be found in the Radical Transcendentalism of the Adept Da Free John. This is not a new philosophy or ideology, not even a novel therapy—as if the world did not abound in "isms" of all descriptions and countless remedial systems for the betterment of Man and the ameliorization of his earthly lot. The term "Radical Transcendentalism," first used by Master Da in his *Nirvanasara*,[10] is, strictly, a concession to the conventional intellect with its insatiable appetite for classification. Master Da himself most frequently refers to it, for reasons that will become obvious, as the

8. J. Meller, ed., *The Buckminster Fuller Reader* (Harmondsworth, England: Penguin Books, 1972), p. 78.

9. See the testimony by Maria von Bertalanffy in M. Davidson, *Uncommon Sense: The Life and Thought of Ludwig von Bertalanffy (1901-1972)* (Los Angeles: J. P. Tarcher, 1983), p. 220.

10. Da Free John, *Nirvanasara: Radical Transcendentalism and the Introduction of Advaitayana Buddhism.* This book is Master Da Free John's critique of the principal Eastern traditions, particularly Buddhist realism and Hindu idealism. In a series of profoundly original essays, he shows how the "languages" of these traditions are inadequate descriptions of Reality. They conceptualize spiritual life as a search for and a solution to the felt problem of existence. By contrast, the radical "language" proposed by Master Da Free John in the form of the Way of Radical Understanding or Divine Ignorance is not problem-based and also does not involve a strategy of escape from suffering, or inversion upon an inner essence. Rather, it is founded on the presumption of prior Realization or Enlightenment: Transcendental Consciousness, Being, Happiness, or Love-Bliss is the always present principle of phenomenal existence.

"Way of Radical Understanding or Divine Ignorance," or simply, "the Way."

Radical Transcendentalism implies a whole life-style whose fulcrum point is the supreme value of Transcendental Realization or Transcendental Identification with Reality itself. It has grown out of the Adept's living At-One-ness with the all-encompassing Being that Master Da also styles "God," "Transcendental Self," "Consciousness," "Truth," or "the Condition of all conditions."

This Reality or Divine Being is not the Christian, Hebraic, or Moslem "God out there" who is charged with the authorship of the world, nor the "God within" of the traditions of esoteric introversionism, nor the abstract projected Absolute of metaphysical speculation. This Reality does not depend for its Realization on any altered state of consciousness or any other form of subjective cognition. It transcends (but does not exclude) conventional types of ecstasy or enstasy,[11] as it transcends all sensation, feeling, or thought. It eclipses all phenomenal conditions, however "high" or rarefied, and, in another sense, it actually constitutes them. This is how Master Da Free John describes this Supreme Condition:

> There is <u>only</u> the Radiant Transcendental Being, Who is One. All beings and things and worlds are ultimately and Really only Identical to That One, Who is God, the Divine Person.
>
> Only God is Alive as everyone and everything. All beings and things and worlds are arising as spontaneous transformations or modifications of That One. God eternally Transcends the world and all beings, and yet the world and all beings are nothing but God. It is a Great and Passionate Mystery.[12]

He further observes:

> Each of us inheres in Radiant Transcendental Being, the Bright or Divine Self, in Whom the Universe of all possibilities is arising as a

---

11. The term "enstasy" is used by historians of religion to refer specifically to the Indian mystical phenomenon of *samadhi*, which implies a "standing in oneself (or one's Self)," as opposed to "ecstasy" (*exstasis*, literally "standing outside"), which is given a more affective flavor.

12. Da Free John, *The God in Every Body Book: Talks and Essays on God-Realization*, 2d ed., p. 70. In this collection of talks and essays, Da Free John criticizes both childish belief in and adolescent doubt of the Divine Reality, and points to the process whereby we Realize our inherence in the Divine as an All-Pervading and Living Reality.

great psycho-physical Process. But we are made superficial by attention to the Play of psycho-physical states, so that we abandon the intuitive position or disposition wherein our own Identity and the Condition of all conditions is obvious. Thus, we develop a state of presumed knowledge and conventional experience in which the physical or elemental world seems to be dominant, such that it appears to cause and also to be the final destiny of the conscious self and all that is mind.

In Truth, there is the Eternal Divine Self, and the total psycho-physical cosmos arises in It. But the conventional view (based on the superficial involvement of attention in phenomena) is that there is, first of all, the physical-elemental world, and mental states as well as conscious being merely arise as individual and temporary effects of that world.[13]

Evidently, Consciousness or Reality is not verifiable, only Verifiable or Realizable. It is capable of being intuitively replicated in the form of a whole-bodily disposition. It is this intuition that forms the backbone of the Way of Radical Understanding. It is a response at the deepest level of one's being, an ego-transcending attitude of being fully present in the world without the superimposition of separateness and without becoming implicated in the self-propagating patterns of reactivity of the body-mind. In a talk entitled "The Religious Ambivalence of Western Man," Master Da Free John explains in vivid terms what this disposition entails:

Then existence is not problematic. It is creative. It is a process of the confrontation of conditions, but it is humorous, already Enlightened. Nothing ultimate is at stake. It is just the game of the universe.

And there is nowhere to look for God. What is God is completely obvious under these conditions, even totally within the limits of your present perception. There is the Divine. It is not a matter of some other vision, some other experience, some inwardness. It is a matter of hearing,[14] *of being awakened from the sleep, the bondage, the problem, the dilemma by which you apprehend your present condition.*

13. Ibid., p. 78.

14. "Hearing" is a technical term used by Master Da Free John to describe the foundation process of intuitive understanding on which spiritual life is based. See p. 80, n. 3, for a full description of "hearing."

*In this hearing you are awakened to the Condition of this moment
without all the concepts and contractions of energy and feeling.*

*When there is no obstruction to feeling-attention, then what is
Divine, without qualification, is completely obvious.*[15]

Master Da Free John goes on to say that, since people imagine
that they do not Realize God under the ordinary conditions of their
lives, they feel compelled to create other kinds of conditions—visions,
auditions, etc.—in order to enjoy that Realization. But, speaking as
one who is familiar with every possible psychic experience, the Adept
firmly discards this notion. *All* conditions or phenomena arise in and
as the Transcendental Reality, and therefore all are equally to be met
with that unobstructed feeling-attention that is coessential with the
unqualified Being-Consciousness.

When this disposition of radical understanding—which is not
simply a mental attitude or exercise—is maintained to perfection,
when the individual surrenders all standpoints, all self-programs, all
clinging, and all aversion toward everything, then feeling-attention
will naturally and instantaneously flip over into Infinity or Objectless
Consciousness, the Ultimate General System.

But what does this flip-over mean? This question is answerable
by responding to another question, which any metaphysics-shy skeptic
is wont to ask sooner or later: What is the ontological status of that
ultimate Being-Consciousness? John Lilly, in discussing Franklin
Merrell-Wolff's "Consciousness-Without-an-Object," digs into this
philosophical issue in his own inimical fashion:

*If states of consciousness are self-programmed, then the basic
question arises: Which one of the states of consciousness is independent of the self-programmatic power of the individual? Is there
any state of consciousness which is not self-programmed?*

*To escape answering these questions we appeal to others, to the
consensus judgment about reality. And we say: "If I cannot trust my
own judgment of the reality of a given state of consciousness, then I
must trust the judgment of others whom I designate as 'experts' in
these matters"—priests, psychiatrists, doctors, lawyers, politicians,
statesmen, legislators, and so forth.*[16]

15. Da Free John, *The God in Every Body Book,* 2d ed., p. 63.

16. J. Lilly, *Simulations of God: The Science of Belief* (New York: Simon & Schuster, 1975),
p. 47.

Of course, as Lilly rightly pointed out, authority alone is insufficient to settle one's doubts. Or else, the history of metaphysical speculation and theology would long have come to a close. His own experience of "something far greater than I"[17] allows Lilly to remain open to the possibility of an "essence" that is not the product of the ego's metaprograms. At the same time, however, he does not have any conclusive answers either. He writes:

It may be that [Merrell-] Wolff, like all the rest of us, is doing an overvaluation of his own abstractions. It may be that he is generating, i.e., self-metaprogramming, states of his own mind and those of others in which the ideals of the race are reified as thought objects, as programs, as realities, as states of consciousness. It may be that this is all we can do.[18]

He then makes the following sanguine recommendation:

If this is all we can do, maybe we had better do it—and see if there is anything beyond this by doing it. . . .

This may be a better game than killing our neighbors because they do not believe in our simulations of God. At least those who espouse these states claim that these states are above any other human aspiration; that once one has experienced them, he is almost unfit for wrath, for pride, for arrogance, for power over others, for group pressure exerted either upon oneself or upon others. . . .

One becomes content with the minimum necessities for survival on the planetside trip; one cuts back on his use of unnecessary articles—machines, gadgets, and devices. He no longer needs motion pictures, television, dishwashers, or other luxuries. One no longer needs much of what most people value above all else. One no longer needs the excitement of war. One no longer needs to be a slave to destructive thoughts or deeds. One no longer needs to organize.[19]

This is all the great Adepts have ever invited mankind to do. They do not ask for blind faith but firm commitment to practical "experimentation."

17. Ibid., p. 54.
18. Ibid., p. 176.
19. Ibid., pp. 176–77.

Lilly's suggestion that the Realization of the Consciousness-Without-an-Object would be desirable even if it should turn out to be a metaprogrammed state is to the point and not to be made light of. However, he appears to have overlooked, or given inadequate attention to, a significant feature of genuine God-Realization. This is the fact that God-Realization presupposes the phenomenon of ego-death. Is it possible for there to be a self-program when the ego or self is transcended? Could the program possibly survive its programmer? The uniform testimony of all the God-Realized Adepts is that it does not. When the self is transcended, there is no way in which the simulation game could be continued. God-Realization is not an experience. It is a permanent condition—*the* Condition. It implies an irrevocable identity shift in which the narrow egoic consciousness, which experiences itself as locked into a particular limited body-mind, is replaced by the All-Identity of Transcendental Being-Consciousness.

This is the clear message of Master Da Free John. And we need not take his word for it. All possible states of consciousness are reproducible, though one may have to fritter away a lifetime in their pursuit. Likewise, the Great Space of Transcendental Consciousness, in which all states of consciousness arise, is Realizable, granted one is willing to submit to the "experimental conditions" that are necessary (though not sufficient) for such a Realization. That the Way of Radical Understanding, communicated by Master Da Free John, is a viable context for this ultimate Opening-up has been demonstrated by the Enlightenment of several long-term practitioners of this Way.[20]

The Way of Radical Understanding or Radical Transcendentalism, anchored as it is in the Wisdom of Transcendental Realization, represents an approach to life that goes beyond the shallowness of materialism in its many forms as well as beyond the dissociative loftiness of idealist systems of thought. It is not limited to either extroversionism, dominated by the sympathetic nervous system, or introversionism, controlled by the parasympathetic ganglia.[21] Rather,

20. These cases of Enlightenment or God-Realization occurred in a relatively short span of time between late March and early June of 1983. For a brief treatment of the significance of these important transitions, see *The Laughing Man,* vol. 4, no. 2 (June 1983), pp. 82–83, and vol. 4, no. 3 (September 1983), pp. 70–72.

21. See Master Da Free John's illuminating treatment of the neurophysiological basis of conventional mystical or yogic states in *The Enlightenment of the Whole Body,* pp. 376ff. This volume, subtitled *A Rational and New Prophetic Revelation of the Truth of Religion, Esoteric Spirituality, and the Divine Destiny of Man,* is a principal source text and the most comprehensive statement of the Way Taught by Da Free John, including a full description of the unfolding of the esoteric process of Enlightenment.

it is self-transcending and hence also world-transcending (though not world-denying). For the practitioner of this Way, therefore, there are major consequences in all areas of his life, notably in his primary relationship to the Transcendental Reality but also in his interpersonal relationships. Some of the moral values and attitudes that naturally grow out of his practice of self-transcendence—such as love, service, harmony—coincide with those of traditional religiosity, but the basis for their implementation is different. Whereas in conventional religion, morality springs from the urge to realize the highest good as postulated by dogma, moral practice in the Way of Radical Understanding is always engaged as part of the overall orientation of self-transcendence through the continuous inspection of, and aperspectival openness to, one's tendencies in action.

Radical Transcendentalism is not concerned with the problem of good and evil as a jumping-off point for ethical prescriptions. Self-transcending practice is senior to all moral conflict or consideration. The moral force of Radical Transcendentalism lies in the fact that it proceeds from the progressive undermining of the very activity that posits the sense of good and evil and all the many degrees by which human life is channelled into the "right" (i.e., "good") direction. That central activity is the ego, the self-sense, or Narcissus.[22] Even the striving for the good, however it may be conceived (and humanity has entertained different, even conflicting, notions about what is moral and good or what is conducive to the good), is a self-program, a manipulation of life.

All occupations derived from the ego-base are necessarily limited to egoity, and all conceptions that feed such egoic occupations are necessarily bereft of a right view of self, world, and God (or the ultimate and Transcendental Reality and Truth).

When the mechanics of egoity are transcended in our understanding, then it becomes obvious that life (or manifest phenomenal existence) is simply a play of opposites. Neither "Good" (or creation

22. Narcissus, the self-lover of Greek mythology, is a key symbol in Master Da Free John's description of Man as a self-possessed seeker, enamored with what he does not recognize as his own image, one who suffers in dilemma, contracted upon himself at every level of the being from all relations and from the condition of relationship itself. "He is the ancient one visible in the Greek 'myth,' who was the universally adored child of the gods, who rejected the loved-one and every form of love and relationship, who was finally condemned to the contemplation of his own image, until he suffered the fact of eternal separation and died in infinite solitude" (*The Knee of Listening*, p. 26).

*and preservation) nor "Evil" (or destruction) finally wins. Nature, in
all its planes, is inherently a dynamic. The play of Nature, in all its
forms and beings and processes, is not merely (or exclusively and
finally) seeking the apparent "Good" of self-preservation (or the
preservation and fulfillment of any particular form, world, or being),
nor is it merely (or exclusively and finally) seeking the apparent "Evil"
of self-destruction (or the dissolution of any particular form, world, or
being). Rather, the play in Nature is always in the direction of
perpetuating the dynamics of the play itself—and, therefore, polarity,
opposition, struggle, alternation, death, and cyclic repetition tend to be
perpetuated as the characteristics of phenomenal existence. Therefore,
the play of Nature is always alternating between the appearance of
dominance by one or the other of its two basic extremes. And the sign
of this is in the inherent struggle that involves every form, being, and
process. The struggle is this dynamic play of opposites, but the import
of it is not the absolute triumph of either half. Things and beings and
processes arise, they move, they are transformed, and they disappear.
No thing or being or process is ultimately preserved. But neither is
there any absolute destruction. Nature is a transformer, not merely a
creator or a destroyer.*

*To the ego (or present temporary form of being) self-preservation
may seem to be the inevitable motive of being. Therefore, a struggle
develops to destroy or escape the dynamic of Nature by dominating
Evil (or death) with Good (or immortality). This ideal gets expressed
in the generally exoteric and occidental or more materialistic efforts to
conquer Nature via worldly knowledge and power. But it also gets
expressed in the more esoteric and oriental or mystical efforts to
escape the plane of Nature by ascent from materiality (or the Evil of
the flesh) to Heaven (the Good God above the consciousness of
Nature).*[23]

For Master Da Free John, the only "sin" there is, is the recoil
from, or the denial of, the infinite Being-Consciousness. Sin, for him,
is the presumption of separation, independence, or identification with
the body-mind. The transcendence of ethical propositions and positions
does not signal the wreckage of moral life, either individually or
collectively.

23. Da Free John, *The God in Every Body Book*, 2d ed., pp. 51–52.

When the devotee has become Transfigured[24] in the seventh stage of life,[25] he is free of all conventional obligations of body and mind, and he abides only in God. Since he is free of all obligations, he can do what he likes, endure whatever arises, and yet remain free. But since he abides only in God, rather than in the modifications of the body-mind, his actions are always God-made, Full of Life, pure, graceful, benign, and auspicious, even when his actions are difficult for others to understand. Such is the paradox of whole bodily Enlightenment.[26]

Ego-transcendence has thus a transforming effect on the body-mind and environment of the God-Realized being. And that transformation is, even in the terms of conventional religious expectation, utterly desirable. For, self-transcendence is synonymous with the disposition of unconditional Love, not as an ephemeral human sentiment but as a constant that informs all the activities of the Enlightened being. Because Realization is not a static, terminal condition but an ongoing or deepening Process of Dissolution in the Transcendental Being, the Enlightened practitioner is engaged in a discipline or *sadhana*[27] of a special kind.

He recognizes what arises, and abides in the Prior Transcendental Consciousness, the Self, or Divine Ignorance. During this phase he may carry on all of his ordinary and natural human activities in the same fashion as in the earlier stages of practice. He appears to be Full,

---

24. "Transfiguration," "Transformation," and "Translation" are technical terms that describe the unfolding process of God-Realization in the seventh stage of life. Transfiguration is the pervasion of body and mind by Transcendental Radiance or Light. Bodily and mental Transformation involves the arising of supernormal signs or abilities, such as healing power, longevity, and psychic capabilities. Divine Translation is the ultimate evidence of God-Realization, wherein the limited psycho-physical body, mind, and world are no longer noticed—not because the consciousness has withdrawn from all such phenomena, but because it has entered into such profound absorptive Realization of the Divine Condition that all phenomena are, as Master Da Free John Confesses, "Outshined" by that Light.

25. Master Da Free John has described the development or spiritual evolution of the human individual in terms of seven stages of eternal life. For a description of this unique model, see the Appendix, pp. 458–63.

26. Bubba [Da] Free John, *The Enlightenment of the Whole Body*, p. 531.

27. The Sanskrit term *sadhana*, traditionally referring to practices directed toward the goal of spiritual and religious attainment, is used by Master Da Free John without the implication of a goal, to mean action generated not as a means to Truth but on the basis of prior understanding and Divine Realization.

and Tranquil, responsible for all of the ordinary conditions of life, and active in a natural manner, even with enthusiasm for the pleasurable conditions of this world. But he recognizes all conditions to be unnecessary modifications of the Radiant Self.

This phase of Awakening[28] *continues for a time, until the conditions of experience begin to become profoundly transparent. Thus, as time goes on, the devotee not only recognizes or "sees through" all conditions of experience, but he becomes more and more Ecstatically Absorbed in the Divine, in Whom all conditions are arising.*[29]

The crisis in which mankind finds itself today is generated and suffered by the separative ego-consciousness. All conventional remedies and solutions—from design science, ecological awareness, and world-wide economic-political restructuring to consciousness-raising methods, back-to-nature philosophies, self-improvement techniques, and medita-tion (however transcendental)—are, in the last analysis, all ego-based measures; they cannot possibly have a decisive curative value. It seems reasonable to assume, however, that a widely shared way of life in which active ego-transcendence is the alpha and omega of everyone's (or most people's) aspiration, will, by removing the engine of the crisis, dissolve the critical situation itself. Problems and solutions are the battleground of un-Enlightened existence, of the self-divided egoic consciousness. The One Reality is not problematical. In *The Knee of Listening,*[30] Master Da Free John writes aphoristically:

We are never at any moment in the dilemma we fear ourselves to

---

28. This is the first of three phases of the *process* of Enlightenment described briefly above as Transfiguration, Transformation, and Translation. For a thorough understanding of this process, see Da Free John's *Enlightenment and the Transformation of Man: Selections from Talks and Essays on the Spiritual Process and God-Realization,* especially "The Three Phases of Enlight-enment," pp. 115–16.

29. Bubba [Da] Free John, *The Enlightenment of the Whole Body,* p. 528.

30. First published in 1972, *The Knee of Listening: The Early Life and Radical Spiritual Teachings of Da Free John* is Master Da Free John's account of his Illumined birth, his years of preparation, testing, and transformation, and his ultimate Re-Awakening as Divine Being. In it he also provides basic instructions for meditation as he himself practiced it, and essays on the nature and significance of radical understanding. Even today *The Knee of Listening* remains the principal statement of Master Da Free John's Confession and Teaching Argument.

be. Only this radical understanding in the heart of life is the ground of real peace and joy. All else is seeking and strife and fear.[31]

3. Religious Provincialism and Scientific Materialism

s I intimated toward the beginning of the previous section, the urge for spiritual maturation alive in some individuals and groups is largely prevented from bearing fruit in society at large by two ideological forces that are as insidious as they are powerful. These forces have a long, intertwined history. Although they are essentially in competition with each other, whenever it served their purpose they would connive at their differences and uneasily conspire to safeguard their shared hegemony over the human mind. Master Da Free John, seeing the larger context, has identified these two cultural configurations as religious provincialism and scientific materialism respectively.

Religious provincialism, as the name indicates, is a narrow, hidebound view of the universe which flies under the banner of religion. It takes the form of exoteric cultism that is intolerant of genuine Ecstasy and the kind of attitudes and practices that are associated with an Ecstatic way of life. Hence it is always antagonistic toward personal, informal religiosity, esotericism, and mysticism. Adepts, and everyone who even seemingly steps outside the established mold, are immediately suspect and likely to be subjected to suppression, recantation, ridicule, anathematization, persecution, banishment, imprisonment, and possibly execution. Religious provincialism seeks vindication for its existence in some sacred revelation or authority and (rightly) fears and (wrongly) discourages independent inquiry and free thinking.

It places dogma over the Living Truth, ritualism over Ecstatic self-transcendence, obedience to the Holy Writ over direct surrender to God, ecclesiastical survival over individual freedom. Its principle is not God-Realization, Emancipation, or Ultimate Happiness, but such goals as moral goodness or personal contentment or the achievement

31. Bubba [Da] Free John, *The Knee of Listening*, 2d ed., p. 224.

of heaven in the hereafter, through prayerful submission to one's "Maker" or "Heavenly Father," or to the "Divine Mother."

All goals are the visions of Narcissus, mere conceptions or simulations of real Happiness associated in our minds with the kinds of extraordinary enjoyments we may have experienced from time to time in our lives. Therefore, our conceptions of the future, as long as we are goal-oriented, are false conceptions because they do not express our prior Happiness. We have only the models of our un-Happy pleasures.

Conventional religious and spiritual pursuits, then, are like ordinary addiction. They are associated with a false goal. If religious and spiritual practitioners really knew What they were seeking, they would Realize It in the present.[32]

Religious provincialism marks and mars most of the traditions and schools of thought which compose what Master Da Free John names the "Great Tradition." By this term he means the total cultural heritage of mankind, all the great and minor religions, philosophies, ideologies, paths, and esoteric teachings by which people, past and present, have organized their lives. In the spirit of the budding world culture, Master Da Free John calls for "the universal acceptance of the total tradition (or Great Tradition) of mankind,"[33] with the stipulation that "we must overcome the provincialism of our minds (and, ultimately, the provincialism that is mind itself)."[34]

He appeals to us to respect and show tolerance toward all traditions. At the same time, however, he asks that this openness be tempered by a healthy attitude of criticism, based on a higher understanding. He does not commend either a naive eclecticism or a simplistic relativism in which all schools of thought are deemed equally true, valid, or viable.

Such a higher understanding is offered by Radical Transcendentalism, which acknowledges the fact that all schools of thought are

32. Da Free John, *The Dreaded Gom-Boo, or the Imaginary Disease That Religion Seeks to Cure,* p. 220. In this major work, Master Da Free John humorously and persistently asserts that the spiritual disease of humanity is an imaginary one: Man is not separated from the Living Divine except by the error of his own presumption. Rather, Man may realize, through understanding, spiritual practice, and the Adept's Help, that he presently inheres in the Happiness, Mystery, and Wonder of God.

33. Da Free John, *Nirvanasara,* p. 199.

34. Ibid., p. 198.

simply representations of, and approaches to, the Truth and that any claim on their part for ultimacy, finality, completeness, or infallibility is no more than propaganda that may actually detract from their potential merit.

It is no longer appropriate or even possible for individuals, cultures, or nations to justify absolute independence from other individuals, cultures, or nations—and it is no longer appropriate or possible to grant absolute or ultimately superior status to any historical Revelation, belief system, or conception of how things work.[35]

Radical Transcendentalism is, by contrast, the tradition of self-transcending, belief-transcending, and knowledge-transcending Realization. Although it is necessarily associated with certain ideas and practices, these are not in any way sacrosanct properties of this Way but are, ultimately, all relativized and transcended by radical understanding: They are founded in the Wisdom of the ultimate Realization. The ideational building-blocks simply serve the Adept as vehicles of communication, whilst the recommended disciplines[36] are designed to free the practitioner's energy and attention for the radical process of self-transcendence. The authority for both theory and practice is rooted in the Adept's Realization, which is not to be turned into an icon of mere belief but to be duplicated by the practitioner in his own life.

In *The Fire Gospel*,[37] which is dedicated to demonstrating the distinction between conventional religious practice and the orientation of Radical Transcendentalism, Master Da Free John explains how traditional religion and spirituality are tied into an archaic cosmology that avows a "Nature realism": The cosmos is seen as an immense hierarchical structure populated by spirit-entities on progressively superior echelons, terminating in the unsurpassable Supreme Ruler of

35. Ibid.

36. The practical disciplines in the Way of Radical Understanding include basic forms of responsibility for work, diet, health, sexuality, exercise, and service to others.

37. *The Fire Gospel: Essays and Talks on Spiritual Baptism* is Master Da Free John's affirmation of the ancient Way that underlies mankind's great religious and spiritual heritage—Spiritual Baptism. In contrast to the conventional water ritual, Spiritual Baptism is the Transmission by the Adept of the Living Force of the Spirit-Power and its bodily reception by the spiritual aspirant. In essays and talks spanning a three-month period of exhaustive consideration, Master Da Free John brilliantly summarizes the self-transcending process of Communion with the Spirit, which alone can purify and Awaken Man.

Nature, the Deity. Today, where the psychic or participatory dimension of religious life is barely existent, this view of the universe has no longer the experiential immediacy it had in the past. It is banished into the exoteric realm of sheer dogma and belief.

This transposition is doubly unfortunate. First, as Master Da Free John points out, the ancient world-view of a spirit-inhabited, multi-dimensional world is in principle correct. Hence it is open to experience, even though there is room and a need for reinterpretation. But the modern taboo against psychic participation in Nature elimi-nates this whole dimension of experience from religious life. Second, because the traditional interpretation of the psychic or psycho-physical organization of the world is antiquated, to give it dogmatic expression and only encourage a response of belief (rather than experience) helps to further undermine the credibility of this model of the universe.

Thus, the contemporary religious leaders find themselves in the unhappy position of employing an archaic language that has little or no communicative value, since the realities of which it speaks are not part of the world experience of the "believers." Consequently, the pious, unless they happen to be completely unsophisticated, do their own "reinterpretation," which usually involves a kind of precipitant demythologization. Of course, the conventional religious mind, though it may discard or allegorize the existence of angels and other higher spirit-entities to whose presence it has become desensitized, is conditioned to accept the one dogma that has no validity—the existence of a Divine Creator who is the *ultimate* Spiritual Agent.

While Master Da Free John does not call into question the possibility of a Patron (or even several such Patrons) at the apex of the political hierarchy of spirit-beings, he certainly challenges any claim to supremacy of that paternal cosmic Principle. The Heavenly Father or Personal God Who is thought to be absolute is, for him, clearly a projection, for which Freud supplied the psychological grounds. Most scientists today would be quick to underwrite this view.

For Kepler,[38] Galileo, Descartes, and Newton in the seventeenth century, Nature was still God's miraculous creation. This changed with

38. In the Dedication to his *Mysterium Cosmographicum* (1596), Kepler could still write rapturously about astronomy: "For here we may behold how God, like a master-builder, has laid the foundation of the world according to order and law, and how He has measured all things so carefully, that we might well judge it is not nature that human art copies, but that God in His very creation was thinking of the way in which man yet unborn would be building one day." Cited in *Science and Religious Belief 1600-1900*, ed. D. C. Goodman (Dorchester, England: John Wright in assoc. with The Open University Press, 1973), p. 8.

the Age of Enlightenment, which celebrated reason above all else. The new spirit is captured in an anecdote about Pierre Simon de Laplace, the French mathematician and astronomer. Napoleon commented to him: "They tell me you have written this large book on the system of the universe, and have never even mentioned its Creator." Laplace responded: "I had no need of that hypothesis."[39] By the third generation of "Enlightened" scientists, God had been analyzed into nonexistence. Thus, modern science came to be an essentially atheistic enterprise. Pointing out that this denial of the Divine could only have arisen on the historical basis of a dualism between God and the world, the German historian of philosophy Wilhelm Kamlah spoke of science as a specifically Christian form of Godlessness—a profound insight, corroborated in a way by the twentieth-century "Death of God" theology within the Christian camp itself.

Although the scientists' faith in the salvific power of reason has been badly shaken through the scientific discoveries of the twentieth century, nevertheless few are willing to don again what they consider the straitjacket of religious superstition. As Albert Einstein observed:

> *The man who is thoroughly convinced of the universal operation of the law of causation cannot for a moment entertain the idea of a being who interferes in the course of events—that is, if he takes the hypothesis of causality really seriously. He has no use for the religion of fear and equally little for social or moral religion.*[40]

Yet, Einstein did not rest content with a rejection of the anthropomorphic Deity of conventional religiosity and its particular morality. He declared his allegiance to the *philosophia perennis* in the form of what he called "cosmic religious feeling," and remarked that "it is the most important function of art and science to awaken this feeling and keep it alive in those who are capable of it."[41] How many scientists would follow Einstein this far? I daresay, exceedingly few. For the majority, religion—whether as a subjective (irrational) feeling or as an organized moral life—is no more than a personal philosophy, perhaps a form of self-indulgence, but most likely a private delusion.

39. Quoted in I. G. Barbour, *Issues in Science and Religion* (New York: Harper & Row, 1971), p. 58.

40. A. Einstein, *The World As I See It* (New York: Wisdom Library, n.d.), p. 27.

41. Ibid., p. 27.

After all, did not Freud expose the neurotic roots of religious beliefs? Can one ignore his conclusion that the "religions of mankind must be classed among the mass-delusions"?[42] Has not Marx affirmed and demonstrated the same truth in the context of economic history? It would be difficult to persuade any hard-nosed scientist otherwise. Nor is this necessary for the present purpose.

There are no compelling reasons to assume that religion is other than an ego-based activity. *But* so is science. And this is hardly ever appreciated by those who like to see religion discredited and discarded onto the considerable pile of follies committed by mankind in its slow advance against irrationalism. Since science, as much as religion, is an activity originating in the ego, it also partakes of the same susceptibilities. Arthur Stanley Eddington, in his Swarthmore Lecture of 1929, unwittingly identified the crucial liability of both pursuits when he remarked: "You will understand the true spirit neither of science nor of religion unless seeking is placed in the forefront."[43]

Seeking is indeed the great principle that animates human beings and that underlies all human endeavor and suffering. Master Da Free John gives it aphoristic expression thus:

Life is the wisdom of seeking, which is no wisdom at all. Truth is the wisdom of no seeking, which is only wiser than life.

Reality is the wisdom of no-dilemma, which is Wisdom itself. There is nothing ultimate about life. Its best wisdom is the knowledge of how to play games.

There is nothing radically useful about the consciousness of Truth. Its best wisdom is the knowledge that all life is seeking.[44]

And again:

Seeking is simply clinging to various concepts, goals, things, methods, and paths that seem to promise release from death, from the

42. S. Freud, *Civilization and Its Discontents* (New York: W. W. Norton, 1961), p. 28. (First published in 1930.)

43. A. S. Eddington, *Science and the Unseen World* (New York: Macmillan, 1930), p. 88.

44. Bubba [Da] Free John, *The Knee of Listening*, p. 251.

knowledge of death, and from all suffering, which is separation and death.

Trouble begins only where there is identification with the seeker. But Truth is not the notion: "I am not the seeker—I am not the dying one who fears and seeks." Truth is simply the understanding of seeking. The man who understands always is understanding, until the movement in him that extends itself as the seeker ceases to arise.[45]

Thus, the scientist is as implicated in this search as the religionist. Both are suffering; both are afraid of their own mortality; both are constantly looking for a way out of their existential dilemma. And neither of them is capable of breaking free by means of their incessant seeking. It takes a fine ear to hear this argument.

The scientific doubter of the religious version of the search may learn *part* of this important lesson from epistemology and the sociology of knowledge. These disciplines will give him a clear understanding of the fact that his own activity is not occurring in a psychological vacuum but that it is necessarily a product of his ego in search of "objective" truth, rational certainty, or at least intellectually satisfying answers to his questions.

What he must be willing to learn next, though, is that the ego is just that movement of seeking, that restless dissociation from the totality of the present moment, that self-inflicted recoil from Reality. It is the clamoring for experiences, sensations, feelings, thoughts, and knowledge in which one can lose oneself with pleasure. But pleasure is only a simulacrum of the Happiness or Bliss of the undifferentiated "Condition of all conditions." To grasp this point the scientist must concede a model of Man that acknowledges Man's multidimensionality and the psycho-physical nature of existence.

This, however, the majority of scientists are unable or unwilling to do. For, the reigning model of Man and the universe stands in the age-old tradition of materialism, first as the primitive attitude of "eat, drink, and be merry," then as a philosophical effort. Materialism treats matter as the primal principle or essence of reality, including all psychic and mental phenomena. Since, in this view, psyche and mind are merely products or epiphenomena of material Nature, it follows that Nature exists independent of the thinking subject. Hence, idealism is a falsity. Furthermore, there can be no immaterial realms

45. Ibid., pp. 229-30.

or entities such as God, angels, or spirits. Therefore, religion is deemed a lie, and metaphysics a waste of time.

Modern scientific materialism is a descendant of the tradition that commenced with the materialist doctrines of the Greeks Leucippus, Democritus, Empedocles, and Epicurus and the Roman Lucretius. More specifically, scientific materialism owes its existence to the materialist revival, after its long eclipse by Christian idealism, in the seventeenth century. Prominent figures were the French astronomer Pierre Gassendi (who still held to the official Church doctrine about God as Father), the English philosopher-statesman Thomas Hobbes (who had fewer qualms about disposing of theological concepts), and the more prestigious French mathematician-philosopher Rene Descartes (who espoused a thoroughly materialistic interpretation of the inanimate cosmos but who nevertheless held fast to the belief in an immaterial and immortal soul).

The eighteenth century, which celebrated itself as the Age of Reason, reaped the first significant technological fruits of the intellectual revolution of the preceding centuries. Its two great landmarks were the monumental *Encyclopedie* of the French Enlightenment philosophers, with their boundless optimism in human progress and the (irrational) belief in the perfectability of Man through reason, and, in the latter part of the century, the Industrial Revolution, which translated scientific insight and speculation into practical reality, thereby transforming the lives of millions of people in a very short span of time.

With the expanding influence of the mechanistic world-view, inspired by Newton, religion receded more and more into the background of popular culture where, however, it persisted to dominate the hearts and minds of the less educated. This trend continued into the nineteenth century, even though the professional culture of science succeeded in freeing itself entirely from the shackles of the Church. Biblical lore and theological speculation proved no competition for a demonstrably successful science that could point to the triumph of chemistry, the formulation of the epochal theory—thermodynamics, Darwin's iconoclastic theory of evolution, and Maxwell's electromagnetic theory—the latter unifying the hitherto separate disciplines of electricity, magnetism, and optics. Science began to stake for itself a claim to the throne of savior of mankind—a role for which it is particularly unsuited but which it is reluctant to resign.

Science has been hailed as the liberator of Man. True enough, science has proved a powerful tool in eradicating many of the emergencies and ills to which humanity has been exposed for millennia. Through the ingenious application of the principles discovered by science, a vast array of machines, apparatuses, and gadgets has been invented that effectively reduce Man's anxiety and labors to stay alive and healthy. The average life span has at least trebled from the time of our Stone Age ancestors. Science has also been responsible for the technical means that now make feasible the cultural and political unification of humanity, liberating Man from his geographic isolation and granting him the possibility of growing beyond his mental insularity. It has even taken Man off his home planet, giving him an altogether new perspective on himself and his future possibilities. The catalog of such benefits is long and obviously open-ended.

Yet, science has its shadowy side, too, which can be symbolized in the single image of the nuclear bomb but which reaches deeper: into the innermost recesses of Man's psychic and mental life. In the words of R. G. Owen:

The successes of science are due to its careful observance of its limitations. It confines itself to the quantitative and mechanical and does not presume to · speak about spirit, values, and freedom; it understands that there may be vast areas of reality that lie beyond its reach. Science, however, because of its accomplishments, has acquired tremendous prestige and has risen in spite of itself to a position of predominant authority in our age. As a result of this exaltation, science, in some quarters, has come to be worshipped as omniscient, omnipotent, and the bearer of man's salvation. Such an attitude to science is, of course, entirely unscientific. It must be carefully distinguished from science proper. We may call it scientism or scientolatry. This peculiarly modern form of idolatry refuses to recognize the limitations of science and claims that its working principles can be used as universal principles, in terms of which the whole of reality can be explained and controlled. Scientism thus transforms the limiting principles of science into all-embracing dogmas which are regarded as absolute and final truths.

Scientology [scientism], therefore, claims that it can solve all problems "scientifically." . . . But when the limits of science are disregarded, when science becomes an absolute authority, when its principles are first converted into the generalized assumptions of a prevailing tradition and then articulated in the all-embracing dogmas of a pseudoscientific metaphysics, then men find themselves, at the end of the scientific age, not free but enslaved in new and more terrible forms of bondage.[46]

What shape this new servitude of Man could take has been portrayed, with chilling imagination, by George Orwell, who envisioned a nightmarish society riddled by scarcity, unbridled aggression, and unparalleled suppression of individual freedom.[47] Aldous Huxley furnished us with an alternative but equally horrifying vision: that of a world society populated by state-controlled, mindless (but not happy) "hollow" citizens.[48] Both "visions" and all other similar novelistic scenarios may, in principle, come true. The stage is certainly set for such a possibility.

Friedrich Georg Juenger, German arch-critic of modern technology, saw science becoming the servant of technology. He astutely observed that "the scientist becomes increasingly an employee in the institutes and laboratories of industry, where his knowledge is exploited for technical uses."[49] His fears, expressed at the time of World War II, were realistic enough. Today, almost four decades later, a large proportion of scientific research is not only government-sponsored but streamlined to meet the requirements of the state.

Science (and scientists) have become a nation's most precious commodity. Understandably, the state intervenes in scientific research and even monopolizes it. The reason for this government intervention in science is well known: to deploy the scientific genius for military ends. In the so-called "Free World," a small number of large corporations have the financial power, if not to openly compete with government, at least to persuade it to share its monopoly with them. Jointly their monies control more or less the whole of the scientific establishment—both at the university level and in the sphere of industry. As a result, scientific knowledge, once freely disseminated across national boundaries, is now jealously guarded and used in the intercompany struggle for increasing economic power and not least in the political game of one-upmanship between the great nations. A sorry and dangerous state of affairs!

46. R. G. Owen, *Scientism, Man, and Religion* (Philadelphia: Westminster Press, 1952), pp. 20–24.

47. See G. Orwell, *1984* (New York: New American Library, 1971).

48. See A. Huxley, *Brave New World* (New York: Harper & Row, 1979).

49. F. G. Juenger, *The Failure of Technology* (Chicago: Henry Regnery, 1956), p. 91.

Equally perilous is the scientistic ideology that, thanks to the successes of science and their uncritical propagandization through the mass media, has infected the popular mind, which is more and more lagging behind the rapidly extending frontiers of knowledge. Science is already post-modern, whereas the ordinary person still occupies a mainly pre-Copernican universe, with an almost magical relationship to the achievements and wonders of contemporary science and technology, which he is able to enjoy passively (and hence suffer) as a mere consumer, but in which he is unable to participate psychically. The knowledge explosion has fragmented his mind and feeling being, leaving him in a state of alienation, confusion, and basic anxiety. Jules Henry concludes his widely read book *Culture against Man* on the following somber note:

> *In Western Culture today one must make a distinction between the culture of life and the culture of death. In the minds of most people science has become synonymous with destructive weapons, i.e. with death. . . . Where is the culture of life? The culture of life resides in all those people who, inarticulate, frightened, and confused, are wondering "where it will all end." Thus the forces of death are confident and organized while the forces of life—the people who long for peace— are, for the most part, scattered, inarticulate, and wooly-minded, overwhelmed by their own impotence. Death struts about the house while Life cowers in the corner.*[50]

4. The New Science and the New Religions: Hoax or Hope?

The concluding remarks of the preceding section reflect one half, perhaps the more substantial half, of the status quo: The problems that mankind faces are very real and serious. However, contrary to Oswald Spengler, who boldly prophesied the decline of our occidental civilization, the outcome of the present global crisis is not predictable. The button that would release a thick swarm of lethal missiles crisscrossing the continents could well be

50. J. Henry, *Culture against Man* (New York: Random House, 1963), pp. 475–76.

pushed accidentally or by an undiagnosed military psychopath. But it need not. Good sense and vigilance might prevail. The nations of the world may even learn to cooperate in time to avoid the specter of economic disaster. That is the promise of the other half of the truth of our present-day situation.

Not all who speak up about the world crisis are prophets of doom. There are many who see new wine manifesting in old bottles. I have already mentioned Jean Gebser, Aurobindo Ghose, and Pierre Teilhard de Chardin. A long list of scholars and writers in the field of the humanities could be added. Among the better-known personalities that would have to be mentioned are Marshall McLuhan, Lewis Mumford, Pitirim A. Sorokin, Buckminster Fuller, Harold Schilling, Charles A. Reich, Abraham Maslow, Carl Rogers, Barbara Marx Hubbard, Theodore Roszak, and Marilyn Ferguson—each approaching this issue from his or her own unique perspective.

Marilyn Ferguson has made the latest attempt not so much to create a new overarching model for the emergent new conditions as to describe what she once called "The Movement That Has No Name." Although in her widely acclaimed book *The Aquarian Conspiracy*[51] she confines herself to charting the "leaderless but powerful network" of reform-minded professionals in different disciplines in the United States, the implications of her findings go clearly beyond the national boundaries of North America. The "Aquarian conspirators" are located in many other countries as well, including some that lie behind the invisible Iron Curtain.

The demolition of the medieval, Christian world-view by the Renaissance sciences left generations of people benumbed, in doubt, or anxiously clinging to demonstrably irrational beliefs. In the eighteenth and nineteenth centuries the intelligentsia—no longer at ease with Christian dogmatism—found its haven in science, which was promptly converted into the pseudo-religion of scientism to meet the meager emotional expectations of the left-brained individual. The population at large, however, continued to profess the Christian faith while at the same time, particularly in the illiterate strata of society, deriving a great deal of practical meaning from astrology, magical healing, divination, and witchcraft—an almost schizoid split that is characteristic even of a large section of our contemporary society. (Significantly, there are about ten thousand "professional" astrologers in the U.S.A. as against some two thousand astronomers!)

51. Marilyn Ferguson, *The Aquarian Conspiracy* (Los Angeles: J. P. Tarcher, 1980).

The extreme rationalism of scientism, not surprisingly, is an unattractive diet to those who look for deeper meanings but for whom the religious establishment is remiss in supplying a wholly convincing way of life. Many do not have the independence of mind to openly confess their apostasy and so continue to pay lip service to their inherited religion. Still, over the last couple of decades church membership, never mind active participation, has overall dwindled significantly in nearly all industrialized countries of the Western hemisphere. The ecumenical spirit, which the anxious clergy hoped would be a timely panacea for their institutional problems, proved rather ineffective. While the great denominations are facing the increasing exodus of their flock, sectarian groups, like the Jehovah's Witnesses and the Pentecostal churches, are steadily recruiting members from among those who dread a fluid, open world and who need the apparent security of the tight, provincial framework of fundamentalist religion: Here seeking is ended before it has begun. Hence, transcendence becomes an impossibility.

If Christianity offered no solace, if the "revivalist" sects of Christianity and the "neo-orthodoxy" of Judaism proved too claustrophobic, if scientism did not satisfy the craving for existential meaning, and if the age-old superstitions and folk mythology were no more than poor substitutes taken with a pinch of salt or in desperation and anguish, then obviously a new answer had to be found. *Natura abhorret vacuum,* "Nature abhors a vacuum"—at least human nature. At first it was hoped that the new discipline of psychology, chiefly in the form of psychoanalysis, could fill the gap left by the rapid decline of civic religion. That decline had of course been precipitated by psychology itself, which in a way led the criticism of religion by the natural sciences to its (bitter) end. However, psychoanalysis was not constituted of the same stuff that religions are made of and was even less equipped to counter existential anxiety and spiritual alienation. The principal reason for this failure was presumably the scientistic slant of psychoanalysis, with its positivistic model and behavioristic program for individual readjustment. Another important reason is, I think, the fact that despite its scientific pretensions, psychoanalysis has not freed itself from the weight of the peculiarly Hebrew and Christian preoccupation with the morbid side of our psychic life and the seemingly all-pervasive sense of guilt. Is it not the psychoanalyst's sacred obligation to exorcise the demons of warped guilt, twisted

Oedipal desires, other oppressive secrets, and a felt sense of unworthiness from the dark niches of the neurotic's unconscious?

Nevertheless, psychoanalysis gave birth to a whole range of new therapies that, today, compete with each other to remedy the psychopathology of our ailing civilization. They are, or propose to be, the secular man's answer to his spiritual emptiness. Their emphasis is on "personal growth," "self-actualization," "consciousness expansion," "aliveness," and "psychic health." Dwelling as they do on the positive (if not hedonistic) side of human nature—on Man's "potential," his creative capacity, and his ability to live a "happy" life—these therapies understandably enjoy considerable popularity, augmented by the fact that many also surround themselves with a messianic aura. They tend to congeal into quasi-cults, with a charismatic, authoritarian leader in the center, whose patients actively live out the neurotic fantasy of "being as little children." Even where such overt cultism does not occur, these therapies often indirectly encourage faddism and a mentality of dependence, which defeat their very *raison d'être*.[52]

Their attraction lies to a large extent in the fact that they take the individual and his problems seriously, giving him an opportunity to tackle his difficulties and to explore himself on his own terms, without having to submit—so the ideology goes—to any external authority. In other words, the narcissistic person is met on his own ground as a consumer of therapeutic experiences. What could be a potentially rewarding approach to self-transcendence generally winds up being a kind of experiential merry-go-round that consoles and gratifies rather than helps to transcend the ego. Where these popular therapies break out of this fun-and-games milieu, they assume a distinctly religious complexion, the inspiration for which comes, as a rule, from one or the other authentic religious tradition of the East—Buddhism, Zen, Taoism, Hinduism, Tantrism, Yoga, Sufism.

In fact, one of the most significant metamorphoses today is the orientalization of the West. This is an immediate consequence of the

52. See M. K. Temerlin and J. W. Temerlin, "Psychotherapy Cults: An Iatrogenic Perversion," *Psychotherapy: Theory, Research, and Practice,* vol. 19, no. 2 (Summer 1982), pp. 131–41. Remarkably, these quasi-religious therapies attract even the cleric. Ralph Wendell Burhoe observes: "Traditional religious and theological doctrines of the soul and its salvation are seldom heard, unless outspoken fundamentalists happen to be around. The older religiously related tradition is increasingly forgotten, and the new secular psychotherapies are openly advocated by churchmen." R. W. Burhoe, "Some Prophecies of Twenty-first-Century Technology and Religion," in *Science and Human Values in the 21st Century,* ed. R. W. Burhoe (Philadelphia: Westminster Press, 1971), p. 41. See also R. W. Burhoe, "Bridging the Gap between Psychology and Theology," *Journal of Religion and Health,* vol. 7, no. 3 (July 1968), pp. 215–26.

*"May I suggest that in today's group-therapy session we
all work on our contact with reality."*

expansion of Western economic and political interest into the East. Widespread disenchantment with Christianity, the first Eastern cult to take root in the occident, and the growing unease about scientific materialism has once again opened up the gates to the wisdom of the East. The ground for this cultural osmosis was prepared by the German romantic philosophers (Fichte, Schelling, etc.) and the American transcendentalists (Emerson, Thoreau, etc.) who influenced the English "metaphysical poets" (foremost Blake, Carlyle, and Coleridge). The activities of the Theosophical Society (founded in 1875), the dawn of Buddhist studies in Europe, and somewhat later the encyclopedic work of C. G. Jung proved singularly potent catalysts in this great process.

However, the influx of oriental ideas and values gathered critical momentum with the blossoming of the so-called "youth counter-culture" of the late sixties and early seventies, which superseded the rootless beatnik generation. Psychedelic experimentation, first vociferously advocated by Aldous Huxley, dealt the death blow to the conventional, if reactionary, attitudes of the earlier Teds, Mods, Rockers, and Skinheads. And it called into question the materialistic establishment itself. Yet, the Hippies and Flower Children grew into adults, many of whom became solid, law-abiding citizens after all. Still, the drug culture of that period, fired by the rebellious minds of Timothy Leary, Alan Watts, and Allen Ginsberg, has left indelible marks on American and European society and culture. These marks are partly wounds, partly auspicious signs.

In his book *The Awareness Trap,* Edwin Schur has drawn our attention to the dangers inherent in the contemporary movement toward what he calls "self-absorption"—the erroneous ideology of awareness as a panacea for all personal and social ills.[53] Without wishing to underwrite Schur's roundly pessimistic appraisal of the social value of individual growth, he rightly pointed out that most of these much-propagandized awareness techniques and programs are a mere travesty, and they all lack the spiritual soundness of the great religious and mystical traditions. Thus, they cannot be expected to heal the Western psyche from its civilizational malaise of "boredom, doubt, and discomfort" (Da Free John).

However, all this seeking over the past two decades has been positive inasmuch as it has greatly promoted the cause of the Eastern

53. See E. Schur, *The Awareness Trap: Self-Absorption instead of Social Change* (New York: McGraw-Hill, 1977).

liberation teachings within our Western culture, thereby sensitizing us to a hitherto neglected dimension of human capability. Most significantly, typically oriental ideas have even penetrated the stronghold of our materialistic civilization—the scientific establishment. The "New Science," like the new religions and quasi-religions, is remarkably orientalized. What is more, both the New Science and the new religions share another feature: They have strong liabilities.

Whereas the new therapies with their pseudo-religious pretensions are pointedly person-centered, the New Science continues the centuries-long fascination with the universe at large. Thus, they perpetuate, each in its own fashion, the artificial value-laden disjunction between individual and world, inner and outer universe. If the new therapies glorify experience and therefore irrationalism, the New Science, although it debunks the simplistic rationalism of the Newtonian paradigm that it endeavors to replace, still holds up the left-brained approach to reality. As always, therefore, scientists are exposing themselves to the anachronistic fallacy of mistaking the facsimile reality conjured up by thought for the Real Thing. Even though quantum physics is mirroring to them an inexhaustibly complex and ultimately inconceivable universe, they are quite undaunted by this. Indeed, their intellects are excited by the prospect of a never-ending voyage of inquiry, just as the experience-hungry therapists and their clientele are encouraged in their inward odyssey by the fact that the human personality is a vastly intricate, multidimensional system. The joy is in traveling, not in arriving, they say. But is it?

Self-exploration and the investigation of the world are basic forms of seeking. And seeking is, as Gautama the Buddha preached and as the modern Adept Da Free John reaffirms, a disease of the ego by which it struggles to block out the knowledge of its own mortality and suffering. But seeking itself is suffering, because it is an indirect affirmation of the fallacious sense of egoic separateness. This becomes clear when the search at last winds down. Before this is possible, however, Man must have come to at least a minimal understanding of the mechanism of individuation through which he singles himself out from the total ecology of existence.

Yet, the new therapies are unlikely to arrive at this point of recognition unless they desist from equating experienced reality with Reality. Likewise, the New Science must come to the understanding that a conceived or thought reality is not identical with Reality. This is an obvious point but one that does not appear to be heeded too much.

Consequently, there is the very real danger that, in their exuberance over knowledge and experience, the new therapies and the New Science might blindly fall in love with each other and authenticate each other's aspirations as alternative religions for the modern age. The guruism of the new therapies is all too apparent, and who would wager that the New Science does not carry the virus of pseudo-religious hubris from which scientism is suffering so mightily?

To be sure, the avant-garde researchers of the New Physics are eagerly turning to Eastern mysticism, delighting in the esoteric confirmations for the paradoxes of quantum phenomena. Gary Zukav writes:

> *The development of physics in the twentieth century already has transformed the consciousness of those involved with it. The study of complementarity, the uncertainty principle, quantum field theory, and the Copenhagen Interpretation of Quantum Mechanics produces insights into the nature of reality very similar to those produced by the study of eastern philosophy. The profound physicists of this century increasingly have become aware that they are confronting the ineffable.*[54]

But, as befits scientists of good standing, these physicists are confronting the Ineffable with the intellect, and therefore the changes in consciousness mentioned by Zukav are only skin-deep. They do not signal the kind of fundamental transformation of the whole being that results from a direct confrontation of the great Mystery, not merely by the mind and its homely icons, but by everything that Man represents, through immediate Realization of the Real. Master Da Free John offers this penetrating analysis of the cerebral approach:

> *Thinking about Reality is not the way to be in touch with It. Thinking is something you do by standing back: You contract, you turn away, you turn inside or become involved in the programmed mechanisms of the verbal mind, hoping to discover something that will give you some excuse, some reason for returning to Reality openly, for feeling good about it. You are trying to find some reason why you should surrender, why you should let go, why you should let yourself be vulnerable in the midst of this mortal circumstance.*[55]

54. G. Zukav, *The Dancing Wu Li Masters: An Overview of the New Physics* (New York: William Morrow, 1979), p. 330.

55. From an unpublished talk given by Da Free John on August 13, 1983.

The Eastern mystics to which modern physicists turn did not arrive at their ontologies by mere abstraction. Their philosophical ideas grew on the soil of mystical experience and were nourished, in at least some instances, by the ambrosia of ultimate Realization or perfect Enlightenment, which transcends all experiencing. Hence also their metaphysical structures, though apparently paralleling those of contemporary quantum physics, are firmly tied into Man's moral life: They serve as maps of spiritual growth, if predominantly through mystical introversion.

While the interpretation of reality proposed by the New Science is to be welcomed, it is still limited and certainly provisional. Therefore, it would be premature to draw far-reaching conclusions purely on the basis of the current research and speculations. And yet, the knowledge of the New Science contains important cues for a healthy departure from the rationalist-mechanistic interpretation of Nature that continues to dominate much of contemporary thought and life. Nevertheless, the lack of a truly comprehensive under-standing—informed not by opinion, belief, or wishful thinking but by Transcendental Realization—in the new therapies or religions and in the New Science greatly hampers their free development and ultimate usefulness for Man. Without the kind of radical orientation found in the Teaching of the Adept Da Free John, the new therapies are likely to fall victim to the "heresy" of religious provincialism, whereas the New Science is prone to succumb to the equally obnoxious error of scientism (perhaps not of the materialist brand, but with the same totalitarian pretensions).

5. The Scientist as Human Being, and the Obligation of Conscious Spiritual Evolution

Science, like religion, is a human activity. In fact, it is an all-too-human enterprise. Contrary to the popular stereotype, "the scientist" suffers the very same limitations and shortcomings that afflict most other people as well. Although his left-brained approach to life may suggest to intellectually less gifted members of our species that the scientist is a superior being, for the most part his abstract orientation is little more than a (seemingly successful) neurotic adaptation. This circumstance deserves to be fully appreciated, because it will shed light on the fateful development of science into scientism.

The mass of humanity lives either in childish dependence or adolescent reactivity to life, that is, in a state of emotional immaturity. Scientists, as Master Da Free John explains, fall characteristically into the latter category by dint of their lopsided intellectual "attack" on the material universe, which they quantify, manipulate, and now even forcibly disintegrate (in nuclear reactors and accelerators). An aesthetically more sensitive temperament might look upon the scientist's experimentation as a brutalization of "Mother Nature"—thus hinting at the undoubtedly existing Oedipal overtones of scientific research.

In its program, science is the rational operation *par excellence*, and *ratio* belongs to the left cerebral hemisphere. However, in actuality, science is an activity that also involves, if only covertly, other sections of the brain. This means that scientific practice—however "pure" it endeavors to be—is always subject to nonrational factors as well. As biologist and science popularizer Carl Sagan put it:

> *In a way, science might be described as paranoid thinking applied to Nature: we are looking for natural conspiracies, for connections among apparently disparate data. Our objective is to abstract patterns from Nature (right-hemisphere thinking), but many proposed patterns do not in fact correspond to the data. Thus all proposed patterns must be subjected to the sieve of critical analysis (left-hemisphere thinking).*[56]

Sagan went on to say that he knew of "no significant advance in science that did not require major inputs from both cerebral hemispheres,"[57] obviously hinting at the role of intuition, synthetic insight, and other integrative functions in scientific research. However, such nonrational-creative breakthroughs occur almost despite the scientist's struggle to operate solely from the cognitive system associated with the left cerebral hemisphere. Because of the nature of his expectations, the scientist can be said to make a deliberate effort at inhibiting the right cerebrum, which is tantamount to a repression of the psychic dimension of the personality: intuition, imagination, subjectivity, sensuality, metaphoricalness, concreteness.

56. C. Sagan, *The Dragons of Eden: Speculations on the Evolution of Human Intelligence* (New York: Ballantine Books, 1978), p. 192.

57. Ibid., p. 193.

While analytical thinking is a valid and useful strategy or cognitive style, it must not become a habitual disposition. For, chronic exercise of the verbal, sequential mind is purchased at the expense of human emotion, or depth of feeling. Scientists are, generally speaking, personalities who are predisposed to emphasize (and overemphasize) the left side of our brain. Thus, Lawrence S. Kubie, a medical specialist at the Yale School of Medicine, made the astute observation that neurotic factors play an important role in the choice and the pursuit of a scientific career. He was even more specific than this:

> There are significant relationships between masked neurotic components in the personality of an apparently normal scientist, and such things as (a) the field of work which he chooses; (b) the problems within that field which he chooses; (c) the clarity with which he habitually uses his native capacity for logical thinking; (d) the ways in which he attacks scientific problems; (e) the scientific causes which he espouses; (f) the controversies in which he becomes entangled and how he fights; and (g) the joy or sorrow which is derived from the work itself and also from his ultimate success or failure.[58]

Since the unconscious is a ubiquitous force in the human personality, it is easy to see how neurotic vulnerabilities would color even a scientist's basic observation of Nature, and subsequent testing and reasoning may only remove some of these initial distortions. This explains, at least in part, why some scientists miss important discoveries by a hair's breadth, why they are resistant to new scientific discoveries,[59] and also why there are "paradigms" and "paradigm shifts": If there were such a thing as objective knowledge, reality would be known as it is, rather than as it appears to be in the successive frameworks of understanding. All knowledge has an a priori foundation, and that foundation is intimately connected with the psychological profile of the investigating subject.

Mostly, the theory-laden character of scientific "facts" remains concealed from us, but we are vividly reminded of it whenever we encounter a scientist suffering from exaggerated neuroses such as

58. L. S. Kubie, "Some Unsolved Problems of the Scientific Career," *American Scientist,* vol. 41 (1953), pp. 597–98.

59. See B. Barber, "Resistance by Scientists to Scientific Discovery," *Science,* vol. 134 (1961), pp. 596–602.

phobic indecisiveness or anxiety-driven curiosity (the equivalent to a
handwashing compulsion, as Kubie pointed out). Most tragic of all is
perhaps the pathological self-defeating strategy of those scientists
who, though extraordinarily gifted, produce works of great ambiguity.
"Some of these men," remarked Kubie, "unconsciously designed their
laborious experiments so as to prove nothing."[60] Judging from the
annual spate of largely irrelevant publications, the conclusion lies at
hand that the scientific population includes not a few such unfortunate
neurotics—unless one were to explain the stockpiling of irrelevancies
as a form of deliberate cynicism or sheer commercialism (to which
scientists fall prey increasingly, dependent as most of them are on the
good will of either Government or University).

Speaking of the social sciences specifically, Stanislav Andreski
made the following acerbic comments about this syndrome:

*What is particularly dismaying is that not only does the flood of
publications reveal an abundance of pompous bluff and a paucity of
new ideas, but even the old and valuable insights which we have
inherited from our illustrious ancestors are being drowned in a torrent
of meaningless verbiage and useless technicalities. Pretentious and
nebulous verbosity, interminable repetition of platitudes and disguised
propaganda are the order of the day . . .*[61]

Andreski's devastating verdict applies, one suspects, with equal force
to the natural sciences, whose professionals increase the mountain of
mostly unread publications by several hundred thousand academic
papers every year.

Are scientists, then, merely pitiable neurotics who are obsessed
with knowledge and factual certainty via abstract thinking, nagged on
by an overpowering urge to doubt? They are probably no more
neurotic than the average non-scientist. However, the form their
neurosis takes, and also the privileged socio-cultural position granted
to scientists in our science-worshipping age, renders their neurotic
liabilities far more perilous for society as a whole. For, it is the
scientific "community" that largely determines the pace and direction
of technology and thus, indirectly, the destiny of mankind. It is also the
scientific community that typically arrogates to itself the right of

60. L. S. Kubie, "Some Unsolved Problems," p. 610.

61. S. Andreski, *Social Sciences as Sorcery* (Harmondsworth, England: Penguin Books, 1974),
p. 11.

passing final judgment on matters that clearly lie outside its province of competence—matters that characteristically concern the cognitive style associated with the right hemisphere of the brain.

Where scientists become obsessed with the mode of the left brain and the reality (or, rather, slice of reality) to which it grants access, they corrupt science into a science-based ideology—scientism. In that case they succumb to their neurotic liabilities. It is then that they also fall prey to what Daniel S. Greenberg called the "folkways" of the scientific community—"chauvinism," "xenophobia," and "evangelism." [62] The first member of this holy trinity is the tenacious belief that science is humanity's greatest benefactor and that therefore it deserves cultural priority over other aspects of human life. By "xenophobia" is meant the irrational attitude of aversion felt by scientists towards "outsiders" who do not honor the scientistic ethos of submission to the formalities of research and who seem to slight the sacred "scientific method." It is this dogmatic exclusiveness that has, for instance, so far curbed the free development of such a "fringe" discipline as parapsychology, which, of course, deals with manifestations of the much-dreaded and repressed half of the brain. The proclivity of the scientific community towards elitist introversion is instinctively balanced by a strong tendency to proselytize: The scientist feels himself in possession of important truths that should be communicated to the lay world. This motivation undoubtedly meshes with economic considerations: After all, it is the lay public that, in the last analysis, finances scientific research.

Of course, science is significant at this juncture in human history. But so long as the psychological susceptibilities of scientists are not fully recognized and handled, science is preordained to slide more and more into mere scientism. How can this be prevented? Lawrence S. Kubie recommended a major revision of scientific education, remarking that "nothing could be more important to science than that scientists should know themselves in the neo-Socratic or Freudian sense, that is, in terms of the interplay between their own conscious and unconscious processes." [63]

If this counsel were heeded, scientific work would in all probability undergo a dramatic change in approach, style, and possibly even content. Alfred North Whitehead, writing a quarter of a century

62. D. S. Greenberg, *The Politics of Pure Science* (New York: New American Library, 1971), pp. 26ff.

63. L. S. Kubie, "Some Unsolved Problems," p. 605.

earlier, tackled this issue from a somewhat different though compatible angle. He observed that only professionalized knowledge is effective, but that this has its inherent dangers: "It produces minds in a groove."[64] This, he further pointed out, causes "serious thought" to be confined to a small, select area or aspect of existence, whilst the "remainder of life is treated superficially, with the imperfect categories of thought derived from one profession."[65] The *idiot savant* who is a genius in his chosen discipline but an imbecile in all other areas, notably practical life, is a typical illustration of such aberrated specialization—the fragmentation of the psyche which parallels the fragmentation of knowledge.

Whitehead also called for an urgent revision of education. He fostered the balanced growth of the individual, which alone, as he saw it, would help to secure real wisdom. He addressed the need to overcome the methodological intolerance of science by means of art and aesthetic education, which includes the life of the spirit. But Whitehead was writing as a scientist-philosopher, not as an Adept. Consequently he had no clear and convincing guidelines to offer. This is the plight of all those who, like him, are acutely sensitive to the imbalances of modern life but even as they criticize the human condition are themselves embroiled in it.

The living wisdom of self-transcendence in its most radical or perfect form is not to be found in conventional religion or in stock prescriptions for self-knowledge or self-actualization. Why? Because conventional religion is ego-based, and the ego balks at the idea of its own negation. It disallows itself to contemplate the possibility of its own superfluousness. Hence self-improvement is substituted for self-transcendence, precisely because the former leaves the ego intact. But utter self-transcendence, or "ego death," is not something that the self would naturally entertain.

And yet, as the German mystic-theologian Meister Eckehart, preaching about true obedience, observed:

When I do not want for myself, God wants for me. Hearken! What, then, does he want for me when I cease to want for myself? When I let go of my I, he must necessarily want all that for me which

64. A. N. Whitehead, *Science and the Modern World* (Harmondsworth, England: Penguin Books, 1938), p. 228.

65. Ibid.

he wants for himself—neither more nor less and in the same manner
that he wants for himself.[66]

Eckehart, who was one of the first to preach in German rather
than in obscure Latin, was well aware of the fact that his sermons
would mostly fall on deaf ears. Nevertheless, he persisted in preaching
about self-transcendence, which not surprisingly landed him in serious
conflict with Pope John XXII. There is an ongoing debate whether
Eckehart was merely an inspired theologian with mystical inclinations
or actually a God-Realized individual. Be that as it may, he dared what
few churchmen today venture to do: He fearlessly and energetically
brought to his listeners the gospel of self-transcendence to the point of
Realization.

Nowadays, almost seven centuries later, the ban on God-
Realization is still in effect in the Christian churches as much as in any
other conventional religion: The consumer mentality of the popular
masses cries out for consolation rather than the wisdom of self-
transcendence. People do not desire the Truth but are satisfied with
the truths of secular understanding. Perhaps this has been so ever
since the day when Man divorced religion from other forms of
knowledge. Today we can witness the nadir of this development. On
the one hand, the sacred or esoteric "knowledge" of religion is no
longer kept alive in the great religious traditions, and on the other
hand, secular knowledge is elevated to the status of Truth by the
ideologues of scientism. But science deals in facts (which, contrary to
popular opinion, are subject to change) and not in Truth, which is
immutable. Thus, what scientists have to offer are more or less self-
consistent and plausible representations of Reality, not Reality itself.
Writes Gary Zukav:

"Reality" is what we take to be true. What we take to be true is
what we believe. What we believe is based upon our perceptions.
What we perceive depends upon what we look for. What we look for
depends upon what we think. What we think depends upon what we
perceive. What we perceive determines what we believe. What we
believe determines what we take to be true. What we take to be true is
our reality.[67]

66. J. Quint, ed., *Meister Eckehart: Deutsche Predigten und Traktate,* "The Talks of Instruction,
Section 1: Of True Obedience" (Munich: Hauser, 1963). (The English rendering is the present
editor's.)

67. G. Zukav, *The Dancing Wu Li Masters,* p. 328.

This is the more sophisticated view that a scientist might entertain. But what of Reality? If both conventional religion and science peddle in substitute truths only, where is Truth to be found? Master Da Free John gives this passionate answer:

If you want to learn about Truth when Truth has become corrupted, then go to an Adept. Go to one who has Realized the Truth. Go to one who has already fulfilled the process completely. If you live in a moment in time when there is no Enlightened Tradition, when all the cults are corrupt, you can be certain that somewhere on Earth an Adept is alive. Such a person appears under exactly those conditions, when Truth is no longer visible in the cults, and when religions have become so corrupted by history and fetishism that they are about to become extinct.

The religious traditions in our time are about to be smothered by a mechanistic, political, and scientific world-view, only because the cults are in doubt. They have held on to their fetishes so tenaciously that they have lost their association with the Living God. They do not even know the Living God anymore. People who belong to churches, religions, and spiritual societies have no unqualified connection with the Living Reality. There is no true devotion in them, and therefore, no Realization. Their association with God is only words and hopefulness. Therefore, they do not represent a living force in the world. They have nothing to offer that is Alive. Only the Adepts, who are God-Realized, through whom the living Power of God manifests, can make a difference in human time. Such individuals are the instruments for the acculturation of humanity.

Periodically, such individuals must appear, and they must be influential. There is a notion that Adepts should be hiding in caves in the wilderness. This is not true. If the Adepts do not speak, the only voice that will be heard is that of ordinary people who are not God-Realized. The Adepts are the Sources of spiritual life. Such individuals must therefore enter into the stream of society, to purify the culture and reestablish the process of God-Realization. If they do not speak and become influential, there is no hope at all for humanity.[68]

The Transmission of Reality is the business of the Adept. The

68. Da Free John, *Scientific Proof of the Existence of God Will Soon Be Announced by the White House!* pp. 381–82.

transmission of doubt is the scientist's karmic concern. He hungers for certainty and yet shies away from absolutes; and rightly so, for there can be no absolutes in the finite or relative realm in which the scientific mind-games are played out, even though apparent absolutes creep into the picture occasionally anyway (e.g., the velocity of light). But the scientist, as human being, must ask himself why he is inclined to opt for doubt—the continuous interrogation of Nature—as his *mood* rather than as an occupation-specific method. Why is he obsessed with elaborating ever more "realistic" representations or symbolizations of Reality? Why does he automatically presume that Reality is inaccessible other than through models? Why does he prefer questions to answers? Why does he so distrust the testimony of the great Realizers or Adepts of mankind? Why does he generally project his energy and attention upon the external world? Why is he typically neglectful of inner life, the intangible psychic dimension?

Science is a falsely optimistic attempt to professionalize Man's instinctive recoil from the Mystery of existence. This the scientist must see before he can make the transition from a mere data processing unit to a fully human being. And only when he has realized human maturity can he proceed to the real life-task of growing beyond ordinary humanness into a self-transcending entity in whom Reality itself becomes transparent. In other words, the scientist must learn to regard his life in the larger context of spiritual evolution and submit himself to the process of conscious maturation. If he does so, not only his life but also his work will assume a new significance.

The scholastics of the Middle Ages made a molehill out of a mountain by putting angels on pinheads and reducing the Great Matter to drivel. The scholars of our period vivisect the Body of God and the Sources of Enlightened Influence and mount them on pins for display, mocking them, making them into scapegoats, and crucifying them on the linear structures of language.[69]

Clearly, once it is understood that the scientific enterprise does not stand apart from human life, but is an integral aspect of Man's mortal existence, science will cease to be a mere handmaiden to technology or the private obsession of a small elite. Instead, it will

69. From notes to the editor by Master Da Free John, given April 5, 1982.

acquire new premises, new objectives. Once science is conducted under
the aegis of a culture that is committed to self-transcendence, it cannot
but serve the enrichment of human life and facilitate the process of
spiritual maturation of our species. What would science be like, and
how would it contribute to the harmonious transformation of the
human environment, if its practitioners were not self-possessed
individuals competing for recognition or economic security and driven
by subconscious forces, but Enlightened beings who were no longer
engaged in a neurotic struggle for survival?

*What happens to life when you are Awake, when you recognize
conditional existence? Well, extraordinary siddhis*[70] *are potentially
associated with that Awakening. And that Awakening is the potential
destiny of beings on Earth, although we are presently in an uncom-
monly crude epoch of evolution on this planet.*

*Even so, the demonstration of that destiny will not be realized in
my lifetime, even if there exists a seventh stage community. The seed
of it can, however, appear in my lifetime, and the appearance of that
seed is what I am here to bring about. Eventually, that seed will lead to
the development in the human plane of the extraordinary arts and
sciences associated with Enlightenment and the native siddhis of
Awakened existence. But until this Awakening moment or epoch is
completed, the arts and sciences that may develop on its basis cannot
become history, cannot become the structure of human destiny
altogether.*

*Science is beginning to explore unusual possibilities, but it does
so without Enlightenment, without acknowledging the inherent
Immortality of existence, of Being Itself, and without tapping into the
reservoir of infinite Being and infinite Energy at the level of human
consciousness. What, then, is science producing? A bastardized culture
associated with political materialism. Therefore, science is failing as a
great benign device, failing to produce a golden age, because the
Awakening epoch has not yet been completed. Science, in fact, is*

---

70. The word *siddhi,* which stems from the Sanskrit root *sidh* meaning "to achieve," signifies
most generally "ability" or "capacity." In yogic contexts, the term is frequently used to denote
paranormal abilities or "powers." In the Way of Radical Understanding or Divine Ignorance such
siddhis may arise spontaneously, in which case they are simply allowed to manifest and are
observed and understood. The Great Siddhi is the Power of the Heart or Divine Consciousness,
which is Transmitted through the Adept's unobstructed body-mind.

culturally predisposed to bypass the epoch of Awakening. It is simply trying to change conditions themselves without Realizing the Truth of existence.

Yet, if this Divine Awakening and science were to characterize humanity, there would exist the great art and science of Transformation, and a completely different kind of life would emerge on Earth. Now, when is that going to happen? This year? In the next couple of decades? Absolutely not![71]

And yet, as Master Da Free John affirms, this kind of spiritualization of human life, though it may take hundreds or perhaps even thousands of years, is our "native and inevitable"[72] potential. Enlightenment is the great principle operative in the universe.

Existence is not for the purpose of Enlightenment. It seems so only when you are not yet Enlightened. But Enlightenment is the Principle of existence, and when there is Enlightenment, then the purpose of existence is obvious. The purpose of existence in manifest form is to Transform manifestation, to Transfigure existence, to glorify Being in form.[73]

---

71. From an unpublished talk given by Da Free John on May 9, 1983.

72. Ibid.

73. Ibid.

PROLOGUE

THE UNITY

THE UNITY

by Da Free John
July 27, 1982

[handwritten: ✓ 8/92]

[handwritten: 1. Lessons in Truth — we are all individuations of One Divine Mind]

The self-consciousness of individual beings inheres in Transcendental Consciousness, or Transcendental Divine Being Itself.
The body-mind of every individual being inheres in the Self-Radiant Love-Bliss of Transcendental Divine Being Itself. Nature, or the worlds of the relations of self-conscious psychophysical beings, inheres in a Matrix of Light or Energy or Life that also inheres in the Self-Radiant Love-Bliss of Transcendental Divine Being Itself.

That in Which or in Whom self-consciousness, the body-mind, and all possible worlds of experience and knowledge inhere is Self-Radiant, Eternal, Indestructible, Perfect, and Absolute Happiness.

We are, in essence or in Reality, That One.

We are not destructible, even by death.

We are, in our conditional individuality, transformable in or by life and death.

We can and, ultimately or inevitably, we will Realize our Identity with That One. And by that Realization we can and necessarily will Ascend into the Domain of That One.

This is the "faith" or intelligent certainty of those who are founded in clear understanding.

2.

The conventional and generally materialistic philosophies that doubt and deny the One Transcendental Divine Being are actually neurotic psychologies that are based on the self-contraction, or the failure to understand the self, transcend the self-contraction, and recognize the worlds or processes of experience and knowledge. Such presumptuous philosophies wrongly attribute utter independence to form and mind and consciousness. Such psychologies are grounded in fear, misunderstanding, recoil, alienation, horror, and death.

Therefore, what is necessary is self-understanding, self-transcendence, and a recognition of all appearances in their Substance or Source-Condition. Then the Unity of Existence will Stand Obvious in the midst of self and world. Then the Way of self-transcendence and Ultimate Translation will be clearly Revealed to the living being.

PART ONE

THE IDIOT
SAVANTS

The scientific community must understand and acknowledge that its positive aspect is its orientation toward free intellectual inquiry. The old exoteric religious institutions perpetuated an "understanding" of the physical universe that was characterized by uninterpretable poetic mythologies and all kinds of absolutist cultic nonsense. Fresh and direct inquiry into phenomena needed to be permitted. That aspect of the emergence of scientism was completely positive. The exoteric religious institutions that existed when scientism began to appear were not founded in universal Truth or a broadly communicated esoteric understanding of the "material" universe and the Way of Man. They were (and remain) downtown exoteric institutions, traditional cultic institutions, without great Adepts and without universal Wisdom. In throwing away this half-baked religion, however, we have also thrown away all psychic inquiry into the universe and its ultimate Condition or Destiny. Intellectual inquiry into the objective phenomena of experience certainly has its value, but psychic inquiry into the experiential universe is not only equally essential, it is primary, and it is more fundamental to the individual. Indeed, such psychic inquiry is absolutely essential for human happiness.

Da Free John
Scientific Proof of the Existence of
God Will Soon Be Announced
by the White House! p. 390

INTRODUCTION TO PART ONE

diot Savants" is a phrase applied to what Pavan Sahgal styled "members of a strange psychological club that, through the centuries, has included wizards of calculation, designers of complicated machines and models and accomplished artists and musicians who were quite helpless at most other tasks."[1] These prodigies, as Sahgal pointed out, are neither idiots (who, strictly speaking, have an IQ of twenty or less) nor savants, because their unusual knowledge and abilities are not the product of systematic learning. They are, rather, genetic accidents. They may be able to extract the square root of a four-digit figure in a few seconds or memorize long passages in a language unknown to them yet have great difficulty in learning simple arithmetic or tying their shoelaces.

In other words, they are highly competent in a narrow area of life but retarded or inept in most other respects. As such they are a perfect confirmation of the popular (and not wholly idle) suspicion that genius borders on madness. At the same time, they serve as a symbol for a trend that is both pernicious and conspicuous in the world of science: intellectual sectarianism, euphemistically called "specialization." In this sense, the term "idiot savants" refers to those "typical" scientists who, figuratively speaking, suffer from a hypertrophy of the left cerebral hemisphere with simultaneous idiocy of the right brain. Master Da Free John supplies the larger context for this insight and criticism:

> To take up the practice of science is a legitimate human activity, but it is also a partial human activity. We must not, therefore, make it the sole judge of human existence, the sole model of human knowledge, awareness, or relationship to the world. To make science, or the particular attributes associated with scientific activity, an exclusive model of human existence would ultimately amount to a

1. P. Sahgal, "Idiot Geniuses," *Science Digest*, May 1981, p. 12.

psychosis. In fact, this is exactly what is taking place culturally today. And this is one of the major reasons why our society is taking such a bizarre turn. The verbal mind, the analytical approach associated with the left hemisphere of the brain, has become the only legitimate way of relating to everything.

The practice of science develops merely a part of the mind, or brain, a particular feature of the nervous system. When you do science, you isolate a specific aspect of the human being to do a certain kind of work. That in itself is fine. But when you make that kind of work and that presumed structure of activity the only one whereby you define yourself as a human being, then you turn that model of the psyche into the model of human relations altogether. If you make the left hemisphere of the brain the psychic model of existence, you become a dissociated personality. You begin to deprogram the whole capacity for participation beyond words, for whole bodily relational association with other beings and the universe.

The kind of knowledge that is characteristic of science is not participatory knowledge. It is analytical knowledge. It is knowledge that is acquired by dissociating from the object of observation, by taking a position entirely independent from the object so that you can simply observe its mechanics. If you adopt such a stance relative to everything all the time, you become mad. You are mad. And such madness is exactly what Narcissus is. Narcissus is the psychic model of science. It is the role or method of science made into a human personality, and it is the dissociative character rather than the participatory character made into Man.

When science is made into the model of human existence, when it defines human consciousness altogether, then it begins to inform mankind with this role of dissociation, with a mind that is about doubt only. It makes the human personality incapable of the process of participatory existence, or the form of knowledge that is associated with participation rather than independence, dissociation, doubt, investigation, and analysis.[2]

The Adept's critique of science or scientism is primarily a critique of the scientist as an *egoic* individual. Secondarily, it is a critique of his particular form of egoity, as expressed in his science-oriented seeking. If the scientist's peculiar orientation to life were simply a personal

2. From an unpublished talk given by Da Free John on October 21, 1980.

affliction without any wider social significance, this would only be a matter of individual concern. But scientists form a quasi-community, and their idiosyncratic approach to life is embodied in a most influential world-view. Hence the scientist's particular style of Narcissism is a matter of grave public interest.

Scientists, of course, are inclined to reject criticisms of their activity—especially when it reflects on their psychological predicament—unless these criticisms bear the hallmark of the scientific approach. The scientist immunizes himself and his world-view against "outside" interference by demanding that any critique of science should proceed on the basis of the "scientific method"—the scientist's pride and jealously guarded central dogma. But what is that method? Paul Feyerabend, iconoclastic philosopher of science, writes acerbically:

> *The image of twentieth-century science in the minds of scientists and laymen is determined by technological miracles such as colour television, the moon shots, the infra-red oven, as well as by a somewhat vague but still quite influential rumour, or fairy-tale, concerning the manner in which these miracles are produced.*
>
> *According to the fairy-tale the success of science is the result of a subtle, but carefully balanced combination of inventiveness and control. Scientists have ideas. And they have special methods for improving ideas. The theories of science have passed the test of method. They give a better account of the world than ideas which have not passed the test.*
>
> *The fairy-tale explains why modern society treats science in a special way and why it grants it privileges not enjoyed by other institutions. . . .*
>
> *But the fairy-tale is false, as we have seen. There is no special method that guarantees success or makes it probable. Scientists do not solve problems because they possess a magic wand—methodology, or a theory of rationality—but because they have studied a problem for a long time, because they know the situation fairly well, because they are not too dumb (though that is rather doubtful nowadays when almost anyone can become a scientist), and because the excesses of one scientific school are almost always balanced by the excesses of some other school. (Besides, scientists only rarely solve their problems, they make lots of mistakes, and many of their solutions are quite useless.) Basically there is hardly any difference between the process that leads to the announcement of a new scientific law and the process preceding*

passage of a new law in society: one informs either all citizens or those immediately concerned, one collects "facts" and prejudices, one discusses the matter, and one finally votes. But while a democracy makes some effort to explain *the process so that everyone can understand it, scientists either* conceal *it, or* bend *it, to make it fit their sectarian interests.*[3]

In sum, there is no such thing as the scientific method, as was noted by R. S. Scorer, a professor of theoretical mechanics.[4]

By the canons of positivist science, the Adept is disqualified from critiquing science. Firstly, unless he happens to be a scientist himself (which is highly unlikely), he is a layman and as such, so the story goes, neither fully comprehends the business of science nor is capable of applying the scientific method in his argumentation. Secondly, since the factual universe of science explicitly rejects the existence of an Ultimate Reality as Being-Consciousness, of which the phenomena investigated by science are only an apparent modification, the Adept's claim to perfect Identity with that Ultimate Reality is not only nonsensical but makes his psychological integrity suspect.

The first apparent "disqualification" is deceptively plausible. As it stands, it might just as well apply to philosophers of science who are not scientists themselves. This is obviously absurd. For, the critique does not concern the myriad details of scientific activity, for which specialized knowledge would indeed be imperative, but it considers the *form* in which science is being pursued. More especially, it addresses the human element in the scientific process. And it does so from the most generic viewpoint possible: the total evolutionary potential of Man.

If the first disqualification is symptomatic of the chauvinistic and xenophobic tendency of the scientific community, the second disqualification is a function of its closed world-view: Certain possibilities *cannot* be the case, because they would undermine the whole conceptual framework of science. In some instances, counter-evidence that clearly contradicts current assumptions can still be accommodated into the scientific world-view—as "anomalies"—but this becomes *psychologically* impossible when the fundamental metaphysical (or, rather,

3. P. Feyerabend, *Against Method: Outline of an Anarchistic Theory of Knowledge* (London: Verso, 1980), pp. 300–302.

4. R. S. Scorer, *The Clever Moron* (London: Routledge & Kegan Paul, 1977), p. 30.

anti-metaphysical) premises of positivist science are directly threatened. In that case, the scientist, like any other human being, will begin to wear conceptual blinders: There can be no such entities as Adepts because they cannot be predicated on the basis of the scientific world-view. *Ergo,* the whole structure of thought (i.e., esotericism, Radical Transcendentalism) built upon the existence of such extraordinary (and scientifically impossible) entities must also be false. Plainly, the limitation pertains to the psychology of the scientist himself. It does not define the Adept or his critique.

Indeed, Master Da Free John addresses just this unnecessary and perilous self-limitation of the scientist who "prefigures" existence but who is on the whole oblivious to the fact that all knowledge is interpretative and hence subject to error and further improvement. He proposes an alternative to the artificial observationism typified in its extreme by behaviorism and espoused by all those scientists still under the spell of the mechanistic world-view of the nineteenth century, which is the overriding majority of the several million scientists alive today. He speaks of existence as a participatory process, and this is perfectly congruent with the findings of modern quantum physics, which, however, is making only very gradual inroads into the predominant world-view of science. The common denominator of the essays and talks in this volume is just this alternative view of reality, in which the Cartesian dichotomy between subject and object is exposed as a root illusion of the ego, an illusion with far-reaching consequences throughout human culture, not least science.

But, as always, Master Da Free John does not approach his subject matter as a theoretician. He is not a scientist or philosopher, but an Adept, even though his considerations greatly enrich both science and philosophy—precisely because he writes and speaks from the participatory disposition that he advocates. Observes Herbert D. Long, professor of theology:

Master Da Free John's writings are an extension of his own being, a form of his agency. They are not scientific tomes in the sense that their bias is one of objective disengagement and description. Neither are they poetry nor autobiography, an extension of his interior life. Both objectivity and subjectivity are present, yet somehow transcended.[5]

5. H. D. Long, "Reflections on the Significance of Da Free John for Our Time," *The Laughing Man,* vol. 4, no. 4 (1983), p. 71.

The essays and talks in this volume have immediate *personal* implications, irrespective of whether the reader is a scientist or a layperson. With his argument the Adept, who has transcended the ego and its projections,[6] purports to penetrate the reader's egoic armor to the point that the reader's consideration of the Adept's argument will become a living experience, bodily truth. Thus, this book calls for participatory cooperation, which is possible only when, in true phenomenological fashion, the reader brackets his a priori assumptions and biases. In other words, the Adept's communication makes sense only when received with intellectual modesty—in ignorance.

For most, if not all, readers this will prove a very difficult task. After all, the reader has much at stake: himself, the apparent sanity of his world-view, his most cherished beliefs and fervent hopes for the future. For, once the message of these essays and talks has been truly understood, the reader will perceive entirely new possibilities for personal and social existence, but also new responsibilities will accrue to him. Certainly, the universe communicated by Master Da Free John is far more magnificent, awesome, and exciting than that pieced together by materialistic science (or scientism). What is more, it can point a way for those pioneering spirits of science who, chastised by the findings of quantum physics, are groping for a new model of reality.

The essays and talks of part 1 provide the setting for the more detailed considerations in subsequent chapters. In chapter 1, entitled "The Cult of Narcissus and the Culture of Participation," Master Da Free John outlines his "methodology" by contrasting ego-based knowledge and activity with the alternative of ego-transcending Realization and "perfect participation in what is." He makes a plea for radical understanding rather than mere intellectual comprehension. The former is always an existential act or process, in which the object is experienced as part of the total web of existence that also includes the human subject.

Chapter 2, styled "The Asana of Science," examines in more depth the conventionally entertained dichotomy between subject and object and shows how science has committed the blunder of taking this notion so seriously as to elevate it to the status of a methodological

---

6. To respond to a widely held misconception about the nature of ego-transcendence, it should be emphasized here that it most definitely does not entail the popularly feared destruction of the personality. For a more detailed explanation of the psychology of transcendence, see the introduction to part 4, pp. 355–58.

absolute. Science, Master Da Free John observes, is a pose, an "asana"[7]—that is, an artificially maintained stance that does not reflect the whole being of Man.

Most practitioners of science, being captives of the particular psychology that is associated with the pose of science, are oblivious to the partial nature of their chosen self-identification as scientists and the lopsided exaggeration of the scientific approach. They think theirs is the best of all rational worlds. Although they have professionalized the attitude of doubt, it is really dogmatic self-assurance that guides them in the maintenance and dissemination of their basic metaphysical premises about the world. In this respect, the position of the scientist is analogous to that of the religionist, who turns faith into his single most important operating principle.

But there are other striking parallels between conventional religion and the religion of science. Thus, science or scientism—the former converts into the latter to the degree that science becomes a substitute for authentic religion—can first and foremost be characterized as the worship of truth. Yet, it is not the Transcendental Truth as the Condition of all empirical phenomena that is the target of the scientist's search, but the multiple (and necessarily ephemeral) truths of phenomenal existence. In other words, the truths of science are the "facts" that it appears to "discover" in the Sacred Book of Nature. Material reality, or Nature, is celebrated as the source of all scientific revelations.

Scientific "literacy" is guaranteed by the scientist's absolute faith in reason. Rational intelligence is valued as the sole decoder of the Book of Nature, because Nature itself is believed to be a supremely rational structure, whose processes unfold according to definite and unchallengeable laws: Nature functions like a gigantic machine or clockwork.

Because reason is deemed Man's ultimate capacity, science as the rational enterprise *par excellence* naturally claims superiority over all other religions. Other scientific creeds are the belief in the uniformity of Nature, the objective "external" existence of the physical universe, the evolution and immortality of matter, and the infinite progress of human knowledge, which will in due course answer all questions and solve all problems. Finally, science or scientism views itself as a

7. The Sanskrit word *asana* is derived from the verbal root *as* meaning "to sit, dwell." It denotes "posture" or "pose," generally a yogic position of the body. Here Master Da Free John uses the term in the broadest sense, to indicate a stance, attitude, or presumption.

benign, humanitarian force in the world, which exists for the ultimate good of mankind.[8]

It is these pervasive tendencies in modern science that Master Da Free John criticizes in chapters 3 and 4, entitled "The Priesthood of Science" and "The False Religion of Scientific Knowledge" respectively.

The last chapter is a fictional dialogue between naive but benign "Sap" (Homo Sapiens) and "Testoob" (the Faustian scientist). Allan Sherman's masterful caricature captures strikingly the peculiar psychology of the individual dominated by the left hemisphere of the brain. This piece adds a right-brain dimension to the present consideration, while at the same time reminding us of the fact that "we use laughter or joking, our worldly humor, to escape from pain"[9]—in this connection, the pain of a human activity that has gone astray.

8. For a book-length treatment of these analogies see W. H. Wood, *The Religion of Science* (London: Macmillan, n.d.).

9. Da Free John, *Scientific Proof of the Existence of God Will Soon Be Announced by the White House!* p. 375.

CHAPTER 1

THE CULT OF NARCISSUS AND THE CULTURE OF PARTICIPATION

an essay by Da Free John
December 3, 1982

4|98

1.

The foundation of my Teaching Argument is this: You are, as a matter of habit, and in every part, conformed to the activity and the results of self-contraction. It is not possible to affirm and Realize the existence of God, or the Living Spiritual Divine, or the Condition of Self-Radiant Transcendental Being until the self-contraction is thoroughly observed, understood, and transcended. Therefore, all other propositions of my Teaching are built upon the proposition of necessary self-transcendence.

The ego, or the essence of every person (personified as "I"), is not an inner entity or subtle essence. The ego is the activity of self-contraction. And it is observable in the person of the "I," the body-mind or psycho-physical persona, as the feeling of separateness and the performance of every kind of separative activity. Therefore, as I have indicated in *The Knee of Listening*, the ego may be recognized and transcended through consistent self-enquiry in the form "Avoiding relationship?"[1]

It is the tendency of the ego (or egoic body-mind) to want to relate to consoling and even ultimate propositions of knowledge and experience, rather than to concentrate in the ordeal of self-understanding and self-transcendence. Therefore, egos may just as likely appear in a religious or spiritual mode as in a secular, atheistic, non-religious, or non-spiritual mode.

There is a long-standing tradition for talking about ultimate matters and making ultimate propositions, without otherwise doing what is necessary in order to enter into the domain of ultimacy. And so the world of egos is busy wondering: "Is there a God? Are we immortal souls? Is there an ultimate Condition that is eternal Happiness?" Just so, there are always ample numbers of self-deceiving and other-deceiving personalities who busily affirm to us all: "Yes, there is a God. We are souls. We can, by certain means, go to a Place of eternal Happiness." And there are always an equal and opposite number of benighted characters who affirm: "No, there is no God. We are mortal material entities. We can only struggle to survive with as much pleasure and as little pain as possible."

But what is the Truth? I propose to you that all of the differing and opposing views of ordinary mankind are developed from the same base. All authorities and all ordinary people are animating and also suffering from the same limitation. The only superior point of view is founded on a unique base, which is freedom from the self-base. All other views are self-bound, self-deluded, and self-perpetuating.

God, soul, and Transcendental Being as well as no-God, no-soul, and no-Transcendental Being can be proposed intellectually, or analytically, or by logical transactions of the mind, but not one of these ultimate propositions (or negations of ultimate propositions) can be proven by the same means. That is to say, the mind, or even the total psycho-physical person, is not in a position to affirm or prove any ultimate propositions to the ultimate degree. This is because the "I," or the bodily based persona, is founded in egoity, or the universally effective act of self-contraction.

1. The enquiry "Avoiding relationship?" is the original form of meditation that Master Da Free John spontaneously discovered and practiced, to the point of perfect Enlightenment, during his own years of spiritual experimentation and Re-Awakening. This enquiry is engaged by practitioners in the Way of Insight, one of the stages of practice for maturing devotees in the Way of Radical Understanding.

Because the usual man or woman is not merely a psycho-physical entity but an actual or active ego, the body-mind-self or "I" is always uniquely expressed as the tendency of non-participation. The unique effect or result of the self-contraction is always present non-participation, or what I call the adventure of Narcissus.

Except in the case of true Enlightenment, the individual personality is an ego. That is, every ordinary personality is rooted in a self-possessed and counter-relational mode of presumption and activity. This root-orientation plays a most profound role in every individual life and, therefore, in every collection or society of individuals. Egoity determines destiny. And the activity of egoity is operative universally—in every function and fraction of individual and collective existence.

Therefore, the world of un-Enlightened human beings represents a Cult of Narcissus. Every feature of human knowledge and experience is an emblem of this Cult—unless the Cult itself is broken. We are all caught in the snare of egoity, all at war with ourselves, and one another, and the world, and total Nature, and the Transcendental Spiritual Divine Condition. We are all by root and tendency involved in an effort of non-participation, countering all possible relations and conditions, and suffering the prime result, which is confinement to self and its experiential solitude and its self-bewildered views. How can this be doubted? How can we fail to take this observation into account?

2.

I propose to you that every feature or characteristic of your psycho-physical existence is merely an expression of root-egoity, or self-contraction. What is more, I Argue that self-contraction is unnecessary. It is something we are adding to the conditions and the Condition of existence. We are simply not noticing the Reality and the realities of our existence, because we are priorly and always established in a state of self-contraction, and thus we are animating ourselves in a self-possessed and separative mode. Therefore, neither body nor mind is set free in the plane of relations, and we are not in a position to know or experience what is. For this reason, our lives, our bodies, our minds, our emotions, and our human world are contaminated with our own presence. We are not free, and, therefore, we are not Happy.

The habit of Narcissus, or universal egoity, is reflected in every destiny, and in every fraction of human culture. And un-Enlightened humanity specializes in the method of Narcissus. True, we are always struggling against these results, but we are also, even unintentionally, always enforcing this cause.

What is "knowledge" in our time? It is epitomized by the method and the accumulated culture of scientism. And the method of science epitomizes the tendency toward non-participation. The method of science is, at its best, a right and useful tool for acquiring certain kinds of information or data about conditional events. But as a world-view, or an ideal orientation toward existence, it is nothing other than the attitude and method of egoity. This is because it is based upon the abstraction or separation of the observer from the observed. It expresses a preference for the non-participation (or non-interference) of the observer in the observed and in the results of the observation. The observed, or what is presumed to be wholly objective and independent of the observer, is the "god" of our scientific path of knowledge and experience. And, therefore, the observer has become the "golem"[2] or even the "dragon" that stands between knowledge and things as they are.

The disposition of scientism has, in our time, become the model or ideal attitude toward what is. Science has come out of the closet, from an esoteric discipline engaged by a few revolutionaries, to a world-view that commands what is acceptable as knowledge for all. I do not object to the factual usefulness of the scientific method as one of the possible tools of Man, but I thoroughly and vehemently object to the culturally enforced notion that it is the single, sufficient, and ideal tool of Man.

The technique of abstraction, or the method and ideal of non-participatory knowledge, cannot be rightly or fruitfully applied to the intimate or inherently relational context of human existence, nor can it be rightly or fruitfully applied to the ultimate context of existence itself. We cannot by non-participation discover what is noticeable only in the context of thorough and perfect participation!

Scientific method and scientific culture, applied as a thorough and singular ideal, only destroy the truly human bond of relations and preclude the human possibility of discovering (and thus participating

---

2. The "golem" is, in Jewish legend, an artificially created man—a monster or automaton. Master Da Free John applies the Hebrew term here to the bias of objectivism that informs science and scientism.

in) the realities and the ultimate Reality of existence. Therefore, in the few hundred years in which the materialistic culture of scientism has been ascending in its dominance, the previous dominance of religious and esoteric spiritual institutions has been steadily declining. And, what is more important, the general ability of people to enter into a truly religious or spiritual mode of existence has been gradually eclipsed in this same period. The reason for this is that the ancient religious and spiritual way of knowing (which was based on the participatory rather than the non-participatory attitude) has been gradually suppressed and even eliminated as a viable tool of humanity.

I call for us to understand ourselves and our cultural history, and so be free to modify and correct our personal and collective destiny. I do not call for the suppression of the scientific method. But I do call for us to accept responsibility for that method and the views and results that become its consequences when it is not applied responsibly. We should accept the fact that there are as many critical and negative results to come from irresponsible application or idolization of the scientific method as there are to come from irresponsible use of the hydrogen bomb or any of the other sophisticated technologies that may be developed by means of our common science. To idolize science and allow it to dominate human life is to idolize egoity, the destiny of Narcissus, and universal separation from Reality.

3.

Science is not love. Science is not surrender. To do science is to stand apart and inspect and analyze. To know without love and submission is to magnify power and the motive of control. Power and control are secondary needs of Man. Such knowledge is, therefore, only a secondary need of Man. Science is only a secondary tool of Man. What is our primary need and our primary tool? We need love, union, unity. Our primary tool is participation. And participation requires submission of self to what is. Therefore, participation is love, or the act of loving or self-transcending submission. If we act as love, submission, or in the attitude or by the tool of self-transcendence, then we also come to know and experience. But the knowledge and experience that come by such means do not enhance or magnify the power of self to control what is. Rather, they enhance and magnify our freedom, our Realization of Reality, and our ultimate Happiness.

To live with one another freely we must love, tolerate, and be compassionate toward one another. Therefore, we cannot live with one another dispassionately, abstracted, as in the mood of science or egoity. We must participate in one another. Just so, we cannot by abstraction notice or Realize what is. We must freely participate in what is to know and experience it (or It). Therefore, in order to know and experience what is we must transcend ourselves—we must transcend Narcissus, the ego, the self-contraction, or the universal avoidance of relationship.

4.

We cannot discover whether or not there is God, or soul, or Transcendental Spiritual Reality by analytical or non-participatory means. The ego cannot discover the Truth. Therefore, science cannot discover the Truth. Science is one of the possible tools of Man. But it is a secondary tool. Even so, the ego is not at all a proper tool of Man. The ego is the primary impediment of Man, and it distorts our use of every tool available to us.

Our greatest need is to discover the Truth. And in order to discover the Truth we must understand and transcend ourselves. If we understand and transcend ourselves, we may then also do science, but we must certainly become religious, which means that we will inevitably become Spiritualized beings.

The domain of science is non-participatory knowledge of apparently objective Nature. But the Domain of Man is participatory knowledge of what is. I ask you: What is when we cease to add our own self-contraction to what is? Analytical, self-abstracting, other-objectifying methods of knowing merely extend the habit of egoity. But if the self-contraction is observed, understood, and transcended, then whatever remains simply evident simply is. And whatever is ultimately is Reality.

Our primary obligation is to be supremely intelligent about ourselves. It is thus that we become capable of communing with and conforming to whatever is ultimately, and it is also thus that we become capable of serving others most truly and profoundly. The ego and the scientific mind also want to serve others by conforming to reality, but reality conceived by means of self-abstraction and the objectification of existence is not what is. It is a false view, an imagined reality, a circumstance presumed on the basis of self-contraction or non-participation. We can know or Realize what is only through self-understanding that becomes not merely self-information but self-transcendence. Therefore, we must first become capable (through self-understanding and self-transcendence) of self-submission and free participation in what is prior to our own self-contraction.

I do not merely propose the idea of God, or soul, or Transcendental Being. Such propositions cannot be rightly believed or presumed by the separate and separative ego. Therefore, the ideas of religion that occupy egos and the egoic culture of self-abstracted scientism are themselves false views, representing a poignant and inevitably frustrated longing for love, release, and ultimate Happiness. On the contrary, I propose self-observation, true self-understanding, and perfect self-transcendence. And if the Way of self-transcendence is magnified as the fullness of participatory capability, then what is will be discovered to be Divine, unbound, eternal, Transcendental Happiness.

5.

The word science comes from a root-word that actually means "to separate"! But the common meaning of the word is "knowing." Therefore, on the basis of this common meaning (rather than the root-meaning) the Way that I Teach may be described as a "participatory science." It is our primary tool, the alternative tool, or the basis for the application of all secondary tools. The Way that I Teach also involves a rigorous experiment. My "method" requires, for its ultimate performance, rigorous and then perfect transcendence of the self-contraction and, on that basis, perfect participation in what is.

Our ordinary science is at best a secondary tool of our manifest humanity. We must not make a "culture" out of it, or dominate our minds with it. Our right and true culture is the super-culture of primary endeavor, the culture of participation. When the ego or self-contraction is transcended, the body-mind or "I" becomes love, or a truly and uniquely human presence. And when "I" is love, what is is self-evident, beyond doubt. I Argue that what is ultimately is Divine, Spiritual, and Transcendental, prior to and beyond the stepped-down complications of conditional Nature. But what is ultimately is not obvious to the non-participatory or self-contracted view of the ego.

Therefore, first of all, I Argue for self-observation, self-understanding, and self-transcendence. The Narcissistic ego and its results are completely evident to our immediate view. If we will transcend that self-contraction and be given up to love and participate in what is prior to the self-contraction, then we will swoon in the Immense Spiritual Reality. That Reality is what is, and It is Obvious when the self-contraction relaxes. Therefore, transcend the Cult of Narcissus, and what I propose ultimately will be Self-Evident in your own case.

"Hear" me by self-understanding and "see" what is,[3] beyond yourself. Do this "science" and I will magnify your "hearing" and "seeing" with the Baptism of Immortal Happiness.

---

3. "Hearing" and "seeing" are technical terms used by Master Da Free John to describe the conscious and spiritual Awakenings that are the necessary foundation of the Way that he Teaches. "Hearing" is the intuitive understanding of the self-contraction and simultaneous intuitive awakening to Divine Consciousness that arise on the basis of disciplined study of the Argument of the Adept. Hearing leads naturally to "seeing," which is emotional and total bodily awakening into faith, or direct feeling-intuition of the Divine Reality under all circumstances. The Adept has also described seeing as conversion from self-possession to God-Communion in, as, and through all relations and all phenomenal experience. Only on the basis of continual hearing and seeing can the practice of true spiritual life begin.

CHAPTER 2

THE ASANA OF SCIENCE

a talk by Da Free John
October 25, 1980

MASTER DA FREE JOHN: Science is commonly described as a way of observing the natural world, a method of excluding or abstracting the viewer from the process of observation, so that what is observed is a "reality" untainted by the presence of the viewer. This process of acquiring knowledge is concerned not with transforming the viewer but with learning about the so-called objective or natural world independent of the viewer.

Now this is an interesting notion of human activity. We are so used to the presence of science and technology in our culture that we accept science as a natural activity, a sort of professionalization or technical elaboration of something that everybody is already doing. But the activity of science may not be natural at all. It is something we are already doing when we conceive of the objective world or the natural world apart from ourselves. Yet, if we become sensitive to the real Condition of our existence, can we truly say that we ever experience or have anything whatsoever to do with an objective world? Do we ever contact anything objective or independent of ourselves?

The common presumption of our daily lives is that there is an objective world, but this presumption is simply a convention of egoic life and of the society wherein we live. Science bases its sophisticated activity upon this conventional view of life. It seems natural enough to say that we live in the physical world. We are all sitting around here in this physical world, right? But to speak of a physical or objective world is simply a convention of our existence, whereas in fact we do not have any actual experience of an objective or independent world. Our actual experience is much more complex or undefined than that convention suggests.

You refer to yourself as "me" or "I," but if you were asked what "I" is, how could you ever come to the end of the description? Obviously you have not entered into an exhaustive self-analysis or observation of yourself before using the term "me" or "I" as a self-reference. If you understand how you presume the reality of a so-called objective world, you will not find an "I" that could possibly have so much as a foot inside a physical world or that can be so defined and confined. This "I," which is ultimately only conscious awareness, this being that is aware of phenomena, has no direct connection to an independently objective world.

The conscious being is related to a so-called objective world through the process of conception and perception. We conceive and we perceive and therefore we presume an objective world, but we do not in fact have any actual contact with the world itself. We are associated with perceptions but not with the world. Thus, we never directly experience a "world" as an independent reality. Yet as we experience this whole affair of perception and conception, we make certain conventional judgments. We establish certain conventions of thought, communication, and action, whereby we say things like, "There is this external world here" and "I am me, and you are you." We say these things, but they are purely conventional statements with no ultimate philosophical stability. The notion of a physical world in which we exist is a conventional notion, an idea, a presumption on which we can act, but a presumption we need not even share. It is not universally accepted that there is an independent gross physical world. Many other cultures have had totally different views of reality, and they have used other conventions to determine their behaviors, relations, and ideas.

Science presumes to seek direct knowledge about a world that is independent of Man. In doing so it has created other effects that have cultural, psychological, and even spiritual significance. Science has become the dominant point of view of our society and thus has established a way of life wherein human beings universally presume that the "real world" is the physical world and that the world of the self, the so-called internal realm, is unreal or merely caused by the external world. Thus, science abandons the primary feature of our condition as human beings. In fact, you could even say that science is not a truly human activity, because in its pursuit what is specifically human in us—the inherence of our consciousness in the Divine Reality—is fundamentally suppressed, abstracted, and separated out.

According to the philosophy of science, we are supposed to pursue knowledge about the external world, rather than participate in a total world wherein Reality includes not only the objects of perception and conception but the process of perception and conception and the being or consciousness in which perception and conception are experienced or recognized. Science does not presume Reality as the total human condition. It presumes reality to be external to the human condition and in its study of that reality it suppresses the human condition as a medium of association with phenomena. The mood of science, therefore, has chosen the so-called external world as the real world and presumes that all the other dimensions of existence with which human beings are directly associated are unreal or simply caused by the "real" world, which is the gross, physical, material, external universe.

In Truth our Condition of existence includes more than the so-called external world. We are always simply existing, simply conscious. Every other feature of our existence is an object to the conscious being. If a thought arises, it is witnessed in consciousness. If a sensation arises, it is witnessed. If a room is perceived, it is witnessed. The fundamental aspect of our Condition, therefore, is spontaneously existing consciousness, which has no features of its own. Everything arises as an object to consciousness through a spontaneous process of perception and conception.

That process of conceiving and perceiving notices and experiences various forms, some of which are related to what we call the external, gross world and others of which cannot be found there at all. For instance, you cannot always find the environments of your dreams in the gross world. At least according to the conventions of our thinking you could say that you cannot find them there. We associate different levels of conceived and perceived objects with different dimensions of experience. Therefore, there is this existing being or existing consciousness, and there are the processes of conception and perception, and then there are various forms, gross and subtle, that we interpret and evaluate according to various conventions. But our actual situation includes all three of these fundamental conditions—existing consciousness, conception and perception, and forms—in dynamic association with one another.

Science is an invention of Man and a development of one specific convention of interpreting reality exclusive of other possible conventions. Thus, in the scientific convention, existing consciousness in association with the process of the conception and perception of forms becomes a single conventional presumption at the level of human relations in space and time. The conception of "me" or "I" is basically the process of conception and perception referring to itself. This body-mind, or the process of conception-perception, calls itself "I." It refers to itself as if it has thoroughly investigated itself and thus knows exactly what it is meaning when it says "me" or "I." But the "I" is just a convention of reference, not necessarily the product of a thorough analysis of its true nature. "I" is a rather intuitive gesture, but it is also just a convention that permits ordinary communication and activity. Therefore, if the process of conception and perception is uninspected, it conceives of itself as an independent self over against all possible forms that arise. Once this presumption is made (and it is made for very ordinary reasons), it is possible to say things like, "There is the external universe." But to call the realm of conceived and perceived forms an "external universe" does not signify that we understand anything profound or that we have understood the true nature of that realm, any more than to say "I" or "me" means that we have thoroughly analyzed and understood the self. It is simply a convention of reference.

Scientific activity is not inherently evil, but it does become an evil or destructive force if it is permitted to dominate our world-view and to remain unaccountable to our total realization of existence. In our time science has been permitted to take a convention absolutely seriously, as if such conventions had ultimate philosophical force, and it has been permitted to do great psychological harm to humanity. By divorcing reality from the realm of our actual existence, science has attributed reality to that which is apparently outside our existence. It has made the so-called physical universe the realm of reality, and it regards everything else to be an effect of the material world.

But science itself tacitly admits that we have no direct connection to an objective universe. If we had a direct connection to an objective universe, we would not have to go to such lengths to find out about it scientifically. We must create tools that abstract Man either mentally or technologically just to find out about the external world. In order to do science, you must "machine" Man, you must define and discipline Man in a particular way, because Man is not naturally habituated to knowing about things in the way that science requires. This discipline can be useful in acquiring certain kinds of knowledge, but if that discipline is permitted to become an absolute point of view to the exclusion of the total reality of Man, then human existence becomes an alienated aberration within the physical universe.

The reality of the external world to which science points has no psychic depth, no depth of being. It is a plastic mass of events. When scientists study Man, they want to prove that the mind, the psyche, the being of Man, is the effect of bodily existence and thus an effect of matter. They conclude that if the mind is caused by matter, then it is basically unreal, secondary, not a primary reality. From that point of view, however, to pursue knowledge about reality one must dissociate from one's own being and find a way to become involved with a so-called external, objective world. Science as such a discipline of knowledge can be of value, but as a point of view about existence, it is destructive and psychotic.

We do not exist merely in a physical universe, you see. We exist in a multidimensional condition, every aspect of which is totally real and mutually related to all other aspects. These many dimensions condition one another and bring one another into existence. As a matter of fact, we never observe anything's ever being brought into existence. Existence is an inherent Condition of Transcendental Being. All these appearances are just transformations or changes. Nothing ever comes into existence. Nothing ever passes out of existence. Things only change. They become apparent and unapparent, identifiable in one moment and unidentifiable in the next. This truth is demonstrated in the law of the conservation of energy conceived by modern physics, which states that energy is never destroyed but is, rather, ceaselessly transformed.

In the ancient world essential human existence, as well as social and cultural existence, was not created and defined by the point of view of science or anything like science. Even though some science-like enterprises may have developed in those times and places, the fundamental conceptions or presumptions that created the model of human existence and established the circumstances and processes of daily life were often based on a total and fully human presumption about the conditions of existence.

Science is a dehumanizing adventure when made into an absolute philosophical point of view, because it chooses a reality independent of Man as the subject of its investigation, makes that reality the force that defines Man, and makes the physical universe senior to, superior to, or more real than the being of Man and the subtler dimensions in which Man participates constantly. Science excludes the subtle dimensions of energy, the dimensions of psyche, and the dimension of being or consciousness. But all these conditions are our true Condition. The mere external or objective physical world, which is only a conventional notion anyway, is a fraction of the total Condition of which we are directly aware in every moment. The physical universe, which science wants to investigate, itself represents only a portion, one dimension, of a much wider, broader scale of dimensions in which we participate.

We exist simultaneously in many dimensions. We fluidly move attention through these dimensions. Our attention can pass from gross physical phenomena into thinking, into visions, into reverie, into a state transcending all gross consciousness, into psychic awareness of what appear to be environments or worlds that have nothing whatever to do with this one, into existent being or consciousness that has no references whatsoever, and then back again through all of these dimensions one by one. We can, therefore, presume a Condition of existence wherein all these dimensions are simultaneously existing, simultaneously real. But since science is not founded upon the observer but upon the observed, it does not have this flexibility of movement through many dimensions, and it is not possessed by the paradoxes of our actual human existence.

Many scientists and people sympathetic with the scientific worldview do not seem capable of thinking about what they are doing. They have no more insight into their presumptions and motives than enthusiastic religionists or "creationists" possess in their domain. Scientists do not rigorously understand that science itself is a chosen, specific development of a single aspect of conventional human understanding. In the enterprise of science the mind and body are used to do a specific kind of work. But apart from that, all the dogma about the total universe and about reality and existence itself, and science's anti-spiritual, anti-religious, anti-psychic point of view, and its Victorian, archaic materialism, and its prejudices against other kinds of knowing, all of this is insidious, not merely nonsensical, because it has such a profoundly negative effect on human beings.

Meanwhile, many scientists who adopt this dogmatic approach act as if they were super-intelligent people with their tweedy, pipe-smoking, slow-talking, complicated linguistic minds. This is the archetype of intelligence, right? This is the way you are supposed to be if you are intelligent. Well, this archetype does not necessarily represent intelligence. It is just a pose. Real intelligence must be fiercely capable of investigating every aspect of existence, including the very process of knowledge that we call science.

Science has now become so legitimized, and we have become so serious about it, that we are beginning to forget that, on a very basic level, we feel there is something ridiculous and even threatening about science. When it first appeared, science was considered heresy by the Church. Then it became thought of as just craziness, and scientists were always depicted as mad. Madness and science were considered the same thing in those days. When science first began to become prominent, before it became really official—at that crossover point from the Middle Ages and the Renaissance into the so-called Age of Enlightenment and Romanticism of the nineteenth century—science was considered to be possibly aberrated. Many stories, such as the tale of Frankenstein, appeared during that time. Science was considered to be a kind of balminess or madness.

On some level we are still very humorous about science. We know that the left-brained, tweedy character is a poseur, and we know that science is a pose, an "asana." Apart from the specific enterprise for which this asana or pose of science was invented, it does not represent the disposition wherein we are Enlightened, free, happy, totally associated with all of the factors of our existence.

To do science one must take on a pose that is not the disposition of Man contemplating Infinity. When science begins to propose that this asana is the disposition we must assume relative to everything, then it becomes mad. We must be able to reconnect with our humor, our primitive sense of the poseur that we can be and of the ridiculousness of our postures. To live all of life in the pose of science, to make the asana of science a style of living, is like trying to eat dinner while standing on your head! There are certain things you cannot do in the posture of science, and when you are seen trying to do them in that pose, you must be laughed at. We must recover our humor by regaining a more complete understanding, appreciation, and awareness of our existence as a whole and understand science as an aspect of existence, a tool, that we can develop as a conventional exercise with ordinary importance, but that could be very destructive to our human existence if it is developed otherwise.

"Up to this point, his logic is impeccable."

The true alternative to the extreme pose of science, however, is not the traditional option of orientalism. The pose and activity of science that we are criticizing is an enterprise of Western Man. It is necessary to begin to see the limitations of that essentially Western exercise and to feel the threats to human life that are created by the absolutism of that pose. Yet, if you only react to the presumptions of science, you start looking to the opposite pose as a solution.

We can clearly see, particularly in recent decades, a developing interest in the oriental approach to life. That interest really represents a nostalgia for the oriental disposition, but we must understand that the oriental asana is also a partial development of Man, an exploitation of only one aspect of our total Condition. If you take the oriental asana too seriously, you deny reality to the conventional relations of human existence. You deny positive value, therefore, to being born and to the conventional responsibilities of being alive as a human being. The oriental disposition of inwardness and withdrawal from life promises infinite regression into security from all the limiting effects of the perceived and conceived universe.

Both the oriental and the occidental views, in their extremes, are reductive. They reduce reality to only one of its features. The oriental disposition attributes reality exclusively to the fundamental self-nature, and the occidental disposition attributes reality exclusively to the objective relations of the self. But when you become dogmatically inclined to attribute reality exclusively to one or another primary feature of our total Condition, you are engineering your consciousness into an illusion, a fault, a dilemma.

The oriental disposition is regressive toward self, but the occidental disposition is progressive to the exclusion of the self. It makes Man into a moral robot whose only significance is the accomplishment attributed to the few individuals who have made scientific discoveries at critical moments. From the point of view of scientific dogma, those are the only human beings who have really done anything other than be confined to illusions. Everybody else is sort of babbling along in fear, believing all kinds of nonsense. Here and there we find some character in a tweed coat with a pipe who is able to break free of all that and see how objects move in space!

In terms of the ability to observe and comprehend, there is something remarkable about such individuals. But likewise other people have accomplished just as many remarkable things in relation to a totally different way of knowing, a more comprehensive or total way of knowing or realizing our existence. Even so, there are many babbling, frightened people, but you can babble and be frightened as a scientist just as much as you can babble and be frightened as a conventionally religious person.

The oriental enterprise—which not only developed in the East but which has been a feature of humanity all along, East and West— has provided the domain for religion, spirituality, mysticism, magic, and all the elaborations of the psyche. Because oriental enterprises attribute reality only to the fundamental depth of the subject and not to the world of forms, they tend to be ineffectively related to the world of forms. Therefore, if the domains of religion, spirituality, mysticism, and magic are not held accountable to real processes, they can develop all kinds of illusions and create views that are purely imaginary, suggestive, or archetypal. Those views may be unified, but the phenomena they are unifying can be totally imaginary, merely psychic and subtle, and only partially objective in relation to the material world. Thus, the mind of Man and the culture of Man, when permitted to develop exclusively along oriental lines, tend to create a culture of illusions.

Science as we know it appeared historically at a time when religious enterprises (particularly Christianity), dominated by orientalism, had become so filled with illusions that early scientific observations were arbitrarily condemned and anathematized, just as science now arbitrarily condemns and anathematizes non-illusory, real features of psychic and spiritual realization. Scientific discoveries were declared heretical because they did not square with the assumed imaginary cosmic picture that had been created by religionists. Then, as science itself began to achieve more and more dominance (because it was discovering some real facts), the Church, the religious point of view, the oriental disposition itself, began to be viewed as wrong. Not only some of its presumptions or ideas were presumed wrong, but religion itself was presumed wrong.

Now we are at the opposite end of this historical pendulum. At one time even the Western world was profoundly associated with the religious consciousness of orientalism (in the form of Christianity, specifically), but now that whole enterprise is presumed to be false. Another world-view, another way of knowledge, another kind of cult has achieved power and has become associated with the State and the machinery of worldly power, and it is using that position to dominate its opposite.

DEVOTEE: Even some meditation groups try to prove their effectiveness scientifically.

MASTER DA FREE JOHN: Yes. In order for religion to remain legitimate in our time, when it is so much out of favor, it must associate with what is in favor—the dominant persuasion and mass of information that has been generated in the cult of scientific materialism. Thus, what in another setting would be called a religious, mystical, or spiritual practice is now called scientific yoga and the like. But science itself is just a conventional expression of the current stage of humanity. The cure for all of this is not to be found in the disposition or enterprise of science itself, nor is it to be found in the disposition and orientation of the oriental asana or point of view. Neither of these two represents the fullness of human realization. They both have, in their extreme and exclusive form, been dominant in one or another time.

To transcend the limitations that are obvious at the present time, we must transcend all of the historical alternatives. We must transcend the limited disposition of science that now dominates as well as the limited disposition of the oriental view that seems to be its primary alternative. In order to transcend all these limited features we must simply and directly observe and consider our condition as a whole, prior to making any of these limited presumptions, prior to assuming or engineering our existence as a choice between the occidental and the oriental dispositions. We must conceive of our condition, our existence, as it is altogether. We must witness it and see that it is altogether existing and real in every dimension, not just in one dimension or feature. And our real existence, our free and happy existence, is to be realized only in the asana, the attitude, of our total Condition, rather than in our choice of a single aspect of that Condition.

CHAPTER 3

THE PRIESTHOOD
OF SCIENCE

a talk by Da Free John
March 13, 1978

MASTER DA FREE JOHN: I have recently read some books that attempt to summarize the current state of physics, astronomy, and cosmology based on scientific observations. These texts summarize the history of the material universe, from the moment of the so-called "Big Bang" to the present, and they also describe its evolution in the future. Each of them is written in a different mood and comes to a different conclusion. In each case, the conclusion has philosophical or spiritual and religious significance, but it has nothing whatever to do with the summary evidence. The conclusions are purely emotional persuasions. One of them has something like a religious feeling about the whole matter. Another has a completely atheistic feeling about it. One sees the universe expanding and contracting in eternal cycles. Another sees its genesis once and its coming to an end only once. But none of these events has actually been observed. The writers of these books are surrounding the collection of physical observations with a structure of childish or adolescent philosophizing that is at the same level of thinking that existed centuries before these physical observations.

Thus, the old dogmas persist. We have different priesthoods, that is all. And the current priesthood is the priesthood of the scientists. Modern scientists certainly perform great services for humanity in many ways, but we tend to misinterpret their influence and their level of understanding. We tend to feel great awe in their company, but they do not have any more sound basis for making ultimate assumptions than people did hundreds of years ago, before our present scientific capacities. In other words, our scientists represent the same mind, the same disposition, the same state of evolution, as men of old, and the same variability of viewpoint, from school to school, from person to person.

It makes no difference whether we are scientists looking at sophisticated measurements and data or ordinary people walking down the street and casually commenting on the weather—we cannot say anything more intelligent than our state of adaptation allows. We cannot enjoy greater insight into what we are examining (regardless of what it is we are examining) than we have the adaptation from which to communicate. We are always the philosophers of our present state of adaptation. Modern scientists are scrutinizing sophisticated data, but they are not making truly sophisticated or higher cultural sense out of it. The data itself may contain all kinds of hidden clues to the same Wisdom that was enjoyed by great seers in the past. But the conventional scientists cannot communicate that Wisdom. They can only communicate the dogma of their own adaptation. Since they have not stepped into a different evolutionary process, they do not know anything about the physics of real meditation and the process that is evolving in the higher structures of the human being. They know nothing about it. Despite their best intentions, then, they are basically just chattering about their own immature or subhuman condition and communicating the vision, the emotional understanding, of which they are presently capable.

People tend to misinterpret modern scientism just as they misinterpreted the priestly influence in the Middle Ages. There is always a kind of glamor surrounding the official priesthood of any time. People presume all kinds of omniscience in these people, but it is the data, the information itself, that glamorizes the people associated with it. The data glamorizes scientists today, just as religious phenomena and beliefs glamorized priests in times past. What they are talking about in itself glamorizes them, but they do not have any capacity to make the greater sense out of it, or to perform a greater service for other human beings than those others can for themselves. Therefore, modern scientists do not introduce into human time another process that would permit human beings to advance on the scale of evolution. On the contrary: They are providing us with highly technical information about the state of adaptation we have already achieved. They are providing us with highly sophisticated information that gives us powers over the elemental life with which it is possible for us to destroy ourselves, because we have not yet developed the evolutionary capacity to make use of this information in a more civilized and benign way.

The more sophisticated the information or the technical powers we acquire, the more we have to mature in the culture of love and freedom, or true psycho-physical morality. Scientists are not offering such a Wisdom-Culture, based on a higher evolutionary level of functioning. But without such a culture, human beings cannot advance, no matter how comprehensive their information.

Thus, it is a matter of great urgency for modern men and women to come into a true understanding of what the true Adept or Spiritual Master represents to Man, and what the devotional relationship to such a one actually entails. The Teaching of the true Spiritual Master serves the moral transformation and ultimate evolution of Man. He incarnates and communicates the necessary Wisdom-Culture of Man. In his Realization and his argument, the Spiritual Master represents a radical criticism of the usual man's standard of functional existence and all the forms of his resistance to the real spiritual process, the life of intelligent sacrifice, or love.

At the present time almost all human beings are more or less mechanically insisting upon the repetition of an essentially sub-conscious, controlled life, not a free and creative and spiritual life. Modern scientism and all the other influences of our day, both secular and apparently religious, represent doctrines and presumptions within that limited, not yet conscious form of life. The conventional institutions that advertise growth, freedom, creativity, and spiritual trans-formation all in fact tend to become spokesmen for that egoic or conventional, Narcissistic logic. But the Way of Life that I Teach is the most serious and profound and radical, or nonconventional, affair. People must therefore begin to distinguish this radical Way from the so-called "spiritual movement" of our time as well as from the conventional traditions of exoteric religion and esoteric spirituality, both Eastern and Western.

CHAPTER 4

THE FALSE RELIGION OF SCIENTIFIC KNOWLEDGE

an essay by Da Free John
October 1980

Scientists tend to imagine themselves to be "humanists," or individuals who possess a superior regard for the well-being of mankind. Indeed, organized groups of scientists commonly promote themselves as a kind of independently superior and humanistic conscience, whereas in fact their general effect on the world is often quite the opposite. (At the very least, their effect is no more superior or ultimately beneficial than that of any other organized and socially powerful point of view, past or present.)

The scientific establishment has been organized in league with the highest levels of concentrated political, economic, and propagandistic power in the world today. Science is simply the primary method of knowing in modern societies, and its rule is established in no less an irrational and authoritarian manner than was the case with any religious or philosophical principle that ruled societies in the past.

The method of science has now become a style of existence, a mood or strategy of relating to the world and to other human beings. That method now describes the conventional posture taken by "Everyman" in every form of his relationship to the conditions of existence. Science has become a world-view, a presumption about the World-Process itself. It has become a religion, although a false one. And modern societies are Cults of this new religion. Can this new religion establish us as individuals and communities in right relationship to each other and to the World-Process? Absolutely not! Science is only a method of inquiry, or knowing about. It is not itself the right, true, or inherent form of our relationship to the conditions of existence. No matter what we may know about the conditions of existence, we cannot account for existence itself. And we are, regardless of our personal and present state of knowledge about the natural mechanics of the world, always responsible for our right relationship to the various conditions of experience, to the beings with whom we exist in this world, and to the World-Process as a whole. Relationship is inherently and perpetually a matter of individual responsibility, founded in intuition, prior to the analytical mind.

The method that is science is inherently incapable of establishing us in a right relationship to the conditions of existence. Love and self-transcendence are realized outside or prior to the play of conventional knowledge. The scientific method is not a moral or a spiritual and intuitive disposition. It is a strategy for acquiring objective knowledge. If it were a moral disposition, then scientists would all be great moral beings. But in fact, ʳhe daily application of the scientific method is not itself a moral practice, or a kind of meditation that transforms the practitioner. Rather, the application of the strategy of scientific inquiry is only a special intellectual discipline, and it forever stands outside the higher intuitive and radical psycho-physical processes whereby the individual may be transformed in either evolutionary or moral or spiritual terms.

Those who embrace the attitude of verbal thinking, observing, analyzing, comparing, categorizing, and so forth must understand that to do so is not the same thing as to exist and live in the most fundamental and responsible terms. Rather, it is merely a way of observing and verbally considering the patterns of phenomena, in order to know about them. And if one abandons the fundamental process of self-transcending Communion and unity with the World-Process, and opts instead and exclusively for the position of the separated analytical observer, then one begins to operate in defiant opposition to the primary conditions of human existence.

Science must again become simply a method of inquiry, and it must be renounced as the universal style of our very relationship to the conditions of existence. It must cease to characterize the totality of Man himself. Rather, it must again become an "employee" of Man—a specialized instrument for certain kinds of work. Otherwise, Man will cease to be capable of either the moral or the spiritual and evolutionary exercise of personal responsibility.

The verbal mind, or the left hemisphere of the human brain, is not suited to be the Ruler of Man. It is only an attribute or potentiality of Man. Therefore the "urge" to science, which is the ultimate method of the analytical or verbal mind, must be disciplined and held in right perspective by a higher or more complete understanding. Every exercise of a part of Man must be understood relative to Man as a whole, and submitted to the process and ultimate Condition that includes and involves Man prior to all his knowledge.

The right hemisphere of the human brain was once the Ruler of Man, in early societies founded in the methods of magic, psychism, and a truly active and inward religious consciousness. But the method of psychic inquiry proved to have severe limitations, because of the variables involved in personal subjective processes and the competitive conflicts between societies organized around different historical accumulations of conventional religious belief. Therefore, the functions of the left hemisphere of the human brain began to evolve and to achieve cultural prominence. And now they are the dominant characteristic of modern verbal and analytical Man. But the results of the dominance of the left brain are equally as limited, troublesome, and psychologically devastating as the results of dominance by the right brain.

The right-brained or "oriental" Man enjoys psychic attunement with the World-Process, but he cannot differentiate himself sufficiently to acquire responsibility for his destiny in the natural world of psycho-physical phenomena. And the left-brained or "occidental" Man, even though he is committed to responsible analysis of natural phenomena and control over the laws that govern the World-Process, is incapable of the higher morality or disposition of self-surrender, self-transcendence, psychic illumination, and participatory Communion with the Radiant Transcendental Reality that may be intuited to be the Truth of the World-Process and the Source of the Happiness of Man.

Therefore, we must awaken from our solid pose of intellectual superiority and our irrational belief that knowledge about the processes of natural phenomena makes a superior humanity. A superior humanity will not be derived from authoritarian scientific decrees, imposed through powerful technologies. Man cannot live happily, nor survive long, without the intuitive certainty of Transcendental Love, or Spiritual Communion with Divine Power, Bliss, and Purpose. Without higher religious consciousness (free of the dogmatic nonsense of conventional religious beliefs), the future made by scientific acculturation is an abominable fiction, a mechanical contrivance in which Man is, paradoxically, both satisfied in his desires and desperate in his being.

And I do not argue this point of view out of despair. I have Realized the Truth, and I see the present and the ancient errors in Man. I am also a knower about the natural world, except that I have been committed to the higher discipline of Man as a totality, and Man as an inherent Sacrifice in God. Therefore, I have seen all the mechanisms of our evolution, and I have understood all the necessary structures of a true culture of Man. But it is extremely difficult to be heard in the midst of a society that is bound and determined to follow its present strategy to the end of its course. The Wisdom of transforming our disposition before we fail is considered disdainfully by the popular and intellectual mentalizing of this day. Everyone is endlessly chatting, comparing concepts, looking for consoling pleasures, fascinations of mind and body. Everyone is possessed by a lust for knowledge about the natural world and about the experiential mechanism of Man. But it seems that very few are interested in being Man at this present time. Very few seem willing to accept the discipline that is the totality of Man and to fulfill the destiny of personal transformation in bodily, emotional, psychic, mental, and Transcendental unity with the Radiant Mystery of the World-Process, which is eternally prior to all our knowing.

CHAPTER 5

CONVERSATION WITH TESTOOB, THE SCIENCE MAN

by Allan Sherman

SAP: What is science?

TESTOOB: Science is a new institution that will change the world. At last man is throwing off the old superstitions and guesswork. Science alone discovers the true nature of reality—and can prove everything it says.

SAP: How?

TESTOOB: By the scientific method. First we *observe* a phenomenon, over and over again. Then we *describe* it. Then we *measure* it, *time* it, *weigh* it. We break it down into its smallest elements and *analyze* those. We *study* its structure. Then we put it back together. If we can *reproduce* it again and again, always the same, that proves our hypothesis.

SAP: So science can prove a hypothesis. But what can science *do*?

TESTOOB: *Anything.* Everything.

SAP: Can you make human life longer?

TESTOOB: Yes. Easily.

SAP: Can you cure illness and pain?

TESTOOB: Yes. And we will.

SAP: Can science teach man to fly like a bird?

TESTOOB: Higher—and faster. We will fly to the moon.

SAP: That's marvelous!

TESTOOB: But that's only half of it.

SAP: What's the other half?

TESTOOB: Science can also make life shorter, inflict pain and blow the moon out of the sky.

SAP: But what about the people?

TESTOOB: What do you mean?

SAP: *People*—like you and me. We wouldn't have any moonlight. The night would be black.

TESTOOB: By then science will invent artificial lighting—much brighter than the moon.

SAP: It doesn't seem right.

TESTOOB: There is no right or wrong. There is only science, doing its job.

SAP: What is science's job?

TESTOOB: Transforming nature into useful things.

SAP: But what about the natural things? I mean—you won't hurt the *flowers*?

TESTOOB: Don't worry. There'll be plenty of flowers. Plastic flowers, paper flowers, any kind you want.

SAP: What is *plastic*? And *paper*?

TESTOOB: Plastic is made from coal and chemicals torn from the bowels of the earth. Paper is made by chopping down trees and mashing them to a pulp.

SAP: Can't we keep the natural flowers?

TESTOOB: Nope. Too haphazard. We'll grind them up to make synthetic smells for the plastic flowers. We'll also have plastic grass and trees.

SAP: As nice as natural?

TESTOOB: Infinitely superior. Nature is unscientific. In nature, no two things are alike—a dreadful waste of time and effort. Science will remedy that. Everything will be mass-produced, with all parts interchangeable.

SAP: Even blades of grass?

TESTOOB: Grass will be replaced by Astroturf. Never changes color. Number 724 No-Fade Midsummer Green. Never needs water or mowing. No weeds. No dandelions.

SAP: I like dandelions.

TESTOOB: For people like you we'll have plastic dandelions.

SAP: Wow. What about animals? My twins love animals.

TESTOOB: There is no such thing as love. But they'll have enough animals. Stuffed animals, mechanical animals, rubber ducks, teddy bears, rocking horses, chocolate bunnies—everything.

SAP: The only natural thing left on earth will be people.

TESTOOB: Only until science is ready to proceed with synthetic people.

SAP: How will you do it?

TESTOOB: We'll begin with simple spare parts and accessories, like false teeth and artificial limbs, to replace those lost in wars or accidents. Then we'll devise glass eyes, though the crude early models will not be functional—purely for looks. Speaking of looks, we'll bring out man-made eyelashes and fingernails; artificial hair, changeable to suit any occasion; prefabricated breasts to please the sexual tastes of Society. For people who want to look different from what nature made them, we will offer skin grafts and change the shapes of noses and ears and chins; we will make fat people skinnier and skinny people fatter.

SAP: What about the brain?

TESTOOB: We'll invent electromechanical brains that can store a million times as many facts as a natural brain, and think three million times as fast.

SAP: What good is a brain like that with glass eyes that don't even function?

TESTOOB: By then we'll have devised machines that function better than natural eyes. Even in the dark. Even on the other side of the moon.

SAP: What about ears?

TESTOOB: Our artificial sound-hearing machines will not only hear things from far distant planets but remember them and play them back—vastly superior to nature's ears.

SAP: Fantastic.

TESTOOB: Yes. But we're only just beginning. At first those parts will be big and bulky. It will take a long time to miniaturize them until they fit inside the body.

SAP: What about the other things inside the body?

TESTOOB: Don't rush me. We have to start slowly. First, we'll replace small sections of the skull with aluminum plates—much stronger than bone. Then we'll manufacture plastic kidneys and livers, and veins and arteries made of extruded neoprene tubing. The natural heart will be replaced by a vinyl pump guaranteed not to wear out, with a perfectly timed synthetic heartbeat generated by an electronic pacemaker.

SAP: Even so, they'll still be natural human beings—just patched up a little here and there.

TESTOOB: Only in the beginning, in the guinea-pig stage. It will be a slow process—a plastic kidney for this fellow, an artificial heart for that fellow, an eye transplant for another fellow. But eventually, *eventually* . . .

SAP: Eventually, what?

TESTOOB: There will be one man in the world who has more artificial parts than natural parts.

SAP: The poor soul!

TESTOOB: There is no such thing as a soul. Besides, that man will go down in history as a great milestone in the march of science. He will be known as SHIT-fifty-one.

SAP: SHIT-*fifty-one*?

TESTOOB: *Synthetic Human In Transition*—the first person who is more than fifty-one percent artificial. From that point on, the project will get easier.

SAP: Why?

TESTOOB: We'll simply remove the rest of his inferior natural parts one by one—and replace them with laboratory-tested, dealer-authorized products. Finally there won't be a single natural thing left in his body. Science will have created the ultimate human being.

SAP: Don't tell me, I know—SHIT-one hundred.

TESTOOB: Precisely. One hundred percent synthetic. Next we will invent a contraceptive chemical and secretly introduce it into the diet of all natural people. This will put an end to babies, with all their crying and wetting and the fuss and bother of growing up. Then we will begin to reproduce SHIT-one hundreds in great numbers.

SAP: Well, at least we'll still have sex.

TESTOOB: Absolutely not. Sex will be obsolete by then.

SAP: How will synthetic man reproduce?

TESTOOB: With an electronic copying machine. A SHIT-one hundred will lie flat on the copying surface of our master copier at Lab Central. Our synthogeneticist will push a button and turn a dial. Out of the plexiwomb slot will come as many exact duplicates of SHIT-one hundred as we need. We will be connected by an electronic network to servo-controlled slave mechanisms in branch laboratories throughout the world. These will automatically produce facsimile people as required.

SAP: But they'll all be the same!

TESTOOB: Yes. Isn't that wonderful? Equality at last!

SAP: Won't you need an awful lot of raw materials?

TESTOOB: Oh, yes. We'll probably use up the whole world.

SAP: Then what good is the project?

TESTOOB: By that time science will know how to get to another planet. We'll use *its* resources.

SAP: What happens when you've used up that planet?

TESTOOB: On to the next planet!

SAP: Do you think that's a good idea?

TESTOOB: Why not? There's lots more where they came from.

SAP: My God, man, you'll use up the whole sky!

TESTOOB: True. But just in time, science will present Syntho-Sky.

SAP: But this sky is beautiful.

TESTOOB: I keep telling you, beauty does not exist. Besides, with Syntho-Sky you'll color your own sunset with solenoid push buttons.

SAP: Sunrise, too?

TESTOOB: No, that you can paint by numbers. And you'll control your own weather. You'll decide when it should be daytime and when it should be nighttime.

SAP: How?

TESTOOB: Just turn on the electro-sun.

SAP: What happened to the real sun?

TESTOOB: We used it up for energy to orbit our simulated planets. The whole thing will be much more efficient than the present solar system.

SAP: Then you'll be satisfied and stop?

TESTOOB: Don't be silly. Then our challenge will have only begun! Science cannot be satisfied until every mystery of the universe is solved; until we control every possibility in the future and can prevent any surprises or shocks.

SAP: Even rainbows? Even falling stars? Even one little unsynthetic snowflake that sneaks through by mistake?

TESTOOB: *Everything*. We'll be in control of *everything*.

SAP: Then what will God do?

TESTOOB: There is no such thing as God.

SAP: Yes, I know. But just supposing there is. Just *supposing*.

TESTOOB: You mean a hypothetical case?

SAP: All right, a hypothetical case. Just assume there *is* a God. What will He do?

TESTOOB: Well, if I were He, I would retire.

SAP: But He'll look around and He won't even recognize anything. There won't be anything left the way He made it.

TESTOOB: Right. And He will be powerless to change anything back.

SAP: And there won't be anyplace else for Him to go.

TESTOOB: No. The whole cosmos will belong to us.

SAP: God will be a kind of prisoner—in a world He never made.

TESTOOB: Not really a prisoner. More of a stranger.

SAP: Won't anybody recognize Him, or pray to Him, or be grateful?

TESTOOB: No. Synthetic humanoids will be free from all religious sham and superstition. Isn't it exciting? I mean, the whole idea? Say— you're not listening. What's wrong? Where are you?

SAP: I was feeling sorry for God.

TESTOOB: Now, now—don't get sentimental. He had His chance.

PART TWO

TRANSCENDING THE POLITICS OF SCIENCE

cience is one of the means of seeking knowledge, but it is not based on the acknowledgment that what we are actually seeking is release. It is based on the presumption that what we are seeking is fulfillment in this plane. However, science has begun to make curious discoveries that border on a higher perception and conception of Reality. Science is beginning, therefore, to conjoin with the perceptions, experiences, and points of view that belong to the higher stages of life. Even so, although science is ultimately compatible with a higher perception and conception of Reality, it is generally devoted toward the purposes of the ordinary plane of experience, such as politics.

Science is, in fact, a part of politics devoted toward the presumption that human pursuits should be oriented toward fulfillment in this world. Politicians, the news, and the programming on television in general all propagandize an idea of human existence as attention devoted to fulfillment in this plane. And there are many taboos against pursuing fulfillment in terms of the higher stages of life.

Da Free John
Easy Death, *p. 234*

INTRODUCTION TO PART TWO

Science, even so-called "pure" science, does not occur in an abstract void, but it is pursued in the context of human life—the politics of the ego. In blatant contrast to the optimistic hopes of the staunch rationalists among scientists, science is not value-free, and its "facts" are not neutral or unburdened by the human element. Rather, facts are value-charged. They are not something to be observed, but something to be stated. That is to say, they are normative statements about the way in which reality is to be perceived. They are not "out there" but the threads and knots of the conceptual net that scientists cast over reality. Indirectly, therefore, they are prescriptions for moral (rational) behavior. Once this is clearly understood, it becomes obvious that science is a highly political enterprise.

It is also exceedingly influential, shaping as it does the world-view and destiny of billions of human beings. However, because the fundamental premises of science are largely uninspected—with the exception of the penetrating analyses of a handful of philosophers and sociologists—science is willy-nilly subject to influence from the unconscious. And this makes a travesty out of its search for objective truth: The scientist's psychology (or psychopathology) governs the parameters of his scientific work. Personal and collective biases and preconceptions predefine the reality horizon of science and thereby delimit (or curtail) the scientist's search for truth. More importantly, in view of the influence that modern science is enjoying, the same unconscious factors that cripple the scientific endeavor are greatly reinforced in society at large and in this way are perpetuated *ad infinitum*.

These disabling unconscious factors converge in what Master Da Free John calls the "objectivist point of view"—the ideology of scientific materialism, which legitimizes the consciousness of the left cerebral hemisphere while simultaneously forcing the human psyche underground.

We exist in a time and cultural circumstance when the psyche has been invalidated. The only dimension of life being affirmed is the grossest level, and there is an attempt through the disciplines of science to create a structure of knowledge in which the gross level of existence is the only or fundamental presumption. But if that presumption were true, then there would not be even a trace of meaning in the entire universe. Nor would human life have any significance whatsoever, and it would not make the least difference what anyone might be doing. It is this desperate point of view that everyone is coming to, and that is the reason why it is so difficult to bring political order to the world.

Why should people maintain order in their lives? Why should they presume moral attitudes, love and help one another, work and be productive, or be happy? Why should anybody pursue any of that if human life is just something driven up from mortal matter, if the whole universe is nothing but a flying flash of mortal stuff?[1]

Scientism is an extension or rationalization of ordinary human psychology, which is essentially non-participatory. In its turn, scientism bolsters that conventional mentality by its persuasive one-dimensional model of reality. Master Da Free John observes about modern science:

What makes science a conventional view is that it expresses the same disposition we entertain in our ordinary presumptions about existence. By virtue of our ordinary identification with the body-mind and its relations, we tend to think we are basically this psycho-physical personality, this limited, defined, dependent structure. That structure is what we mean when we say "I." We regard our own consciousness to be dependent on and conditioned by our physical existence, and consequently we feel profoundly threatened by the changes and mortal destiny of the physical body.

Contemporary scientism develops this conventional presumption into laws about the universe, models of human existence that have in principle the same psychological content as the ordinary presumptions on the basis of which people operate in their daily lives. So—science extends this ordinary presumption of identification with a physical or psycho-physical personality into models of existence, such as the key notion of science that consciousness is a feature of matter, that it is

1. From an unpublished talk given by Da Free John on November 19, 1980.

*dependent on brain activity, that it comes about only because we are
born into this molecular robot state of a human entity, and that
therefore when the molecular robot dies, the necessary conditions for
the existence of consciousness cease to exist.*[2]

But even scientists cannot quite live in a universe bereft of all
existential significance. Therefore, ever since its separation from our
religious heritage, science has dallied with the philosophy of humanism, with which it shares an unbounded faith in the supremacy of
reason and the futility of "supernatural" explanations of life. Deriving
much of its credo from the principles and premises of scientific
thought, humanism understandably has a strong appeal for scientists
who are, moreover, supplied by it with an irreproachable justification
for their scientific activity: to work for the betterment of all mankind.
Humanistic scientism is thus a full-fledged anthropocentric religion.
As was to be expected, therefore, self-transcendence is not part of its
vocabulary. Man, the measure of all things, has Nobody or Nothing to
look up to. This is clearly articulated in the Humanist Manifesto, a
document signed by thirty eminent individuals representing a very
much larger community of humanist believers. Its concluding para-
graph runs thus:

*Though we consider the religious forms and ideas of our fathers
no longer adequate, the quest for the good life is still the central task
for mankind. Man is at last becoming aware that he alone is
responsible for the realization of the world of his dreams, that he has
within himself the power for its achievement. He must set intelligence
and will to the task.*[3]

When the ego perceives naught greater than itself, it necessarily
falls back on itself and replaces the transhuman value of self-
transcendence and Transcendental Realization, which forms the
bedrock of authentic religion, with values that vouchsafe the survival
of the ego: self-improvement and social cooperation. These are
certainly noble goals, but they do not express the total potential of
human existence. For, paradoxically, Man comes into his own only

2. From an unpublished talk given by Da Free John on December 18, 1980. For a detailed
examination of the relationship between consciousness, brain, and death, see Da Free John, *Easy
Death,* especially chapters 2 and 31.

3. "A Humanist Manifesto," *The New Humanist,* vol. 6, no. 3 (1933).

when he moves beyond himself and his numerous projections, when he steps outside his skin, which does not define his being. But such a possibility is not given in the program of humanistic scientism, which does not recognize the primacy of Consciousness. Hence the Adept's vehement critique of the essentially reductionistic stance of humanism. Master Da Free John makes his point by singling out Albert Einstein, the greatest hero of twentieth-century science and one of the most benign advocates of humanistic philosophy. Speaking about Einstein's *My Views,* he comments:

> *You can see how Einstein's position corresponds to the traditional position of science, of humanism, of materialistic scientism. You can also see how it corresponds to the merely conventional egoic or objectivist point of view elaborated by science to the absolute degree.*
>
> *Einstein himself had no intention to produce an atomic bomb. The bomb was the product of a politically organized scientific culture, exploiting not only the possibilities of what Einstein had discovered, but also the egoic principle itself in the form of the objectivist, dissociated point of view. Even though Einstein would of course not deliberately want to destroy the quality of human existence, or the human capacity for Realization of Truth, he did in fact just that, despite his humble humanitarian aspirations.*
>
> *Not all materialistic scientists are good, homely men like Einstein, but they are all riding on this same opinion. And the ultimate results of that opinion are absurdities that amount to a negation of the principle of our inherence in the Ultimate Condition of Nature. The principle of objectivism—or egoity itself—prevents the Realization of Truth. In effect, it makes taboo all efforts at ultimate self-transcendence.*[4]

Science, and the associative pseudo-religious belief system of humanism, are thematizations of conventional egoic existence. Therefore, they suffer the essential frailties that afflict the un-Enlightened human personality itself. Directly or indirectly, both endeavors augment the egocentrism that is rampant in our civilization and that is rapidly driving it into a *cul de sac* from which there may be no return. This is the topic of chapter 6, entitled "The Transcendence of Ego and Egoic Society." Here Master Da Free John shows how the

---

4. From an unpublished talk given by Da Free John on October 26, 1982.

egocentric style of life, which characterizes present-day mankind, is the source of untold suffering and destruction. Not only is it marked by the absence of Wisdom and Happiness (which depends on the literal Realization of the Real), but it actively opposes the realization of such Wisdom and Happiness.

The exclusive obsession of science with factual knowledge makes science a dangerous tool. Chapter 7 is a sobering exploration of "The Destructive Mood of Western Science." In this talk Master Da Free John argues that science has a uniquely Western flavor, epitomized as it is in the attitude of confrontation with Nature. In the latter part of this talk, the Adept considers with a small group of spiritual practitioners the personal consequences of the fact that we are living at the brink of global annihilation. The conversation conveys a sense of the lively and penetrating "samyama"[5] in which Master Da Free John tends to spontaneously engage for the purpose of instruction. The talk is also a fine example of the way in which he always integrates theory with practice, the abstract with the concrete, and the impersonal with the personal.

Ego and suffering are coextensive. In fact, traditional religions like Buddhism and Hinduism have made suffering the starting-point for their philosophical and soteriological programs. The considerations of chapters 6 and 7 may give the reader the impression that Radical Transcendentalism, as Taught by Master Da Free John, proceeds in a similar vein. This possible misunderstanding is explicitly corrected in chapter 8, entitled "Man's Three Afflictions and the Business of Science." Here Master Da Free John develops his description of the psychology of "boredom, doubt, and discomfort," showing, in the second section of this talk, how science has institutionalized the attitude of doubt. In the third section he returns to the theme of the inherently destructive orientation of science and technology. He describes modern science as an adolescent enterprise and challenges scientists to forestall the impending crisis by consciously opting for the kind of self-transformation that is at the core of the spiritual process.

---

5. In his writings Master Da Free John has adopted the Sanskrit term *samyama*, as classically presented by Patanjali in his *Yoga Sutra*, where the word is understood as "a process of one-pointed but ultimately thoughtless concentration and exhaustive contemplation of a particular object, function, person, process, or condition, until the essence or ultimate obviousness of that subject is clear" (Da Free John, *Love of the Two-Armed Form*, p. 1). Master Da Free John has also used the term "consideration" to describe this living process in his own life and Teaching Work.

In contrast to the founding fathers of science, contemporary
scientists do not appear to be particularly creative or even particularly
intelligent. For the most part, they are not even overly concerned
about the larger implications of their research. Perhaps most of
today's scientists are little more than glorified technicians. They are
very knowledgeable about the minutiae of their specific field of
inquiry, but are often astonishingly ignorant of even the wider context
of their own discipline, which alone could give relevance to their work.
On the whole, scientists are disinclined to philosophize about their
investigations and tend to confine themselves to formulating working
hypotheses and perhaps, occasionally, second- or third-order theories.

And yet, in another, broader sense, scientists can be said to be
inveterate philosophers. For, as Master Da Free John points out in
chapter 9, they meet the great Mystery of existence with chronic
thinking; and broadly speaking, systematic thinking is a form of
philosophizing. It is also, as the Adept explains, a stress-based activity.
As Master Da Free John puts it, it is "a dramatization of the stressful
acknowledgment that you are not in control of existence." It is, in
other words, a manifestation of human seeking—the eternal motivation of the ego. Concluding his talk, the Adept confesses that he is
here to awaken an altogether different disposition in those who are
willing to listen to his Argument—the disposition of Enlightenment,
which is not inimical to science or philosophy, but the only principle
that could transform both branches of human inquiry and defuse their
potential destructiveness.

Master Da Free John does not uphold the rigid opposition, forced
by science and endorsed by religion, between sacred and secular forms
of knowledge. Rather, he regards both as valid polar expressions of
human intelligence (and biology). One actualizes the capacities of the
right cerebral hemisphere, the other those of the left hemisphere. But
they do not, either singly or together, represent the fullness of Man.
He writes:

*Both the left and the right hemispheres or zones of functioning
of the human brain contain specific or built-in functional limits as well
as limiting presumptions. And, therefore, both science and mysticism
represent only partial or half-human forms of understanding. Only
the whole body or total body-mind of Man can provide the structural
point of view for right and ultimate human understanding. Only the
whole body (or total psycho-physical being) of Man can provide the*

foundation for a truly human and harmoniously integrated culture.
Science and mysticism both represent archaic or partial cultural
principles. Each is the point of view of one half of Man.[6]

And:

The culture of science is the ultimate achievement of the
"occidental" mind, or the primary mood of Western Man. And the
culture of mysticism is the ultimate achievement of the "oriental"
mind, or the primary mood of Eastern Man.

But what of the culture of Man in his totality—including his total
brain and totally integrated bodily being? That culture has no great
representation in the human world as it now exists. Man is yet only
evolved or adapted to the lower structures of his possibility, and his
cultural achievements still reflect only his internal conflict. Therefore,
East and West are in conflict, and the parts of human consciousness
are culturally at war.

I am at work to awaken a new understanding of Man in his
totality, and to help establish a whole bodily cultural movement in the
world, that will replace the half-bodily cultures of science and
mysticism. That understanding includes the total mind and nervous
system of Man, and it produces a culture that is not founded on self-
possession, self-division, doubt, exploitation of Man and Nature, or
the flight from relationships, or even the flight from bodily existence.
Rather, the whole bodily understanding of Man produces a culture of
self-transcendence, relational love, bodily service, and spiritually
illumined consciousness. Therefore, by this new or radical under-
standing, East and West will create a World-Synthesis of human
culture, on the basis of aspiration and adaptation to the Total World,
or the World of Light.[7]

The "culture of self-transcendence" of which Master Da Free
John speaks is the social correlate of the personal commitment to, and
practice of, radical understanding. Thus, he proposes not only a new
individual response to the world, but an alternative form of living in
community with others. Self-transformation, apart from responsible
living in association with other human beings, is the ideal of oriental

6. Da Free John, *Scientific Proof of the Existence of God Will Soon Be Announced by the White House!* p. 116.

7. Ibid., pp. 117–18.

quietism, whereas individual "salvation" through social transformation is the ideal of Western humanistic-technocratic politics. The former approach is all head without trunk and limbs, the latter is a beheaded body. For Master Da Free John, genuine self-transformation and self-transcendence can take place only in the context of a participatory community where intimacy is cultivated. This is the subject matter of his essay "The Ancient Sacred Ordeal Is the Model for Intimate and Personal Culture," which forms chapter 10. It is in such an authentic community that the routine politics of State and of science can be converted into a truly human affair.

CHAPTER 6

THE TRANSCENDENCE OF EGO AND EGOIC SOCIETY

an essay by Da Free John
May 6, 1982

1.

The un-Enlightened or egocentric body-mind-self is founded on the action of self-contraction. The self-contraction is expressed as the differentiation of self from the Transcendental Source-Condition and from every other form of presumed not-self, and it is likewise expressed via the independent definition of self, and the constant concern and search for independent preservation of self. The self-based or self-contracting and self-preserving conception of existence is manifested via the psychology of fear and conflict relative to all that is not-self. Therefore, the psychology of egocentric existence is inherently disposed to seek control and dominance over all that is not-self. For this reason, individual lives are a constant expression of anxiety, mechanically involved in techniques of self-manipulation (in order to preserve self) and other-manipulation (in order to control or dominate whatever is not-self). The moods of human egoity are always very close to fear, sorrow, and anger. And the collective or group life of egocentric human beings is likewise dominated by the same exclusiveness and the same motives toward self-preservation and control of what is "outside."

Human societies are always tending to be modeled after the un-Enlightened pattern of the individual ego. The political and social

117

systems of the present-day world are not generated by literally
Enlightened or even highly evolved leaders, ideals, or institutions. We
live in the "samsaric" or un-Enlightened world of egoic society—and
this is why the signs of the times are so profoundly negative.

The entire world is now nearly out of control with egoic motives.
Mankind, tutored by materialistic philosophies, ego-serving technologies, and gross political idealisms, is possessed by the mechanical
efforts of self-indulgence, depressed by the frustration of the inherently
Spiritual motives of being, anxious for the achievement of release, and
trapped in the devices of anger. The ego, whether individual or
collective, is eventually reduced to sorrow and despair by the inability
of life to generate Happiness and Joy and Immortality. And that self-
contained depression finally becomes anger, or angry confrontation
with the total world and every form of not-self (including the
Transcendental Identity or Condition, which is made into an "Other"
by the egoic mind and thus conceived via the conventional or merely
exoteric ideas about God). And when anger becomes the mood of
societies, the quality of fire, or the primitive and destructive intents of
the frustrated ego, invades the plane of humanity. That fire is
expressed as all of the sufferings and all of the painful illusions of
mankind, including all of the ego-based politics of confrontation, and it
is finally summarized in the acts of war.

2.

The differentiation of existence into self-possessed units yields, in
the case of each "one," the craving for entirely pleasurized and
unthreatened existence. This craving (or obsessive motive of self-
preservation and self-glorification) in turn yields inevitable conflict,
fear, sorrow, anger, and all kinds of destructive acts in relation to
others as well as to self (because the extreme exercise of self-
preservation is ultimately an aggressive and self-defeating motivation
that destroys the self in the final effort to dominate the not-self).
Therefore, all egos (or un-Enlightened centers of identity, whether
individual or collective) are in aggressive conflict with all other egos
(and all that is not-self, or outside the defined egoic center). All
individual and collective egos are involved in programs of self-
destruction (via patterns of self-possession, self-seeking, self-
indulgence, reactive emotion, un-Enlightened thinking, and so forth)

as well as other-destruction (via all kinds of reactive activity, based on self-concern, that seeks to control and ultimately dominate whatever is "outside" the self-center).

The search for the independent preservation and ultimate enhancement of self is the universal model of un-Enlightened egoity. Therefore, suffering, power struggle, and war are inevitable in egoic society. And if the capability for political manipulation and war becomes technologically profound, universal suppression via aggressive political efforts and universal destruction via war become the common expectation and destiny of all human beings.

We live in just such a time of technological sophistication, in which the egoic model of Man and human society is the universal basis of mind. Gross materialism (in science and politics) gives human beings no option in the mind except that of the trapped and threatened animal. Therefore, a fiery mood is abroad, full of gross desire, frustration, fear, despair, and aggressive reactivity. The egoic motive of self-preservation is approaching its most destructive mood— the mood that appears in the moment of ultimate entrapment. In that mood, there is no longer any will to preserve self or world or any others. There is simply explosive fire, based on the deep motives of egoic self-preservation, but reduced to action that is most primitive and wholly destructive of both self and not-self. In the collective mind of humanity in the present and growing extremes of entrapment, the explosion of great nuclear bombs merely represents the archetype of anger itself. And it is for this reason that the possibility of a nuclear holocaust, in the extreme moment of the now rising political confrontations, is an irrational and therefore entirely possible (if not inevitable) event.

Past societies have, in their extreme moments of confrontation, destroyed themselves as well as their opponents. This is because ego-based societies function in essentially the same manner as egoic individuals. Individual human beings kill others and themselves every day. Therefore, groups and societies, confronting one another in egoic fashion, likewise threaten one another with destruction. And in the extreme moments of confrontation, when self-preservation achieves its peak of righteous irrationality, it is profoundly likely that nuclear war will result.

The motives of present-day society are the same as those of past societies. The only difference is that in the present day the technology of confrontation has become profound. Therefore, when confrontation

reaches its peak of irrationality, our war-motives will willingly destroy
the entire world, just as readily as, in the past, less technologically
sophisticated war-makers have wiped their petty tribes from the face
of the Earth.

3.

Many people are now trying to influence governments to
abandon nuclear weapons. But even if they succeed, irrational individuals and groups can still threaten and destroy the common order
with "terrorist" tactics and "home-made" bombs. And the "limited" or
non-nuclear warfare that might still erupt between governments that
agree not to make nuclear war is just as much a threat to us all as any
nuclear war.

It is time that we accept the political necessity for an end to
confrontation politics. We must abandon our ancient egoic principles
and renounce our political, social, and cultural provincialism. Individuals
within the collective order of mankind may yet suffer the un-
Enlightened and immature disabilities of egocentric personality, but
governments themselves, as well as institutions and leaders in every
area of human endeavor, must abandon the egocentric, subhuman,
merely materialistic, non-cooperative, and intolerant or loveless posture and style of life. Indeed, we must all demand that a new
leadership of this kind come forward and accept responsibility for the
representation of our interests.

Haven't we had enough of the brute, stupid, childish, and
exploitative representation of our existence that is played out daily (in
our name and on our lives) by governments, politicians, militarists,
scientists, technocrats, social planners, educators, exoteric and fundamentalist religionists (who aggressively propagate the provincial and
pharisaical religions of ego-salvation rather than practice the universal
and ego-transcending religion of love), and media hypers (who thrive
on the invention and exaggeration of conflict and dramatize our worst
instincts in the eternal "gotcha" game that denudes and exposes and
trivializes both the highs and the inevitable lows in the dynamic
efforts of humankind)? Isn't it evident in your deepest feeling psyche
that this Wisdom-renouncing world is being controlled by our worst
and most superficial conceptions of existence? It is time for us to
understand ourselves and reclaim the world from the dictatorship of

the ego, and from all of those who play at politics (and life in general) as if it were a sporting event that is supposed to excite and entertain us all on television.

Nuclear disarmament is a relatively positive but still too superficial effort. It is not a curative means, but only another palliative and temporary move in the midst of our traditional advance toward future trouble. There is something more fundamental than the disarmament politics whereby <u>enemies</u> come to a gentlemanly agreement on how to kill one another without destroying one another! What is more fundamental, necessary, and curative is that we understand and transcend that which is in us that makes us confront one another as opponents and enemies.

It may sound naive to speak of the necessity for the present childish and brutishly adolescent crowd of governments and institutions to understand themselves and renounce the self-imagery and the techniques of enemies, but the feeling that it is naive to speak in such terms is a reflection of our egoic frustration and despair. We must transcend that very frustration and despair if we are going to prevent the enslavement and destruction of mankind.

Humanity is now living in bondage to egocentric and materialistic idealisms that are suppressing our human freedom to live by Wisdom and Realize the Truth. If we do not shake loose from this regime, we are going to suffer the extreme fulfillment of collective egoic destiny in a Narcissistic holocaust that will either enslave mankind via a technologically robotized political and social order or else destroy mankind via technologically engineered warfare.

It is not naive to demand a new leadership when those who are led number in the billions. Nor is it folly to try to educate mankind when the only alternative is slavery and death. Therefore, I say to you that we must all commit ourselves to understand the patterns by which we are now (and have traditionally been) living (both individually and collectively), so that we can then change those patterns and the destinies those patterns will inevitably inflict upon us. The egoic model must be educated out of the collective order of mankind. A new leadership must appear, which is awakened to an understanding of the primitive egoic basis of the present and traditional collective order. That new leadership must, above all, provide an <u>educative</u> role, and it must transform the techniques whereby governments and societies enter into relations with one another. Only such a leadership can, by strategies based on the wit of free intelligence, cause all the governments and institutions of the world to voluntarily change toward a cooperative and benign mode of association with others. (And this can be done by establishing profoundly undesirable economic and other practical consequences for not participating in the cooperative process.) If this kind of approach is not made soon, we will be entering into the most destructive period of political confrontation in human history.

4.

An Enlightened (or non-egoic and at least higher evolutionary, if not Spiritual and Transcendental) view of existence (and thus of politics) must soon arise in the leadership of mankind. At the present time we are all being led to enslavement and destruction by un-Enlightened materialists and self-seekers in every area of common human endeavor. The ideal of "Wisdom" has been replaced by the ideal of "knowledge," and knowledge has come to mean traditional "science," or all that can be achieved or supported exclusively by the intellectual efforts of materialistic philosophy. Science (which has traditionally identified itself with the archaic and false philosophy of materialism) has itself thus become identical to technology (or the materialistic machine of the known), and materialistic technology (along with its like in the form of all the materialistic idealisms that appeal to human egoity) has become the primary instrument for the political manipulation and control of collective humanity.

The political ideals and means of the present time are materialistic, based on a gross and egoic conception of human existence. There simply cannot be any ultimately effective change in our collective situation until a new leadership arises that is founded on the intelligence and higher evolutionary capacity of ego-transcendence and, ultimately, the Wisdom of non-sectarian Spiritual and Transcendental Enlightenment. Only such a leadership can rightly educate the collective order and relieve it of the burden of the egoic and materially confined view of life. And only such a leadership can transform the technique of governments from a process of self-preserving and other-controlling confrontation (of their own members as well as other societies) to a process of cooperation, unification, and a worldwide creative order based on pluralism, tolerance, and freedom.

The problem of the automatic and even unconscious creation of suffering and destruction is inherent in the egocentric form of individual existence. It is this principle that I call you to observe and understand. We must learn from this observation of the ego (in personal and collective terms) and so equip ourselves to freely abandon the egoic model of existence. This essay has, thus far, primarily spoken to the necessity for such education and change at the level of the leadership and collective order of mankind. Now I must move on to consider the implications of this education at the level of individual practice.

5.

The ego is self-contraction, or the conversion of manifest existence away from the free orientation to its Source or Real Condition and so back upon the individual center of functional experience. I see that this conversion represents the orientation, habit, and destiny described by the myth of Narcissus—which I propose as a symbol for the process of egocentrism.

The egocentric form of conditional existence is a kind of entrapment that leads only to more and more elaborate (and confining as well as deluding) states of limited and un-Enlightened psycho-physical personality. In the egocentric form, conditional existence cannot Locate Happiness, Truth, or Reality, but it is confined entirely to the visions and sufferings of independent selfhood. Therefore, many who have seen this to be so have called humanity to escape conditional existence itself by a strategy of self-suppressive means. What I call for is self-observation, self-understanding, and self-transcendence in the midst of free participation in the play of conditional existence. If this is done, the motives either to exploit or to escape the conditional self are inherently transcended. A more natural course of life-practice develops on the basis of the orientation of self-transcendence (rather than self-exploitation or self-suppression). And that practice leads naturally to the Blissful and Free Realization of the Real or Transcendental Condition in which there is inherent transcendence of self and world.

We must observe and understand the self as contraction. We must see the self-contraction operating inherently in pain, as all the kinds of conditional desire, reactive emotion, conflict, and destructive aggressiveness (rather than creative and liberating power). On the basis of this observation and understanding of self (or the individuated psycho-physical personality), we should freely abandon the principle and the strategies of egocentricity. We should yield the body-mind and attention to That Condition which precedes the self-contraction— That Transcendental Freedom, Love-Bliss, Happiness, Consciousness, and Being in and from which the self-contraction is generated in each moment. By our practicing self-observation, self-understanding, and self-transcendence in every moment of manifest, conditional, and relational existence, the habit and the effects of egocentricity are gradually released, thereby liberating energy and attention for the Realization of the Freedom, Love-Bliss, Happiness, Consciousness, or Being that is the Real and ultimate Condition of self and not-self. And that Realization ultimately Translates existence from the domain of conditional Nature and into the Domain of Transcendental or Divine Fullness.

This Way of ultimate practice may not be accepted by many in this yet Adolescent Age of Man, but at least the principles of the Way (in terms of abandoning the gross style of ego-based political confrontations and ego-based social participation, or non-participation) must become a matter of practical commitment on the part of the leaders and educators of mankind—or else we will collectively move toward intolerable enslavement and even nuclear destruction. Therefore, I call everyone to consider at least the political and broad social fulfillment of the Way that I Teach via ego-transcending tolerance and creative cooperation.

Beyond this, I call and look for those who can understand and utterly transcend the pattern and destiny of the self in this world and all higher or subtler worlds. I am calling and looking for those who will go beyond the outward and bodily improvement of self and its world, and who will also go beyond the inward and ascending improvement of self in the higher or subtler worlds. I am calling and looking for those who will go directly to the Source-Condition of self and all worlds. I am here to serve everyone with ego-transcending understanding, but I am especially looking for those who will embrace the Way in its ultimate form, so that the ultimate form of the Way may be fulfilled by them and passed on by them to future generations.

The ultimate form of the Way is the free (or non-problematic and non-strategic) renunciation of self based on the intelligence of direct understanding. It is not the ascetical, self-suppressive, or, in effect, suicidal path (which is not based on inherently self-transcending understanding but on the egoic presumption of a problem to be strategically escaped). The radical Way of understanding is not strategically self-destructive and world-denying. It is based in participatory intelligence, expressed as love and surrender, and matured as simplicity and freedom.

The path of this egocentric world is recognizable as suffering, delusion, fear, and death. Even all resistance to self and world only reinforces the self-mind, and the strategy of resistance only duplicates suffering in its stark disciplines. The Way that I Teach inherently transcends confrontation with self and world. It is the Way of inherent peace, not the fruitless search for peace. That peace is beyond all understanding, but it cannot be Realized except through understanding.

CHAPTER 7

THE DESTRUCTIVE MOOD OF WESTERN SCIENCE

a talk by Da Free John
October 19, 1980

ASTER DA FREE JOHN: We think that we acquire scientific knowledge and then naturally use it for our various purposes. To do such science seems natural or automatic, but it is not. Rather, it is the way the Western mind works. The Western mind pursues knowledge of a certain kind and then uses it in a certain way. The Western mind is always in confrontation with matter, or Nature, assuming power over natural laws and events, over masses of human beings. Such a process seems natural, but it is not. It is a cultural disposition that creates Western technology and that also creates the tools that produce this technology. Science, as it is commonly practiced, has a uniquely Western orientation.

Since ancient times there have been intelligent men who were just as rigorous in their pursuit of knowledge as scientists are today. They were not all just hallucinating or imagining things in some sort of balmy, religious fashion, but they conceived of knowledge in terms other than Western Man and therefore put their knowledge to different uses. They were characterized by a different disposition. It is the Western disposition, with nothing else controlling it, informing it, or modifying its behavior, that is producing our present political and social difficulties. It has been doing so for a long time—long before the enterprise of science, as we now know it, existed. Whenever Western Man has found a way to achieve power, and therefore advantage, over

126

natural forces, that is what he has done.

DEVOTEE: This approach to life seems to represent Western Man's alienation from God. He feels a certain innate sense of inferiority, for which he compensates by the way he uses science. It seems a way of glamorizing himself, feeling somehow superior to the world he is living in.

MASTER DA FREE JOHN: It certainly communicates the attitude of somebody who feels superior to other people or at least superior to other ways human beings can live. In our day it is science, not religion, that is persuasive. It is science that is dominant. The whole frame of mind and orientation to the world created by scientism is the popular persuasion in our time. Religion has become a secondary popular persuasion that no longer has the force of science.

It is always possible to adhere to the Truth, but to do so today you must criticize the popular persuasiveness of the scientific point of view, just as in another time perhaps you must counter the popular persuasiveness of conventional religion—and on one level modern science is a form of conventional religion, simply a popular religious movement. Both science and religion are ways of knowing, and science is a doctrine about knowledge as well as a summary of knowledge acquired over time. There is even what can be called exoteric science— the popular world of technology, the mass of scientific ideas, and the materialist view of the world. The materialist view is a basic principle of exoteric science, and it qualifies as a structure of knowledge, belief, and relations, just as past religions did. The materialist view is just as full of superstition and one-sidedness or one-dimensional thinking, just as capable of dissociation from Truth, as is religion.

The "truth" that science pursues is not <u>the</u> Truth. What science pursues is knowledge, but knowledge <u>about</u> things. Thus, science opposes conventional ignorance or the state wherein one knows very little about things, but the Truth is not knowledge <u>about</u>. Knowledge about something can be true, but it is not the Truth.

Likewise, the absence of knowledge about something is ignorance only in the conventional sense. In fact, the Truth is one with Divine Ignorance, which is not the absence of knowledge about things. It is that Ignorance which represents the fundamental Condition of, and orientation to, existence. Truth or Ignorance in that sense represents another way of knowing—not knowing <u>about,</u> but knowing in the sense of Realization or intuitive comprehension of the Condition of existence. When we abide in that intuitive Realization, there arise Wisdom and a sensitivity to the Condition or Process of existence in which a higher understanding becomes active and through which we can make certain kinds of observations directly, as human individuals, without using machines or any other intermediary devices.

The Way of Divine Ignorance, which relates to the Truth, is a different way of knowing than that conceived by science. The Ignorance whereby we are related to the Truth is a different kind of ignorance than the ignorance that science is trying to remedy. From the conventional point of view, ordinary ignorance should, as a general ideal, be overcome, particularly insofar as the absence of knowledge makes human beings dangerous or threatening or otherwise out of balance. Such ignorance does need to be cured, for it is a real human disability, but this goal of science is a conventional enterprise that has nothing to do with the Truth. Science provides knowledge of what is true about things, but to restrict oneself to that form of knowledge is to restrict oneself likewise to that form of relationship to things.

Science is essentially a dissociated, analytical way of relating to things, and its mood is doubt. Science never transcends this mood of doubt because it never transcends its way of knowing, its habitual, moment to moment way of associating with things. Thus, when the attitude of science becomes the way of life, the mood of doubt becomes the mood of existence and the condition, mood, and emotion of dissociation, and all the habits of dissociation become the program of one's existence. And that is precisely what has occurred in the culture of science. When it becomes the popular attitude, science produces the dissociated human being.

Thus, science today is uninformed, just as the attitude or disposition of the West was uninformed when gunpowder was introduced there. The Chinese invented gunpowder, but they were also characterized by a different way of knowing, a different way of associating with things, a way that was about the Truth. The "Tao" was about Ignorance with a capital "I."[1] Founded in the disposition of Ignorance, Chinese discoveries yielded harmless results—for example, they used gunpowder to make firecrackers for celebrations. But Man's

---

1. Thus, Lao Tzu observes in his *Tao Tê Ching* (chapter 70) that people do not know him because they have knowledge, whereas the sage who is one with the Tao ("Way") is beyond all knowing. For, "the Tao that can be expressed is not the eternal Tao" (chapter 1). Ch'u Ta-kao, *Tao Tê Ching* (London: Unwin Paperbacks, 1972).

discoveries tend to produce harmful results when he is not founded in the disposition of Ignorance. Western Man received the same knowledge as the Chinese sage about the substances that could be made into gunpowder, but not enjoying the Chinese sage's disposition, Western Man used it for warfare, in the attitude of dissociation and disharmony with life.

The pattern of thinking that is associated with knowledge about things is created by real observation and corresponds to the way things actually work. One whose thinking is thus patterned thinks he is somehow in unity with this universe. He has a mystical feeling about it all. But an individual who is characterized by the pattern of analytical thinking and who feels that pattern to be in strong correspondence with the way the world works is not a benign character. In any case, any pattern one could have in mind is not a complete or perfect rendering of the universe as it is. It is always only a logical pattern, a linear pattern—not to mention the fact that it is just a reflection, just a pattern, in the mind. It is not the universe itself.

The physical universe that science studies is revealing itself to be an inconceivable realm of space-time paradoxes. If you became of "the mind" of such paradoxes, you would "lose your mind" and transcend your patterns. To truly understand the universe, even in the terms in which modern science conceives it, is to transcend knowing about the universe. It is to be in the disposition of Divine Ignorance, of patternless mind, of unqualified awareness. It is to feel in unity with the universe, in which and with which one is related to a pattern of mind that is unqualified. To truly understand the universe is to relate to it through a disposition of unqualified feeling. This disposition is not dissociative or analytical at all. Thus, there is another way of knowing that is about the Truth, and this way of knowing is about Ignorance in the highest sense.

DEVOTEE: Master, you have been describing the scientific-analytical approach to knowing and its limitations. In contrast, I have been looking at the *Yoga Sutra*[2] in the past few days, particularly the section on the process of samyama[3] as a form of knowing about things. Swami

2. The *Yoga Sutra* of Patanjali, composed c. A.D. 200, is the fountainhead of Classical Yoga. Consisting of 195 aphoristic sentences, outlining the theory and practice of Yoga, this work has inspired the composition of numerous Sanskrit commentaries and subcommentaries.

3. The Sanskrit term *samyama* means literally "constraint." In Classical Yoga it is a technical expression for the combined practice of concentration (*dharana*), meditation (*dhyana*), and ecstatic absorption (*samadhi*) in regard to the same object of concentration. See also p. 113, n. 5.

Vivekananda, in his commentary,[4] discusses how the combination of concentration, meditation, and samadhi, with reference to the same object, leads to a superior form of knowing . . .

MASTER DA FREE JOHN: . . . by attaining a condition of unity with the object, rather than a condition in which you abstract the object and transform it into a mental category only.

DEVOTEE: What is so interesting about this way of direct knowing is that it is based on the earlier stages of human maturity and responsibility relative to pratyahara[5] and the yamas and niyamas[6]—all those disciplines that are so obviously not even considered by the scientific community.

MASTER DA FREE JOHN: Yes, it is possible to be a proficient scientist with very few positive human qualities in evidence. You can be a totally degenerate, corrupt, maniacal personality, absolutely dissociated in your behavior, filled with illusions and negative, cynical views, and still be a scientist. Whereas, since ancient times, practice of the way of knowing in the higher sense has required positive human characteristics.

A different kind of preparation is required to be a spiritual practitioner. Many dimensions of one's human character must be brought into alignment with the spiritual process, whereas to practice science, very little needs to be brought into alignment other than the mechanics of the observer's intelligence and his ability to make deductions.

DEVOTEE: Apparently Pythagoras established a community around him who practiced disciplines of diet, meditation, and so on, and only the inner circle were taught geometry. Pythagoras is reported to have said that geometry should only be taught to saints because someone with such knowledge could have tremendous power and unlock the secrets of the natural universe.

4. See Swami Vivekananda, *Raja-Yoga, or Conquering the Internal Nature* (Calcutta: Advaita Ashrama, 1962).

5. The Sanskrit word *pratyahara* means literally "counter-grasping." It refers to the yogic technique of withdrawing the senses from sense-objects—a practice that precedes concentration.

6. The Sanskrit terms *yama* and *niyama*, "discipline" and "restraint," refer to the moral requirements and basic practices of self-restraint that form the foundation of the eightfold Yoga taught in the *Yoga Sutra*.

MASTER DA FREE JOHN: The schools in Greece, as well as in other cultures, were complete schools of philosophy. They were academies, ashrams,[7] that provided every level of human training and initiation. One did not just go to class every day, read books, and merely think and use the tools of analysis. Rather, one was trained in, and one practiced, a whole, rather than a fragmented, disposition toward existence—and only then, having become founded in that disposition, would one think.

Thinking is definitely an aspect of an authentic human life, of spiritual life. You must be able to think clearly. Much of what all of you are suffering is ambiguous thinking, bad thinking, lack of thinking, the arbitrary inheritance of unconsidered persuasions. These persuasions must be re-cognized, known again. They must become the subject of clear comprehension or "hearing."

DEVOTEE: It is interesting too, Master, that we tend to view thinking as a negative activity when we see it employed in the imbalanced way the scientist tends to employ it, without being founded in the disposition of Ignorance. The scientist seems so full of doubt and of "wisdom" without love. His exaggerated thinking makes him seem almost inhuman.

MASTER DA FREE JOHN: The scientist has abolished true Wisdom from the realm of knowledge. He has thrown it out with all the garbage that was associated with so-called wisdom in the past. Today scientists inform us that we can destroy this Earth or at least render it uninhabitable. Well, where at the present time can you find in the character of humanity—which is epitomized by the scientist, for instance—a disposition that could prevent the destruction of the Earth? How can we possibly prevent the destruction of the Earth with the attitudes that are dominant in the whole play of science? You may find among scientists some humanists who would not be inclined towards certain kinds of destruction, but their humanism is not sufficient to prevent the destruction of the Earth, nor is the humanist disposition sufficient to make human life really worth living.

The universe described by scientists is such a meaningless mass of plastic garbage. It has no light and no fullness or significance. It is a

7. An ashram (Sanskrit: *ashrama*) is traditionally a place where a Spiritual Master gathers the community of his devotees in order to live with them, instruct them, and communicate the Living Force of his Presence. Master Da Free John sometimes uses the term to include the entire community or fellowship of devotees, wherever they may be located.

totally insignificant mass of moving matter that has no meaning
whatsoever. The only attribute that makes the universe seem to be
non-chaotic is the regularity of its movements, but even that regularity
is temporary. It is a universe utterly without significance, and if the
universe you conceive of is utterly without significance, then you are
also without significance, human existence is without significance.
And if human existence is without significance, then why the hell
should anybody prevent the destruction of the Earth?

The destruction of the Earth is just a social extension of self-
destructiveness, of degeneration, of the misapplication of knowledge.
Western Man in particular has always misapplied knowledge—either
prevented it through the persuasions of false wisdom, or exploited it
through a false scientific persuasion to the point of destruction.
Another dimension of presumption must therefore be brought to the
culture of scientism. Otherwise no integrity, no balance, can be applied
to the discoveries of science. The Chinese were founded in a
disposition that prevented them from using gunpowder for destructive
purposes. Likewise, Western Man—and the whole world has been
Westernized in some basic sense through science and technology—
must achieve or acquire another dimension of persuasion, of conception, of knowing, of realization, that will naturally control the
technological uses of science. Otherwise there will be no motive in
common humanity to prevent destruction.

Western Man has always been destructive because of his orientation to existence. It is just that we have come to a point where the
adolescent game of Western Man is associated with forces and
technological inventions that could destroy the entire world. Gunpowder was used in the past to slaughter people right and left without
any higher sense of life at all, but it was not capable of destroying the
Earth. Today, Western Man uses atom bombs as he used gunpowder
centuries ago, but atom bombs can annihilate the entire Earth. There
was no wisdom then, and there is no wisdom now.

I heard that a young teenager was able to determine how to make
an atom bomb small enough to fit into a suitcase based solely on
articles he read in *Scientific American*. The atom bomb is a fairly
simple device, and it is now common knowledge how to make such a
bomb, the kind of device that could be used by any terrorist group.

Do you not think terrorism is inevitable? What will change and
prevent it? It is far less likely that the Russians and the Americans will
use their atomic weapons, even though, in the stupid political conflict

that exists between these two great powers, there is constant talk about the possibility. In the meantime, however, some little terrorist group could produce an atom bomb sufficient to blow up a city.

These terrorists are not controlled by the international politics and persuasions that characterize the Russians and Americans. The Russians and Americans do not want to blow up the world, because they would destroy themselves in the process, but terrorists do not give a damn. Terrorists are always ready to give up their lives and the lives of everybody else to create some political advantage. And they are, you see, the extension of scientism in its popular form, the extension of Western consciousness.

That consciousness is the real threat, not the argument between Russia and the United States. The argument between Russia and the United States is suggestive of threat—a lot of little skirmishes occur, many games are played—but that argument is constantly economized to prevent the ultimate atomic holocaust. The terrorists do not play such games.

Super-destructive weaponry that could destroy the mass of humanity, if not the entire Earth, is now available to the popular Western mind, the mind of the ordinary, unillumined being who has always been destructive. Where in the Western consciousness, or in the common consciousness of mankind, can be found a higher view that would prevent such a scenario? The truth is, a higher view cannot be found there. The Western mind in itself is just insane, and scientism in and of itself is simply a form of insanity.

On one level scientism represents a conventional way of knowing that could be used for positive or negative purposes. Scientism is not inherently good or bad, but it is associated with a habit of use that always acts in the direction of power and manipulation. Scientism expresses an attitude, a way of relating to the universe, that is inherently dissociative, and scientism is not informed by a higher and integrative point of view.

The psychology of the political motives of the so-called great powers, as well as of terrorists, is very primitive. It is the same level of motivation that existed hundreds of years ago, that led tribe to beat tribe—the "wipe-out-your-enemy" kind of consciousness. It is a disturbed point of view that is not in any way whatsoever an expression of Illumination. That same psychology, the same orientation to existence that used clubs and then gunpowder, now employs atomic weapons.

The known world has been destroyed a number of times already,
except that in the past the known world was only a portion of the total
Earth, and generally only human populations, and not the Earth itself,
were destroyed. Today, in the age of science and technology, it is not
the rare unique individual who is being informed and persuaded and
controlled by science and its technologies. Science is informing and
persuading many kinds of people who are not so intelligent. They are
the ones who have atomic weaponry at hand, and such individuals are
as unillumined and dangerous now as they ever were. Yet, they have
the capacity to manipulate mankind as a whole and to destroy the
entire planet.

The higher motives of Man in the past have always been
associated with harmony, contemplation, a unified view wherein one
could intuitively associate with everything at Infinity. This disposition
enabled individuals to control all the hard-edged factors of existence
and to regulate their behavior in a benign fashion. Such higher
individuals and their cultural extensions maintained harmony in past
societies, but that disposition is not informing the world at the present
time. The man of science commits a great disservice by dissociating
himself and mankind from this higher disposition, by making it look
like foolishness. The man of science understands and argues that we
should save the Earth, but he himself has discarded the only
orientation that could make it possible for mankind to avoid such a
calamity. Mankind in the disposition of dissociation will never save
the Earth or make life livable.

In addition to the threat of a technology capable of totally
destroying the Earth as a habitable environment, there exist the
continuous destructive influences of technology, which manifest in the
degenerative and dehumanizing effects of its common social uses.
These influences are magnified by the influence of scientism, which
grows and grows and which accepts no other kind of wisdom. The
denial of another kind of wisdom is more dehumanizing than the
suppressive influence of technology. The rational mind, the form of
knowledge that has become the only acceptable one, excludes all other
possibilities from human life, including the highest possibility of
Enlightenment or God-Realization. Thus, the threat of the total
destruction of the Earth as a habitable environment is only one aspect
of the worldwide technological movement that is oppressing human
existence at the present time. All the other destructive aspects of
technology will continue to influence mankind as long as the Earth is
habitable.

Then what should one do? Should one not only Realize God, but also get seriously involved in a different orientation to life? In times past, when people have reviewed their situation, some have come to the philosophical conclusion that this world is an inherently negative creation and that existence is an inevitable round of suffering. Such judgments have led them to dissociate from the conventional stream of life. Others have simply reviewed the state of humanity in general, as well as what is available as human existence in the relational form of common life, and, made the decision to dissociate themselves, to minimize the requirements for their existence, and to turn their attention away from this world for entirely non-metaphysical reasons.

Today, we are facing a situation that is, it seems to me, much more definitive as a negative statement about the state of things than any situation could have been hundreds of years ago. Should we make the same decision and just abandon the game? Should we basically stop trying to fulfill our human existence?

DEVOTEE: Fulfill it minimally.

MASTER DA FREE JOHN: To do that, not only would you have to fulfill it minimally, but you would have to turn your attention into another sphere of existence. Rather than commit suicide, you would simply do whatever was necessary for mere survival, to pay your debt to the fact of your personal existence in this world. But you would not engage in any enterprises—cultural, personal, relational, intimate—for the sake of the elaboration of human existence. Rather, you would accept your individual existence merely as a given factor, which could be satisfied with very minimal attention, very minimal food, a little bit of shelter and clothing, and essentially social isolation.

DEVOTEE: But I think one should be able to enjoy oneself! (Laughter.)

MASTER DA FREE JOHN: But if you were to fulfill human existence minimally, you would also not involve yourself in any kind of activity that would satisfy you more than minimally.

DEVOTEE: Master, you have talked about the Jain philosophy of fasting until death,[8] pointing out all the limitations of mere asceticism,

8. Fasting until death is recognized in the extreme ascetical tradition of Jainism as a valid form of exiting from this world. Known as *itvara,* this ritual practice of suicide through starvation is a curious anomaly in a religious tradition in which nonviolence (*ahimsa*) holds a place of central importance.

or spiritual suicide as you described it. And then you mentioned the necessity of knowing the art of dying, the capacity to transcend human existence.[9] In fact, you spoke about the great virtue of the capacity to enter into samadhi at will, and you said that if you received a report that bombs were being dropped, you would realize the natural benefit of being able to enter into samadhi, transcend the body-mind, transcend the world.

MASTER DA FREE JOHN: You must already be in Samadhi,[10] because you may not get any warning. You may experience sudden death, sudden snuffing, with no time to go through a meditative procedure! You will, in fact, go wherever your attention or your tendencies tend to take you. Through need, or desire, or the search of the subliminal mind, you will spontaneously pursue things associated with your human existence, and if the world is blown up, you will not have any place to go.

DEVOTEE: But the practice you have given us, Master, is self-transcending and world-transcending from the very beginning.

MASTER DA FREE JOHN: If it is really practiced.

DEVOTEE: Yes, I know the Way of Radical Understanding or Divine Ignorance is not about going to another place. It simply indicates that the more positively a spiritual human being lives, the more positive his destiny would probably be, but that whatever his destiny, he would be able to transcend it through the process of surrender.

MASTER DA FREE JOHN: But attention determines destiny, you see. You may purify your habit of attention by being good or positive in some human sense, but it does not follow, then, that the orientation of your attention will go beyond being human. You will still be human, albeit minimized and transformed and made positive. But such an orientation suffers just as much from the absence of the possibilities of

9. See Da Free John, *Easy Death: Talks and Essays on the Inherent and Ultimate Transcendence of Death and Everything Else*, pp. 58–59.

10. Here, the word "Samadhi" does not refer to the conventional mystical or yogic state of acute inwardness or immersion in higher consciousness. Rather, it is the ultimate Condition of Enlightenment or God-Realization. For, egoic tendencies still exist at the level of yogic ecstasies, where they activate attention and thus, in the event of death, would prevent the individual from transcending the world altogether.

Earth as the aggravated, degenerate, desiring personality suffers from the absence of the capacity to be born on Earth. If the Earth is destroyed, therefore, both the virtuous and the degraded suffer because the destiny of all is controlled by attention. It is only when attention transcends the disposition toward human existence that it is liberated from the whole connection to human existence and therefore from the consequences of what happens to the Earth and to the capability of rebirth on Earth.

DEVOTEE: Master, I just remembered that you have said in the past that our Work might most truly flourish among significant numbers of people only after some really terrible event had occurred, because the patterns of attention would only be broken by such a negative event.

MASTER DA FREE JOHN: As far as I am concerned, such a negative event has already occurred. Humanity has already dissociated from the Truth and is on a degraded course. People are living degraded, unillumined lives. What I have had to deal with in people to date has therefore been nothing on a very high level, you see.[11] Thus far, I have been given to deal with only the accumulated patterns of this degraded, self-possessed destiny, and not accumulated patterns of a higher human destiny, a positive, virtuous human destiny.

The terrible event has already occurred, and the entire Earth is already embroiled in war, in political and social confusion, in habit energy that is self-possessed and degraded. If you can see what has happened in your own case, see what you represent personally, and see the common world, then, if intelligence is enough, you should already be sufficiently motivated to engage the spiritual process. But the more self-possessed you are, the more degraded or lazy your so-called nature, your accumulated tendencies, then the more likely you must experience some calamitous event to learn anything. Even calamitous events, however, do not necessarily change anything for the most degraded and self-possessed and ordinary beings. In any case, to engage the spiritual process requires intelligence, and free energy and attention.

DEVOTEE: Master, it seems obvious that the only possibility for changing the situation of humanity is Transcendental Work as you have described it.

---

11. This comment was made before the transition of several practitioners into the Enlightened disposition in the period from late March to early June of 1983.

MASTER DA FREE JOHN: Yes, but it must be Transcendental Work done with great energy.

DEVOTEE: Would it have to be done by a significant number of people as well?

MASTER DA FREE JOHN: It makes not a damn bit of difference if anybody else does it. If it is the Truth, it is the Truth. If somehow you have gotten in touch with It, then spiritual practice is there for you to do whether or not anyone else is persuaded to practice. If some others are persuaded, then that is good for them.

Perhaps all of you can make cooperative arrangements for your living conditions and somehow practice together. But be conscious that the living conditions people tend to want to develop cooperatively are extensions of the whole notion of fulfilling human life. When I talk about cooperation, I am considering it in spiritual terms, in basic, real, human terms, and therefore it is something that can be engaged only by people who are truly practicing. People who are not truly practicing conceive of the whole game of cooperation in elaborate human terms of satisfaction, fulfillment in one way or another, survival for its own sake, without any other consideration added.

Individuals in the past who renounced the world for one or another reason did not engage in elaborate plans of cooperative community with one another. They might have moved somewhere as a group, but they did only what was necessary for minimal service to their mere existence. They did not try to create a utopia in the desert. Usually they looked for a place where everything fell out of the trees so to cultivate anything would not even be necessary, where the weather was moderate, and where the natural availability of things made survival almost an automaticity.

Thus, they looked for a circumstance in which the minimum requirements of existence were satisfied either automatically or with minimal attention and activity, and apart from that they did not have the slightest impulse toward fulfillment or perfection or survival of life. Their life was one wherein their entire being was committed to Transcendental Communion, and they just did not do anything else. They had no other concerns at all, either to convince anyone else to live as they did or to elaborate their personal daily life in any way that was entertaining.

DEVOTEE: Master, it still seems that the mere fact that you would spend your time working on a book such as *Scientific Proof of the Existence of God Will Soon Be Announced by the White House!* indicates that you feel the communication of Truth in the world can somehow make a difference.

MASTER DA FREE JOHN: I do not know if it makes any difference. It is just something I have tended to do to try to be helpful to others, to be available to Teach them. I have observed, however, over years of tending to be helpful in this way that it is a relatively fruitless activity. It does not produce much on a great scale in terms of persuading and changing others. To the degree that others are persuaded and changed, it has required tremendous effort on my part. I have paid much personal dues to be available to help others. The whole effort of serving others is, on one level, a karmic intention.[12] Like any other intention, therefore, it must be transcended.

DEVOTEE: Master, the Buddhist Tantric schools claim that it does not make any difference what the Siddha[13] does, whether he communicates or whether he does not communicate. They say that the mere Force of the individual's Realization is effective or operative on so many levels, in so many worlds, and in so many so-called individuals that It is not even measurable by ordinary human terms. It is said that the Siddha's Work is going on constantly.

MASTER DA FREE JOHN: That is the other dimension of Transcendental Work, which has nothing to do with karma. As long as the situation is workable, I will Teach and I will write. If it becomes unworkable, then I will not Teach or write. But I will not cease to be

12. In his writings, Master Da Free John has described how the principle of karma or moral retribution can remain operative in the case of the Enlightened personality, but on a higher level: "There are higher karmas and lower karmas. The Narcissistic karmas, the more conventional individual karmas, fall away. In the seventh stage of life certain higher karmas may be animated, particularly in the case of the Adept, who does spontaneous 'Crazy' Work sometimes, to Teach. The higher karmas—if one could call them karmas at all—the higher expressions of action, which are basically devoted toward the Awakening of others and the Demonstration of the Way, may remain intact" (*The Bodily Sacrifice of Attention,* p. 82).

13. A Siddha is literally a "Fulfilled" or "Perfect One." A Siddha (also Maha-Siddha, "Maha" meaning "great") is one who has Realized God permanently and beyond doubt. Master Da Free John uses the term to refer to the Free Adepts who have appeared in many cultures and who, because of their own Awakening, are naturally moved to Awaken others through the spontaneously transmitted Consciousness, Presence, Power, and Intelligence of the Divine Being.

Realized or cease to do what I do fundamentally. I will not doubt the spiritual process and abandon it. Nothing like that would be the consequence, you see. What I have done thus far is just a spontaneous expression, and when that more apparent level of it becomes unworkable, then it is transcended or falls away. Thus, that level of it could be conceived of as being something like karma, something that could be abandoned, something that comes into play when the conditions for it exist.

Another dimension of Transcendental Work is simply the expression of the quality of Enlightenment Itself, of the Realization of the Radiance that is Infinite. That Disposition accomplishes various things when there are circumstances amenable to It, but if the appropriate circumstances do not exist, that Disposition does not seem to have any effect. Thus, under some circumstances I may <u>seem</u> not to be doing anything anymore. I have done what I have done thus far because circumstances permitted it, but now I am moving in the direction of non-confrontation with the world.[14]

DEVOTEE: I have always observed a strange paradox in your Play in relationship to the world, Master. At times you seem to be very aggressive about the state of the Earth, very much directed toward what is going on. Then at so many other times you state that this world does not make any difference, that the separate self sense does not make any difference. What I find interesting about it all is that, in either extreme, I have always felt your Freedom from whether or not this world exists. And that is a mad thing to realize about your Spiritual Master! We are all very much aware that your Realization is totally independent of what happens.

MASTER DA FREE JOHN: Yes, because I have taken into account the fact of death. If you take the fact of death into account, all the ways whereby death may occur are already transcended, you see. The destruction of the Earth and its inhabitants by atomic warfare is just another means whereby death may occur. You are not any deader when you have been killed by a nuclear bomb than you are when you

14. This is a reference to Master Da Free John's transition into the "hermitage phase" of his life. Having established a community of spiritual practitioners and provided them with all the Agencies necessary for their maturation, Master Da is now moved to intensify his Work with devotees in the more advanced stages of practice to facilitate their transformation and bodily demonstration of God-Realization. (See p. 180, n. 12, for a description of the Agencies, or vehicles of spiritual Help, created by Master Da Free John.)

have died from a heart attack or old age. You are still dead. Realization of the spiritual Disposition already takes death into account, and therefore, the Realized individual has a free relationship to death's possibilities.

But for those who are not utterly associated with this matter of spiritual Realization, it is useful to consider the realities of the time. Such consideration is a way of invoking inspection and awakening intelligence relative to spiritual practice in general. Mediocre spiritual practice is based on a conscious or unconscious choice of possibilities for human experience that depend on continuation and on death's occurring in the future.

If you knew you were going to die next Friday at noon, if you knew this, your human activities would be transformed dramatically, and you would suddenly become capable of bringing things to an end, of handling those karmic matters that are necessary for releasing attention from this life. As long as you think death is indefinite and even far into the future, your attention is associated with programs of fulfillment that depend on the continuance of life and that have nothing to do with the consideration of death.

If this is your frame of mind, you practice the Way not in its radical form, and not with profoundly free energy and attention, but conventionally. In other words, you practice the Way in the midst of an orientation to existence wherein you are not conceiving of death presently, wherein you are basically trying to fulfill human desires, to glamorize and pleasurize your existence until death. You are conceiving of living presently, and death is an event you do not really feel you need take into account at the present time. But nuclear bombs or not, death can occur at any time from any number of causes.

DEVOTEE: I was just remembering a story I know you have heard, Master, that is a humorous way of pointing out how taking the fact of death into account can change one's disposition. An Englishman is captured by Indians, and the chief brings his sick son to him, telling him that if he does not heal the child by morning, they will kill him. So, the Englishman prays to God, promising that if God heals the boy, He has got Himself a convert!

MASTER DA FREE JOHN: Yes, that is a humorous version of it. There is also the story of a man who visited a sage who was a king. The man was sent on a tour of the palace carrying a bowl of water filled to the brim, with a swordsman following behind him. He was told that if he spilled so much as a drop over the edge of the bowl, he would have his head cut off. Conceiving of death as a present, imminent condition transformed his relationship to everything.

It would be the same for you, except you do not view your actions as consequential to death. You view death as something that happens a long time from now, decades from now, and in the meantime you do not see your actions as something that could bring about sudden death. You see your actions as devoted to consequences you conceive to be positive, life-enhancing, and human. You do not think of death as a possibility that could result from a moment's inattention, a moment's fluctuation of concentration.

DEVOTEE: Master, there is also the hope that death is just an occasion where you simply go to sleep and everything is preserved, whereas if an atom bomb dropped on you, you would be splattered all over creation. That is a much more horrifying thought.

MASTER DA FREE JOHN: What if in order to live you had to beat your own heart? What if the heart were a voluntary activity like extending your hand to grasp something? What if breathing and circulating the blood were voluntary, and you had to maintain them by keeping your attention in that physiological process, and if you abandoned it for more than a few moments, you would interrupt the cycle and cause your own death? What if this were the way it were? You could not sleep, for one thing. It is said that sharks never sleep because they only maintain oxygenation through motion, by making the water pass over their gills. If they were to sleep or to stop moving, they would drown. What if you had to do something similar to the shark? It would relate you to existence in an entirely different way.

But your existence is an involuntary process. It is happening automatically. Your attention is occupied, instead of with surviving, with glamorizing and extending your existence. You are associated with other kinds of relational designs, with social and subjective inventiveness, because your existence is something you need not take into account. It is arising mysteriously and automatically, and you take it for granted. You can do whatever you like and just keep on existing, except that you know that the process will be interfered with at some point through some external interference or the degeneration of the body. But for the time being, your existence is automatic, and thus your attention is associated with the self-glamorizing play of life. If existence were voluntary rather than involuntary and automatic, this would create a totally different habit of attention.

DEVOTEE: It seems that once we realize that true life is only possible through Transcendental Communion, then we are obliged to practice the Prayer of Remembrance[15] moment to moment. The Source of our true life is in simply fulfilling that obligation. We would necessarily have to practice the Prayer in order to remain "Alive," just as we would have to beat each heartbeat to remain physically alive if it were not occurring automatically.

MASTER DA FREE JOHN: Basically, what you are saying is that your existence—in the fullest sense—is not automatic. Your mere existence is automatic, but to exist consciously in the Condition that truly is your life, you must intentionally practice, and the spiritual process is an acknowledgment of that Condition. You must intentionally stay alive. You must intentionally associate yourself with That Which is Life. Otherwise your life is reduced to the automaticity of mere existence without any great significance, and your attention wanders in realms of insignificance or self-glamorization that are ultimately deluding.

DEVOTEE: Master, the devotee who practices the Prayer of Remembrance reminds me of a samurai soldier. The samurai soldier cannot even get into the bathtub without having his sword with him. He would not go anywhere without that sword.

MASTER DA FREE JOHN: What if each of you had another devotee behind you who would cut off your head with a sword if you abandoned the Prayer of Remembrance for even one half of a breath cycle? (Laughter.)

---

15. "Remembrance" is a foundation practice in the initial stages of the Way of Radical Understanding or Divine Ignorance, as Taught by Master Da Free John. Remembrance is the whole-bodily exercise of invoking and surrendering body and mind into the Divine by means of the Name "Da," which denotes the "Giver" or the Divine Being in its personal aspect. For Master Da's instructions on this practice, see his *Bodily Worship of the Living God*, pp. 141ff.

CHAPTER 8

MAN'S THREE AFFLICTIONS AND THE BUSINESS OF SCIENCE

a talk by Da Free John
December 15, 1980

1.

MASTER DA FREE JOHN: Let us talk about affliction. In the classical Buddhist description, Gautama contemplates existence and develops the presumption that existence is suffering. This analysis is the basis of the conception of the Way in Hinayana Buddhism, in which existence is conceived as a problem to be solved through overcoming or vanishing all tendency toward association with manifestation. Yet, even if existence itself is not conceived as inherently a problem, if existence is not definable as suffering, it is still possible to observe one's existence as something that includes suffering or has the potential for suffering.

When we think about the fact that life can involve suffering, we tend to think in terms of extreme difficulties: death, disease, war and famine, separation, sorrow, and all the rest. Such suffering is extreme. In other words, it is not common. Although some people in some places in the world at the present time commonly suffer these difficulties, human life in general does not involve continuous suffering at the level of extremes. But human existence, bereft of higher understanding and Enlightenment, is in general afflicted. It contains the quality of suffering. That suffering may be exquisite or profound, but it is not extreme in the usual sense of being afflicted by terrible disease and disasters.

If we observe our ordinary lives, apart from extreme forms of suffering, but also apart from the natural transcendence involved in full Enlightenment or God-Communion, we can see that certain kinds of affliction are more or less constant. It is interesting to observe one's moment to moment existence and to see what those afflictions are. Perhaps all of them could be summarized in terms of boredom, doubt, and discomfort. We can suffer extremes, but in our moment to moment existence, which is generally not associated with extreme forms of suffering, we are still tending to be constantly afflicted by boredom, doubt, and discomfort.

The Enlightened point of view does not presume that existence is inherently qualified by suffering. Apart from Enlightenment, however, existence does appear to be inherently a form of suffering because it is constantly afflicted. People are aware of the fact that they are trying to avoid extreme forms of suffering, but they are less aware of the fact that in every moment they are trying to avoid the natural or ordinary forms of suffering. They are constantly trying to avoid the subtle afflictions of boredom, doubt, and discomfort.

In our profound anxiety, at the level of fear, we are trying to avoid the extreme forms of suffering. But we also maintain an ordinary level of anxiety, a kind of tension, in which we are trying to avoid being overcome by the feelings of boredom, doubt, and discomfort. It is the desire to avoid these forms of ordinary affliction that produces our habits of self-indulgence. We animate ourselves constantly to avoid these three forms of affliction.

Boredom is a form of suffering that we very much want to avoid. So we keep ourselves interested. We disturb ourselves with interest to avoid boredom. We console ourselves with beliefs to avoid doubt. And we indulge ourselves physically in food, sex, drink, drugs, and so forth to avoid discomfort. Independent of Realized understanding, people live in fear of extreme suffering and maintain a level of anxiety or tension, developed through the form of self-indulgent habits, to avoid the ordinary forms of suffering. In other words, people live as if existence were inherently a form of suffering.

It is interesting that in the sacred traditions people take up methods of self-application that in fact enhance the qualities they are ordinarily trying to avoid. Extreme ascetics even devote themselves to

maintaining association with extreme forms of suffering. But other
practitioners, who devote themselves to practices independent of both
extreme self-indulgence and extreme self-denial, maintain a habit of
self-application wherein the qualities of boredom, doubt, and discomfort are in fact made the continuous companions of their existence.

The Buddhist tradition in particular tends to dissociate itself from
extreme ascetical application because of its original mood. Historically,
Gautama tried the extreme practices of asceticism that began to involve
extreme suffering. And the life-style of his youth had afforded him all
the possibilities of avoiding ordinary affliction. He had grown up in a
royal court with all the wealth required to keep people amused,
consoled, and pleasurized. According to the historical report, then,
Gautama came to a point where he realized that neither of these
extremes is the right foundation for Enlightenment. For that reason,
Buddhism historically conceives of the Way as a kind of middle path, a
middle ground, where extremes are avoided. Nonetheless, the
Buddhist's middle path of reasonable discipline involves a kind of self-
application in which the ordinary forms of affliction—boredom,
doubt, and discomfort—are in fact intensified.

Religious belief is a convention of human consciousness that is at
the service of our ordinary anxiety about the form of affliction called
doubt. To be a believer in the conventional religious sense is a way of
avoiding doubt through belief and religious consolation. Through the
same motive people also try to avoid the various kinds of discomfort
involved in life. Likewise, they try to avoid boredom. Ordinary
application to a religious way of life, then, is not a high calling. Rather,
it serves the usual intention of people to avoid the ordinary forms and
levels of affliction.

In contrast, serious application to a religious or a spiritually
conceived Way of life in fact tends to enhance these qualities. Because
this is so, people find it difficult to associate themselves with a
consistent discipline. If you apply yourself for days and then weeks and
then months on end to the discipline of real religious or spiritual
practice, you begin to suffer the afflictions of boredom, doubt, and
discomfort. As a result, you find yourself wanting to introduce forms
of self-indulgence, consolation, and entertaining occupation in the
midst of your practice. For this reason, you see, even those who
somewhat seriously practice a religious or spiritual Way of life tend to
remain mediocre. Even though they may be avoiding extreme forms
of suffering (for the moment at any rate), and even though they may

be in general avoiding extreme self-indulgence, they are still, by virtue of their practice, unable to avoid the ordinary discomfort that ordinary people in their anxiety are also trying to avoid.

Self-indulgence in its various forms, then, is a primary method that ordinary people use to escape these afflictions. But religious preoccupation in the conventional form, the "believing-in-Jesus" kind of mechanism, is another method ordinary people apply in their anxiety to avoid the basic discomfort of existence.

If you study the historical reports of serious meditators or serious practitioners, in which they describe the various states through which they pass prior to their Realization, among those descriptions you will find descriptions of the extreme encounter with boredom, doubt, and discomfort. The real course of religious practice, you see, is not a conventional means for escaping affliction. It is a practice that avoids extremes perhaps, but by virtue of the very practice of avoiding extremes the ordinary states of affliction are intensified. And to fulfill the Way of practice, you must be able to encounter, endure, and ultimately transcend the fundamental afflictedness of egoic existence. If you do not pass through it, if you cannot endure it, if you cannot understand and transcend it, then you will inevitably return to the conventional state of the ego and become disposed toward self-indulgence and illusion. You may even become self-destructive and thus inevitably suffer the extreme forms of disease, calamity, and distress.

Serious and real application to a religious or spiritual Way of life is therefore not a conventional method for avoiding the states about which human beings are ordinarily anxious. When you read the commentaries of psychiatrists, people who conceive of things from the point of view of conventional knowledge and scientism, you find that they criticize religion as if it were simply an "opiate of the people," a conventional method for avoiding the realities and real discomforts of life. As I have pointed out, religion in the conventional sense is just that. It is not superior to the usual methods of physical self-indulgence. It is just another one of the basic routines available to people to help them avoid the discomforts of existence. But real practice intensifies these states to the point of a crisis in which the real Fullness of existence replaces the ego-bond, the ego-contraction, which is the root of conventional discomfort.

Doubt is not ultimately transcended through beliefs. Doubt is a state of mind that is fundamentally without content. It is an expression of the contraction of the being. It is not cured with positive beliefs that are the opposite of doubt. It is cured by the release of this contraction so that there is a continuity between consciousness and forms and relations, an unobstructed continuity between the being and Reality altogether.

Boredom, likewise, is not transcended through application of attention to what is interesting. That activity is in fact a way of escaping boredom, not transcending it. Boredom truly does not have any content. It is an expression of the contraction of the being. And it is transcended only through the release of this contraction.

Discomfort, again, has no content. It is not truly released through self-indulgence, but through transcendence of the contracting power of the being.

In some sense you could say that boredom, doubt, and discomfort represent the contractions of the three fundamental levels of the being, if we conceive of the being in physical, emotional, and mental terms. Doubt is an affliction of mind. It also tends to have an emotional aspect, but we could say it is fundamentally an affliction of the mind, an expression of the contraction of mind. Boredom could be said to be an affliction or contraction of our emotional nature, although it also has a mental aspect. And discomfort is an affliction or contraction at the physical level of the being. Thus, if the conventional ego, the limited self-sense, is simply a contraction of the total psycho-physical being, then we read that contraction through these ordinary afflictions.

2.

MASTER DA FREE JOHN: Scientism is a development of conventional knowledge or of conventional existence—existence as it is viewed from the point of view of the ego. The method of scientism, which is a rigorous development of conventional knowledge, makes use of doubt. People in their ordinary frame of life make conventional or ordinary use of doubt, but science is the rigorous application of doubt. Scientists tend to describe themselves as skeptics. They doubt everything until it is proven.

Science has thus found a way to make doubt into a tool of conventional knowledge. And, rightly used, that tool has its place. But as a psychological state that defines our existence and that is developed into a view of the universe, doubt is a form of affliction, something to be understood and ultimately transcended. In the course of real spiritual practice, doubt is encountered in its purity. It is not regarded to have philosophical content. It is regarded to be simply a sign of the contraction of the being. In other words, it does not contain all kinds of meanings about Reality, and it should not become a method for viewing Reality, for interpreting the world. If it does, then we are not only engaged in the usual reactivity of self-contraction, but we are making the self-contraction into a world-view. We are making it the medium, the foundation, the seed of knowledge. For this reason people who suffer chronic doubt also chronically suffer a mortal and rather dark view of Reality, bereft of God and every kind of positive or Divine sign.

Boredom and discomfort must also ultimately be encountered in their purity, not as signs of what is outside the self but as signs of the activity that is the self. Only by observing these conditions in their purity and persisting in spiritual practice even while they appear are we cutting through the disability that is the self-contraction and transcending the conventional orientation to life. Therefore, the pure qualities of boredom, doubt, and discomfort are a part of spiritual discipline.

There really is no method of true spiritual practice for avoiding these qualities. Religion should not be conceived as a method for avoiding these states. True religious or spiritual practice is not a servant of anxiety and fear, or of our search to be consoled or to escape the ordinary states of the ego. Rather, it is a Way of life in which the ordinary states of the ego and the fundamental activity that is the ego are clearly observed, understood, and transcended on the basis of such understanding.

The usual individual is not only bored and in doubt and uncomfortable, but he or she communicates a view of the world that is based on those aspects of the ego-disposition. Conventional knowledge in general is an expression or development of this ordinary state of affliction. Scientism, which is a rigorous development of conventional knowledge, is an expression of the egoic point of view toward reality. It has developed the ego-position as a world-view, a point of view about things that are apparently outside the ego. Scientism investigates what is outside the self, and it tries to eliminate interference by the self with what is being studied and the procedure of the study. But the point of view at the root of its investigations is nonetheless the self, or the ego-contraction, and the signs of the self, which are boredom, doubt, and discomfort.

The description of reality, therefore, that has developed at the rather adolescent level of present scientific culture is a duplication of the egoic point of view whereby boredom, doubt, and discomfort are ultimately justified. The same individuals who try to promote the viewpoint of scientism and all its wonderful discoveries are in fact promoting a view that, if you took it seriously, would ultimately lead you to become extremely bored, to enter into the extremities of doubt, and to suffer inevitable personal discomfort.

Why should one feel positive about existence in human form in this universe if existence is nothing but a mechanical development of a universal, mechanical Nature? If we truly are mortal, nothing but the robots of DNA and other material features of the universe, then even though one has discovered that that universe is a great complexity, a really wonderful machine, how can one feel anything but doubt? How can one be anything but depressed and bored? How can one feel anything but uncomfortable in the face of inevitable death and trial and discomfort that serve no purpose whatsoever, in which each individual seems to be an expression of the universal machine of Nature that ultimately does not give a damn about any of its single manifestations, but is somehow a great material god who will go on and on and on, reproduce itself in millions, and therefore need not have any concern whatsoever for the fate of any single individual? Why should happiness be the basic mood toward such scientific discovery?

If, however, we not only do the work of scientific discovery, achieving conventional knowledge, but also engage in the sacred ordeal or the highest spiritual process, then we transcend the conventional mood of the ego and all its artifacts, all its signs, expressions, and ordinary forms of destiny. Then we may also be able to make use of scientific discoveries and technological developments, and we may be able to feel good about those discoveries in which science seems to be involved. Those discoveries will not oblige us to view existence negatively because they will not represent the limit of our understanding and our presumption about the nature of Reality. Only by committing ourselves to the spiritual process and to the more radical propositions about Reality that are founded on Realization do we transcend all the signs and disturbances of the egoic nature—both the expressions of our individual self-bondage and the extensions of that self-bondage in cultural and social forms and the forms of conventional knowledge.

3.

DEVOTEE: Master, it is interesting that when people presume a negative view they create negative things. I was thinking about the hydrogen bomb, for instance. It seems that people could use that energy for something creative rather than something destructive.

MASTER DA FREE JOHN: Our technologies reflect the state of adaptation of mankind in general and the disposition of the political and other social powers that take scientific knowledge and develop it in the form of technological tools. Science is not inherently disposed to be destructive except to the degree it is an expression of conventional consciousness. Then it is quite easily used by negative expressions of conventional consciousness when it is converted into technology.

It is possible for science to serve positive purposes. But it can do so only if those who make use of it are Enlightened or disposed toward a spiritual Realization of existence. And that, of course, is not commonly the case at present. Technology, therefore, often tends to be used for destructive purposes, and science itself tends to develop models of Reality, models of Man, and models of the universe that are conceived in limitation. Such models do not really justify a liberally Happy disposition, but rather exploit the bondage of the ego.

On one level, the ordinary hearers of the discoveries of science and the models projected by science feel stimulated, because these discoveries show a vast, complex pattern that has a certain order. But at another level, scientific models and discoveries tend also to justify the mood of doubt, the Godless mood, the mood of mortality. That mood cannot be escaped by keeping yourself constantly stimulated by the possible technological manipulations of your own existence and by your fascination with science and all that it is discovering. That state is, rather, a conventional development like the ordinary stimulations people bring to their bored and distressed lives.

DEVOTEE: Master, some scientists suggest that perhaps beings in other physical worlds are in a different disposition.

MASTER DA FREE JOHN: Yes, I have heard scientists say that we are in danger of destroying ourselves, and they wonder if there are other civilizations out in space that have been able to go beyond this stage of adolescent technology. In fact, one scientist who appeared on a TV program recently constantly referred to the fact that we may destroy ourselves and that civilizations that develop technological capability may typically destroy themselves.

The only way civilizations can go beyond this point is to achieve a higher view of existence, in which conventional knowledge and technologies can be applied according to a wise, Free disposition, one that is Happy in the context of the universe. This means that we must achieve a different cultural status at the same time that we are developing our technological, scientific capacity. Mankind is in a rather primitive cultural state at the present time, yet we have a very sophisticated capability at the level of science and technology. It should be obvious that we are tending toward the possibility of self-destruction because of our low level of cultural development, our primitive state of realization. Only by advancing the capacity for Realization in the spiritual sense, in the high philosophical sense, can we make right use of technologies and of the scientific method.

It should also be understood that this is much too early in the game of science to start proposing models of the universe, models of Reality, and models of what Man is. We can summarize our discoveries to date and see that they point to a rather limited and mortal framework of Reality, but at the present time we should not presume that that framework is Reality. The history of serious scientific inquiry is very short. We could say it has been taking place for a few hundred years, perhaps. It was only after the Victorian era that we really began to see the real development of technologies. Thus, we have enjoyed perhaps a century of serious scientific application, including the development of a world-view based on science. It is much too early in the game, then, for scientists to be developing models of Reality that are fixed, mortal, and materialistic. Such models themselves are an expression of a primitive, archaic human state.

People should understand the limitations of knowledge at the present time. They should understand that science itself must go on and develop to the point of maturity. Science is still in its adolescence. It is in no position to be controlling mankind at this stage. Science must enter into a more advanced form of understanding and technological capability, and likewise mankind as a whole must begin to develop more advanced cultural forms of participation in the universal Reality—forms of participation that go beyond this egoic, mortalistic view and the archaic presumptions of materialism. Such higher cultural participation is based on radically understanding the nature of Reality and is not limited by the conventions of the archaic mind and mortal consciousness nor by a deprecation of the domain with which we are associated at the level of the psyche. Therefore, science has a great deal more to discover before it can propose a model that approaches or approximates the Truth of things, the real Condition of things. Likewise, it is much too late in the game of existing as human beings to be defining ourselves in terms of the ancient, exoteric, archaic, philosophical views.

A great transformation must occur culturally at the level of both conventional knowledge and spiritual Knowledge, or Realization, before mankind will be able to go beyond the threat of self-destruction. The threat of the destruction of mankind as a whole is simply another version of the tendency of the individual toward self-destruction. The same tendency that seems to be evident at the level of our global existence is present in the features of ordinary consciousness in which every individual is involved. Under the pressures of fear and anxiety, individuals tend toward self-destruction. Therefore, mankind as a whole, depressed or suppressed by the same emotions, the same illusions, and the same despair, tends to be self-destructive.

Only when you transcend the model of existence that pressurizes the being in a self-destructive manner do you transcend the possible destiny of self-destruction. Mankind must pass through the same transformation that every individual must endure. It is not just a matter of being intelligent and sober about science. It is a matter of engaging in the sacred ordeal of existence and transcending the limiting power of your own unillumined existence. Mankind must go through this ordeal, and that means that every individual must go through this ordeal. And we must witness, over the next decades or centuries, a profound transformation of human consciousness. If we do not see such a transformation, then simply in order to prevent mankind from destroying itself, powers of State must assume more control over people while people continue in their rather childish and adolescent adaptation to life.

In our time we do in fact see the powers of the State growing and interfering more and more profoundly with the capacity for free

individual exercise and intimate cultural experiment. Those trends will
inevitably increase and may even become absolute over the coming
decades unless a cultural revolution places every individual into a
cultural process wherein the self-limiting features of existence are
transcended, including all the reflections on Reality that develop on
the basis of these self-limits. Powers of the State or unifying media in
the setting of human societies will always exist, but the kind of
oppression that occurs when a State controls people who themselves
have no self-control will disappear. The State will represent simply a
conventional mechanism of order and communication in which the
people are fundamentally Happy, Enlightened, and associated with
conceptions of Reality that are benign, Free, and Happy.

At the present time, however, no other process of communication
parallels the strength of the communication associated with political
powers, scientific activity, and the dissemination of conventional
knowledge. No process of communication that would lead people
toward radical understanding, a Liberated view, a spiritual Consciousness, has strength equal to that of the communications media of
scientific and political materialism. The overriding and dominant
levels of communication are extensions of egoic self-possession.
Therefore, the level of communication proceeding via the State and
other secular instruments is increasingly developing the tendency
toward holocaust or the alternative, which is the strict control of
humanity via the powers of the State.

At the level of daily life, of people downtown in touch with one
another, we do not see any signs whatsoever of a higher cultural
disposition. Nothing of the kind is developing, but only TV, which is
the fundamental source of mind and persuasion, and the street
consciousness that is dramatizing conflict, distress, boredom, doubt,
discomfort, disease, un-Happiness, despair, bewilderment. More and
more technological advantages are presented to people in the form of
products they can use to stimulate themselves out of boredom. But at
the level of ideas, at the level of a communicated sense of existence,
there is only more and more justification for despair and emptiness.

As a result, people are becoming either desperate and empty or
fiercely interested in illusions. Paradoxically, then, at the same time
that we have this great movement of secular knowledge and scientism,
we have the resurgence of conventional religious cults. We still find
masses of people fanatically associated with the Jesus movements,
Sunday preaching, and the archaisms of ancient religious dogmas and
cults.

We do not see the development of a Wisdom-culture that Awakens people in the radical sense and Liberates them from the features of their own existence that make them dangerous to one another, that make them sheerly distracted egos—egos comforted by illusions and relaxed by physical self-indulgence. Unless another dimension begins to appear at the level of cultural communication and association, we will witness more and more a movement toward ultimate threats. That movement can go on just so long before the powers of the State begin to intervene and start to control populations. At the present time, you see, everybody has the sense that politics is heating up, that there are all kinds of threats out there. There are Communists over against so-called free states, there are Third World states and revolutionaries, and there is a great deal of technological capability with which all those people can be in touch.

Every day we hear about conflicts in various parts of the world that increase the possibility of a nuclear confrontation. Many people are already being snuffed out by these political conflicts. And everybody has the sense, reinforced every day, that a great heat is building toward an inevitable conflict. Whether or not the inevitable conflict occurs depends on just how reactive become the people who have control over weaponry. Perhaps there may be some use of nuclear weapons and even some terrible events. But more likely than the universal destruction of mankind will be the strict control of the world's populations by the power of the State. By then, mankind will have become psychologically habituated to the view that the holocaust seems inevitable. Therefore, people will accept more readily that it is right and appropriate for the State to assume totalitarian control.

This, then, is one possible scenario of the future. It does not seem likely in the near future that any kind of great Wisdom-influence will be communicated universally and with the same kind of strength with which the forms of conventional knowledge are communicated. Thus, it seems likely that we will move more and more toward the holocaust or its alternative. In other words, we will be conditioned more and more to accept the fact that there is a great threat and that at some point the political powers will develop a kind of totalitarian world state. Perhaps only some time after that will a new cultural influence begin to develop.

DEVOTEE: Master, there is a decline in human morals, but at the same time there is also an increase in the turning to true religious values, at least among some groups.

MASTER DA FREE JOHN: Yes. But while there is some popular movement toward spirituality, particularly in its older forms, the real powers in charge—the powers of the State and the powers of conventional communication and education—are propagandizing against spirituality, against religion, against all the human kinds of occupation, development, and experience that have always been part of religious and spiritual acculturation. Even though there is a slight popular trend toward a spiritual Way of life, it is very difficult for that trend to achieve any kind of strength because it is constantly being undermined by the conventional powers that are threatening us in the first place. Those conventional powers are also the ones that will make the judgments about how to solve the problem created by the threat produced by technology.

No popular movement toward Wisdom will change things. Such a popular movement will perhaps continue even under a political regime that profoundly controls individual existence. However, if such a popular movement begins to achieve the strength people have when they actually enter into the domain of Realization rather than popular interest in spirituality, then perhaps at some point in the future the force of Realization among the group of Enlightened practitioners will begin to be reflected in the conventions of the universal culture of humanity.

At present there does not seem to be any cultural capacity for a universal cultural transformation of mankind, in particular of those who are practically in charge. It does seem possible, however, that a holocaust could be avoided by using the machinery of State.

Once the threat of holocaust is somehow contained by a new political organization of humanity, then there will perhaps be the potential for a cultural revolution toward a more radical understanding, a Transcendental Realization of life. But that revolution could still be centuries away. After all, humanity has already gone on without a Realized point of view for millennia! There have always only been a few people seriously involved in the ultimate consideration of things. Most people have been basically controlled by the conventional powers, and humanity has already learned that it can survive that way merely by controlling the benighted masses through superior influences such as the powers of the State.

That same design could be maintained for hundreds of years into the future, though under a World State dominated by the highly developed view of scientism and its technologies. After a time—particularly after science has had the opportunity to continue its investigations to the point of making discoveries beyond the archaic presumptions science itself continues to maintain—a cultural revolution of human existence may occur, both because the people begin to develop an urge toward Transcendental Realization, and also because science begins to develop an understanding of the nature of things that justifies such a cultural transformation.

However, the present broad scientific presumption does not justify a spiritual Way of life. Rather, it propagandizes against such a Way. Only when scientific knowledge develops beyond its adolescent phase, by making more advanced discoveries that do not support its present presumption, will it tend to justify the cultural revolution of human consciousness. Until the powers of knowledge and control in the world begin to justify a radical spiritual view of life, it is not likely that a radical spiritual view of life will become the context of existence for the mass of humanity.

Thus, two levels of development must go hand in hand. One is at the level of that percentage of individuals in any given moment who are seriously inclined toward a spiritual Way of life—and they are only a fractional percentage of mankind as a whole. The other level of development concerns the regime of conventional enterprises of knowledge, whose experiments must be continued until they develop a point of view that justifies the Awakened disposition at present cultivated by a small group of people through their own energy and inclination. When those two enterprises come together, when they can see the likenesses in one another, then it becomes possible for mankind as a whole to become informed by a cultural enterprise that reflects a transcendental view of Reality.

DEVOTEE: Do you mean that science will inevitably lead toward a time when something other than fixed, materialistic assumptions must be acknowledged?

MASTER DA FREE JOHN: Well, you can always hope. But science, you see, does not develop sacred commitment. As we have considered together, it represents a different way of knowing. On the basis of its investigations, it can begin to see that the world is a much more paradoxical and expanded affair than is presumed from the conventional point of view of scientific materialism. Science may not necessarily be able to generate a kind of sacred tradition on that basis, but those who are inclined toward the sacred ordeal of life will always be able to remark that the discoveries of science are synchronous or utterly sympathetic with an ultimate spiritual process. And as long as such people have freedom to communicate, there is the possibility that a sacred cultural movement can develop.

Hopefully, that is the way it will be. Hopefully, there will not be such wholesale suppression of the alternative way, or of the fact that there are really two dimensions to our life, one at the level of conventional activity and conventional knowledge and the other at the level of sacred activity and sacred knowledge. Humanity must come to an understanding that these two dimensions exist. Just as there are two halves to the brain and two halves to the nervous system, there are two fundamental aspects of human activity. One is of a conventional kind, and the other is of a sacred kind. It is not a matter of one or the other's being dominant. Both must be exercised by every human being and reflected in the order to which all human beings are related.

If this understanding can somehow be generated through conversation, through cultural processes, then the movement into the future will be along the lines of tolerance for this understanding. But if my Argument cannot achieve any kind of force, if people do not understand its intelligence, respect it, and organize themselves along the lines of this radical understanding, then we will see a continued movement in the direction of the secularization of humanity. This will mean that, apart from the possibility of a holocaust, there may be hundreds of years of an extremely secularized human order. That which is repressed and suppressed—this sacred dimension of human enterprise—will eventually create a revolution somewhere down the line. But it could take centuries, and who knows what kind of form it might take?

In any case, humanity, through some groups or sacred enterprises, will ultimately demand the recognition of another dimension of human activity. That recognition will require a cultural revolution, perhaps even involve war and disturbances. Such changes have always been required in the past for the sacred dimension to arise and flourish. Before all of that takes place, however, before the secularization of the world has become absolute, extreme, and one-sided, if an understanding can be generated through such consideration as my own of the real nature of our existence, and if an acknowledgment of the two-sided nature of human enterprise can be generally shared, then, as we move into the future, social, cultural, legal, and political structures will develop along the lines of this understanding and guarantee tolerance of the sacred.

But there is absolutely no evidence in the world at the present time of any movement in any direction whatsoever except extreme secularization. Thus, one of the reasons why I have appeared here is to introduce this sacred consideration. But the Teaching I bring will not amount to a damned thing unless numbers of people begin to hear it, unless it begins to represent a cultural conversation, a cultural force that will transform the tendencies toward extreme secularization that are present in the world today.

CHAPTER 9

PHILOSOPHY IS A
STRESS-BASED ACTIVITY

a talk by Da Free John
May 17, 1983

MASTER DA FREE JOHN: Is there any need for philosophy whatsoever? Spiritual or otherwise? Is there really any need or use for philosophy? You might feel that there is a need for it based on some stress or problem-conception. But is philosophy of any use? (Laughs.) Is it of any use at all?

DEVOTEE: Master, are you using the word philosophy in the sense of something that is conforming or identical to Truth?

MASTER DA FREE JOHN: There is no philosophy that is identical to Truth. Philosophy is a process that may be associated with the Realization of Truth, but philosophy itself is a process. The word "philosophy" means "love of wisdom." It is usually associated with some mental or discriminative activity, a way of considering things as they are or as they seem to be and coming to conclusions about reality. There are high philosophies, low philosophies, false ones, true ones perhaps, great philosophy, lesser philosophy—but it is all philosophy. It is all the same enterprise. Is there any use for it?

DEVOTEE: Well, I would say there is no use for it in and of itself.

MASTER DA FREE JOHN: You might ask, "Is a leg of any use in and of itself?" And there is no use for a leg in and of itself, but if you are going to do any walking, then a leg comes in handy! Well, what I have to say, in and of itself, is just a pile of words. Does this philosophizing have any use as a leg has a use?

DEVOTEE: It helps to bring people here.

MASTER DA FREE JOHN: We could just as well have sold them tickets to get them here! If that is the only purpose of it, then I am working awfully hard. If my purpose were just to get people to associate with me or enter our community, I could do all kinds of things, including selling tickets. That does not seem to be a very high purpose.

DEVOTEE: Master, maybe people have thoughts and opinions on all kinds of things that limit their perception of reality. Philosophy, in terms of your Teaching and your consideration of the Great Tradition, seems to be necessary to undermine all that.

MASTER DA FREE JOHN: I myself have suggested on occasion that it is useful to study religion and spiritual philosophy in terms of the Great Tradition. The reason such critical study is useful is that you already have all kinds of inherited, thought-up, and propagandized ideas that correspond to ideas that can be found in the traditions. Thus, you can see how those ideas traditionally get elaborated as a way of life, and you can see their limitations. Doing philosophy in these terms, then, can be said to have a purpose. Doing philosophy is thus a way of undoing philosophy.

DEVOTEE: Master, one of the ways by which you express the ultimate Truth in the Teaching is the statement, "You do not know what a single thing is." That certainly contradicts the usual notions people have about philosophy and about the use of the thinking mind.

MASTER DA FREE JOHN: You could say that philosophy is a very basic activity of human beings because they are mind-oriented. Almost any kind of mental process can be thought of as a philosophical exercise. Therefore, the rigorous activity we would call philosophy is a species of something that is typical of human beings. And perhaps that typical activity which is specialized in the form of the rigorous work of philosophy is the basic activity of trying to account for everything.

Now, science is philosophy. Humanity in general is philosophizing. We are all trying to figure it out. We are trying to account for our existence, for everything that is appearing. Perhaps this is the basic reason why we think, why human beings started to think to begin with, and why they developed this specialized, functional process of thinking that is relatively unique, at least in terms of its extent in the human species on this planet. Perhaps the basic reason for thinking is the felt need to account for everything, to figure everything out.

You are always thinking, it seems. But if you examine the root of your perpetual thinking, there is a stress beneath it, a kind of emotion that is not itself a thought, but that motivates thought. That stress is associated with the feeling that you cannot account for things, that you have not figured them out and are therefore vulnerable. Then, feeling vulnerable, feeling threatened, you engage in thinking.

When thinking becomes rigorous, a profound exercise of insight, then we call it philosophy. When it is a little less rigorous, we call it philosophizing. Then there is all the rest of our thinking that is something like philosophy. But all our thought is basically built upon a stressful feeling or emotion that arises in every moment simply on the basis of our encounter with manifest existence.

It seems to be natural to us, we feel, to try to account for everything, to figure things out. We feel that if we could do that successfully and fully, then we would not be threatened. We would relieve ourselves of this stressful emotion, this stressful sense of existence. Thus, the origin of philosophy is this stressful feeling, associated with the rudimentary presumption, which is not even a concept in its root origins, that we cannot account for things, have not yet figured them out, are not in control of them, and therefore are obliged to seek to know. Philosophizing and the activities of philosophy are an effort to know, to figure things out, to account for things. We feel that if we do that, then we will relieve ourselves of stress.

The origin of philosophy, then, is not pure in some abstract sense. The origin of philosophy is the same as the origins of desire in general. It is the same as the origin of seeking altogether. It is the origin of the sexual motivation and of all kinds of pursuits. Perhaps in general we are activated by this stress, this need to gain control by figuring things out, accounting for everything, accomplishing control over everything.

This stress, it seems to me, is a basic source of much of what we are doing. It certainly is the source of the complex emotion behind what we are doing typically, moment to moment. We could say that in every moment we are stressfully trying to account for everything. The history of human culture is filled with such accountings. And we could say that those accountings are the philosophical conclusions or answers that have been developed on the basis of this stress. Of course, most evidence of human activity apart from philosophy is not at all conclusive, not an answer, a philosophy, a fulfillment of any ultimate kind. Human beings, then, are always philosophizing, always seeking.

DEVOTEE: Master, you speak of theories that are just the mode of the acceptable understanding of the way things operate and of what can be understood about them at a given time. But it is always understood that such understanding is not the fulfillment of knowledge at any point. When a new theory is proposed, we always recognize that there is more to be understood about the matters it treats.

MASTER DA FREE JOHN: Some people recognize that, but many others do not. Many people accept a scientific proposition, or a proposition coming from any other quarter, as an answer, and then they cling to that answer, that proposition, that theory, that description, and they defend it very emotionally, even irrationally. People frequently get involved in irrational defenses of apparently rational propositions.

Why? Because what we are seeking through philosophizing and science or philosophical effort in general is relief from the stress of not being able to account for everything, of not having figured everything out, of not knowing, of not being in control. Human beings are motivated in a primary sense by the feeling that they are not in control of their existence. What we are doing in every domain of our living, then, is animating that stress, the feeling that we are not in control, through desire, through mental activity, through all kinds of activities. We are elaborating this stress, dramatizing it. We could say, then, that philosophy, even in its most sophisticated form, its most academic or scientific form, is a stress-based activity, a dramatization of the stressful acknowledgment that you are not in control of existence.

Something is controlling existence itself, and your existence in particular. Somehow it is all controlled, and human activity is basically devoted to finding out about that which is in control. If we find out about it, our discovery puts us in a position of apparent control. As soon as we put ourselves in a position to feel that we are somehow in control, we want to stay in that position. Therefore, people defend philosophical points of view, scientific theories, social structures, political systems, and unusual, strange, or conventional human arrangements, because they feel that, at least in some sense, that which they are defending represents their portion of control over existence. What we are seeking, then, is this control, the status of being in control over that which otherwise seems to be controlling us.

Science and philosophy are simply rather professionalized academic developments of a basic, stressful, neurotic impulse. But to be involved in these pursuits, to be seekers, has become a convention for human beings. We do not think of these activities as being fundamentally stress-based and neurotic. We think of them as necessary in fact, or ordinary, natural, normal. The whole human race is seeking, you see. We are called by various institutions and systems to believe certain propositions and to seek in certain ways in common. But then each of us has his or her own private domain of seeking founded on the same stress, the same need to gain control.

DEVOTEE: Master, I remember that once in considering the origins of scientific knowledge you pointed out that the actual origins of scientific knowledge, mathematics, and related fields are in the spiritual traditions. The Taoists, for instance, didn't seem to seek power through their knowledge.

MASTER DA FREE JOHN: They were not necessarily seeking power in the sense that we conceive of power, in political and institutional terms. But they were seeking power in the sense that they were pursuing freedom from being controlled, which is itself a kind of control over whatever it is that may otherwise seem to be controlling you.

DEVOTEE: You mentioned the other night that knowledge, like desire, is basically an attempt to gain power.

MASTER DA FREE JOHN: Yes, in biblical language, you see, to have sex with someone is to know them. Knowledge is always a form of control. Sex-desire or sexual motivation is, among other things we may say about it, an effort, like all our efforts, a search to control something that seems to be controlling us or that could potentially control us. So, our sex relationships are games of knowledge, games of getting to know one another and getting to control one another, getting to control the force of sex itself, getting to control the other or the otherness by overwhelming it, by getting it attached to us, by trivializing it, by containing it or systematizing it in one fashion or another. Our sexual activity, by tendency at any rate, is part of our effort to gain control over what we fear is controlling us or about to control us. It is an irrational effort to control what is outside ourselves and to free ourselves from the feeling of being controlled.

Unfortunately, if you dramatize this impulse profoundly in sexual relationships, you tend also to destroy those relationships, to destroy the force, the fullness, the energy that can be involved in them. Thus, it seems that somehow you must give up this search to become intimate with Life, Energy, Happiness. This is so in sexual terms. Perhaps it is so in all terms. Perhaps what we must do altogether is transcend this stress, this effort to control, this need to account for everything, this need to know about or figure out everything and everyone, or the "other," epitomized by whatever individual or group of individuals with whom you are dramatizing this effort to control.

Paradoxically (or not so paradoxically, perhaps, if you understand), Freedom and Happiness are not found through our seeking or effort to control what we fear is controlling us. Freedom, Happiness, and Realization of Truth require us to relinquish this effort. To relinquish this effort, we must understand its impulse. Therefore, if there is useful philosophy, it seems to me, it is an activity whereby we specifically regard this impulse, understand it, and transcend it.

Useful philosophy is not the stuff of thinking, the strings of concepts that become an end in themselves to those who never relinquish this search, those who are just seeking control, who love philosophizing, love concepts, love explanations, love answers in scientific form, religious form, psychological form, or whatever form—discursive, aesthetic, even sexual. Those who pursue control based on this stress achieve various ends or models of existence and want to hold on to them fiercely. Such people we might call philosophers, scientists, lovers. But they are not truly that. They have not brought their regard to inspect that which is motivating them.

In fact, if you examine it, what is controlling you most profoundly is this negative, stressful reaction. Thus, it seems to me that the proper object or consideration of philosophy is the origin of philosophy itself, the motive of philosophizing itself, the motive to know, the

PART TWO: TRANSCENDING THE
POLITICS OF SCIENCE

motive to find out, the motive to account for and thus to control or be immune to the apparently controlling forces of existence. That Which is controlling you apparently is also That Which I̲s̲. Your resistance or stressful reaction to being controlled and, therefore, everything you do about that resistance, are what distinguish or separate you from Reality and Its Realization.

Philosophy, then, is a conventional enterprise, whether it takes the form of academic philosophy or science or human cultural and social and political efforts, or even sexual seeking. Any form of seeking whatsoever is a neurotic or stress-based effort that we must understand. Ultimately, that seeking controls us or separates us from Happiness, the Free Disposition in the midst of this great Present, the great Configuration of immediate existence.

DEVOTEE: Master, in *The Liberator (Eleutherios)*,[1] you write that no ultimate knowledge is derived from knowing any objects. It is the knower who must be transcended.

MASTER DA FREE JOHN: Yes. And the knower is not just a one. The knower is this complex of stress, this dissonance, this contraction from the Force of existence that arises when you acknowledge "an other" or "the other" or forces outside yourself that are controlling you. As soon as you feel controlled or in the mood not to be controlled, you become the ego. That mood of resistance is the essence of egoity. It is the essence of the origins of conventional human activity. This stress— not any kind of subtle, inward entity, but a motion, an activity in the midst of what is—makes you a seeker, an ego.

True philosophy, then, is not a development of concepts to account for everything, to figure everything out, to solve problems, to answer questions. True philosophy is the most direct regard of the origin of your impulse to philosophy itself, or to figuring things out, or to controlling existence through knowledge in one form or another. We are involved together in such philosophy, not in the development

1. *The Liberator (Eleutherios)*, by Da Free John, is the most concise summation of the Way of Radical Understanding or Divine Ignorance. Commencing with the Adept's confession that there is only Transcendental Consciousness, the book describes the essence of the spiritual process. On the basis of a life of discipline, in which the Transcendental relationship to the Adept is cultivated, the practitioner's attention and energy are gradually freed from the bond of the ego. The resultant equanimity enables him to turn fully to the task of understanding and transcending the self-contraction, leading to an ever more profound identification with Consciousness or Reality Itself.

"... Professor Schlemmer just proved he doesn't exist ..."

of a heap of concepts that make sense when strung together such that we can feel immune to the powers of existence. Such stringing together of concepts is ordinary philosophy or what I would call false philosophy. It is an end in itself, a form of seeking, not true philosophy, which transcends seeking and which is the very process whereby or wherein we transcend seeking.

You must be sensitive by now to the fact that in every casual moment of ordinary reverie, just by being here in any moment, you feel somehow subtly motivated to do something, to think some final thought, to figure something out in an ultimate sense. Always there is this stress. It becomes thinking, cycles of emotion, desire, activity, complicated arrangements, and reactions in every moment. In any moment whatsoever, if you are sensitive to yourself, you can find yourself out and see that you are under stress. You feel controlled subtly but emotionally, and you want not to be controlled. All the wondering about God and sex and death comes from this stress, from an already existing or primitive reaction to manifest existence. It is the sign of a contraction in the midst of manifest existence.

On that basis you have built your entire life. And you are still thinking. You are still trying to figure it out. You are still wondering about existence. You are still moving through cycles of emotion, always trying to feel good. You always have to work hard to feel good, you know. Your life activities are constantly taking the form of an effort to feel better. Your desiring is always an effort to feel better. Your physical activity is always an effort to feel better. Your thinking, therefore, is an effort to feel better, no matter what form it takes. No matter how abstract, aesthetic, scientific, or intellectual your thinking may be, it is, like every other form of your activity, an attempt to feel good, because in every moment it seems that you do not feel good. You feel under stress. And what is the content of that stress? A feeling that you are threatened and controlled by whatever is altogether and immediately. Thus, you want to find That out. You want to account for It: You want to figure It out and gain control over It so that you do not have to feel this stress, this un-Happiness. This is always true. Isn't it?

DEVOTEE: Yes, absolutely.

MASTER DA FREE JOHN: To understand this is the essence of philosophy. It is the essence of human consideration. To know this fact about yourself, to have found this out about yourself, is to have discovered something most profound: that this stress characterizes your existence—period. This stress is what you are always about. Always. Everything you are doing, then, is a search based on this stress. And you are never doing anything else until this stress itself is understood and directly transcended so that you Exist or Stand in that Condition Which is prior to the introduction of that stress. After all, the stress is not native to you. It is a reaction to whatever is really the case altogether and ultimately. You are adding this stress reaction to existence in every moment, and this primitive stress takes the form of your character, your activities, your relations, and your entire way of living.

At the root of your life, then, and primitive or immediate to every moment is the same stress, the same self-contraction, the same reaction that is felt as a disease, what I have called the Dreaded Gom-Boo.[2] In any moment it could take on any form and any kind of emotional color. It could be fear, sorrow, anger, anxiety, passion, lust, hunger, intellectual fascination, political or social motivation, an interest, a desire. Therefore, it can be characterized in different ways in any moment of living. But, nonetheless, in every moment of living it is the same stress. One could call it anything—the x-factor, the ego, the Dreaded Gom-Boo, the Impossible Three-Day Thumb-and-Finger Problem.[3] It makes no difference what you call it, you see. I have called it all kinds of things. But I am always pointing to that—Narcissus. And until we regard that, until we understand and transcend that immediately and Stand in the Position prior to the introduction of that, we are just crazy. We are the ego. We are suffering. We are un-Happy. We are diseased beings seeking relief, seeking stable good feeling and stable Happiness, and making great efforts to be free of being controlled, limited, and on the verge of being snuffed out.

You are anxious about this always, in every moment, are you not? You could die in any moment. In any moment you could die from apparently external or apparently internal causes. Well, how can anyone know this yet have that knowing not become stress? You are always under stress. You are never not under stress. You may cover it

2. "The Dreaded Gom-Boo" is Master Da's term for our presumed separation from the Divine Reality, which traditional religion treats as a form of disease to be cured by conventional means such as prayer, fasting, meditation, and all kinds of beliefs. See Master Da Free John's *The Dreaded Gom-Boo, or the Imaginary Disease That Religion Seeks to Cure: A Collection of Essays and Talks on the Direct Process of Enlightenment.*

3. Master Da Free John has used this phrase in one of his talks. See chapter 1 of *The Dreaded Gom-Boo, or the Imaginary Disease That Religion Seeks to Cure.*

up with the extended mechanisms of the body-mind or the manifest self—pleasures in the body, good feelings developed in some circumstance, or mental configurations you find satisfying and consoling—but underneath there still exists this stress. You are being controlled by something you cannot account for and you are trying to protect yourself against it. And that is why you are doing everything you are doing, physically, emotionally, mentally, psychically, altogether. You are never doing anything but reacting to stress. Is this completely clear?

DEVOTEES: Yes.

MASTER DA FREE JOHN: This is remarkable, is it not—that there is something so basic and that it could be acknowledged universally? What else is there to do, then, but consider this? What else is worth doing, since you know that everything else other than the direct consideration and transcendence of that stress is simply a development of that stress itself, a play upon it, the enterprise of it? It is all Narcissus, all un-Happiness, all disease.

DEVOTEE: The other night during our gathering I went to my room to get a shirt, and as I was walking, I noticed that I was presuming something fearful, almost as if I were going to be attacked. I just kept walking. When I came back, the same thing happened. And there wasn't anything there. It became clear to me that I had added something to the moment that did not really exist. It was simply that contraction.

MASTER DA FREE JOHN: You were having a miniature anxiety attack?

DEVOTEE: Yes, and there was nothing there. I was just going to get a shirt.

MASTER DA FREE JOHN: But there is something there.

DEVOTEE: Well, the ego—yes.

MASTER DA FREE JOHN: The stress itself, the reaction itself. And in certain moments you do not have anything you can do that will successfully remove it. So what is there? Just that stress. Then you become very anxious, very afraid, resistive, tormented in one way or another, very un-Happy, very grave, very depressed. All kinds of symptoms can appear. The Way that we consider, then, involves the criticism of our ideas and of the conceptions we develop on the basis of this uninspected stress or self-contraction. Therefore, it involves the criticism of certain traditional ideas. But it is a process of moment to moment inspection, observation, understanding, and transcendence—directly and immediately—of that stress or reaction or self-contraction that dissociates us from the Transcendental Reality, that divorces us or makes us unconscious of our uncaused, Free Status.

If we inspect and understand that contraction in every moment and directly transcend it, then we cease to superimpose this contraction, and all the concepts and efforts by which we dramatize it, on the moment. We stand in that Condition and Disposition that precedes the introduction of this contraction, this stress, and all the enterprises we build upon it. In that case, then, the Status in which we Exist is tacitly Obvious, inherently Realizable, and, therefore, ultimately Realized. And if It is Realized, then the Status of phenomena becomes Obvious. There is no need to justify the world or participate in it simply because it seems to exist. But there is also no need to dissociate from it because we are un-Happy, or controlled or limited by it. Neither of those activities is the case.

We are inherently Free Consciousness, inherently Blissful, Self-Radiant. And everything is That. Just That. That is the Status of everything in every moment. We are utterly free of this contraction or this stress and therefore free of all the efforts and concepts we build upon it. We simply Stand in the Position in which we always already Exist. And in that Position the Status of phenomena is always already Obvious. This is the same as to say, "Brahman is the world,"[4] or, "Nirvana and samsara are the same."[5] These are just verbal equations intended to be signs of the radical, Free Disposition that is inherently and priorly Free of this stress that everyone acknowledges to be the base of his or her moment to moment existence.

4. This is a well-known formula of Advaita Vedanta, the Hindu nondualist tradition. It is based on the Transcendental Realization of the inherence of the phenomenal world in the Divine Being, or Brahman.

5. This equation is peculiar to Mahayana Buddhism, which sought to overcome the notion, typical of Hinayana Buddhism, that Nirvana or Ultimate Realization could be a goal. Nirvana is, rather, here and now. It is, ultimately, not different from phenomenal existence (*samsara*).

Thus, our consideration is about noticing, acknowledging, being sensitive to, and observing, understanding, and transcending this activity, this stress that motivates existence and generates enterprises psychically, mentally, emotionally, physically, at the level of life-energy, at the level of relationships of all kinds. It is a matter of inspecting that, understanding it, and in every moment directly transcending it so that you Stand in the Position Prior to the introduction of that stress into the realm of phenomenal existence.

And if you do not introduce that stress, then phenomenal existence is whatever it is. And what is it? That is What is Realized. It is not known on the basis of the self-contraction, but It is Obvious when the self-contraction is not introduced. We can say It is Brahman or Nirvana. We can say It is any number of things. We can say It is God. We can give It any name whatsoever, but It is simply the Condition in Which we Stand. It is Self-Radiant Being. It is not anything but Consciousness Itself. It is inherently Free. And everything is just That.

When That is Realized, therefore, then whatever we may do, apparently as the body-mind, there is simply That. Then the actions of the body-mind are Free and not subject to false conceptualization, false views, ego-based activities, and summary presumptions about Reality that are expressions of un-Happiness.

This Realization being the case, anything can be done. In other words, the participatory disposition is fully allowed, but not on the basis of the idealistic conception of Reality. The life of Love or Radiant Existence proceeds, but without the ego-based conception of God. And there is inherent Freedom from the problem of conditional existence. Thus, there is inherent Freedom from the disposition to dissociate from phenomena, to become inverted to the point of unconsciousness of phenomena or to escape the world. There is simply the life of Free action, Self-Radiant, in which conditional existence is Transfigured, Transformed, and, without any dissociative effort at all, ultimately Outshined, not by being separated from, but by virtue of being utterly recognized as nothing but That Which Outshines it or is it.[6]

Therefore, inspect this primitive mood or motivating stress in every moment. Hear me and see me. Enter into my Circle of Influence, the Sphere of my Existence. Practice the Way of Faith or

---

6. The terms "Transfiguration" and "Transformation," together with "Translation" (which is synonymous with the term "Outshining" as used here), have been described on p. 27, n. 24.

the Way of Divine Communion,[7] or practice the Way of Insight, practice enquiry.[8] If you do so, then you will naturally come into sympathy with the Witness Position, or the Stance or Disposition of Consciousness. But you will not claim the Witness Position on the basis of some self-based, stress-based effort to dissociate from phenomena. It will simply be naturally obvious to you that that is the Position in Which you Stand. And then, because you are sympathetic with that Position, you will become more and more profoundly sensitive to the Status of that Position, the Status of Consciousness Itself. And when you are most profoundly, intuitively aware as Consciousness and Its Status, then you will likewise be profoundly aware of the Status of phenomena.

All that is inherent in the Witness Position. But you must enter into It sympathetically, by hearing and seeing me, by passing through the Argument of Ignorance and Narcissus and the practices associated with the Way of Faith or the Way of Insight, so that you are sympathetically established in the Witness Position. And then you must Realize It Itself. You must enter into It sympathetically, most profoundly, in the form of the second stage of the Perfect Practice,[9] until you Realize Its Status. To Realize Its Status is not only to Realize the Free Position of Consciousness, or Self-Radiant Being Itself, but it is to Realize the Status of conditional existence altogether.

---

7. Practice of the Way of Radical Understanding or Divine Ignorance is described as a sequence of stages leading to spiritual maturity. The preparatory stage for all practitioners is the Way of Divine Communion, a period of transition from ordinary egoic life to true spiritual practice, characterized by devotional surrender of oneself to the Divine Reality. When the capacity for self-transcending practice has stabilized, the practitioner assumes either the Way of Faith (in the case of those naturally inclined to the disposition of feeling-surrender) or the Way of Insight (in the case of those naturally capable of self-transcendence via the application of discriminative intelligence). When both energy and attention have been set free so that the body-mind has realized a stable condition of equanimity, then the transition to the ultimate stage of practice, the Perfect Practice, can be made (see n. 9 below).

8. For a description of the practice of enquiry, see p. 74, n. 1.

9. The Perfect Practice, as described by Master Da Free John in *The Liberator (Eleutherios)*, is the epitome of the consideration and practice of the Way that he Teaches, and the basis on which all of the philosophy and every discipline associated with this Way are developed and fulfilled. In the first stage of the Perfect Practice the discipline is to "Be consciousness" in daily life and meditation, until the body-mind accepts the discipline of equanimity. Attention is thus freed for the second stage of the Perfect Practice—"Contemplate consciousness"—wherein attention (or self-consciousness itself) is yielded into the Source-Condition from which it is always arising. This practice gradually becomes profound Identification with Being or Consciousness Itself. The third and Enlightened stage of the Perfect Practice—"Transcend everything in Consciousness"— begins when this Identification becomes complete and the being simply Abides as Transcendental Divine Consciousness.

Then the third stage of the Perfect Practice naturally unfolds, in which all phenomena are recognizable. That is the beginning of the Way. Everything previous to it, everything that precedes the Enlightened Confession, is the yoga of consideration.[10] The Enlightened Confession is founded on Awakening, or the fulfillment of this process that I just outlined, and is itself a Way of life. It is not the end of life. It is not even the goal of life. Rather, it is the Real Status of life. In other words, it is the mature, human disposition. The Way begins from that point, and it is Demonstrated, on the basis of Self-Abiding recognition of phenomena, as Transfiguration and Transformation of conditional existence in this life and in any life or phenomenal state that may arise after or during it.

The Way is ultimately Demonstrated as the Outshining of conditional existence, not dissociation from conditional existence. A clay figure placed into an oven at first is transfigured by the heat, transformed. Its chemical composition and everything about it is changed. Then, when the heat becomes most intense, one cannot see the difference between the clay figure and the sphere of heat or energy surrounding it. The figure is outshined by the brightness. There is just a field of brilliance. Translation is of that kind. It is not a matter of dissociation from conditional existence. It is not founded on the motive of dissociation or on the motive of stress, the motive of egoity.

Therefore, if you simply go on as you tend to be, in this psychophysical form, and do not inspect the root origin, new and alive in every moment, of what you are tending to do, then you will inevitably function in either the idealistic or the realistic manner. Only some people, you see, become idealists finally, or realists finally. Most people flash between these two all day long. Sometimes you feel rather depressed and wish you could just be completely free of all life-experience. You wish you could just cut it away. In another moment, you feel that life is great, that the world is full of light, that "God made everything," "God is Present," "I am in love." In the million-dollar moments you are an idealist, and in more ordinary moments of

---

10. The "yoga of consideration" is the practice of devotees in the Way of Radical Understanding through the first six stages. It involves the consideration and exploration of all aspects of conditional existence (or all the forms of manifest experience and knowledge with which the egoic consciousness tends to be associated) from the transcendental point of view and understanding of the seventh, or fully Enlightened and ego-free, stage of life. The "yoga of consideration" is thus the necessary preparation for practice of the Way of the seventh stage of life. For a complete discussion, see *The Yoga of Consideration and the Way That I Teach,* by Da Free John.

basically feeling all right you are still an idealist. But then in the moments when things are not really going too well, you become a realist, and when things are really rotten, you become an incredible realist, or you wish that God would somehow poke through and tell you that you are the child of God and everything is all right. Thus, hour by hour you rotate between idealism and realism and all the shades of conventional consciousness or psychology that in one way or another represent these two positions, because you are living in this self-contracted mode, living in this body of stress. In each moment you are saying either yes or no to what is controlling you and to the state of being controlled.

To be an idealist is to say yes, and to be a realist is to say no. And that is all you are ever doing. If you are saying yes, you are an idealist, and you can get all the religion you want along with that. And if you say no, you are a realist and a materialist perhaps, and you can believe in the doctrines of materialism and scientism and get involved in all the kinds of aggravated activities that people create politically, socially, sexually, psychologically, emotionally, and intellectually.

Everyone is just playing out these two possibilities in one or another complex fashion. Life is just that play. It is never anything else. Neither point of view is founded on Happiness Itself, but only on the search for It. And on what is the search for Happiness based? This uninspected stress, which is felt primitively. It is a feeling, yet it is nonetheless an activity, an action you are apparently involuntarily performing in reaction to what seems to be an action that has already been performed by everything altogether. It is the apparent action of everything's having to come into being, even your own body-mind, which you did not make. You are involved in an equal and opposite reaction—the ego—which you feel as primitive stress, un-Happiness. On that basis you are saying either yes or no in the form of every kind of functional process in the realm of this body-mind.

If you were to inspect yourself directly in every moment, in other words if you were to give your regard to this essential reaction—rather than just be blithely playing out your yes-ism and no-ism and gravitating toward all kinds of points of view and desires and your effort to get free of being controlled, or to be Happy, in effect in control—if you were to inspect this primitive feeling and the action that is within the realm of your own responsibility, then you would Stand in a Position that is prior to everything everybody is doing and everything you are tending to do. Then you would Stand in the native

Position, which does not know about anything, which is in a state of
Ignorance, Divine Ignorance, not stupidity, not unconsciousness. That
Position is naturally Conscious, fully Alive, without the addition of this
reaction.

Well, you must do that to hear and see me at all. You must
magnify that Position to practice the Way of Faith or the Way of
Insight. When either the Way of Faith or the Way of Insight has
become mature in some fundamental sense, you will Stand naturally
sympathetic with the Position that is prior to this reaction. It is
Consciousness Itself. It is apparently functioning as the Witness—It is
regarded as such in the first stage of the Perfect Practice—but It is just
Itself. It is Consciousness, and It is regarded as such in the second stage
of the Perfect Practice. And when Consciousness Itself is thoroughly
entered into, identified with, when Its Status is discovered as Self-
Radiant Being, then the Status of phenomena is also Obvious. And
that is Enlightenment. That is full Awakening. It is a natural process
that begins when you enjoy the capacity to examine, to be sensitive to,
to observe, to understand, and to transcend this primitive reaction to
manifest existence.

Is this not so?

DEVOTEES: Yes.

MASTER DA FREE JOHN: Then why could it not have been so clearly
stated thousands of years ago and become the basis of human culture
and society, instead of the nonsense of idealistic and realistic views, the
insanity of ego-based society, the neurosis of ordinary human life that
you suffer? Why has there not been such a clear presentation of this
Argument? Why has it not become the dominant form of human
education? Then we would have been able to live entirely differently,
not just as individuals who perhaps now come into my Company, but
as a world order of beings. If we were educated in this fashion and
truly entered into this process or disposition, everyone would live
differently! Everyone! The whole world would be different!

The level of scientific knowledge in any epoch does not make the
difference. Just this factor alone would make human life entirely
different. Then we could go on and do whatever else we want. We
could even pursue knowing about things in scientific fashion, but
without the element of egoity, without the false views associated with
egoity, without the false philosophy of realism and materialism. We

would be religious without the false views of idealism. We would already be a Free society of beings. It could already have been so now for thousands of years. But it is not! Life is absolutely <u>not</u> that! Absolutely not that! It is everything else.

How could such a situation have arisen? It is because wise men or Enlightened beings are not in charge and are not allowed to be in charge. They are rarely even allowed to be heard. And most of those who are heard, if anyone, are not Enlightened. Most of those who are heard are so-called wise men in the framework of the first six stages of life, or within the framework of the two concepts fundamental to egoity. They are advocates of the idealistic and realistic paths associated with or made inevitable by those points of view.

Therefore, this consideration I bring to you is radical and also revolutionary. If it were taken seriously, and taken seriously at large, all of human culture and all of human society would change dramatically. We would in practical fashion take care of our business to provide the best environment we can for one another. We would do so as a matter of service and without false views. But such service is not what is going on at the present time, not at all. There is still a profound disinclination to consider this Argument. This is why it is very important for practitioners of this Way to make clear the unique principle this Teaching communicates and serves. Otherwise, we will be lumped in with the idealistic and realistic forces of the Great Tradition of religion and spirituality and we will be made invisible by the conventional or egoic forces of human society.

We must stand as we are, in the unique position of our advocacy, and we must champion this Teaching profoundly and clearly. In order to do this, we must have people who can hear me and see me and practice, people who can enter into this unique spiritual process. Only practitioners can really communicate about the spiritual process to others. You see, then, why I am so urgent about getting people to practice. I myself have already spent nearly two decades of my lifetime at this advocacy, and nothing much is changing yet. Why not? Because of a reluctance in the ego position, at the level of the stress itself, to examine this fault, to become responsible for it, to transcend it utterly, and to transform existence completely, entirely, thoroughly, and radically. The ego does not want to do that. The stress in which you live does not want to do that. You will be moved to do this work only if you hear me and see me, only if you Stand in the Position That precedes this stroke, this imaginary disease that all of mankind are suffering.

Literally every single human being on Earth is suffering from what I call an imaginary disease. The Dreaded Gom-Boo is literally a universal disease. It is real enough, but it is unnecessary. It is merely being presumed. It is not cured by the usual efforts. One need only cease to presume it. It can be instantly relinquished. It does not require a process of cure. One must regard the disease directly and enter directly into the process of this Way, beginning with the yoga of consideration and its various aspects, until—as soon as possible—that yoga becomes this Enlightened Disposition. The more individuals who have entered into this Enlightened Disposition, the more effective this institution can become as a communicative, educational force, and then the more and more people there will be who apply themselves to this unique, ego-transcending education.

The education in which people are generally and typically involved all over the world is ego-reinforcing, ego-based, ego-serving. For this reason the world is mad—and for no other reason whatsoever. Nothing is causing that madness. God is not making it. The world is not an illusion in the sense that it is a horror we should just abandon. We are doing the madness. We are completely responsible for it. We need not appeal to any One or any Force outside Man to deal with this matter. To become responsible for madness is the stroke that Man makes before Man Awakens. Man must Awaken. Nothing need change about the universe at all.

Man need not even evolve in terms of functional activity and knowledge for this transformation to occur. When the Awakening of Man does occur, mankind will continue to learn about Nature and how it works and do a great work on this planet and elsewhere. But first we must outgrow our infantile and adolescent life of egoity. That is the payment, you see. Only by such means will we make the transition into the higher domain of universal activity. There is no other means whatsoever. No accumulation of scientific knowledge and technology will accomplish that activity at all. It is absurd to think that flipping diseased egos out into space in rocket ships and all the other technological and political things that we can do materialistically in this world are going to change our situation. Those events in themselves cannot change the situation. To think so is to embrace a kind of mortal idealism that is founded on materialistic or realistic ideas but expressed through an idealistic face: "Let's just get our technology together and make everything good!"

It makes no difference how much technology and scientific advancement you introduce into human society. You can plug everybody into TV and computer banks and high-tech daily work, but it does not change anything. Everybody is still a bewildered, un-Happy personality who is rather chaotic and threatening and therefore who needs to be controlled artificially. No peace will ever come of that approach. No Happiness and no order—other than the strained order of suppression—can possibly come of all that. And the more there is of a fascinating technological society, the more there will be the need for control.

Therefore, what is necessary at this moment, as in any moment in the past, is a new form of human education into which every human being enters. Out of that true and effective education, and out of a race of beings who are Awakened to their true Condition, we will realize the basis for order and a creative life. Such education does not bring an end to science or technology or philosophy. Rather, it gives them their true base. It releases human enterprise from the false and chaotic views of idealism and realism and places it into the domain of Transcendental Freedom and true creativity.

Am I right or wrong?

DEVOTEES (laughing, clapping): You're right! This sounds wonderful, Master.

MASTER DA FREE JOHN: Well, everybody go and do it, I guess!

This is a good speech. It sounds great—and it is absolutely true. It is absolutely straightforward and simple, and there is no ultimate reason why what I am suggesting should not be done. On the other hand, I am appealing to people who think that they are diseased, and who are motivated by that disease whether they presume themselves to be motivated by a disease or not, and who do not readily give their attention to this consideration.

Now, I have lived for the last decade and more with a select group, a kind of cross section of humanity, a fraction of one percent of the total world. I have lived very intimately and directly with them all this time and I am still struggling with them more or less as I have always been struggling with them. Our association certainly has changed to some degree. But, even that change has required tremendous effort on my part, and I never know from day to day whether it is all going to fall apart. I must still talk even to the people who have been with me for a decade and more as if they had just arrived, as if they had never heard me at all, as if they had never seen me at all. I observe them to be involved in precisely the same kind of orientation and animating the same motivations they always animated before they had anything to do with me.[11]

It is not easy to effect this great change in the world. It is something that we can, however, understand rather directly. If you will give your attention to me, this change is comprehensible. It is simple in conception, but it requires tremendous effort to do anything about it, or, in other words, to make the consideration consequential. Thus, rather than going out and giving lectures in the world, I have just stayed day after day with whoever wanted to come to me and worked with them, and created this institution and the other Agencies of my Influence.[12] As soon as the spell of egoity begins to break for some significant number of people, then it can begin to become effective more broadly as well. As an effective institution, though, we are still in our infancy.

DEVOTEE: Master, two months ago, when Nananu-I-Ma was Enlightened,[13] you said, "I assume no limit upon the number of devotees who will be Enlightened." And then later on you said, "If human beings would just get hip to me, the whole world could be transformed."

MASTER DA FREE JOHN: Yes. I am not playing the role of superman and trying to keep you un-Enlightened just because I want a bunch of people around me to support an expanded self-sense. I am not indulging in any of that "star" bullshit. I am actually here to Work for your Enlightenment. I am looking forward to an Enlightened community. I am not in any sense trying to prevent it. I am not threatened

11. This passage reflects Master Da Free John's unrelenting demand on even the most mature practitioners to intensify their practice and to demonstrate the signs of higher practice and, in some cases, of the Enlightened Disposition itself.

12. During the years of his Spiritual Work Master Da Free John has created vehicles or "Agencies" of his Wisdom, Help, and Blessing-Transmission. The primary Agencies are his written and spoken Teaching; the sacred Sanctuaries, Holy Places, or physical Seats of Divine Power and Grace that he has purified and Empowered here in the West; and the devotional Culture and Community of those who have received his Transmission and who practice the Way that he Teaches (particularly those devotees who practice in the advanced stages of the Way). These Agencies, created by Master Da Free John during his life, are intended to perpetuate the Fullness of his Enlightening Influence beyond his human death for future generations.

13. Nananu-I-Ma is the first of several practitioners of the Way of Radical Understanding to be Enlightened. Her Awakening occurred on the Fijian island of Nananu-I-Ra in March 1983.

by the fact that more and more people become Enlightened. The Enlightenment of many people does not threaten anything! And my Work does not come to an end if such Enlightenments occur. My Work really only begins then. For the present I am still having to clean up after the ineffectiveness of previous interventions in human time by Awakened personalities. I am not truly even doing my own Work to date, except insofar as you could say that part of my Work is to do this cleanup, this initial, preparatory work with people.

My real Work begins when people enter into the seventh stage of life and when there is a community of individuals thus Awakened who can in a simple and direct fashion function as Awakened people do. There must be many such people, because all kinds of Enlightened talents are required to make a difference in the world. There must be a great number of such people with many kinds of capabilities, and they must create a remarkably capable institution and form of human community. We have yet to see the appearance of this Enlightened culture. But I am here for that Work. That is what I am here to do, you see. That is what this Work is all about.

CHAPTER 10

THE ANCIENT SACRED ORDEAL IS THE MODEL FOR INTIMATE AND PERSONAL CULTURE

an essay by Da Free John
December 5, 1980

1.

What is sacred or holy is, by definition, "set apart." When some feature of existence is acknowledged to be sacred, various taboos and formal rules of association are immediately established in order to manage the sacred game of relations with the sacred form.

Since ancient times, primary features of the world have been acknowledged and set apart for holy games. Thus, mountains and trees and rivers, the sun and moon and stars, extraordinary people and all uncommon things have been made holy.

Whatever is prominent and whatever is extraordinary or uncommon tends to be made holy in "participatory" cultures. And it is only when the principle of participatory consciousness itself is abandoned that holy things become the subject of knowledge, to be casually touched and controlled by Man.

Once a mountain climber was asked why he climbed. His answer was, "Because it is there." Truly, he climbed because mountains were once holy, whereas now they are the presumed domain of Man. We who live in the new scientific or analytical culture of knowledge and power are moved to explore and conquer and know what was once set apart by taboos. We climb mountains and go to the moon and stars— not merely because they are there, but because we want to claim them as our own domain, as known things subject to our control, emptied of the threat of the unknown, and also emptied of Mystery.

Among the prominences we now seek to climb and claim is our own evolutionary structure, which was once holy and denied to common Man. (The *Old Testament* story of the "fall" of Man is a testimony to the ancient taboos against knowing the holy things of our own manifest being.) [1] Thus, ordinary people now research the secret parts of Man and Nature. This represents a new epoch in our world. But even though this growth was necessary in order to transcend our childhood, we must yet overcome our adolescent vulgarity relative to the knowing of once holy things.

To know something in the analytical sense is not to Realize it in the holy sense. Knowledge of the holy was permitted even in ancient times, but a sacred trial was required, and when the holy prominence was embraced, it was the awesome Mystery of Truth that was revealed. In contrast to this process, analytical knowing tends to violate every sanctuary and to replace the Truth with Man. Thus, unless we go beyond our aggressive adolescent method, we will not see the Truth in the once sacred places. Instead, we will only see ourselves, like Narcissus at the pond.

It is good that we have decided to go beyond our childhood and to know the world. But we must also go beyond our adolescence and so also know the Living God as we increase.

2.

The sacred order of ancient participatory cultures did not deny esoteric knowledge to Man. It was simply that it could be gained only by fulfilling the appropriate and necessary requirements for growth. Thus, a sacred ordeal was required for esoteric initiation. For those who were not yet mature enough either to desire esoteric knowledge

1. The esoteric significance of this *Old Testament* tale is revealed in the essay "Jesus Is the Whole Body," by Da Free John, *The Enlightenment of the Whole Body*, pp. 448-52.

or to embrace the ordeal, a structure of cultural limits was established. Such structures prevented casual access to esoteric knowledge, but they did not prevent access to the Mystery of existence. Indeed, the purpose of such limits was to ensure continuous contact with the Divine Mystery, but within the limits of knowledge appropriate to each stage of life, or each division of human culture. (Such was the situation even in ancient Israel, although the esoteric initiate culture is implied rather than made explicit in the exoteric books of the *Old Testament*.)

The culture of scientism is a rather adolescent development of Man, which abandons the taboos and violates the sacred domains in order to acquire the knowledge previously reserved for initiates. But this new enterprise also abandons the total culture of relations with the Divine Mystery. Thus, even common people are denied access to the Divine Truth in our time, whereas everyone enjoys common familiarity with elaborate knowledge about the intimate interiors of Man and Earth and the stars.

At its worst, scientism is a kind of moden "pharisaism" that grants technical knowledge about Nature to everyone while denying intimacy with the Divine even to children and ordinary men and women. At its daily level, the pursuit of science is a kind of Adam-and-Eve adventure that explores the unknown in regions once denied to all but the most heroic and self-sacrificing aspirants. At its best, science can be a tool of mature humanity in the midst of our universal sacred ordeal of evolution and growth into Wisdom. But for science to function as such, we must again Awaken to the Divine Mystery. Even if we move beyond the restrictions that once surrounded "holy things," we must not fail to submit to the undivided Mystery and Truth that is the Eternal Context of Man and the world.

                                         3.

This is a time when it is presumed to be appropriate and even necessary for the political and secular arms of scientism to explore, know, control, and even violate every feature of the once sacred domains of Man and Nature. And no holy purpose is pronounced by those who make these explorations and control our lives. All of it is an enterprise of Man for his own sake, pursuing knowledge and power as ends in themselves.

At the same time, it is presumed to be entirely inappropriate for those who yet speak for a religious or spiritual Way of life to speak or act in any fashion that departs from the ancient exoteric prescriptions or taboos. But even in the ancient context, it was precisely in the setting of sacred culture that the taboos relative to "holy things" were systematically abandoned in the sacred ordeal of esoteric initiation.

In our time, it is expected that sacred culture and the sacred ordeal be abandoned and replaced by the secular order of analytical knowledge and power. And religion is only tolerated if it retains the exoteric face of the common man's conventional limits. But I say that the new order has abandoned allegiance to the Divine Truth, and we must not permit the Way of Enlightenment and Transcendental Realization to be destroyed.

If the secular forces of scientism are going to be permitted to explore and inhabit every aspect of Nature, then Man at least must be permitted to explore every aspect of potential growth in Realization of the Mystery or Truth of existence. If the ordinary politics of secular knowledge is going to be allowed to become the common environment of our larger society, then there must also be a new tolerance for the religious, spiritual, or sacred experiment of Man within the context of intimate communities and personal endeavor.

The sacred communities of ancient times established limits on esoteric knowledge that permitted growth in knowledge only via a sacred ordeal. For those who did not engage in that ordeal, behavioral and fundamental social rules and taboos were established as a condition for association with the Divine or Transcendental Mystery. It is from such exoteric programs that we inherit our common views about personal behavior, daily morality, and social contracts or laws. But in the same communities where such exoteric rules were in force, there were esoteric rules and rituals and behavioral models that specifically violated or went beyond the common model. The sacred ordeal has always been associated with the pursuit of higher forms of knowledge and power as the context of Divine association, and thus the Way of that ordeal has always involved going beyond the consciousness that defines itself in terms of the exoteric human model.

At the exoteric level of sacred culture, the ordinary things of life are taken very seriously. And the rules whereby those ordinary things are managed or transmitted are likewise taken very seriously. But when an individual enters into the sacred ordeal, it is expected that he or she transcend all of that seriousness. For this reason, entrance into initiate circles has generally been associated with vows whereby the individual abandons attachments and concerns relative to ordinary things. And this tradition of vows has taken two basic historical forms. One is reflected in the tradition of asceticism (or abandonment of ordinary things) and the other is the tradition we might call "crazy ecstasy," wherein initiates embrace ordinary things in a spontaneous or chaotic manner, free of the rules that ordinarily pertain to such things at the exoteric level of culture. (In the crazy ecstasy schools, such rules as dietary restriction and conventional sex control were among the things relative to which a free orientation was expected.)

In our time, even ordinary men and women are given access to secular knowledge about everything science explores, and such people are also both controlled by the secular State and denied access to the Divine Way by the propaganda of the new knowledge. Therefore, it is also both appropriate and necessary that the Wisdom-Influence become prominent via the literature and activities of sacred communities. But even for such sacred communities to form, there must develop an uncommon tolerance for higher human experimentation along the lines of the sacred ordeal, even as there is now the general tolerance for the secular and political experiments of scientism.

Such tolerance must represent an understanding about the sacred esoteric ordeal of Man. Therefore, it must be accepted that sacred communities and sacred cultural organizations must be free to engage in the cultural experiment that goes beyond ordinary or exoteric expectations relative to human behavior. It must no longer be considered strange or unacceptable that religious or spiritual communities sometimes experiment with social structures, psychological structures, sexuality, and even drugs (or chemical agents that relate to evolutionary structures in Man), just as they also explore the techniques of ecstasy and love, or participate in esoteric psychic processes and powers, or perceive a Power in the world that makes everything extraordinary possible for human individuals, whether or not they also embrace all the exoteric conventions of common society and the new knowledge and technologies of scientism.

There must be this new tolerance for the broader and esoteric cultural expressions of religion and spirituality, because religion and spirituality must, under the conditions of our time, become more openly visible in terms of the hidden, esoteric, or secret aspects of what has always gone on in sacred traditions. This must be understood, so that mankind will know that no absolute limits have ever been set on the Way of Truth.

The sacred experiment is a form of free inquiry, just as science is presumed to be. And if science is to be tolerated as a free exercise relative to every aspect of our existence, then so also must the sacred experiment be tolerated. At the level of the intimate, personal, sacred, and fundamental cultural exercise of human existence, we must demand our freedom. We must not permit the secular order to abolish such freedom and the cultural or sacred experiment that should take place in the setting of that freedom. The State must acknowledge that such rights are the inherent rights of all citizens, and common society must learn to tolerate all kinds of human variations at the level of personal, private, and intimate cultural behavior. If this is not done, then the sacred experiment of Man will tend to be cancelled by the dogmas and the politics of this time, and then not only every mountain but every man and woman will be conquered simply because they are there.

PART THREE

THIS WORLD
IS AN
INDEFINABLE
REALM

The entire human world is building existence out of the convention of attention that is ordinarily determined by the brain and nervous system. All human pursuits of the common kind are therefore directed toward the investigation and fulfillment of this particular state of attention. Our sciences, our politics, all our cultural activities in general are devoted to this investigation and this fulfillment. On the other hand, every human being is suffering. Every human being feels mysteriously confined, feels somehow curiously trapped, feels unfulfilled. This motivation toward fulfillment is also part of human endeavor. Because we are trying to make our life fulfill itself on the basis of an arbitrary selection of Reality, there is no universal state of peace or fulfillment in the world to date. This appearance that is arising at the present time is an artificial reality. In some cases, it can achieve a more or less sattvic or balanced condition, but it cannot fulfill itself in the Absolute sense, because it is not Absolute. It is only a selection of Reality, a selection of possibility.

Da Free John
Easy Death, *p. 233*

INTRODUCTION TO PART THREE

We are witnessing today a profound "reality shift" of which technological change and social transformation are only the surface symptoms. That switch is currently wrenching us out of the "reality space" defined by the combined genius of Newton, Galileo, Kepler, Bacon, and Descartes and the other giants of the mechanomorphic, deterministic paradigm. This world-view has been shaping the perceptions, thoughts, and emotions of so-called Western Man for over three hundred years. In many respects, it is still a potent influence in our lives, but it is no longer uncontested. Ever since the turn of the century, the clockwork universe of the preceding periods has been called into question by such heroes of twentieth-century science as Einstein, Planck, Bohr, Heisenberg, Dirac, and more recently Bohm. Their research and thinking is gradually shifting us into the paradoxical "quantum reality."

The findings of modern high-energy physics have not only demonstrated the limitations of the mechanistic paradigm. Their real significance lies in the fact that they have uncovered the limitations of the *metaphysical premises* underlying that paradigm and, what is more, of the *style of thinking*—ratiocination—that has always been hailed as the highest human faculty. Quantum physicists have learned to accept that Nature, or reality, holds irresoluble paradoxes and that it is not as "rational" as their predecessors, under the spell of Newtonian thinking, had been prone to believe. Ignoring for the present purposes the fact that there are several competing interpretations of quantum mechanical data, the universe of the new physics is definitely not the homely, causally-determined world of classical physics. Rather, the quantum mechanical universe is a welter of probabilistic processes that assaults common sense and the scientific method alike.

Easily the most significant and perplexing deviation from the mechanistic world-view has been the recognition that scientific observationism—the *sine qua non* of all science—is a myth. Quantum mechanics has shown that the observer is really a participator. Fred Alan Wolf, a leading-edge quantum physicist, explains:

191

Quantum physics has taught us that we, the observers of reality, are, at the same time, the participants of reality. In other words, "observation" is not a passive noun; "to observe" is not a passive verb. However, our classical, Western upbringing has preconditioned us to think objectively, to see the world as preexistent.

In a preexistent world-game, there is no room for players. Like a computer machine, which goes on endlessly doing its thing and following preset rules, all the game can do is continue. And all we can do is watch, never touching the dials. We are simply passive, nearly nonexistent observers of that prechosen world-game.

Objectivity takes its toll; the cost is your awareness of your awareness.[1]

This states the observer-as-participant argument in its extreme form. Originally, the discussion revolved around the fact that the measuring devices used to investigate subatomic matter actually interfere with the object. From there, the consideration was widened to include the observing subject, the human consciousness. Wolf, following Nobel-prize-winning physicist Eugene Wigner, appoints the mind as the principle that creates our reality. This represents a remarkable departure from the metaphysics-shy mechanistic paradigm. It is also a very daring "long-shot" interpretation of quantum mechanical events, which stands in need of much further philosophical reflection and refinement. Yet, it is this kind of avant-garde speculation that has created an important point of contact with the imponderable world apprehended by the mystics East and West. Michael Talbot writes:

The views of the physicists are changing. It has been fifty years since Heisenberg delivered his monumental statements concerning observation; slowly, the tremendous mass of the scientific establishment begins to feel the first tremors of a radical and awesome new age. For centuries the mystic has asserted that matter and consciousness are different aspects of the same something. For all those who have spent their lives trying to penetrate the secrets of matter, the new physics has a message, not a new one, but one that may well turn out to be the most important rediscovery humankind has ever made. Perhaps the change will be felt like a roll of thunder as old

---

1. F. A. Wolf, *Taking the Quantum Leap* (San Francisco: Harper & Row, 1981), p. 146.

constructions fall and new ones take their place. Perhaps the change will be so subtle and gradual that we will have no more sense of it than the anti-Copernicans during the time of Galileo, who did not feel the earth move. Whatever the case, the message of the new physics is that we are participators in a universe of ever-increasing wonder.[2]

Human consciousness is inextricably inserted into the symphony of cosmic life. Precisely how it is inserted is not for quantum physicists to decide. It is not even a matter to be left to philosophers or psychologists, who, unless they happen to be transpersonal psychologists, have a mere local interest in consciousness. Ultimately, the mechanics of consciousness and its participation in the total field of existence is the province of the mystics and Adepts—those who take the participatory nature of reality at first hand.

The talks and essays of part 3 offer an Adept's view of the universe—a view that is in basic consonance with the most advanced scientific models mustered to explain the paradoxical, multidimensional, and interconnected reality of manifest existence. Over and above that, it is a panoramic vision—engendered by the Adept's transcendental Realization rather than by memorizing or theorizing—which potentially can fertilize scientific speculation and research. For, the Adept's understanding of the *structure* of the total world exceeds the current comprehension of science. Why? Because he has transcended the very mechanism—egoic attention—that by an interlocking play of "objective" forms and "subjective" molds of cognition creates those partial frameworks of reality to which sentient beings relate as their world and to which they tend to ascribe ultimacy.

How, then, does phenomenal reality appear to one who has fully Realized the Ground in which all these partial, "omnijective" realities or reality dimensions have their existence? Master Da Free John gives this answer:

If attention were free to simply see the universal mechanism in which the phenomena of near-death experiences [and, in fact, all phenomena] are arising, what would be seen is a Mandala[3] *of light, or light-energy, made of concentric circles.*[4]

2. M. Talbot, *Mysticism and the New Physics* (New York: Bantam Books, 1980), p. 42.

3. The Sanskrit word *mandala* means literally "circle." Specifically, the term is applied to those Tibetan geometric designs that are "psychocosmological" representations used in advanced meditation and visualization practices. The Cosmic Mandala is the actual structure of which these graphic depictions are simplified mythological models.

4. Da Free John, *Easy Death*, p. 258.

And:

Each of the levels of this Great Mandala represents a quality of energy or light. In each of the rings or portions of this Mandala which move out from the central whiteness are infinite numbers of possible worlds and kinds of embodiment. In this world, this gross plane in which we now exist, we are manifesting, in visionary form, a portion of the golden-yellow field of the Mandala.[5]

Furthermore:

We are presently existing in the outer frame of the Great Field of the Cosmic Mandala. Unless there is responsibility for attention, there will be no movement closer to the center. Unless there is Enlightenment, there will be no permanent residence in the Center, or the Source, and there is no permanence anywhere but in the Source.[6]

This Mandala, in the literal sense an archetypal structure, which discloses itself partially to the waking consciousness ("inhabiting" part of this structure) and in a different aspect to the mystic or the dying person, is not to be stamped as a mere visionary hallucination. Or at least, it is no more or less hallucinatory than the physical realm—a minute slice of the total Mandala of existence—which is apparently "given" to the senses, but which is really a curious amalgam between datum and construct: Remember, the neat categories of "objective" and "subjective" are simply heuristic devices of limited practical value but not reflective of reality as such.

This unique model of the hierarchically organized total field of the cosmos is not intended as an exhaustive description of the primary structures of existence. The Adept does not cast himself in the role of a phenomenologist. As is evident from the following quote, his extraordinary disclosures about the cosmic Matrix serve a different—spiritual—purpose.

The Cosmic Mandala is not in you (the egoic body-mind or subtle self-soul). You are in the Cosmic Mandala. The ego is not Perfect. The ego must be transcended in That which is Perfect. If you seek the Cosmic Mandala in yourself—or even if you seem to find It in

5. Ibid., p. 259.

6. Ibid., p. 260.

yourself—you are deluded, limited, and bound by yourself. Therefore, do not seek within yourself and high in yourself for the Great Form. Such is only the path of Narcissus, or self-worship. First transcend the ego-base (or the causal, separate and separative phenomenal self-contraction) in its Subjective Source, the Transcendental or Divine Self-Condition. When the Transcendental Self, rather than the ego or self-contraction, is the Realized Base of manifest individuality and attention, then the Objective Mandala of the Cosmos is inherently recognizable (as a whole and in every part) in Its Transcendental Source-Condition (and so the Cosmic Mandala may be Penetrated, or Transcended in Its Core).

The ego cannot Penetrate or Transcend the Great Mandala of Apparitions. The ego is not the Way. Transcendence of the egoic self-contraction is Preparation for the Way. The Transcendental Self is the Way. In and by the Transcendental or Divine Self, all the realms of conditional appearance are ultimately Outshined by the Self-Radiant Condition and Domain that is both the Subjective Source and the Objective Core of the Cosmos.[7]

To the scientist, voracious for knowledge as he is, it must seem as if Master Da Free John were dangling before him a tantalizing, spectacular vista, merely to tell him that he could share the same view only if he were to give up his burning curiosity. And he would be right! Even to enter dimensions of the Cosmic Mandala other than the physical realm, the scientist would have to abandon some of his egoic ballast: his conceptual presuppositions about the organization of the manifest world and his much-vaunted scientific method. Instead, he would have to adopt the discipline and attitude of the mystic. That is to say, it would be incumbent on him to *participate* in, rather than passively (or even actively) observe, the phenomenal processes. But even then, he would never come to know reality in any exhaustive sense. For, typically, his mystical excursions—through introversion—would dissociate him from the physical ("external") environment. There is no such thing as omniscience, in the sense of absolute analytical knowledge. "Knowledge," states Master Da Free John aphoristically, "has nothing whatever to do with Truth."[8] Therefore,

7. Ibid., pp. 278–79.

8. Bubba [Da] Free John, *The Paradox of Instruction*, p. 40. In *The Paradox of Instruction* Master Da Free John summarizes his Argument about Divine Ignorance and contrasts the Way of Radical Understanding with the traditional paths of gradual attainment.

neither has curiosity or scientific doubt (or certainty for that matter).

Nevertheless, participatory knowledge and the psychological disposition that is associated with it are significant elements in Man's spiritual maturation. In order to move beyond the essentially dissociative, schizoid disposition to which modern education inclines us, we must learn to understand and experience the world as a *psycho-physical* process.

This fundamental notion is conveyed in chapter 11, a brief essay styled "The View That Must Be Tested." Here Master Da Free John points out the dreamlike quality of the "waking world" that is the foundation of all scientific inquiry. In *The Paradox of Instruction*, he expresses this idea thus:

> *In fact and in Truth this manifest appearance in which we are animated to one another in the waking state is an hallucination that occurs in consciousness. All these trees, buildings, bodies, hairs, thoughts arise as modification of a single and absolute field that is Perfect Radiance. The world is a conception, as completely unnecessary as a thought or a dream. And it is just as silly, just as humorous, just as arbitrary and unserious, as any dream.*
>
> *There is no need for this present configuration to appear. There is no reason for it to persist. There is no need to overcome it or to enjoy a victory as it. It is completely arbitrary, just as arbitrary as any dream you might have had recently. The dream came to an end—it became obsolete because you realized it was not necessary. You woke up.*
>
> *You must be awake. Your awakening is what the communication of this Teaching is all about. The Teaching is a penetrating criticism, a goad to awakening to the non-necessity of things. The communication of Truth, the Argument and Influence of the Spiritual Master, works to undermine the droning trance in which you exist in the waking state and in all other states of experience.*[9]

The next chapter, entitled "The Ultimate Vision," approaches the same theme from a slightly different angle—that of the energetic nature of existence. Master Da Free John employs such physicalistic metaphors as "energy," "field," "atomic particles," and "space" in order to paint a more palpable image of the extraordinary plasticity of what the left brain is programmed to decipher as a most "solid" state.

9. Ibid., pp. 291–92.

Chapter 13, called "Even Science Is a Magical Activity," applies this insight into the psycho-physical nature of manifest existence to scientific research as such. Master Da Free John's argument is straightforward: Since the world in itself is not object to a subject, but a process in which subject and object are equally "enfolded"—to use David Bohm's term—in the total configuration of existence, science does not actually confront an "objective" universe. As a product of human consciousness, which is itself a phenomenon of the psycho-physical Total, science is in effect a psycho-physical or—more specifi-cally—a psychic response to existence. To emphasize this point—and not without humor—Master Da Free John styles science a magical activity. This term is doubly pertinent: firstly, because a psychic universe is magical in the sense that it is replete with power connections (traditionally conceived as "spirits"), and science is greatly concerned with power (using Nature's resources to conquer Nature); and secondly, because magic is the acknowledged predecessor of science. Both magic and science seek to manipulate the world by exploiting its apparent laws. In the former case, these laws are psychic correlations, and in the latter they are causal connecting principles. But, as has become clear through the findings of quantum physics, the causal laws (ostensibly read off by science from the Book of Nature) are simply high probabilities, and therefore what seems completely determinate, rational, measurable, and predictable is still only the same indefinable realm that once mystified the prescientific mind.

Conditional existence is a magical world, but, as the Buddhologist Edward Conze observed, scientific habits of thought reinforced by the success of science-inspired technology have increasingly confined Man's sensibilities to the physical, "objective" level. And yet, as Conze recognized:

All the meaning that life may have derives from contact with the magical and spiritual world, and without such contact it ceases to be worthwhile, fruitful and invested with beauty. It seems rather stupid to discard the life-giving qualities of these realms simply because they do not conform to a standard of truth suited only to the natural world, where to the scientist phenomena appear worthy of notice only if they are capable of repetition, public observation, and measurement. They are naturally more inaccessible to natural experience than natural things are. The methods of science, mighty and effective though they be, are useless for the exploration of two-thirds of the universe, and

*the psychic and the spiritual worlds are quite beyond them. Other
faculties within us may well reveal that which the senses fail to see.*[10]

In chapter 13, Master Da Free John graphically depicts existence
in psychic terms. How, the reader may ask, does this differ from the
kind of *participation mystique* that is characteristic of the thought and
life-experience of primitive mankind? Does not Master Da Free
John's recommendation to relate to the world as a psychic process
signal a return to this archaic (and hence anachronistic) mode of
cognition? Do we have to discount the rational mind in favor of the
magical, "natural" attitude?

First of all, it must be stated that the Radical Transcendentalism
Taught by Master Da Free John in no way condones or constitutes a
nostalgic regression to a lost state of innocent communion with
Mother Nature. This could only be accomplished by sacrificing the
wakeful consciousness that has been the gain of a long process of
biological and cultural evolution. Reason is not to be shunted, merely
chastised. Its proper function lies in dealing with the universe from
the pragmatic viewpoint in regard to the apparently tangible or
"material" realm. The intellectual approach to life becomes vapid only
when it achieves predominance or even exclusiveness, because then an
unimaginably vast aspect of the Nature-Man Field is blinked and
human life becomes fragmented, impoverished, and rootless.

Master Da Free John does not ask us to abandon either intellect
or individuality (both being complementary developments) but to
become whole: to *extend* our functional capacity by developing our
sensitivity to the psychic dimension of Nature. This is not accompanied
by a reduction or loss of consciousness, and therefore this "magical"
participation must not be equated with the primitive *participation
mystique,* as described by the French scholar Lucien Lévy-Bruhl. The
latter represents, as C. G. Jung correctly recognized, a *participation
inconsciente* and is based on an as yet ill-defined sense of individuality.
Psychic participation in the former sense, however, is a fully conscious
and mature response.

At any rate, this sensitization beyond the mere physical level of
existence (which is a construct primarily of the non-participatory
intellect) is not the goal of Radical Transcendentalism. Rather, it can
be understood as an integral part of the "normalizing" program of the

10. E. Conze, *Buddhist Thought in India* (London: Allen & Unwin, 1962), p. 24.

Way of Radical Understanding Taught by Master Da Free John, through which the spiritual practitioner becomes capable of freeing his energy and attention for the actual task of Realizing what the Adept calls the "Divine Domain," which is beyond both the intellect-dominated material dimension and the psyche-dominated immaterial dimension of Nature and which is, in fact, no dimension or location at all, but the eternal Condition of all the transient states and processes of phenomenal existence.

So, the point of awakening to the psychic aspect of existence is not simply to improve Man's life or expand his reach, but to help him break out of his intellect-fashioned conceptual cages and to allow him to intuit the ultimate Condition, the Transcendental Self of all so-called subjects and objects.

Chapter 14 consists of a talk explaining the unusual premises of an essay entitled "The Exoteric Taboos Are in Nature." Here Master Da Free John links the desired awakening to the psychic nature of the world with Man's potential for higher, spiritual evolution. He makes the astute and unexpected observation that the psycho-social taboos against spiritual evolution are actually rooted in inhibitory factors peculiar to Nature itself. This explains why spiritual discipline, or the voluntary adoption of a self-transcending Way of life, is a transformative ordeal: Spiritual evolution is based on a moment-to-moment conscious reorientation counteracting the blind mechanism of identification with the material—cellular, molecular, and atomic—being or dimension. In this talk, Master Da Free John further considers the multidimensional structure of the cosmos and the failure of science to go beyond the mere physical dimension.

Chapter 15, which bears the title "Is Consciousness Exhibited by Flowers and Bees?—Beyond the Mechanistic Model of Nature," is a discourse on the amazing "intelligence" detectable in Nature. Master Da Free John points out the astonishing cooperation that is seen to exist between different kinds of apparently non-intelligent species, whereby they serve their mutual survival. He argues that these "helping relationships" cannot be satisfactorily explained by a materialistic interpretation. He counter-proposes that Nature is not the unconscious, "blind" force that materialistic thinking is positing. Evolution is, therefore, not "the product of an enormous lottery presided over by natural selection, blindly picking the rare winner from among numbers drawn at utter random."[11] Referring to the fact

11. J. Monod, *Chance and Necessity: An Essay on the Natural Philosophy of Modern Biology* (New York: Vintage Books, 1972), p. 138.

that modern physics has already overthrown the classical concept of matter by resolving matter into energy, Master Da Free John takes the next step and equates energy (or rather, Energy) with Consciousness.

While not casting out the notion of random evolutionary processes altogether,[12] he criticizes the materialistic slant of conventional biological theorizing in which the principle of causality plays the role of inviolable dogma. The theory of evolution in particular is beset by many unresolved conceptual difficulties and unsolved empirical problems. Biologists undoubtedly hope to resolve and solve these by newer and better conceptualizations and mathematical-statistical procedures, but they may very well find themselves, sooner or later, in the same precarious position as their colleagues in physics, who are forced to postulate ever more subatomic "particles"—the latest being the mysterious "quark"—to adjust their model of the universe (or, as most of them would say, to accommodate in their theory the newly discovered "facts").

Master Da Free John is drawing our attention again to the psycho-physical nature of things. The intelligent connection of which he speaks is immediately Obvious in the Realized condition, but it is not so evident to the analytical mind. The scientist, therefore, feels beholden to go out in search of "verification"—a long, circuitous route—among the "facts" that present themselves to his inquiring consciousness (and that are predefined by his model of the world, which few would admit). Instead of offhandedly discarding the Adept's views, which are not so much a description of phenomenal processes as an argument for Consciousness, the biologist would be wise to welcome them as a stimulus for reexamining his approach. It is good to know that some mavericks are in fact breaking away from the established biological paradigm and that their conclusions, which offer a more sophisticated model of life processes, are consonant with the Adept's perspective. Here the work of the English biochemist and plant physiologist Rupert Sheldrake must be singled out as offering the most convincing hypothesis to date,[13] and, as we will see, Master Da Free John has put Sheldrake's insights to good use in explaining the function of the Adept in chapter 23.

12. Even if one were to assume, as does David Bohm, a total contingent interconnectedness of all phenomena, this would nevertheless represent itself for all practical purposes as apparent chance events, because the mind cannot trace the most remote linkages between things.

13. See R. Sheldrake, *A New Science of Life: The Hypothesis of Formative Causation* (Los Angeles: J. P. Tarcher, 1981).

Rejecting reductionistic-mechanistic approaches informed by materialism, which seek to explain complex behavior from the bottom up as it were, Sheldrake revived and refined the notion of "morphogenetic fields," first postulated by the Russian biologist Alexander Gurwitsch (in 1922). These fields, which are without mass or energy, are the hidden variables behind the formation and organization of any given "system"—whether biological, chemical, physical, and even mental. As Sheldrake made clear, his hypothesis does not invalidate materialism altogether, though it does force it to redefine itself. On the other hand, coupled to a non-materialistic metaphysics, the explanatory value of this notion is greatly magnified. In that case, it would help to explain how the apparent "laws" of the physical cosmos could arise out of a condition of pure chaos prior to the "Big Bang." For, it would lend credence to the idea of an all-encompassing morphogenetic field, the unmanifest Matrix of the manifest world—the *prakriti* of Indian philosophy.

This whole notion can fruitfully be combined with David Bohm's equally fundamental concept of the "implicate order," which accounts for the time dimension and thus for (intelligent) creativity in the process of reality by showing how there can be feedback between morphogenetic fields and their related singularized phenomena. However, Bohm balks at the suggestion, put forward by a number of avant-garde quantum physicists, that consciousness is tied up in the quantum mechanical processes (and hence in the implicate order of the universe). Yet, if we were to side with the Adepts who testify that Consciousness is the ultimate "Field," then we would see that this suggestion is not as far-fetched as it seems. We could then conceive of an information dialectic (perhaps even using Bohm's "projection-injection" dynamics) involving Consciousness and the phenomenal body-mind exhibiting individualized awareness, in a relationship that is essentially non-material and non-local.

In chapter 16, which consists of a talk entitled "The Game of Perception," Master Da Free John turns to a consideration of consciousness and, more specifically, the way in which it constructs an external, "objective" world. The key question he asks is this: Does the perceptual world exist in fact or only in effect? In answering the question, he is mainly interested in making the point that we take our "clay models" of reality too seriously, instead of recognizing the humor of it all by Realizing the actual Condition in which the subject-object game is mechanically enacted.

The purpose of all of Master Da Free John's considerations with practitioners is not merely to educate them, but to draw them into the direct intuition of the ultimate Condition. For, when the intellect has exhausted all possible explanations, it always ends up confronting the same sheer Mystery that is the Real. Science and philosophy treat that Mystery either as a temporary setback remediable by further progress in scientific analysis, or as a philosophical conundrum that simply frustrates the intellect but otherwise leaves the philosopher untouched. However, Master Da Free John engages his considerations with practitioners to help them transcend the limiting categories of rational understanding and to lead them into the disposition of radical understanding or "Divine Ignorance." Then the Mystery reveals Itself as the Living Reality.

Chapter 17 is called "How Does This Room Appear When Seen from All Possible Points of View?" Master Da Free John starts out with the statement that unless we deliberately complicate things, the uniqueness of consciousness is self-evident to all of us. He then argues that its uniqueness lies ultimately in the fact that consciousness is Transcendental Consciousness or the primary Principle of mental *and* physical existence, prior to space-time and hence prior to evolution. It is transhuman, but Realizable via the human body-mind by transcending the illusion of subjectivity (and objectivity). One can resonate with this Truth even while the functional consciousness (arising on the basis of the false identification with a particular body-mind) is operative. But perfect verification of the Adept's confession of the transcendental nature of Consciousness is possible only upon unmediated Realization of Consciousness Itself, or full Awakening.

What is the relationship between consciousness and Consciousness? The finite or functional consciousness, which experiences itself as the subject of countless objects (in the shape of thoughts, feelings, volitions, perceptions, etc.), is inherently Transcendental Consciousness. It is a modification of the Being-Consciousness that is Reality, or That Which Is. In his book *Easy Death,* Master Da Free John describes attention, which can be equated with functional consciousness, as moving in "a great electronic field," whilst itself being pointlike and capable of shifting its position rapidly within that field.[14]

Master Da Free John next speaks of the two "conventions of awareness" that have their biological correlates in the bimodal

14. Da Free John, *Easy Death,* p. 274.

organization of the brain: the convention of common-sense pluralistic reality and the convention of reality as a unity. He then observes that because of the association of the functional consciousness with a particular organism and nervous system, awareness is necessarily localized and perspectival. But what, he asks, would this room look like if it were viewed from all possible (infinite) positions? What lies beyond the conventions of the curious coding-decoding machine of the human brain? In *The Liberator (Eleutherios)*, Master Da Free John reiterates the testimony of all the great Adepts of mankind:

All objects are only apparent relations of Consciousness.

Objects appear to Consciousness when It consents to be active as attention in relation to a body-mind in the conditional realm of Nature.

Consciousness Itself is never separate, limited, individual, conditional, or unhappy.

Consciousness is the Transcendental, One, and Eternal Principle of existence.

When viewed by the Transcendental Consciousness, all objects are inherently recognizable as the Happiness or Radiant Love-Bliss of Transcendental Being.

There are, in Truth, no objects, but there is only Radiant Transcendental Being, Consciousness, or Happiness.[15]

From the Adept's point of view, it is altogether absurd to live under the spell of separateness, rationalized by one convention or another. But some conventions are more absurd and separative than others. Thus, materialism or materialistic metaphysics hypostatizes the model of reality gathered by the lens of common sense and the sensory capacities of the body. Its basic dualism between subject and object enforces an acutely nonparticipatory lifestyle. Participation, by contrast, is the hallmark of the nonlinear orientation to reality. However, Reality Itself transcends not only all conventional, angular views of existence, but also participation and nonparticipation. Since Reality is the Whole of existence, it could be said to be Total Participation, except that it is impartite and does not take (*capere*) part (*partis*) in anything. It is the ultimate Individuum or Indivisible, the transcendental Atom of pure Being-Consciousness.

15. Da Free John, *The Liberator (Eleutherios)*, p. 35.

Chapter 18 is a talk, entitled "The Body as Energy and the Universal Field of Consciousness," that resumes the critique of scientific materialism as an ideological device exiling Man to the gross realm of manifestation while depriving him of participation in the nonmaterial—subtle or psychic—dimension or dimensions. Master Da Free John explains in vivid bodily terms what this banishment means: We live a stifling counterfeit existence in the shadow of the gross material forms that we believe to be our sole reality, and needlessly suffer the pain of the amputation of a significant part of our bodily reality. Sensitization to the energetic aspect of our bodily existence, or awakening to the psychic field, is therefore a crucial preparatory step in any authentic spiritual discipline. For, it is only by experiencing firsthand the "alternative" reality of what Master Da Free John calls the "etheric" [16] and "astral" [17] (psychic) dimensions that we can begin to break free from the highly suggestive ideological fabrications of materialism. Only then can we assume responsibility on the psychic level. Until that time, we are literally at the mercy of the unconscious—the submerged part of our reality—as well as the phenomenal forces of the subtle dimension (which, as Master Da Free John makes clear, is not merely a personal subjective experience but a quasi-objective environment populated by other ostensibly independent subjects).

The notions of multiple "sheaths" enveloping the physical body and of associated subtle spaces are a prominent feature of the psycho-cosmology of most religious traditions and form an important part of

16. "The etheric dimension of force or manifest light pervades and surrounds our universe and every physical body. It is the field of energy, magnetism, and space in which the lower or grosser elements function. Thus, your 'etheric body' is the specific concentration of force associated with and surrounding-permeating your physical body. It serves as a conduit for the forces of universal light and energy to the physical body.

"In practical terms of daily experience, the etheric aspect of the being is our emotional-sexual, feeling nature. The etheric body functions through and corresponds to the nervous system. Functioning as a medium between the conscious mind and the physical being, it controls the distribution and use of energy and emotion. It is the dimension of vitality or life-force. We feel the etheric dimension of life not only as vital energy and power and magnetic-gravitational forces, but also as the endless play of emotional polarization, positive and negative, to others, objects, the world itself, everything that arises" (Bubba [Da] Free John, *Conscious Exercise and the Transcendental Sun,* pp. 27–28).

17. The astral dimension of the being, the "star body," is simply a stepped-up frequency of the same fundamental Energy that also composes the etheric body and the physical body. All these bodies should be understood as interpenetrating fields of energy. The astral body is the energy configuration that is conventionally referred to as the mind or psyche. Beyond all these psycho-physical fields is the Ultimate Field of Being-Consciousness that Modifies Itself into the countless individuated fields of conditioned existence.

the secret knowledge of esotericism. Empirical-analytical science, of course, knows nothing of these topographies of the nonmaterial cosmos. It is not even programmed to know anything about them. This, however, says nothing about the ontological status of such subtle levels of existence; rather, it is a commentary on the self-limitations of mainstream science. And yet, quantum theoretical considerations combined with the evidence of parapsychology definitely move the esoteric models of "transpersonal" locales into the orbit of scientific respectability. Michael Talbot writes:

> *Are these other realities actually places as we conceive of them or do they exist within our heads? In the paradigm of reality offered by both mysticism and the new physics, such a question becomes meaningless. . . . The universe itself is not a* place *in the paradigm of the new physics. As don Juan warns, there is no world "out there," only a description of the world. With the advent of the participator principle the entire matter-space-time continuum of the physical universe becomes merely a* state of being.[18]

Thus, the material realm is only one in a whole series of frequency bands of finite states of being. The universe is fields within fields within fields of being-consciousness, arising in its totality in the Ultimate Field of Being-Consciousness. The Adept takes all this for granted. His primary interest lies in communicating the Ultimate Field Itself, the Radiant Transcendental Consciousness. In this spirit, Master Da Free John ends his talk with an ecstatic confession of his perfect Identity with Being-Consciousness, transcending all individuated forms and levels of conditioned reality.

The concluding chapter of part 3 is the autobiographical testimony of a practitioner of science who, after a lifetime of pursuing personal meaning through his scientific research (with occasional and always disappointing departures into the domain of religion), has become a practitioner of authentic spirituality. His is one of many similar "lilas"[19] that attest to the transformative power of the Adept's "morphogenetic work" with students of the Way of Radical Under-

18. M. Talbot, *Mysticism and the New Physics,* pp. 164–65.

19. Literally meaning "play," the Sanskrit word *lila* is used here to refer to instructive stories relating to the Teaching interaction between Adept and practitioner, even where there is no personal contact.

standing or Divine Ignorance. Ben Pierce's story conveys a sense of the profound personal change that is necessary to break the hypnotic spell of the left-brained orientation to reality and thus to become available to a different point of view: that we are not observers or victims of reality but that we are Identical to the Shoreless Ocean of Reality in Which all the countless interpenetrating realities of finite perception arise as waves, bubbles, and foam.[20]

20. This metaphor is borrowed from the *Ashtavakra Gita* (2:4). See *The Song of the Self Supreme: Ashtavakra Gita,* trans. Radhakamal Mukerjee (Clearlake, Calif.: The Dawn Horse Press, 1982).

CHAPTER 11

THE VIEW THAT MUST BE TESTED

an essay by Da Free John
January 20, 1977

T he waking world is not a "place," a fixed shape, but a sizeless realm, an undefinable dimension, just as the condition or region into which you enter in dreams is an undefinable realm. The world of our experience is not fixed, like a moon or any object, but it is fluid, like space or light. It is operative as a play of possibility, rather than fixed mechanical destiny. And its conditions in every moment arise not merely according to physical laws, but according to psycho-physical laws. The universe in which Earth appears is a psycho-physical system (psycho-spatial and psycho-temporal), not a mere physical or material one. The same world or realm, in other of its aspects, is seen in dreams and sleeping too. This view is ancient and must be tested. It is native to man and makes him wonder, fear, seek, and hide.

Every human individual represents only a limited realization of the psycho-physical scheme of appearances. The more psychic or conscious he becomes, the more he sees the world as a Psychic or Conscious Process. It is not only the man who is a psycho-physical process. His world is also. Free life begins only when we begin to operate from this profound premise. This thesis is itself the most significant consideration of Man. To enter into the Truth of our condition we must enter into psychic, heartfelt relationship with the world. Then we see not only the body of the world, but its mind also, its subjective or subtle places, and its degrees of self.

207

But when even this soulful knowing shows itself to be suffering, then Enjoyment is awake, prior to the birth of worlds, and beings, and you that contemplates the Mystery. The waking world is a psycho-physical realm. Everything appears, then, as in dreams, in correspondence with the tendencies, high and low, which are the individual. When this becomes clear, one ceases to identify with preferences, judgments, perceptions, reactions, experiences, forms of knowing, or the pursuit of strategies, high or low, since it is all illusory, changing, and held in place by these very actions. When you awaken, you are no longer concerned about the dream world, since it is all phantoms, created in a moment by tendencies that are the real creators of every circumstance of dreams. Just so, when this waking world is seen truly, it becomes clear that the phantoms of its appearance are endless, appearing out of a formless depth, and that true responsibility is relative to the forces of one's own apparent psycho-physical activity, which creates the theatre and calls up all that is good or bad. The realm itself is not to be valued or rejected in terms of any of its content. The realm cannot even be defined. Where do you dream? Where is a place? Rather, one's own action, one's very self must be seen as a contraction from the Condition of Radiance, or Love, in which the very world is floating. There must be Awakening to that Condition which is prior to the Play. Such is the only real responsibility. The rest is the destiny of complication. When the true Condition is realized, the reality of all distractions, of self, of action, of world, of God apart, is undone. There is no necessity to the dream, but there is apparent persistence of the dream. See it truly and abide in the Presence and Radiance that is Real. That Communion is truly Awake, even as the dream conventions remain, since it notices nothing, but abides as itself, whatever arises.

We appear in this waking world by the very same process by which we appear in dreams. And the solid waking world is, when seen in Truth, no more real, necessary, fixed, significant, or true than any random dream place. When this begins to become even a little obvious, a process of Awakening has begun, similar to waking in the morning from your dreams. When you begin to suspect yourself a little, then you begin to become distracted by another and formless dimension, much as the sleeper begins to sense his bed cloth, his solid body, and his room. At that point, one may become sensitive to the Spiritual Master, the Presence of the Condition of things, one who is already Awake, the paradoxical man. He is, in person, that dimension which is Truth. He calls you constantly and roughens your feet. He intensifies the sunlight in your room. He does not awaken you to another place or dream, as if your mother shakes you awake to play in rooms protected or threatened by your father. Rather, he serves an Awakening in which there is no realm, no implication, and no adventure. He does not awaken you to another place. He Awakens you in place, so that even while the dream of living survives, the destiny or even noticing of all effects escapes you.

CHAPTER 12

THE ULTIMATE VISION

an essay by Da Free John
July 20, 1979

The idea of a solid or objective world of "matter" and "one shot" mortality is an archaic and even "Victorian" concept that survives to this day in popular pseudo-scientific descriptions of the world and of human existence. But the now firmly established modern scientific conception that applies to all events (whether "material" or "mental") is that all phenomena and all beings are actually temporary states of atomic energy, or light. And energy, or light itself, is an eternally continuous process of transformation. Form always changes, but energy is always conserved. Therefore, individual beings, experiences, and worlds themselves are, each and all, only temporary events, or moments of the everlasting play of energy. But since all phenomena are changing and passing into new forms or states of energy, all beings, human or otherwise, since they are only energy itself, will also be conserved forever, although forever in new forms.

This conception of the world and of human existence is modern and also ancient. The ancient sages comprehended the world as permutations of energy and saw that a human lifetime is only a single event in a beginningless and endless procession of transformations (or births and deaths in all the subtle and gross or high and low realms of phenomenal possibility). Some interpreted the factuality of eternal survival to be the ultimate Truth. These were the religious mystics, yogis, and magicians, who became enamored of experience and perpetual devotion to self-existence. Others, such as the classical Buddhists, were psychologically disposed to interpret the endlessness of factual survival negatively, as inherently a matter of suffering, since living beings appeared only to be constantly changing and dying and being born again, sometimes rising up and sometimes falling again, under the perpetual force of mechanical necessity. Even since ancient times, those of a superficial and unillumined mind have been possessed by the self-indulgent and world-resisting fear of mortality, while others, being more profoundly informed by experience, have been consoled by factual immortality, and still others have been determined to bring a factual and final end to the perpetual cycles of mechanical and self-centered experience. But what is the Truth? What is the Realization that transcends both positive and negative concerns for mortality and immortality?

The Truth that must ultimately be Realized is spontaneously Awakened when the body-mind and the world and all experience become suddenly "transparent" to the fundamental consciousness. This "transparency" is not generally or necessarily associated with a visual experience. Rather, it is at first a matter of ego-death, or the establishment of natural identification with the deepest or "native" position of ordinary consciousness. Then the "eyes" of intuition must open. That is, the state of the atomic energies that compose or define the body-mind, and the world, and all experience, must become obvious.

It is like having one's visual awareness suddenly established in the plane of the atom. Then, instead of viewing the body-mind, and the world, and all experience as "objective" or solid phenomena that cannot be penetrated by consciousness, there is the sudden awareness that all phenomena are made of transparent fields of apparent "particles" of energy that are suspended in "space" and moving about in mysterious and ever-changing associations with one another. Thus, even the empirical "self," the total body-mind, is viewed or understood as a transparent field of suspended particles or vortexes of energy. The body-mind is mostly "space," and none of its suspended particles seem to touch one another, but only to move relative to one another as if controlled by invisible flows of pervasive magnetic or electronic energy. And the difference between the particles that compose the body-mind and those that compose the world "outside" is not any longer profound. Only certain magnetic or electronic influences make the difference between the form of the body-mind and that of the world, but the space between the particles of the body-mind and the space between the particles of the world are the same continuous or absolute space.

Once this "vision" or intuitive understanding is Awakened, the idea of a solid and separate self, or a solid body that somehow materially creates or contains consciousness, is instantly (or inherently) dissolved. Only the absence of "transparency" (or self-transcendence) creates or implies the illusion of a limited consciousness necessarily bound to a fixed physical entity. In fact, consciousness is limited only to the degree it identifies with the solid personal appearance of the body-mind, the world, and the conventions of psycho-physical experience. The deeper the personal consciousness enters into its psycho-physical situation, the more its perceptions and conceptions project beyond the limited self into psychically expanded space-time phenomena. And when there is intuitive penetration of the total body-mind, the solid or objective world, and all the limits of experience, it is Realized that consciousness is Infinite.

The internal or personal consciousness is actually identical to the Infinite Space in which the particles of atoms that compose all phenomena are suspended. When the illusion of the atom itself is penetrated, so that the Mystery of Transcendental Space becomes obvious to consciousness, then the ego-conception is Released, and only Transcendental Consciousness becomes obvious in the Radiant Transparent Infinity of energy motions. This obvious Transparency is Liberation and God-Realization.

When this Liberated Realization occurs, the "problem" of manifest existence dissolves and all necessity is transcended. The changing conventions of psycho-physical existence may remain, but they are not any longer viewed as a problem to be overcome. There is simply Radiance, Love, Humor, Happiness, Delight, Wisdom, Strength, Freedom, and the capacity to Serve the world of living beings with the Transfiguring Power of Divine Truth.

CHAPTER 13

EVEN SCIENCE IS A MAGICAL ACTIVITY

a talk by Da Free John
October 27, 1980

1.

MASTER DA FREE JOHN: The attitude, asana,[1] or method of science is one that treats the processes of experience as objective phenomena. The forms that are cognized and perceived by the method of science are treated as phenomena that exist in and of themselves, independent of cognition and perception. The forms of cognition and perception may obviously be regarded in this way, and in treating them as such we simply put ourselves in a position to study or find out about those phenomena as a process of forms.

We are mistaken, however, if we make this attitude or procedure the only allowable or justifiable procedure of human existence. In doing so we make various philosophical presumptions about the nature of Reality that are clearly false and that suppress and depress various other ways of human knowing and aspects of human existence and in general deny the possibility of equanimity, or harmonious Realization of the Condition of our existence.

The attitude or asana of science is a method based on analysis, made possible by the objectification of phenomena and the assumption

---

1. The term "asana" is defined on p. 71, n. 7.

of a point of view wherein the viewer is conceived to have either no fundamental effect or a rigorously reduced effect on the things observed. When this attitude becomes the only possible human stance, Reality tends to be defined in terms of that objective dimension of things, and the other dimensions of our Condition tend to be reduced to the description we propose of the objective world. Thus, the psychic dimension of the being, including the process of cognition and perception and conscious existence itself, is typically reduced to a secondary development of matter.

We have already discussed that there are other ways of knowing, in particular the way of knowing that I have called participatory knowledge. Historically, when participatory knowledge became the exclusive way of knowing, the psyche and the essential condition of being or consciousness tended to provide the limiting structure we define as reality. When the self-Essence and the psyche are deemed to be the only "real" reality, then the forms that arise and anything that may be proposed as an objective world become secondary, even unnecessary and illusory.[2] That attitude characterizes the extreme oriental disposition. Even so, this process of participatory knowledge, without being made into an exclusive and dominant approach to things, is a natural dimension of our existence, a simple, ordinary expression of the totality of our condition, to which we must adapt and with which we must become naturally familiar.

Now, if we do not define Reality simply in terms of the conscious essence of the subject or self, if we understand that Reality is the Transcendental Condition of all the features of our condition, then we can presume various asanas in the midst of our daily living. One of those asanas is the left-brained, analytical approach to forms of phenomena in themselves so that their laws and interrelations may be inspected and understood. But we may also presume the participatory way of knowing without making it reductive—in other words, without passing into the inverted state of the subject independent of forms. We can simply make use of the process of participation in all possible phenomena, a process that is native to our condition.

We have already considered that we do not in fact have any awareness of a world that exists in and of itself. Our awareness of the world is always in the form of cognition and perception. And the

2. The "self-Essence" is the essential consciousness or atman prior to Enlightenment, that is, before it Realizes its absolute identity with the Divine Reality or Brahman.

world itself is always in the form of a perception or a cognition. In other words, our fundamental association with the world is participatory. There is no distinction in our basic Condition of existence between the psyche, consciousness, cognition and perception, and the forms that arise. They are a single process, no part of which is the only reality, the "real" reality, and no part of which causes any other part. All parts arise simultaneously in a condition of mutuality as modifications of the Transcendental Being.

Since we do not realize the world in any terms other than psychic ones, and since the world for us is always apparent in the form of states of cognition and perception, it is reasonable to participate in the world as a psychic phenomenon. It is quite natural to do so. We already exist in that psychic and participatory circumstance.

In other times and places, the participatory way of knowing was dominant, particularly in the oriental setting. Until the dogmatically dominant appearance of the mood of scientism and the left-brained model of Man, other ways of knowing and the fundamental disposition of participatory knowing were common in the schooling of human life.

But the convention of knowing that is dominant and popular in our time is essentially a development of the one way of knowing seen in the discipline of scientific activity. This activity is otherwise animated by everyone in the form of a left-brained, verbal, or waking mentality primarily associated with motor activity, wherein attention is moved bodily into gross relations. This is the primary attitude or asana to which we adapt in present social circumstances. We are therefore not very well schooled in the disposition of participation wherein we realize our existence to be a Condition of continuousness with all phenomena or all beings. We tend to exclude and suppress the participatory disposition. We do not enjoy a high level of adaptation to that way of knowing or relating to the conditions of existence.

We would do well to generate tools for investigating the world in and of itself. Such investigation is a useful development of our association with the world, so long as it does not become an exclusive philosophy. But if our association with the world is fundamentally psychic to begin with and is never anything but that, then even this scientific activity (in which we presume to be analytically differentiated from phenomena in order to know them in and of themselves) is itself a psychic phenomenon.

Even science, then, is a psychic development, a psychic process, a way of relating to the psychic phenomenon we regard as the so-called objective world. But when science presumes to provide the basis for an exclusive point of view toward life, we forget this truth. We act as if it were not the case, and then the principle of scientific knowing becomes destructive.

The participatory way of knowing is a way of psychically inhering in the World-Process and becoming sensitive to it as a psychic phenomenon, becoming active in it through psychic processes, and observing in it the effects of psychic processes. We could call that way of knowing "magic." It is a magical activity. There are many kinds of magical activity, but if we simply understand our relationship to the world as I have just described it, then we realize that that form of relationship is naturally magical, because we know the world only as a psychic phenomenon.

We may consider the world to be an objective phenomenon, but then we are actually treating a psychic phenomenon as if it were an objective phenomenon. To do so produces a certain kind of knowledge and a certain strategy of association—an asana or a disposition—but it does not change the fact that we exist essentially in a participatory association with the phenomena of the world. We are inherently related to the world in a magical fashion. The world itself is inherently a magical process, a magical or psychic phenomenon.

Science is therefore a kind of magical activity, a way of relating to and using the magical nature of our existence, a disposition of relationship to a phenomenon that in its totality is psychic or magical in nature. Of course, those who advocate the scientific point of view would not in general want to equate science with magic. More likely they would propose science as the antithesis of magical activity. But because of the inherently psychic nature of our association with the world, science must nonetheless be understood as a species of magical activity.

Yet, the disposition of science could be called antimagical. Science presumes the antimagical disposition to pursue a certain familiarity with or knowledge about the World-Process. When the disposition of science becomes exclusive and dominant, its antimagical quality becomes obvious as a kind of dogmatic inclination, a cultural effect that is dehumanizing—antimagical activity is antihuman activity.

Now, we could not say that science simply as a rigorous method for acquiring certain kinds of knowledge is antimagical in the negative sense. But when its point of view is made exclusive, then the effect of the antimagical disposition is negative because it suppresses and argues against the fundamental nature of our association with things, as if by doing science and acquiring knowledge by its means, we could ultimately magically cease to be human, magically cease to be magically related to the universe, and magically eliminate the magical and psychic nature of the universe!

Antimagic is itself a kind of magic, and when developed in an exaggerated fashion, it becomes bad magic, negative magic. To presume the scientific disposition exclusively depresses us psychically. It demands that we identify with what is mortal, what is limited, what is material, what is not psychic. To confront this dogma and the force of this antimagical disposition is to suffer the suppression of the fullness of conscious existence.

Fundamentally, then, we could say that the fault of our science-dominated time is its dehumanizing effect, its antipsychic or antimagical effect, which is tending to destroy our inherent understanding of the nature of our existence and to suppress and delegitimize the naturally magical process of associating with the world.

As a result of the Westernization of mankind through the movement of scientism and its extensions, we have seen a gradual disappearance of the profession of magic and the esotericism of religion, spirituality, and mysticism. These ancient cultural processes are being studied today, but most of that study is based on the scientific, antimagical inclination to reduce magical processes to explanation via the antimagical, scientific model of Man.

Thus, in our anthropological and other scientific studies of magic, mysticism, and shamanism there generally exists a prejudice to perceive those activities and the individuals associated with them as infantile versions of Man operating on the basis of illusion and false models of the world. Likewise, scientific commentators constantly point out that modern mankind is not supposed to be capable of relating to the world through magical processes and that furthermore we should not try to relate to the world in such fashion. To do so would be dangerous, they warn. We would be getting involved with illusions, unreality, even madness.

I once went to see a woman who was a principal student of Carl Jung. In the psychological school of Jung there seems to be a level of tolerance for the psychic process and the forms it has taken in various cultures—magic, yoga, mysticism, shamanism, and so forth. But the

conventional, occidental model of Man and the mood of scientism
continued to inform even the investigations of Jung and his followers.
When I spoke to this woman about the spiritual process in which I
was involved, she immediately warned me against having anything to
do with mysticism, kundalini,[3] or spiritual esotericism. She said that
anything like that would be dangerous for a Westerner, anathema,
leading definitely in the direction of insanity. She was clearly expressing
the conventional prejudice of scientism and the exclusive view of the
occidental mind.

It is true that from a certain disposition of adaptation, such as
may more or less characterize people in the West, to take up the way
of life strictly as it appears in the orient could well be either
impossible or ultimately deluding. But the principles of the participatory way of knowledge are true of all of us wherever we happen to
have been born and raised. Merely Western Man is a partial
development of Man, just as merely Eastern Man is a partial
development of Man. Ultimately, all the features of Man that have
developed separately in both the East and the West must be awakened
in us and organized in a different fashion to give rise to Complete
Man, who is neither Eastern nor Western, but who is Transcendentally
Occupied, and in whom all features of the body-mind and of the brain
are in a condition of equanimity, fully awake and functional.

Considering the degree to which mankind has become Westernized, it is perhaps no longer appropriate or even possible to develop
the way of participatory knowledge precisely in the terms of oriental
esoteric spirituality or even in the terms of the vitalistic magical

---

3. The kundalini or kundalini shakti, the "serpent power," is that manifestation of the Life-
Current which lies dormant in Man, traditionally described as coiled three and a half times at the
base of the spine, blocking with its open mouth the axial channel. Conventional yogic esotericism
strives to awaken this Force in the spiritual practitioner and guide it along the axis of the body to
the crown of the head, thereby producing all the various forms of inner or mystical experience.
Master Da Free John has criticized this position as follows:
"The modern traditions of yoga generally fail to discriminate between the Life-Energy in the
human nervous system (or the egoic body-mind) and the central or root-process that is self-
conscious attention. Thus, the 'Way' is typically and mistakenly interpreted as the raising or
ascent of attention via the internal or subjective (egoic) ladder (spinal column) of the central
nervous system (culminating in the subjective mysticism of the brain-mind). However, the most
ancient Wisdom distinguishes between the display of phenomena in the body-mind (the total
nervous system, including the brain) and the root of attention (or egoic self-consciousness) in the
heart" (*Bodily Worship of the Living God*, p. 145).
The Way of Radical Understanding aims at the dissolution of attention itself, while
simultaneously relaxing or surrendering the whole body-mind into the Life-Current, which is
beyond all manifestations of the nervous system.

cultures of the world. But the psychic structures that originally were culturally adapted from the oriental point of view are still there to be developed—not simply from the oriental point of view, but from this total point of view. To become whole, Western Man must develop the capacity for participatory knowledge and therefore must develop a kind of magical consciousness in new, present, living terms.

If we understand ourselves in this manner, then clearly we must begin to adapt to another dimension of our existence. We must include this other dimension along with our capacity for analytical objectification of the world and the mood of doubt, so that we can observe phenomena through psychic means, without attributing patterns to what we observe that are not inherent or fully integrated. We must begin to operate on the basis of the obvious, on the basis of the presumption of the condition, with all of its features, that is obvious to us in our moment to moment existence.

That means we must begin to participate in the world as a psychic phenomenon, as a dimension of forms that is a direct expression of the psyche, just as dreams are a direct expression of the psyche. We must transcend the conventional bias against the discovery and observation that the world of the waking state is full of psychic phenomena. The world is that kind of psychic event, but we are prejudiced against seeing it as such. The scientific disposition, as a point of view, as a tool or method of activity, is prejudiced against this discovery because it is prejudiced against this psychic way of relating to things.

In science or other similar activities, we are not participating in the magical process in its positive sense. But so long as science is just a portion or part of one attitude by which we associate with things, there is nothing inherently wrong with it. It is in fact a kind of discipline that can help us associate with phenomena as they really are without becoming psychically aberrated. But even the activity of science is a magical activity, a way of using the fact that we are psychically involved with a psychic phenomenon.

And the world is a psychic phenomenon. In other words, we never experience the world except psychically. We never experience it except as knowledge and perception. We never experience it except as a condition that includes us. We are not separate from it. What we are at the level of the psyche and at the level of consciousness is just as much an inherent part of the world as the so-called material, objective forms. When we associate with the world on the basis of the totality of all the conditions of our existence, we participate in the world of forms as a psychic process. By participating psychically in the psychic phenomena of the world, we learn the laws whereby we can influence the phenomena of the waking state. We generate a process wherein we can become sensitive to the phenomena of the waking state so that we can observe unusual coincidences of form and psychic significances that our verbal mind tends to exclude from what we are observing.

If we examine the presumptions and activities of people involved in magical culture, such as mystics, shamans, medicine men, and psychics of a certain kind, we find them noticing phenomena in the features of the so-called objective world that correspond to psychic states. They are always seeing in the world the very things that they say they see in visions. From the magician's point of view, the world is populated by psychically significant beings, forms, and processes. The magician has a magical relationship to all the things that can change. All the things that can appear and disappear in the waking state are conceived and perceived by the magician as psychic or magical phenomena.

In the early years of my own sadhana,[4] when I went from Columbia College to graduate studies at Stanford University and was living on the beach, I was involved in a process of the bare observation of all the conditions that arose, whether internal and subjective or so-called objective in the external world.[5] Whatever they were, I put myself in a position to observe those things unqualifiedly without bringing an attitude to them. I developed this capacity over time. I simply presumed the disposition of the observer and did not presume any left-brained or right-brained dogma about the nature of things. I did not presume any absolute distinction between the internal and the external. I just allowed experience to be whatever it was. Nor did I presume a relation between internal and external. I just observed things as they were. And over time the nature of things as they are began to become more and more obvious.

I presumed that I was performing an activity out of which I would create a work of fiction, a kind of novel. But I discovered over time that the process in which I was involved was what was significant, not the results, not the boxes and boxes of notes and writings I produced over those years. Eventually I just burned all those

4. The term "sadhana" is defined on p. 27, n. 27.

5. For an account of this period of Master Da Free John's life, see his spiritual autobiography, *The Knee of Listening*, pp. 16–35.

papers when I moved to New York and became involved with Rudi.[6] I recognized and acknowledged that all those notes and writings were basically without significance or use and that I could not convert them all into a book. I had to somehow throw them into a fire and allow them to become unified as a psychic form rather than as boxes of notes that could no longer be integrated.

The process in which I was involved, however, ultimately demonstrated to me that there was no distinction between the internal, psychic, subjective world, so-called, and the outer, objective world, that all states were essentially psychic states and crossed over into one another. In some sense the waking state affected dreams and the subtle, psychic, and hallucinatory activity. But the opposite was also true. Things that were going on in dreams and at a purely psychic level crossed over into the objective world of the waking state. A kind of story began to develop wherein I would sometimes observe some character or event in a dream or a flash of consciousness, and then I would observe that event being played out in the phenomena of my external life. The characters in the internal world appeared in the external world. Pieces of the events being worked out in the external world carried over into the internal world. My experience was a single, fluid, psychic plastic.

As a result of this process, the phenomena of the objective world began to achieve psychic force. They became recognizable as states and signs of the psyche. The beings in the objective world became psychically significant beings. I became sensitive to my daily life as a psychic process, even in the terms of the simple perception of objective events. A psychic unfolding was taking place, much as in dreams.

I began to become profoundly sensitive to certain processes in the so-called natural or objective or material world. I developed the ability to read them, to observe them, to see dramas proceeding in the phenomenal world that from our ordinary, verbal, self-abstracting, objectifying point of view would not be observable. Thus, I achieved a psychic inherence in world forces, forces of weather, natural phenomena, and creatures of all kinds. I became unusually associated with certain animals and patterns in the natural world such as the weather and the ocean. The ultimate outcome of this development was the

6. Rudi (Albert Rudolph, 1928–1973) was Master Da Free John's spiritual Teacher from 1964–68. He helped Master Da prepare the foundation for the mature phases of his spiritual life. For an account of Master Da's years with Rudi, see *The Knee of Listening.*

awakening of a state of brilliant equanimity and awareness of the coincidence of all phenomena. And when this awakening occurred, there was a breakthrough in the process of my sadhana, and I went on to find a human spiritual teacher.

Eventually—several years later—I actually did write the novel I had originally presumed to be working on. The novel, which I have titled *The Mummery*,[7] was one of the outcomes of that process of submission to the totality of my existence, in which the external and internal worlds were perceived and lived as a single process, and through the observation of which archetypal characters and archetypal configurations of destiny and tendency appeared. The novel, then, is itself a magical text, not like a realistic novel. It is full of cryptic meanings, like a complex dream. It is magical language.

The novel is not filled with arbitrary archetypes, but it is the product of a profound consideration that took place over several years. And there is a great magical message in it, discoverable only by those who are sensitive to it, perhaps never completely discoverable, you see. *The Mummery* is like magical texts that have appeared in magically based cultures in the past—a book of magical beings and magical creatures, a magical story, an archetypal adventure. It is a secret book, a sealed book, an esoteric book.

DEVOTEE: Master, many of the events you prophesied in *The Mummery* have already come true.

MASTER DA FREE JOHN: All kinds of slices of meaning, slices of space-time, appear in that book. It is full of paradoxes. On one level, it seems to be a story about something happening in this world. But time in that text does not really work the way time works in this world, and the transitions between places are all magical transitions.

Well—having made this discovery of the coincidence of the subjective and objective domains through the rigorous sadhana to which I applied myself, I then went on to develop the other aspects of my sadhana, which became conclusive in the six years following that initial stage, from 1964 to 1970. The conclusiveness of that six-year period depended on my entering into it with the disposition that had been generated in the earlier sadhana. I did not go to Rudi and to India

---

7. Master Da Free John's unpublished novel, *The Mummery*, was written in 1969. It is an archetypal, poetic, and non-linear story told in the form of a "prose opera."

like an ordinary Western college boy, in other words. I had already passed through a phenomenal transformation that fitted me for the sadhana to come.

DEVOTEE: Even your discovery of Rudi occurred in a magical way, through a vision of his art store.

DEVOTEE: And around that same time you also came to understand about life beyond death.

MASTER DA FREE JOHN: Yes. In other words, the Reality, the unkillable Force of our essential existence, our psychic existence, was proven, demonstrated, and brought back to life in the face of everything that suppresses such a Realization in the current context of human life. An ordinary, Western, left-brained character doing yoga and performing various psychic disciplines would not necessarily enjoy a comparable awakening.

You must awaken from the suppressed state of the being, transcend the dogmas in the common world that suppress the being, and rediscover the psychic nature of the world. You must rediscover your own existence as a psychic process that is not threatened by the apparent limitations of the physical world and that does not come to an end simply because one feature of your existence—physical, bodily manifestation—comes to an end.

This coming to the front of the psychic being, the essential character of your existence, is a necessary preliminary for the spiritual process. Another vision, another model of existence, in other words, must achieve reality for the spiritual process to be true, or for it to be anything more than a consolation for you and your mortal understanding. All the capacities that can develop through the spiritual process will seem unreal to you unless you can achieve the point of view wherein such phenomena are real and comprehensible.

Otherwise you can have unusual experiences by disciplining the body and concentrating yourself in a certain way, but those experiences will always be doubtable to you. You will always be able to explain them, it would seem, in scientific terms, using the ordinary mortal model of the nervous system. No great change will have occurred then. You will just have made your mortality a little more elaborate, a little more complicated, a little more showy. But you will be essentially in the same condition or disposition as you were at the beginning,

unless you can pass through this crisis wherein the psyche ceases to be
dominated by the phenomenal world that is proposed to be the only
reality by the dogmas of our time.

DEVOTEE: Master, it was not until my conventional model of
existence began to break down and I began to see that in Truth the
world is a psycho-physical realm in which I am involved and to which
I am psycho-physically related, that a kind of opening and awakening
in the being itself occurred that allowed me to participate in life with a
fuller understanding and consciousness.

MASTER DA FREE JOHN: Yes, the confession that "I" is the body-
mind,[8] whatever that is in its totality, is more than a confession that
you are the body as you conceive it from the analytical, left-brained
point of view. It is the confession that the body-mind, the totality of
your existence, is altogether, thoroughly, psycho-physical. In other
words, what you regard to be body is not merely body. It is psycho-

8. This idea forms part of the "Ignorance consideration"—the three-pronged Teaching
Argument that (a) " 'I' do not know what anything is"; (b) " 'I' is the body"; and (c) " 'I am the
body' is love." In *The Bodily Sacrifice of Attention*, Master Da Free John writes:
   "Confronting anything, any particularity, putting your attention on it clearly and directly, what
do you understand? It is tacitly obvious that you do not know what it is. You know all kinds of
things about it, but you do not know what it is. You cannot account for it in any absolute terms.
You cannot account for its being there. You cannot account for the 'where' itself. You do not
know where a thing is. You do not know what it is. You do not know how it arises, where it
arises, in whom it arises, where it is going. You do not know what its substance is, you do not
know what its ultimate nature is. You know a number of things about it, but what you know
about anything does not include any ultimate knowledge. In other words, the form of your
relationship to everything is Divine Ignorance, not knowledge!" (p. 57).
   Master Da Free John next spells out the implication of this understanding:
   "The ultimate import of that consideration, which is summarized in the form ' "I" do not know
what anything is,' is the statement, ' "I" am the body,' or ' "I" is the body.' This is the next step in
the realization of Divine Ignorance.
   "The 'I,' the subjective 'I' in the mind, is nothing but a reflection of the body. It is a conception
that arises on the basis of bodily self-contraction.
   "Ordinarily we identify with this 'I' and we generate our adventure of existence on the basis of
this conception of ourselves as a subjective personality, an independent self. There is no real,
actual, present, independent self. It is an idea based on the body. The body is the source of this
notion of a separate 'I.' If we recognize the 'I,' we realize it to be nothing but the body, and the 'I'-
thought disappears. Ultimately, we become Free, then, to Realize the Nature of the bodily self,
the ultimate Condition of the bodily self" (p. 59).
   The third part of the whole Argument is expressed in the formula " 'I-am-the-body' is love."
As Master Da Free John explains:
   "Through recognition of the 'I' (and even the entire mind) as nothing but the body,
contraction of the body upon the 'I' or the mind is transcended. Thus, the internal 'I' and the
compulsive activity of mind are released. The separative and self-directed life of Narcissus
relaxes. The self-transcending life of harmonious bodily surrender into the Living Spirit begins.
Such is the life of Divine Ignorance, wherein we live as love, free of the binding contraction of
self, mind, knowledge, and experience. 'I am the body' is love" (p. 64).

physical. It is mind. It is psyche apparent in a particular fashion, but it is not merely body, not merely matter.

The magical disposition, then, must reawaken in us if we are to achieve the human process in its fullest terms. To reawaken this disposition is not necessarily to revert or regress to, or reassociate with, the cultural disposition toward magical activity to be found in the orient or in vital cultures. On the other hand, the development of this psychic disposition will clearly show some of the signs that were present or were made available to experience in those cultures. A likeness naturally exists between those who live the spiritual Way and those who are otherwise yogis, mystics, shamans, magicians, medicine men, witch doctors, and so forth. It is simply that we today have our own cultural and spiritual uses of the psychic faculties.

Throughout these many years I have had a magical relationship to all kinds of things. The world is for me a psychic, magical phenomenon. I work with it directly as such. I work with every individual as such. I live my daily life as such. Therefore, I am associated in my daily life with forces in the world that are psychic in nature. Things that become apparent in my environment, in the apparent coincidences of possible changes and the appearance of beings, are magical and are observable to me in psychic terms. I have dreams and then things occur in life that directly correspond to them. I see the world as a psychic process. My association with the world has developed on one level similar to the way life develops for a shaman. For instance, I have had many occasions of unusual association with animals and the recognition of a kind of empowerment that comes with association with certain creatures.

An example of such magic occurred here yesterday. A shaman from Mexico was brought to this country for a few days. He was contacted by the Communion[9] and was invited to stay in a place near The Mountain of Attention.[10] I did not meet him personally, but some of the community's doctors and a few other practitioners spent some time with him. He is not a shaman who also has a Western, intellectual understanding of what he is doing. He is literally an Indian shaman who lives way out in the country in Mexico in a tribal setting

9. The spiritual fellowship of practitioners of the Way Taught by Master Da Free John is called The Johannine Daist Communion.

10. The Mountain of Attention is a principal renunciate sanctuary and meditation retreat of The Johannine Daist Communion. It is located in northern California.

where he has lived all his life. He is now in his nineties or perhaps around a hundred, and he has practiced as a shaman in the traditional way all his life. He has never had any association with downtown, urban society. He was just lifted out of his circumstance and brought here for a few days—I do not know how long he was in this country. He came to us yesterday and then zipped back to Mexico last night.

DEVOTEE: Without a plane! (Laughter.)

MASTER DA FREE JOHN: He was a sweet character but not really very outward, not really into what occupied everybody else. While devotees were visiting with him yesterday, I just sat here alone, psychically tuning in to him and to the mass of psychic forces associated with such people.

In the shamanistic tribal culture of this man the primary animal is the deer, the being seen in the world and in visions that helps us to pass through the portal to the other reality, the other side of the world, the visionary dimension.

Today I left the house for a little while. As I walked, I was thinking about this shaman and about the magical process in which he is involved and in which I am involved. I was walking the path beside Great Food Dish[11] when I saw an acorn. This acorn seemed unusual to me because it was complete, not broken. It still had its "cap." I picked it up and I began thinking about the multitude of oak trees here on the Sanctuary and about how the acorn is a kind of ritual symbol, a sacred object in this place.

Then I walked over to the Tree of Life at Skyway Temple[12]— which is an old oak tree—and as I looked at the site there and thought about the deer in this man's practice, suddenly I heard a thumping. I looked up, and right next to me was a deer, a stag with antlers. It came right next to me, stomped around a bit, and then moved across the lawn. Now and then he would stop and then start again, giving me the clear impression that I should follow him and that he would guide me. I watched him run off, cresting the hill.

I walked to where he had disappeared, generally feeling where he had gone and recognizing that this event duplicated the shamans' following the deer into the visionary world. The shamans get the idea

11. Great Food Dish is the central dining facility at The Mountain of Attention.

12. Skyway Temple is an outdoor sacramental site at The Mountain of Attention. The primary physical characteristic of this site is a massive oak called the Tree of Life.

when they see a deer. If you see a deer, you only see it. You cannot grasp it. It is always off, away. You can see it, and it leads you and then disappears.

When I reached the corral, I saw the deer grazing up the hill by my office. I still had the acorn in my hand, and it occurred to me that it was a kind of spirit offering. Just then the deer lifted his head and saw me. He kept grazing, and I kept walking. He showed no inclination to run off, but when I came within a hundred feet or so, he started again to move. I called him—"tchick-tchick-tchick"—and started making noises toward him, holding up the acorn. He looked back at me, then leaped up and down, and then leaped off. It seemed that he leaped off the hill right at my office.

I quickly walked up the hill, but the deer was absolutely nowhere to be seen. From the prominence next to my office and below The Manner of Flowers,[13] the football field, the garden, and the whole area of this valley are visible. And the stag was nowhere to be seen. He had disappeared.

Well, that is how the shaman tracks the deer. To relocate the deer you must allow it to lead you into vision.

The deer is regarded as a magical creature, and it is a prominent creature in the magic of various peoples. Each tribe or group has its prominent animal figures, and the deer is particularly valued in some, as it is in the culture of the old Mexican shaman. The deer is also a prominent creature on this property. Deer live all around here. The presence of deer, like the presence of other creatures, has magical significance to the right ceremonial and sacred use of this ground. When you are doing magic, you associate with the creature world. Creatures can come and be around you, or they can be absent. That they have mobility, can come and go, appear or not appear, is a prerequisite for magical association with them. They move freely. They are not contained. Thus, their appearance on any occasion is naturally acknowledged to be auspicious from a magical point view.

Whenever a shaman or medicine man is doing magic, he is always associating with the powers of the Earth: the weather, the living things, the creatures and their coming and going. He looks for signs when he performs any magical act. He will choose to perform that magical act by observing features in the area that seem to be auspicious. The time seems to be auspicious. The conditions of the day,

13. The Manner of Flowers is the name of one of the primary temples at The Mountain of Attention.

the weather, the wind, and all the play of the elements seem auspicious. The feeling seems auspicious. Certain creatures are also associated with the place that is auspicious. So the magician usually looks for creatures to appear during or after the ceremony. And, in the magician's feeling, the appearance of creatures always confirms the potency of the magic. Whenever he performs magical activity and animals in one or another way associate with him during that time, the magician acknowledges a kind of empowerment that comes through that association.

Over the years, I have had a number of auspicious conjunctions with animals of all kinds and psychic, visionary association with them preceding or following my meetings with them. I have had a long history of empowerments and magical associations with creatures. I have talked to you about a number of them, such as lions, snakes, birds of all kinds, horses, spiders, the scorpion that appeared on my genitals once when I was meditating in the dark. The ultimate truth of this psychic process is to be able to engage in moment to moment existence as a magical event, to always be tending the Spiritual Fire, which is the Universal, Radiant Current.

I was tending the fire today, you see, and that stag's appearance was a magical sign. I was not tending a physical fire. It was psychic. The recognition of the world phenomena as psychic phenomena permits us to be awakened psychically in the midst of those phenomena. In other words, it is not only closing one's eyes and seeing a deer in a vision that is a psychic phenomenon. The magical conjunction is itself a psychic phenomenon. Yes, there can be visions associated with exalted states of awareness. There can also be dream phenomena and hallucinatory reveries. These are other features of the magical process. But the magical moment should coincide with the recognition of the fact that you are not existing in the world of science. You are in the Divine World, the same world in which you are psychically alive—not merely the world in which you are bodily present, not merely the world in which your foot is standing or is placed, but the world in which your entire being resides.

Therefore, it is a world filled with magical conjunctions. That is its significance. That is its meaning. The meaning of a bird and the description of the part of the cosmos to which it relates may also be apparent to you. But the recognition that you are in the Divine World, or the psychic world, is the essential force of such phenomena.

You must awaken to the exhilaration that comes through such recognition, instead of just falling back into the mood of doubt, saying, "Oh, there's a deer there—deer live here all the time," or "Lightning—oh, there's a storm coming up," or "Birds—well, there are always birds flying around." (Laughter.) See? Right away you want to think that you are in the mortal world instead of recognizing that you are in the Divine World.

DEVOTEE: Master, the shaman said that two things would happen when he got home. First of all, he said his people missed him very much, and the radio was going to announce his return, and he gestured how they would all be cheering and singing. Then he said he was going to go up into the mountains far away for a few days.

MASTER DA FREE JOHN: You see, he came into a different world. He came into the world that is presumed to be non-psychic, non-magical. The world is transformed by our presumption about it. Those who live in a magical disposition toward the world change their world in one characteristic way: They do not seem to do very much with it as a natural phenomenon. They are very protective of it as a natural phenomenon and want to interfere with it as little as possible, because it is only by letting the world be what it is as a natural process, without interference, that it has the opportunity to produce magical signs and therefore to permit them to engage in magical relations with it.

The disposition of scientism changes the world. It is a magical activity in the form of antimagic, and so the world at large is at present being transformed from the point of view of antimagic. And that activity is all about interfering with the World-Process, interfering with changes in the Earth, and producing human environments that systematically exclude the features of the natural world that are otherwise interpreted magically by those who are so disposed.

The city is the world as science creates it. It is the world of the left brain, the antimagical or non-psychic world. The forces and magical beings you can observe in a natural setting are eliminated there. It is a wholly controlled, "interfered with" environment. It is Man becoming the master, Man controlling all forces, Man eliminating the arbitrariness of change that Nature represents. No creatures wander in the cities except for a few domestic little characters—a few dogs and cats and canaries and parakeets. Basically, the life cycle of animals living free is eliminated or contained so that it no longer has the ability to reflect itself magically. Animals may perhaps be kept off somewhere in a zoo in the city, but they no longer live and act as they would in their own domain. Their magical force is systematically eliminated by the way we cage and contain them.

The entire effect of scientific Man, occidental Man, non-magical Man on the world is to eliminate the magical content of the world as well as to eliminate magical association with the world. Because this view is dominant, we are seeing the world being changed, in ways that people who still exist in a magically based culture are always complaining about. I understand that one of the reasons the shaman came from Mexico is that his tribal way of life is being interfered with by the encroachment of urbanization and other forces detrimental to the life of natural Man as well as animals and natural forces of all kinds.

Tribal Indians in this country are all very much associated with a way of life of relative noninterference with Nature, using its bounty in various ways, yet not controlling it or interfering with it, but rather relating sympathetically and magically to it. Their complaint is that the white man, scientific Man, is destroying the whole natural world and is doing so because he is presuming a false relationship to the natural world, a dissociated and power- or dominance-oriented relationship to things. This abstracting feature of the scientific mind, therefore of the Western mind, with its thirst for control is systematically destroying the capacity of mankind to enter into magical relationship with things as a human activity and to be related to a world that is unchanged by the scientific attitude.

It is difficult nowadays to find an environment in which to do magic even if you were personally disposed so to live. People who are disposed toward a freer, more total psychic existence usually try to get out of the cities, the urbanized, downtown, TV world, and they look for places in the country. It is very difficult to find such places in the United States anymore. Mexico is still a place where, to some degree, this wild natural world survives, but it is only a matter of time before it will also disappear.

2.

MASTER DA FREE JOHN: Only one human force is dominant on Earth at the present time. It wants to take over and change the entire world.

It wants all human beings to conform to a model of existence. It wants to change the total environment of Earth into a technologically mastered condition. And when mankind leaves the Earth and physically goes out into space, this force wants to do the same thing in space. (Laughter.)

But people have been associated with outer space for thousands of years through the medium of psychic association with the universe! People have visited other parts of the physical universe and the total cosmos through psychic means. Through the medium of psychic association or participatory knowing, people have already left the sphere of Earth. They are being prevented from doing so now by the anti-psychic trend of the new Man. The only way the new Man can envision getting off this planet is through the medium of technology and scientism. The only relationship to the universe, therefore, of which such people conceive is to move around in association with analyzed, technological environments, pursuing that one kind of knowing and entering into relations of power with all forces. Science fiction is always conceiving of the ultimate human destiny in outer space in very much the same territorial, power-mad terms people live on Earth, in which there are galactic wars and people blow one another to pieces with superior machinery and all the rest of that nonsense.

DEVOTEE: Master, you mentioned the American Indians. It always seemed to me that the story told in the book *Black Elk Speaks*[14] describes the end of the magical way of relating to the world.

MASTER DA FREE JOHN: That epoch was the end of magic for that particular cultural group, or at least was a profound end of a certain part of its history. Some of those people are still active, but they do not have the same world to live in, nor the same freedom nor even the same intention to live in the old, magical ways.

In other parts of the world other kinds of ancient human groups are still active in this magical fashion. Magic, you see, is of many types. There are vitalistic, older magical cultures, of which the American Indian is an example, as are the Mexican Indian, the South American Indian, and the Hawaiian Indian. Many vital magical cultures still exist in little pockets of activity. First they are usually studied by anthro-

14. J. G. Neihardt, *Black Elk Speaks* (Lincoln, Nebr.: Univ. of Nebraska Press, 1961).

pologists, then the missionaries come, and then the territorial politics starts enclosing them. Eventually they are assimilated.

Other magical cultures of a higher type exist, although calling them a higher type does not mean that they rightfully or in absolute terms dissociate themselves from the domain of vital magic, but they presume a more expanded, spiritual purpose for magic and are less associated with the negative or black magic that tends to be pursued obsessively in vital cultures. These so-called higher magical cultures include certain aspects of Hinduism or the culture of India in general.

In our own time and very recently we have seen the destruction of such a culture in Tibet. There has been no great outcry about what has happened in Tibet, and yet one of the principal philosophical magical cultures that has ever appeared on Earth has been systematically destroyed within our lifetime by the encroachment of the Chinese in Tibet. Many Tibetans have had to flee from their homeland. Those who stayed have been systematically washed out of their magical world into the idealism of Communism and a kind of objective, occidental Man's view of things. The Tibetans have been dispersed, just as were the American Indians, the Jews, and many other groups. Today these peoples are trying to survive as groups by regenerating their traditions in other places. But in general we see a movement all over the Earth to destroy all vestiges of the spiritual, magical disposition and the kinds of culture and human life created on its basis.

As a just-coming-to-life spiritual culture, we too are being met by the same kinds of intrusions. The same forces are threatening us and would want to complicate us. Those same forces are in you because you have not been born into a spiritual culture. You have for one or another reason come to the point of entertaining the possibility of wanting to generate the spiritual Way of life, but there exist features in your disposition that work against your practice and the development of this Way of life in your own case as well as in this community and in this institution.

The disposition in Man at the present time is opposed to this Way of life, and the evidence of opposition is visible all over the world. We are witnessing the worldwide development of insane, power-mad, analytical Man and all the self-destructive and other-destructive habits that that kind of man generates when he is otherwise bereft of Wisdom—in other words, when he does not have the ability to bring into balance what he discovers through the one way of knowing called science. The scientific man cannot bring science into balance with a total understanding or a higher Wisdom about life and this world.

For that reason, we see warfare everywhere on Earth, which can produce the terrible consequences we have already discussed, nuclear explosions and the technological and political domination of mankind by the point of view inherent in the psychology of science. But the true war is not occurring at the level of technological weapons. The true war is taking place at the level of consciousness. It is a war between the species of Man who lives according to the model reflected in scientism and the species of Man who lives in his old form, which is magical and tends to be more exclusively subjective and unable to understand and control certain of the forces that perhaps human beings should try to control or associate with in a more sophisticated fashion.

Ultimately it is a war between the left-brained model of Man and the transcendental development of Man, which is not magical in the old sense but Magical in the perfect sense, wherein Man is unified and enjoys a unified understanding of the universe and his position as a process or as an expression of the active Principle that is manifesting and evolving in the apparent world.

The urban world in which we all tend to be crammed reflects a basic human—or subhuman—attitude. Even in the country the urban design of Man still encroaches. Living out here in the country trying to safeguard this place, trying to survive as a sacred institution, we therefore endure all kinds of problems. The city is a form of consciousness, not merely a place in space. It reflects an attitude, a way of life altogether. It is a dogma, a psychological field. It is a vision. And it is antithetical to magical culture.

In the culture of magic the world is approached as it is, not as it becomes after human beings have manipulated and changed it. The world to which the magician looks to relate himself is the spontaneously living world into which he is born, not into which he is educated and with which he is combined through human strategies. People who work to develop the magical process in an advanced form usually dissociate even from their villages or tribes for a while. They go out into the wilderness to dissociate themselves, as a temporary technique at any rate, from all kinds of ordinary human activity, to readjust, to balance themselves out, to become resensitized to the larger dimension of their existence. Having become magically active, they then see the given world in magical terms, and they simply and sensitively observe the changes that take place and then perform various activities that constantly generate and regenerate the magical forces in the world.

From this magical point of view the features of the observed world—even the gross, so-called outer world—are understood to be magical. In particular certain characters of that world, certain of its characteristics, are considered magical—especially those that are in a state of free flow rather than unchanging. The animals, the patterns of weather, human others apart from the ordinariness of daily social obligation—these features of the world are conceived in magical terms, are constantly observed for any changes, and are approached via magical activity to generate certain kinds of changes. These magical features of the world are conceived to be a bridge to the total world. The so-called objective world is not viewed as a thing in itself, but it is always a form of connection to the total psycho-physical world.

The deer, for instance, is not just an animal in the objective world. It is a living psycho-physical feature of the formal universe and is therefore a bridge between the various dimensions of the formal universe. The deer is not merely an animal in the objective physical world but a psychic presence. It is a way of relating to the more fluid, psychic dimension of the world. Likewise, this fluid, psychic dimension of the world makes its bridge to the objective world through these creatures and forces.

From the magical, shamanistic point of view everything is alive. The cosmos is a living process. A little while ago we were talking about accepting the positive as well as the magical significance of creatures other than Man. From the magical point of view, so-called inanimate objects are also conceived as being alive and participating in a living, magical cosmos. And this is certainly true. The more psychically awake you become, the more you are aware of the psycho-physical nature of what you call the objective world. Once you see that the world is psycho-physical in nature, you begin to appreciate the living condition of everything that arises in the field of experience— not living, perhaps, in the sense that a chair can get up and walk out of the room, but living in a magical sense. Your association with so-called inanimate objects can go through many changes. Association with an inanimate place, even just a room, can change. There are feelings associated with it, a sense of energies, emotions, moods, influences, all kinds of factors to which you become sensitive relative to so-called inanimate things, just as you can be sensitive relative to moving and living things.

It is not that you should just arbitrarily take up a view that everything is alive, as if everything were a creature. Rather, you must develop and mature in your psychic sensitivity to things and then begin to appreciate just in what sense everything is alive, and in what sense everything has effect and should be acknowledged as a force. Living things are significant to us because a force is associated with life. Inanimate things are also living in the sense that a force is associated with them. They are living in this sense rather than in the sense that they are mobile. (Perhaps it is also true that they can move around. This is not totally out of the question, but it must be observed.) At any rate so-called inanimate objects are alive as forces and influences, and the forces can change and vary in our association with them.

This, then, is part of the magical consciousness that is natural to us: to awaken to this sense of the total cosmos as a living presence, a circumstance of forces. At the root of all these things, animate and inanimate, is Radiant Being, the Utterly Living Conscious Reality. Inanimate things, lower creatures, Man, Nature, the Earth, everything is a modification of That Which is ultimately perfectly Alive, Radiant, Forceful, Conscious, Existing. Thus, to have this sense that everything is alive is not illogical or somehow strange. Everything is alive as force, as energy, as psychic reality.

You all can see that table, right? You call it a thing, and in calling it a thing or an object and getting involved in the objective consciousness we analyze with our left brain, you tend to reduce that object to something not alive. But if we naturally relate to that table, first of all we realize that it is a perception. I say, "There is that table over there," but this table is a perception, a development of my own nervous system. It is made to seem a table by virtue of a convention, a process of the nervous system, a process of cognition and perception. I do not see the thing itself. I see this perception. The table exists only as a psychic condition. It is itself a psychic condition, because it is not other than a perception. If we relate to it openly, without defining it, excluding it, or analyzing it into something not alive, we realize its natural livingness, its natural psychic condition.

Even to understand things in analytical, scientific terms, we must recognize that everything is a species of Light, a modification of Force. Even from that point of view, then, without otherwise sympathetically participating in everything as energy, you must presume that everything is Light. To enter into open psycho-physical participation with this world is to recognize it as Force, as Energy, as Light, and therefore as something alive and something that is not absolutely separable from Consciousness, from Being, from the psychic Condition of our existence.

The world participates in Conscious Being utterly because we have no way to dissociate ourselves from the world to the point that it is no longer a psychic phenomenon. Therefore, we cannot have any association with that table without being involved in a psychic phenomenon, because our perception is nothing but a psychic phenomenon. It is never not that, in other words. We presume in some sense that the table is "over there," but in between "over there" and "me" there exists this game of perception/conception.

Ultimately, all that arises to perception is transparent, and something about the nature of so-called reality begins to become clear to us. We are all the time chattering about the external world and presuming ourselves to be separate from it. But when we enter into the deepest recognition of the actual circumstance of our existence, we realize that we are never involved with anything but a psychic phenomenon. Our entire existence is for us a psychic phenomenon, a perception of Energy, a convention of Energy. Therefore, it is temporary and changing. It is to be gone beyond. It is not forever, and as it appears now is not the only way Reality or Light can modify Itself. It is just modifying Itself in this way at the present time.

If a particular kind of psycho-physical mechanism were not in operation in us, if a particular kind of brain-mind and nervous system were not active, we would not observe this world as we now do. We would be in another state altogether. And some day you will be in that state, and it will be perfectly natural for you. It will just be a development of the same State that is fundamentally yours at the present, except that you are not acknowledging It as such. You are presuming another convention, another design. You develop a convention of presumption about the world that is based on bodily relations as they are perceived and analyzed by this nervous system. But that convention is not otherwise necessary. It is just a convention, a temporary model, and it does not describe Reality as it Is. Rather, it is a description of a particular way Reality gets modified. Reality otherwise transcends the description.

What is Reality? Is it the objective, material world? What is that, anyway? Even science is finding out through its investigations that space-time is a paradoxical affair and that our consciousness is determined by the local "Earth-universe" game in which we see things in a certain temporal and spatial frame. But if you get out beyond this local consciousness, the universe is a very paradoxical affair. Space-time is not always as linear and fixed as it seems to be here. Space does not always look precisely as it does here, cannot always be cognized or perceived as it is here. Objects have a different kind of locus, a different kind of process. Light appears differently, modifies itself differently. Mind, therefore, would presumably be entirely different under those expanded conditions. Psychic states would also, therefore, be entirely different in that context of awareness. The knowledge and experience we can develop under the present conditions are therefore local knowledge and local experience. They are not absolute in any terms. And therefore, ultimately, they are transcended.

In the *Bhagavad Gita* Krishna says, "I am the Recipient and Lord of all the sacrifices."[15] All the dharmas[16] can be reduced to the one Dharma of sacrifice to the Universal, Transcendental Being. However, we are all used to a monotheistic notion of the Divine wherein very little evidence of the Power of God is demonstrated in people's lives. People believe that there is only one God and that all these other gods are untrue, that there are no ghosts, that there is nothing but one God—but there is also no God-Power. This is because people do not understand this world as the Divine Domain, as a psychic realm fundamentally, and they do not see that in fact all conditions and all beings live in God and are a bridge to God.

All things and beings are a bridge to the Infinite. They are not simply things in themselves, but they are in fact such a bridge. Merely to think, then, in terms of the One Transcendental Being is not necessarily to generate a process wherein the Power of God and the Person of God, or the Being That Is God, is directly contacted through practice of your Way of life. You must Awaken and discover the Divine World wherein everything is a bridge to the Infinite, One Being.

That Awakening is what is primary. It is not merely an awakening to the mental truth that there is only one God. It is a matter of Awakening to the Nature of your Condition and therefore to the Nature of the Condition of everything that you are observing. Because that Awakening is primary, when it occurs you begin to

15. *Bhagavad Gita* 9:24.

16. The Sanskrit word *dharma* has many different meanings. Here it stands for "way of life," "attitude," "disposition," etc. The supreme Dharma is the Law of sacrifice which, in human terms, is self-transcending surrender.

become sensitive to the world in a new fashion. And in that sensitivity you will see in magical terms how various presences, beings, and events—in gross visibility or only in subtle visibility, or altogether invisible and only sensed—are bridges to this One. Therefore, you may become aware of magical association with beings or forces, states of presence and the like, that are actually part of the magical apparatus of your association with the One Divine. Having made this discovery, you may continue to enjoy magical association with those entities, forces, or conditions, but you will not fall prey to the error of worshipping those features of the world in themselves. Rather, you will be making use of your association with those forces or beings as a bridge or medium of association with the Living Divine.

All beings are that One, but they are each still the being each appears to be, with the particular characteristics each obviously has. You acknowledge and recognize that One, but in the form of every particular individual and the particular relationship you have to that individual. Likewise, you must become sensitive to the total world, to the great features of the world and its fluid, magical features.

The four cardinal directions are associated with the movement of the Earth, the movement of the sun, and the movement of the winds. Therefore, they are associated with energies, and the field of those energies corresponds to the directions or aspects of the field of energy in the body. In this way we are associated with a complex of forces that can be understood to be wholly integrated and to abide in One Great Universal and Transcendental Reality. But we must not abstract that One from the complexity of the magical universe. We must recognize that One in the complexity of the magical universe and use the magical universe as a bridge, a form of association with that One.

We should not merely associate with the power of the north wind and the deer, you see. We should associate with the One, but through these characteristics, and we should observe and understand and feel that these characteristics of the moving universe exist, with their particular dynamic features, their particular proportions, the particular quality of Energy or Force that they represent in this complex Unity.

The shaman has a magical cosmos in mind. He has names for everything. He has a diagram of the universe. But the true shaman does not simply have this scheme in mind, as if he learned it from somebody or a book. The true shaman has realized this scheme. He is in the habit of recognizing things in magical terms, and he therefore begins to become sensitive to what they are indicating about the world. Once he sees what is shown, then he names it or spontaneously feels a name for it, regards it in a particular fashion, and introduces a certain feature into his magical process or his sacramental life that will continue to acknowledge that which he has realized.

Therefore, as a spiritual practitioner you must be able to acknowledge and recognize all the powers that combine in your perception and conception to be the magical representation of the One Who is Alive as everything and everyone. The body-mind is just such an incarnate representation. It is not an ego. It is a total, complex configuration of the One Being. Just so, all beings are That, and the total environment is just such a Singleness, if we Awaken to understand, recognize, and acknowledge it as such. If you begin to engage in this recognition and acknowledgment through sacramental activity and through daily life, you will discover that much more Power appears in your practice. You will not just be performing rote rituals. You will see that an even greater Power, a greater Dimension of influence and of actual change, appears in your daily practice and in your sacramental practice.

Your practice must become true magic. You must be a shaman, but you also must be more than a shaman. You must practice beyond the limitations of the vitalistic shaman, but you must be at least as good as that, at least as conscious as that, at least as aware of the magical nature of everything, at least as perceptive and sensitive, and at least as capable of acknowledgment, so that you can see what is trying to influence you through the medium of all kinds of relations, odd appearances, and coincidences.

Everything altogether is trying to be a revelation for you. It is just that you are not sensitive to it in your ordinary habit. The shaman, you see, has entered into a discipline to make himself sensitive. It is not that he is making the magic happen. The magic is already there. He is just not sensitive to it, not in a position to observe it. Thus, he must engage in a discipline that enables him to participate in what is already happening. Then all of a sudden he sees all kinds of magical things.

We likewise should not devalue the media of association with the Divine. We should not fail to allow this world to be a bridge of association with the Divine, just as we should not fail to allow the body-mind to be such a bridge. We should make all our relations such a bridge. We should recognize the world as sacred and therefore value its particular features and not desecrate it. We should rightly use and

value those features, not as fetishes we value for their own sake, but as
what they truly are, as media of Divine Association, recognizable in
the One Divine.

                                        3.

MASTER DA FREE JOHN: The trouble with conventional religion is
that it has broken down the bridge to the Divine World. Conventional
religion talks a great deal about God, but it has no bridge to God, in the
form of either esoteric practices or an understanding of the world as a
sacred universe. In conventional religion the universe has been
emptied of its sacred significance as a bridge and as an expression of
Divine Communion. The Divine is therefore considered only in the
abstract. People are everywhere crying out for help from God, but
there is no Power in their cries because they have established no link
to the Divine. Without the link there is no Power. The medium of
connection, the actual connection, the bridge, makes the Power
possible, makes prayer and all sacred activity workable, makes such
activity effective and not merely imaginary.

     We must value all the links, all the media, of Divine Association.
Such valuation is the significance of the body-mind as "the temple of
God." It is not such a temple in and of itself, but when rightly related
to the Divine, the body-mind is a bridge, a form of Divine Association.
It is in this sense that it should be valued, not merely for its own sake,
as an egoic temple to oneself.

     Likewise, the entire world is a temple of Divine Association. All
temples are really summations or descriptions of the total cosmos.
They are empowered as the summary of the cosmos, as a perfect
bridge to the Divine. The Divine is perfectly apparent in Holy Places,
therefore, and may be contacted directly there through right kinds of
association. The body-mind is such a temple, but worship is not to be
reduced to self-possessed activities of indulging one's body-mind. Such
a view justifies Narcissistic immersion in oneself, inversion only.

     No, the total universe is a sacred manifestation, an incarnate
expression of the Divine. It is a perfect link to the Divine if we are
Awakened. Then, when Awakened, we see the magical significance of
the cosmos and of the present moment and no longer discount the
features of this world because we are in mortal fear. Rather, we use all
the features of this world as a bridge to God, as a medium of God-

"I THINK YOU SHOULD BE MORE EXPLICIT HERE IN STEP TWO."

Communion, as a Vision in fact of the Divine—not a vision in and of
itself but something that is transparent to God, and a medium
nonetheless, not something that is supposed to be discounted and
emptied of Divine Power.

This world is God Present. God is not merely behind the world
and elsewhere and up there and inside. God is Omnipresent, absolutely
Present, unqualifiedly Present. Not to see God in the terms of
manifest reality is to fail to Realize God. Therefore, we must awaken
to the magical nature of this world, see the Divine, and enjoy the link
or bridge to God that all our relations, the body-mind itself, and all the
media of this world represent, particularly all its outstanding features,
those unique magical entities, places, and substances that show
themselves to be of great significance in the course of spiritual
practice. These things, above all, must be valued in the ritual terms of
sacred activity.

To live such a sacred life, you must be free of all automatic asanas,
prejudices, and habitual ways of adapting the nervous system and
accumulating presumptions totally independent of clear thinking or
experience. You must free the body-mind, the nervous system, the
being altogether from the entire concoction of suffering that is just an
obstruction even to seeing what is before your eyes at this moment.
Therefore, apply the discipline of being unreservedly associated with
what is. Make that your occupation, instead of spending your lifetime
spewing out the logic of your own suffering and calling it knowledge.
Apply yourself to that discipline of unqualified association for a period
of time, and something remarkable about the nature of things is
bound to break through it.

This is what I did in college. I just gave myself up to that
discipline. It was very difficult, no doubt about it, but it is the only
option you have when you recognize that your life is nothing but
accumulated suffering. If life is nothing but a mortal cage and "when
you're dead, you're dead," then let that really be seen, and then the hell
with all of it! If mortality is all there is to life, the hell with the whole
machine! Who gives a damn! Why should you even suffer then?
Pleasurize yourself into oblivion! Kill yourself with pleasures! What
difference does anything make, if mortality and annihilation really are
what life and death are all about? But find out if that really is the way
it is!

To find out, however, you must apply yourself to another
discipline altogether than just presuming that that is the way it is.
Those who simply presume that this is the way it is have not applied

themselves to the difficult affair of existence with sufficient energy to really find out about life. They have just suffered in a bind, a box of ideas and presumptions, a certain logic of the nervous system, one particular asana or attitude. Such a state is of no value and cannot produce anything of significance. Therefore, really find out the way it is for yourself.

Having done that personally, it has not at all been my discovery that "this life is a mortal cage" and "when you're dead, you're dead." Not at all. But I have not come to this point of view merely by thinking in some predecided fashion or by wanting to believe something like that. I simply gave myself up to the Process of existence. I allowed its Revelation to take place. When you live in that sensitive disposition, the universe moves and breaks up, you move and break up, and What is Alive begins to show Itself.

Now if it had turned out that life is a mortal cage and when you're dead, you're dead, then I myself would have said the hell with it. But that is not what became obvious. Likewise, all of you must do the same thing. You must go through the same trial. I am not suggesting that you believe a certain bunch of propositions based on whatever authority you may want to presume exists in my case. We simply consider this together. And you must consider it to the point of understanding, practicing, associating yourself with the Real Process of existence, and seeing that revelation.

This Way is about finding the Real God, the Actual, Living, and Present, Revealed God, the God Who is Tangible, Obvious, not merely believed in, not merely thought about, but directly, obviously Revealed. And it is a Way of associating with That One in which you can participate with your entire being. The Way is about developing that capacity. If you are weak and afraid and in doubt, then obviously you are not very close to that capacity. But know that the actual development of the Way involves the transcendence of fear and weakness and doubt, not by working on fear and weakness and doubt or on other characteristics in yourself you feel you must somehow press out or cease to notice, but by discovering, through the submission of yourself to the Totality of things as they are, whatever That is, and entering into association with That in the Presence of Which fear and weakness and doubt simply do not arise.

If you are hungry and there is lunch, then hunger ceases to be your attitude. You simply eat. In the Presence of the literal Divine, in the moment of actual Communion with the Divine, fear and weakness and doubt do not come into play. The only reason they exist at all is that we are involved with ourselves and not with the Real God.

The fathers and prophets of Israel would wander around in the wilderness calling for God. Then suddenly they would have a direct Revelation of God. Wherever that Revelation took place, they would build a temple and settle the tribe there. That is how those early patriarchs became part of the ancient history of the Jews.

In the earliest days the Jews were not a single great tribe. Theirs was an accumulated culture whose alliances were based on the wanderings of individuals who would perform this exercise of surrender, calling upon God and waiting for the Revelation. They did not just arbitrarily believe in God. They kept praying, wandering, actively looking for God. Then, when the Revelation came, they would build a temple on that spot and settle. The individual patriarchs acknowledged by the Jews were originally principal figures in single tribal groups. Over time these various tribal groups began to become integrated with one another, and they collectively acknowledged all the individuals who had made this discovery. Eventually, as a single culture they came to certain opinions about the nature of God.

You must do the same thing. You do not know what anything is. You do not know what this entire existence is. You have no reason to presume any of the ideas you have, positive or negative. Thus, you have no option but to surrender yourself completely to Whatever It Is and wander and call upon It, Whatever It Is, until It Shows Itself. Then when It Shows Itself, you settle down and relate to It.

People should get out of their houses and out of the cities and go screaming into the countryside and do whatever the hell they must do just to maintain their attention in discovering the real nature of their existence. If they did this for a few years, instead of just carrying on as everybody is, there would be much positive change. Let all those politicians abandon their mansions. Let them take off their damn clothes and go out into the desert somewhere and find out what is happening. Everybody is upset, crazy, negative. Well, kick them out into the desert. Do not place them in positions of power. Let them go and find It as It is. This has been done in times past. This is exactly what ancient societies used to do with aberrated people. (Laughter.) Youth was supposed to be devoted to finding It out, rather than being idiotic and a threat to everyone.

But in our time you are not expected to find anything out. You are expected to believe life as it is given to you, you see. We were all naive in our childhood and willing to accept what parents told us, what everybody told us. But after a few years, you realize that life is rotten, that you are just an unhappy, confused son-of-a-bitch, and that everybody is suffering. The whole affair is insane!

Rather than settling down to an adolescent life of complaint, you should kick your ass out of the house and submit yourself to the bare facts of existence. Wander until you find It. This was an obvious course to me. There was no way I was just going to take a profession or a job and settle down to a middle-class life. To do so was insane from my point of view. I did not see any Happy people. I only saw people burdened with their lifetime occupation, their dumb ideas about existence, and their endless neurotic fretting. What is the purpose of organizing that into a career? What is the purpose of devoting yourself to a life of preserving that?

Since my own inheritance was lacking, since I really received no inheritance but suffering, there was no possibility, then, from my point of view, of just assuming the life of an ordinary householder, working and paying my dues to society. Since, in spiritual terms or real terms, I only received a negative inheritance, it was obvious to me that there was no option but to take up a life of wandering, of submission, in order to discover the Truth, whatever That was going to be. My intention was simply to discover Reality altogether as It Is, rather than presume It to be anything whatsoever.

You likewise must do this in some essential sense before you can actually take up the Way. You must become capable of real consideration, real observation, submission to the Reality of your total existence. You will take up the Way when that consideration has become conclusive, when the Revelation is in some sense basic enough to initiate the further process whereby the Revelation becomes total Enlightenment.

I have seen some people wandering in my lifetime, but they have a lot of baggage with them. They are just walking around, tasting everything and settling for all kinds of nonsense. I have not seen many real wanderers. I have not encountered many people who have actually confronted the Revelation of the Truth, because you must submit yourself to the extreme to Realize that Revelation.

A little bit of the Truth covered over by a lot of nonsense, you see, is as aberrating as no Truth at all. And I have seen people with a little Truth who were aberrated like everyone else. Your commitment to the Truth must become so profound that you are willing to become aberrated by that commitment. You must be willing to go mad with it. You must be willing to be destroyed by it. Your commitment must be complete.

At the beginning, of course, there is no guarantee of anything whatsoever. My engagement of this Way of life was totally open-ended. There were no guarantees. Thus, it is a dangerous proposition to submit yourself, not to that which you know, but to That Which you do not know at all. After a while, perhaps, you know something about It, and maybe some of Its features begin to brighten up, but you never know It. You are still always submitting yourself to What you do not know.

The trouble with people in general is that they are submitting themselves, consciously or unconsciously, to all kinds of things they think they know. The discipline is to submit yourself to What you do not know. Most of what people think they know is not knowledge at all. It is just presumption, imagination. Ultimately, you must be in an utterly mindless, uncontracted disposition of total submission to the Infinite.

In that disposition the Revelation can take all kinds of forms. It is Crazy Wisdom,[17] you see. All Wise Men are Crazy. You must be Crazy to surrender so hard that the room gets bright! If everything looks bright to you, you must be a little mad. But do not even look for brightness. Just surrender, because if you demand brightness, the Brightness may start glaring at you like a five-million-watt bulb and drive you insane. Merely to see brightness is not to be Enlightened. Schizophrenics see brightness and become terrified.

Do not look for all kinds of psychic stuff, therefore. Psychism can be deluding and maddening. Simply surrender the total body-mind into the Infinity that you do not know. Do not demand any kind of experience. Whatever experience occurs for you could very well drive you mad and disturb you unless you are simply in a surrendered

---

17. "Crazy Wisdom" is the spontaneous Humor, Freedom, Understanding, and total Liberation from all conventions (personal, social, psycho-physical, religious, spiritual, universal) that characterize the Free Adepts wherever and whenever they appear. The Realization at the root of Crazy Wisdom Teaching is expressed in such paradoxical formulas as "Nirvana (the Transcendental Reality) and samsara (conditional, manifest existence) are the same." Crazy Wisdom, to which Adepts may be Awakened upon full entry into highest Enlightenment, is thus unpremeditated, Free action, without regard for the egoic taboos and strictures of either conventional secular or conventionally sacred society. It is a Divine Manifestation, often temporary, for the sake of the Awakened Teaching-Instruction of others.

disposition. Enlightenment is not necessarily associated with all kinds of psychic phenomena. It is very likely that such things will develop, but it is not necessary that there be psychic phenomena, visions of light, or anything of the sort. There can be just utter surrender, an intuition of Bliss, and Freedom, tacit but Real nonetheless, and utterly Liberating.

Therefore, let existence take whatever form it is going to take. Do not demand that it take on some sort of extraordinary psychic form or any extraordinary form in the world. Simply surrender. The Revelation will take whatever form it is going to take in your case. And when it takes place, and when it is real, it will be obvious and also sufficient. Therefore, you should make no prejudgment about what form it is supposed to take. Simply put yourself in a position to observe all its forms.

Do not arbitrarily make the decision that you exist in an objective, independently existing, material world. You have no reason to believe such a thing. Conventionally you are associated with forms and others, but you need not assign independent existence to all of that. Your perceptions are all psychic in nature. They are developments of the mind and nervous system. They are not really associated with something independent of a process of psychic perception and cognition.

Do not be so quick, therefore, to presume that the world is of that objective kind. Submit as you are. Submit in human terms. To submit in human terms, you must submit in consciousness. You must submit psychically. You must surrender into existence as a psychic being, a conscious being, who is not associated with objective, independent events, but only with a mass of psychic states. That is the way it is in any case. You cannot make it any different. Surrender as that, therefore, and look for all the peculiar signs of the nature of things.

My experience is that it is utterly and directly confirmed that what we call the physical world is just a dimension of the psyche, a dimension of the world in which we exist psychically. The so-called physical or material universe is passing through changes according to psychic laws. All the physical laws ultimately coincide with psychic laws and with the whole domain of subtlety that cannot be differentiated from the mode of existence we call the psyche. You know that anything positive or negative can arise in the mind, but the same is true of this physical universe. It can seem to be dark and dismal and mortal. It can also seem to be totally different from that—bright and immortal and magical. It is not that one or the other of those perceptions is true. Both possibilities exist, and the one you perceive depends on your habit of association with existence. You command the karma of your destiny by virtue of your technique or habit of association with things.

You must become responsible for the attitude—mental, psychic, and emotional—whereby you relate to moment to moment existence. The place where we are thinking is the same place we see with our open eyes. The changes of mind are changes of the same universe we see with open eyes. It is simply that we apparently cognize these mental phenomena in a different dimension from this physical one. We do not see the coincidence between them, and so we are stuck with a mind that seems to be inside and separate from the world. We must ultimately recognize that there is no dividing line between the psyche and the body and the world. They are an infinite plastic. They are one Process. And when the psyche and the world begin to coincide and the barrier breaks down, then we begin to become Happy, because the Energy, the Being, That Is Inherent in the universe is then allowed to Move freely and to Saturate our existence.

You can see through the mind and the physical world at the same time. There is no obstruction between oneself and God. There is no self between oneself and God. We reside simply in the Seat of Being. And we are totally capable of being Happy simply to Radiantly Exist. It is just that we have all kinds of habits of mind that involve us in formalities, patterns, adventures, and limitations. So we cease to recognize things and we forget our Position, which is simply the Domain of Infinitely Radiant Being.

We will not achieve That Condition in time. We are already resident in That Condition. If you will recognize all these psycho-physical phenomena, then it becomes obvious that you are in that Position. You become Happy again. The body-mind begins to Shine. It begins to become blissful, transparent, and unnecessary. Its being unnecessary does not mean that you make the decision to dissociate from it. Paradoxically, its being unnecessary makes it possible that it continue, because it is not binding. It is not caused.

In our suffering and despair it seems that it would be nice to die and be taken out of here into some better place. But the discipline of our existence is to Realize the Brightness in this incident. Only on that basis, paradoxically, are we released from it. Thus, we are obliged by the very Law of our existence to transcend the limitations that are themselves only presumptions and that seem to exist by virtue of birth. We must become Happy and Outshine this body-mind, Outshine this world, Outshine all the doctrines of this world.

Ultimately, then, the secret is not to become psychic and peer through the hole in your forehead to the other side. It is rather to recognize this world totally, become free of all of its limits, outbreathe it, outlove it, outlive it. Achieve such Force through submission to God that the God-Force overcomes the world.

In our natural or usual condition there seems to be a consciousness, simply, and there seem to be processes of cognition and perception, and there seem to be forms of all kinds. But in the Enlightened Disposition of total Communion with the Reality That is the Condition of all of those features of our existence, they all become transparent. They have no significance or limiting existence. Everything is tacitly recognizable, transparent. There is no self. There is no mind. There is no perception. There are no forms. There are no relations. There is no world. There are no limits. There is no past, no future, no place. There is simply the Radiant Being, and it is to This that we must resort ultimately. It is This to which we submit all forms, all states, every sense of independent existence, to the extreme, to the point of Ecstasy, to the point of Translation.

In the seventh stage of life such Translation has already taken place. It seems to others, perhaps, that the individual is still current in the ordinary fashion. But from the point of view of Realization there is already no self, no mind, no body, no world, no time or space. Everything is recognizable, Shined through. In the Bhava[18] of that recognition there is no sense of being a self behind anything or in any place. There is no thinking, no psychic or mental form, no bodily perception, no otherness, nothing concretely arising. There is only Radiant Transcendental Being.

18. Master Da Free John here refers to Bhava Samadhi, one of the two forms of radical Samadhi pertaining to the seventh stage of life. The transition to the seventh stage of life, sometimes called "open eyes," is Sahaj Samadhi, the natural disposition of Identification with the Transcendental Reality *and* moment to moment recognition of phenomena as non-binding modifications of that Reality. Bhava Samadhi is the ultimate form of God-Consciousness. It is the natural "Mood of Ecstasy" in which there is Divine Inherence without any noticing of arising conditions. In that case, at death there is the complete dissolution or Translation of the individual into the Divine Being.

CHAPTER 14

THE EXOTERIC TABOOS
ARE IN NATURE

an essay and talk by Da Free John
December 31, 1980

MASTER DA FREE JOHN: I have an essay to read and discuss, titled "The Exoteric Taboos Are in Nature."

We have talked about how the Semitic tradition maintains certain cultural taboos against the evolutionary development of human consciousness and against casual entrance into the domain of esotericism, which only the initiates, or those in the inner temple, may enter. In many other traditions as well taboos exist against casual access to esoteric knowledge. This essay argues that structures in Nature itself are constructed in such a fashion that in effect they act as taboos against evolutionary development.

Evolutionary development is possible in Nature and in the human frame, but it occurs only under certain conditions, just as entrance into the esoteric frame of a sacred culture requires a certain maturity and the passing of certain tests. Likewise, in Nature itself exist structural categories that prevent casual association with higher phenomenal awareness. This preventive structure is the subject of this essay.

The Exoteric Taboos Are in Nature

an essay by Da Free John
December 31, 1980

There is, in fact or in effect, a taboo structure in the cellular, molecular, and atomic regions of our psycho-physical state. Our conventional knowledge, psychology, and social mores, and our states of mind, emotion, desire, and body are controlled by mechanical barriers, or unfathomable paradoxes of structure and force, that keep us conscious in the "exoteric," subhuman, or conventionally human mode. It is the seemingly "given" or impenetrable force of such mechanisms that prevents people from transcending the idiot norms and unillumined models of conventional humanity. Thus, human beings can "go beyond" only by confronting, understanding, and intuitively transcending the deep mechanics of our nominal or conventional psycho-physical condition. Persuasive argument and clear thinking are not enough.

Until the "outer" or cellular, molecular, and atomic mechanics of the Great Paradox of Nature are penetrated by higher understanding and the self-transcending gesture of being, human individuals are either bound to repetitive and superficial conventions (and their attendant illusions and confusions) or else they animate their motive toward expansive freedom merely in exercises toward more exotic fulfillments of the "exoteric" possibilities of money, food, and sex—or more energized concentrations of the "exoteric" or gross organism.

I struggled with people for years to help them break through the limits of conventional bondage and conventional aspiration. And the Way I communicated to them is precisely the Way of "going beyond" the limits of conventional destiny.

But there is a higher Way that develops spontaneously when the process of "going beyond" the "hedge of Narcissus," or the ring of paradoxical mechanics that enclose or define the contracted self-idea, has become mature to the point of Realization of the Identity that transcends all possibilities. In the seventh stage of life, which is beyond even the conventions of egoic esotericism, the ultimate esotericism is spontaneously activated. In that disposition, the cellular, molecular, and atomic paradoxes that act as an effective barrier to Wisdom, or knowledge and experience that directly relate to the native inherence of phenomena in the Transcendental Radiance of Divine Being, are inherently transcended. Such transcendence is native to that seventh stage disposition, because the conventional identification of being with the cellular, molecular, and atomic machine of the body-mind-self has been replaced with prior Identification with Infinitely Radiant Transcendental Being. Thus, existence is not conceived and perceived from the cellular, molecular, or atomic point of view, looking back at the Ultimate Condition through the blind of paradoxes or structural limits. Instead, the total field of Nature, or the psycho-physical universe of conventional selves, is viewed from the Transcendental or All-Pervading "Position" which is the Free Matrix of all events.

Physicists conceive of an original state of the physical (or atomic, molecular, and cellular) universe just prior to the "Big Bang" that initiated the present Great Cycle of universal manifestation. In that original state, all of the matter that now composes the total physical universe and all manifest beings was reduced to the size of the head of a pin. After the "Big Bang," consequent beings consider "Reality" from the point of view of extended matter, or the effected structures of manifestation. The ultimate esoteric process of existence is to view all manifest existence in an atomic state, as a potential of paradoxical possibilities, but from the "point of view" of that Condition wherein the "pinhead" of the original concentration of all manifesting forces was established. Wisdom is, therefore, to see and understand phenomena from the "point of view" of God, or the Transcendental Being, rather than from the conventional point of view of the already manifest cellular, molecular, or atomic self.

Ordinary people, self-bound, explore the possibilities of the cellular dimension of the manifest being in the exoteric plane of money, food, and sex. They do so in fear, and so they establish many limiting psychological and social conventions to protect themselves from the effects of their own self-existence and self-exploitation.

Uncommon people, more self-expansive in their will, explore the possibilities of the molecular dimension of the manifest being, in the conventionally esoteric (or fifth stage) plane of mystical psychism and either the psychic (and magical) or intellectual (and technological) manipulation of cellular matter characteristic of beings in the fourth and third stages of life.

Those who go beyond the conventions of the cellular and molecular mechanics that define conventional self-existence intuitively Realize the Living Identity that is prior even to the atomic identity or self-essence of individual existence discovered in the sixth stage of life.

They abide in the Plane of that Identity, recognizing all levels of events, all permutations of attention, as paradoxical and uncaused or spontaneous modifications of Radiant Transcendental Being. In their case, there is an explosion of being in the Infinite Field of Radiant Existence, wherein consciousness is associated with the original Matrix of all possibility prior even to atomic identification with conditional states in manifestation.

MASTER DA FREE JOHN: There are several points in this essay on which I should comment.

The mechanics of the so-called physical universe or the material world are described here in terms of three basic dimensions or aspects of appearance—cellular, molecular, and atomic. These are common terms used in the domain of contemporary physics. They describe three fundamental dimensions of physical expression. The physical universe may be viewed in terms of just one of these dimensions, or it may be conceived as a play of all three dimensions, somehow mysteriously related to one another. The language of physics, when it comes down to describing the nature of reality, tends to associate with one or the other of these three dimensions of possible description.

When the human being, or rather the model of Man, is discussed in the culture of contemporary science, the discussion tends to focus on the cellular level. It is presumed on the basis of the studies of physics that the human individual is composed of molecular and atomic material, but it is no longer thought that we are human at the molecular and atomic level. That level of our existence is mere "matter." Our individuality, our conscious existence, tends to be conceived relative only to the cellular or biological machine. The molecular level of our existence is that complex dimension of phenomena associated with the DNA structuring that is responsible for our appearance in the material realm.

All of Nature can be conceived as a cellular machine at the elemental level that corresponds to cellular existence in the human form. Or it can be conceived as a great molecular process of complex molecules made of elementary atomic structures. Or, again, it can be conceived in atomic terms as a kind of electronic field in which, ultimately, even the total physical universe we conceive of relative to the original "Big Bang" that produced this vast complex of galaxies may be viewed as a system of atoms, or even as just one atom.

The conventional descriptions of science tend to treat our human existence as basically a biophysical or biochemical process. Thus, in that analysis all our features are reduced to a biochemical, biophysical description. But the universe as a totality is a living process, even at the molecular level and the atomic level. It is just that there are prejudices, based on conventions of understanding human existence, that make it impossible for contemporary science, at any rate, to conceive of our existence with consciousness at the level of molecular existence or atomic existence or even beyond those.

Therefore, the models of Man that are proposed by contemporary science tend to be mortal models based on the notion of a cellular or biophysical machine in which consciousness itself originates only as a result of biochemical or material processes. And this description of Man corresponds to the common or conventional understanding human individuals have of themselves in the unillumined or unevolved state of consciousness.

Therefore, in terms of its model of Man to date, contemporary science is basically a professionalized extension or rigorous application of the conventional understanding of Man. And until human individuals begin to develop the higher exercise of being, founded on real understanding and free yielding of self, they tend to develop their adventure of existence sheerly on the basis of this cellular or biophysical conception of their existence. Thus, in general, people who have not developed beyond the third stage of life conceive of their existence in conventional terms—which means in biophysical or cellular terms—as mortal machines. They may be associated with secular or sacred presumptions about their existence, but those presumptions are exoteric in either case.

Such a lower-adapted human life may become a highly degraded, disoriented state, or at best it may achieve a kind of conventional harmony as a cellular process. People in such a disposition tend to be defined and limited in their consciousness through association with the exoteric realm of phenomena, which I have described in brief as the domain of money, food, and sex. People who are not in the least inclined toward transcendence of conventional existence maintain their attention in the realm of money, food, and sex—the ordinary, lower-adapted dimension of cellular life—and they construct their destiny via association with cultural taboos that apply brakes to what individuals can do in general and to what they can do to one another. It is a system of taboos for maintaining existence at the level of the cellular ring of self-definition.

The taboo structure expressed in cultural terms at the cellular level of life corresponds to the third stage and below. A somewhat more evolved dimension of self-application may appear at the conventional level of the fourth stage of life (not the fourth stage as we understand it in high philosophical terms). The conventional, fourth stage self-application is in general an extension of the third stage point of view, in which the magic of psychism is used to manipulate cellular existence and is not oriented toward higher evolutionary realization.

Likewise, science, as technology and as intellectual knowledge about the world in cellular terms, manipulates the world for very much the same purposes that are served in conventional magic. Those who achieve a level of understanding, though still from the egoic or self-bound point of view, become liberated in their will toward a more expansive possibility of realization. They enter into the conventional realm of esotericism, which is also culturally presented in traditional systems that have both an exoteric and an esoteric domain.

Thus, in the fifth stage of life, we see the development of capacities that in general are associated with notions of Divine Realization but that are really only evolutionary capabilities. They involve the passage of attention out of the strict confinement to the cellular or biophysical conception of our existence and, based on a certain level of understanding, they pass into the next level of our existence, which is molecular in nature and therefore to some degree relates to the whole process of atomic forces.

The sixth stage of life is that level of intuition wherein one enters into the most essential or atomic level of the being. By means of the process of the sixth stage, the spiritual practitioner enters, intuitively, not into the molecular structures of expanded subtlety but into the essential, atomic centrality, or the point of the arising of being in manifest terms.

The seventh stage of life, however, which represents the ultimate esotericism, involves the transcendence of the ego-principle or the self-defined state in which we are defined by cellular, molecular, or atomic forces. Cellular, molecular, and atomic forces tend to define our sense of existence in one form or another. Therefore, even the evolution of Man is an egoic play within those structures, involving passage from one ring or level of subtleness to the next, involving an expansion of self but not ultimate transcendence of self and Realization of the Condition or Matrix of existence in ultimate terms.

The seventh stage of life represents the ultimate esotericism of which beings are capable. It involves utter self-transcendence or transcendence of the limiting force, the paradoxes, or the rings of manifestation or levels of manifest energy. It involves transcendence to the perfect degree so that the entire force of manifestation at every level becomes recognizable from the point of view of ultimate Self-Identification rather than conventional self-identification at any level of manifestation. In this essay, then, I am relating the stages of life, including the disposition of the seventh stage, to the conventional structures of reality as conceived from the point of view of physics as well as from the point of view of the forms of human consciousness.

Entrance into these subtler or broader dimensions of existence in the evolutionary scale of manifestation, passing from cellular to molecular and then to atomic realization of the state of the self, generates the uncommon phenomena regarded to be supernatural or miraculous because they do not seem to have anything to do with the laws of Nature. What they in fact have nothing to do with are the laws of Nature as conceived from a lesser point of view. In fact, the arising of siddhis or psychic powers and extraordinary phenomena is simply a matter of the transition of attention through the various rings or limits of manifest Reality. In each dimension there is a uniform expansiveness that includes kinds of phenomena not presumed at any previous level. Therefore, the passage of attention, or the awakening of the consciousness of the being, from the cellular mortality of this biophysical machine into the molecular domain develops more advanced evolutionary capacities of mind simply by virtue of the entrance of consciousness into another actual dimension of physical existence.

These evolutionary capacities and experiences, then, are not really miraculous phenomena or, in other words, phenomena that have nothing to do with the laws of Nature. They are phenomena associated with dimensions of Nature that are not presumed to exist from the cellular, mechanical, material point of view.

Unfortunately, contemporary science still persists in considering Man in terms of this most lowly based, material, cellular model of existence. In searching for the ultimate descriptive model of human existence in those terms, contemporary science is forming a negative philosophical work. It is confining human consciousness to its lowest common denominator. But there are branches of science—in particular, or most outstanding perhaps, the domain of physics—wherein the

nature of matter is being contemplated and wherein a new understanding of the nature of the universe itself is arising. And it is only a
matter of time until the conventions of science begin to consider Man
in the same light that the universe is now being considered. At
present, however, the behavioral sciences and other descriptive
sciences related to Man are not themselves functioning on the same
plane on which are operating the advanced physical sciences that
examine the universe.

DEVOTEE: Master, it is paradoxical that scientists say we are all made
of "star stuff," and yet they do not really carry that statement to its
fullest implication.

MASTER DA FREE JOHN: Yes, in a TV program we were watching
yesterday, a well-known scientist mentioned that in the moment
before the entire physical universe began to develop through the "Big
Bang," all the material out of which everything whatsoever is made,
that is, everything—the entire universe, all the galaxies, all of that
material—was the size of the head of a pin. It is utterly inconceivable
how all that material could have existed in such a condensed state. Can
you imagine taking even just everything in this room out into the yard
and trying to pound it down to something the size of a pinhead? It is
impossible. The forces necessary to reduce matter of such mass to that
highly energized but almost infinitesimal size are not conceivable.

DEVOTEE: Is it true?

MASTER DA FREE JOHN: Not in reality. However, all the available
physical data point to just such a fact. And the universe may be
conceived as a cyclic process in which everything expands seemingly
out of nothing into infinite expressions of all kinds, then eventually
the whole affair collapses on itself again in a kind of gravitational
implosion, and then the cycle begins again. The ancient Hindu
cosmology contains this very description and has very detailed, even
mathematical descriptions of these cycles and the periods within it, the
periods of change, the cycles on Earth, cycles relative to planetary
bodies and the sun, and so forth.

    These very technical, ancient descriptions are based on the
intuitive observation of the nature of the manifest universe. Such
observation was achieved through rigorous application of the partici-

patory sacred ordeal by geniuses of the ancient Way. Now science, using another method—the analytical method of knowing about things independent of participatory self-sacrifice—is arriving at the same conclusions. Ultimately, the two will come together: The sacred Way and the secular way will in the end be talking about the same thing.

There are many dimensions to the sacred Way. There are also many exoteric traditions, fashioned by ordinary people, that will pass by the board as time goes on. But the fundamental and profound aspects of the Great Tradition,[1] which has had its representatives all over the Earth since ancient times, will eventually be found to represent a description of the universe that corresponds to that which is now being developed and will ultimately be developed by the sciences. Necessarily, then, as time goes on, a Way of life quite different from the present cellular politics of conventional humanity will become the norm.

DEVOTEE: Master, would you say that the most advanced form of physical science at the present time, speaking from the secular point of view, is physics?

MASTER DA FREE JOHN: Among the sciences physics seems to be the most developed, but all the sciences have the potential to develop to a highly advanced form. It is just that the other sciences, say, for instance, the sciences that describe Man and his psychology, still base themselves on archaic, materialistic notions of human beings as cellular, mortal machines. These sciences do not understand that human existence participates by its very nature in the other dimensions of Reality and that our consciousness and the ultimate processes of which we are capable involve living participation in these other dimensions.

We enjoy a potential for conscious existence in the molecular and atomic dimensions of the universe and likewise in the Transcendental Dimension that is the Matrix of the universe. The traditions of the sacred Way verify and point to this fact and generate all kinds of propositions in relation to it. But science in its present mode is not generally disposed to acknowledge the verity of those principles because scientists have not yet proven them through the mechanism

1. For an explanation of the term "Great Tradition," see the General Introduction, p. 30.

of science itself. They do not want to presume points of view arbitrarily. And that is good. They should rigorously apply their own method.

However, in the meantime they are acquiring power and increasingly dominating human consciousness through certain models of Man that are unillumined, incomplete descriptions based on partial study and a product of the adolescence of science itself. This is the problem with science, not that it has not yet proved these evolutionary and transcendental principles, but that it is gaining power prior to its own maturity, which causes it to arbitrarily cancel out the culture of the sacred Way and the propositions that must be realized by human beings in order for them to be Happy and to realize a full existence, free of fear.

DEVOTEE: Master, your earlier comment suggests that the scientist's point about the universe fitting on the head of a pin is spiritually untenable.

MASTER DA FREE JOHN: From the scientist's point of view, yes. He is not qualified to make such advanced judgments based on the data he acknowledges. He claims that everything was originally an undifferentiated substance the size of the head of a pin, but that now we are all somehow independent cellular blobs, mortal little molecular machines that have no Transcendental Consciousness, but only have the kind of consciousness that can allow the development of conventional science through the application of the intellect.

He further asserts that we have no hope of existing beyond death or of entering presently into active existence in more subtle or invisible dimensions. Yet, if everything was originally one substance the size of the head of a pin and only later became elaborated as all of this complexity, it should be obvious that all of this is somehow connected, that there is necessarily a great Connecting Principle, not merely all this individuation and mortality. In other words, there is room for an altogether different conception about the nature of things. But what the scientist dogmatizes about at present is that such an alternative conception is utterly improbable or impossible. He is closed-minded and unwilling to entertain this possibility. He assigns great things to the universe and nothing to Man.

DEVOTEE: Master, how does this relate to the Hindu idea of the blue bindu[2] as the seed of all manifestation?

MASTER DA FREE JOHN: That idea is a mystical conception, but it does relate to the notion that all manifest forms and forces are ultimately congealed in a point without dimension. It is possible to achieve a state of consciousness wherein one can look into all possibility as into a hole at the end of an egg and thus, by the movement of attention, conceive of all possibilities. At present, we exist in the exploded state of this bindu and only see certain parts of it, depending on our state of consciousness. Commonly, people see only the so-called material dimension of that explosion, whereas there are many other dimensions to be perceived. From the Enlightened point of view one sees the manifestation of phenomena at the point of origination, at the level of bindu rather than from the extended point of view looking back. Wisdom is inherent, therefore, in the truly Enlightened stage when the self that arises within the exploded bindu of manifest Reality is transcended in ultimate Identification with the Divine.

Some people do not think of Man from the point of view of the conventional model. They tend to popularize a model of Man based on the analyses of matter or the physical universe advanced in contemporary physics. Therefore, you could consult their works and also the specialized literature of physics itself to appreciate how this essay we are considering relates to a rather comprehensive discipline or understanding of the universe. Ultimately, however, we must be able to apply this same understanding that we and today's physicists are gaining in the study of the universe to the study of Man, because Man is just a feature of the total scheme and inheres in all the planes in which the physical universe also inheres.

Because Man exists in all those dimensions, we have the capacity for unusual phenomenal states of consciousness, which are either discounted as mere nonsense by the scientific understanding or are conceived of in terms of the cellular, lower-based model of human

2. The Sanskrit word *bindu* means literally "drop." The blue bindu referred to is a visionary phenomenon associated with the *ajna cakra* ("command center"), the psycho-physical center that is located in the head, midway between the eyebrows. The blue bindu is an experiential expression of the zero-dimensional Force or Potency that is the Matrix of all creation, material and immaterial. This bindu corresponds to what Master Da Free John describes as the "white star or flash of light" at the center of the Cosmic Mandala, the total structure of psycho-physical existence. In order to enter the God-Realized or Enlightened Disposition, this bindu must be pierced, that is, the experience associated with it must be transcended.

beings. Conventional scientists do not introduce a dimensional under-standing of human existence, and physicists in general do not tend to think in terms of a dimensional physical universe. The cosmologies tend to be cellular and molecular, in other words only material or basically elemental cosmologies that express the cellular view of Man. Thus, conventional physicists are stuck in material conceptions of the stars and ideas such as the "Big Bang" as the origin of physical events. They do not conceive of the subtler and Transcendental dimensions in which those processes are taking place.

Likewise, contemporary science does not tend to conceive of Man in terms of dimensional existence, but rather thinks of Man only in terms of the conventions of cellular life, the biophysical, biochemical, psycho-physical, mortal organism that lives for a while and then is snuffed out. Conventional scientists have great difficulty conceiving of the possibility of human survival after death. They simply lack a model that can account for this eventuality. Thus, they doggedly confine themselves to an interpretation of Man in which existence beyond death is an impossibility.

The same tendency causes them to think that more expanded kinds of conscious processes are nonsense. Thus, everything from after-life experiences to ESP, witches and ghosts, and all the other supernormal phenomena tends to be thrown into the same bag of primitive nonsense that has no reality. Contemporary science is stuck with primitive models of Man and the universe. Ultimately, the paradoxes and forms of dimensional understanding that are currently being developed in the advanced sciences will have to be applied to Man as well. This application will account for all the unusual kinds of phenomena that are associated with evolutionary development, psychism, ESP, survival of death, and the like.

The extraordinary phenomena that are now associated with just a few uncommon people belong to the domain in which we inhere that is subtler than the mere cellular, material, or elemental level of our existence. When mind enters into the field of manifest existence that is subtler than the cellular one, it begins to function in extraordinary ways. Suddenly, consciousness begins to become associ-ated with the ability to see past and future, to see places without being there physically, and so on. Thus, unless there is a model for the dimensional understanding of human existence, such phenomena must be discounted as nonsense, or else some interpretation must be superimposed on them that confines the being to the mortal model.

Humanity is still suffering from archaic ideas and ordinary presumptions that were first expressed to some degree in the conventions of exoteric religion and of ordinary life, and are now being systematically applied as descriptive models in a yet adolescent science.

DEVOTEE: Master, science has pressed on in its investigation of the cellular level without any spiritual guidelines or laws. Scientists have just jumped in and discovered all kinds of things. I was thinking that science could tap into the molecular level without any spiritual understanding and cause all kinds of difficulties.

MASTER DA FREE JOHN: Science has achieved considerable power at the cellular, elemental level. However, because human beings do not possess Wisdom, science tends to represent a destructive influence. And, yes, as soon as scientists begin to gain power in subtler dimensions, without subtler or radical Transcendental Consciousness, they have an even greater potential for disturbance.

Hopefully, however, as science becomes more sophisticated, the consciousness of humanity will also begin to change. It will be transformed by the evolution of the information and presumptions common among people. It would be good if this could begin to happen now. Instead, scientism is acting as an arm of conventional illusions and the primitive cellular consciousness of Man. It is not serving an Enlightened consciousness. Although it is serving an advanced technological advantage over the elemental world, there must be a corresponding growth in consciousness. This can only come through the generation of more advanced models of understanding of the nature of things and a more mature cultural application of that understanding, both at the secular level and at the level of sacred community and the sacred ordeal of individual life.

CHAPTER 15

IS CONSCIOUSNESS EXHIBITED BY FLOWERS AND BEES? —BEYOND THE MECHANISTIC MODEL OF NATURE

a talk by Da Free John
January 26, 1983

MASTER DA FREE JOHN: I had an amusing idea. I was thinking that right here in the natural world, which is presumed by the materialists to be just a material domain of elements changing and evolving in various forms, many curious things happen. One thing that occurred to me to notice is the case between flowers and bees.

You see, the bees are attracted to certain colors and patterns in flowers. In fact, flowers develop specific colors and patterns on their petals that function as pathways to guide bees and other insects into their center, so that the flowers can reproduce. The bees see these colors and are attracted to them. Certain insects are attracted to certain colors, other insects are attracted to other colors, in some flowers certain colors and patterns do not appear, and certain insects will not go to flowers with a certain color and pattern, and so forth.

As an interesting argument against the materialists, it is at least amusing to consider that the flowers, which, we presume, do not see, become involved in creating appearances for the sake of beings that do see. If flowers do not see, how do they take into account the process of seeing in creatures other than themselves and develop visibility in response? How does something that cannot see create visibility if it does not see? I made a little note about this:

The bee is attracted to the colors of the flower. The bee is attracted through seeing. The flower evolves colors and patterns to attract the bee. The import of these colors and patterns is that they ought to be seen. Then by whom or what or by what means does the flower see itself and know its colors? It must be that the processes of Nature are associated with consciousness and means of perception which are not taken into account by the materialists. If the flower does not see and know, then how does it consider and adapt to the bee's sense of color or work with color as visibility?

How does this inert organ evolve over time to be seen? How does it know it is seen? The result of the flower's being seen is that the bee lands on it. The flower may have some tactile response to that, but how does it become involved with being seen? How does it know what seeing is? How does it make something for the purpose of being seen if it itself does not see?

How could all of this possibly occur within the framework of the material model of the universe concocted by materialistic scientists? That which is the case in Nature must be something greater than the model of the materialists. That which is the case in Nature must be something like capacities associated with consciousness, perception, and cognition even in the case of organisms and creatures that apparently do not have these senses.

DEVOTEE: The materialists' argument is that all of this occurs purely by chance, and that there are billions of ways that flowers could have developed. Only the one that happened by sheer chance to be red lived, and all the other flowers were not pollinated and died.

MASTER DA FREE JOHN: But how did that one get to be red? How did it get to be seen?

DEVOTEE: Just by chance. It had no intention to be red.

MASTER DA FREE JOHN: Yes, it may have been red by chance, but how did it get to be seen by chance? How did it enter into the realm of being seen?

DEVOTEE: I don't know.

MASTER DA FREE JOHN: (Laughter.) Well, this is what the materialists are supposed to be arguing against. How does the flower enter into the realm of being seen to begin with, and then how does it function further, in terms of being seen, if it itself does not see?

DEVOTEE: "This Maya[1] is great!"

MASTER DA FREE JOHN: And if it is originally without difference, how does organic Nature produce individuated form? How does it enter into the domain of form if it does not have the capacity to stand outside form and to regulate or know itself? There are remarkable examples all over the natural world of cooperation between different species, between flowers and insects, and between species of insects working with other species of insects, and certain fish associated with other fish.

There are all kinds of helping relations in Nature that are not just the result of chance meetings that happen to be working out right. The various creatures actually have very discrete organic features that make it possible for them to cooperate with one another. If they did not cooperate, neither would survive. This fact expresses a kind of relationship between these apparent organisms in Nature that requires much more of what we might call awareness than the material model provides.

In fact, it is obvious to me that Nature is made of Consciousness. It is made of Conscious Force. All of this apparently inert matter is Conscious Energy. It appears to be objective to us because we are already objectified, discrete entities, functioning in relation to these forms. But if we were to transcend ourselves and enter into the Source

1. *Maya* is a classical Sanskrit term that literally means "she who measures" but is used currently and in traditional Hindu philosophy to convey the sense of "trick, deceit, fraud, or illusion." The deluding force of the Creative Power of manifestation.

of our own existence, we would discover that all of this objective, material, solid Nature is Conscious Energy.

It is even admitted by the schools of contemporary science that Nature is made of Energy. All I am saying beyond that admission is that Energy is Consciousness. The whole world is pervaded by Consciousness and by Energy, and everything is but a play on Conscious Energy, or Shakti.[2] Nature is associated with Consciousness everywhere. Even though they are not ultimate, all the forms evolving in Nature are nonetheless developments of Consciousness, and the overriding function of Consciousness can be seen in these bizarre and wonderful organizations of life, such as the simple relationship between flowers and insects, wherein flowers, even though they are apparently without eyes, develop the capacity to be seen and exploit being seen for the sake of their own survival and the survival of other creatures as well. And those other creatures that do have sight—from what did they develop sight? From no sight? How did they even get the impulse?

In other words, the ultimate features of existence are being manifested mysteriously by limited forms of manifest being. Therefore, everything in Nature is an expression of both Energy and Consciousness. Everything in Nature is, mysteriously, completely known somehow. Every flower that grows arises within an infinite Domain of Consciousness and Energy, which is full of Wisdom, bizarre and marvelous, and which makes it possible for all kinds of cooperative organisms to appear and for beings such as ourselves to arise. Even though as mere human beings we are not ultimate beings, except in the case of Enlightened Realization of the Absolute Condition, nonetheless what we are is a magnification of free Energy and Consciousness. We therefore bear all the features and all the qualities of That in Which we ultimately arise. Thus, we are conscious. We can perceive. We can think. We not only perceive but we are perceptible in every sense. We not only see but we are visible, we are seen. We not only feel, we are touchable, tangible. We can smell and taste, but we can also be smelled and tasted.

Now, all of that, you see, has nothing to do with chance. There is the whole affair of randomness and casual meetings that produce temporary changes whereby some creatures may survive and some

2. The Sanskrit term *shakti* means literally "power." It denotes the feminine or Power aspect of the Ultimate Reality; it is the Force of Transcendental Consciousness, the Energy of manifestation.

may not. There is a kind of evolutionary game of chance going on in Nature—that is true enough. There is no reason to deny notions of evolution absolutely, although many limited conceptions are associated with the philosophy of evolution. But the material model does not provide us with the right understanding of the context in which all of this activity is now occurring, always has been occurring, and always will occur.

Apart from their own apparent, limited condition, the flowers exhibit the influence of Consciousness, of a capacity for perception and knowing that is beyond their apparent organic capabilities. Otherwise, how could the flower respond to its visibility to the bee and magnify its visibility? Somehow or other the function of Consciousness, the Wisdom inherent in Energy Itself, is making this happen. We cannot ultimately account for this phenomenon until we enter into the stage of true Enlightenment, or at least until we become highly evolved and are able to see things quite differently than the left-brained materialists. But it is still obvious to us in our ordinary, gross, egoic state, or at least it makes us wonder to observe how things are working out in Nature and to notice that these processes are far more profound than the material models of chance organization suggest.

Why is there something rather than nothing? How could there be anything at all? Not just how does a flower appear the way it does—how is there anything? Why is there anything? How can anything be? I mean, how could something come to be by chance if there is nothing to begin with? How can there be anything like chance to begin with? Why is there anything? How can there be something rather than nothing? Why should there be something if all there is is mechanical chance in Nature? Why should there be Nature to begin with? You cannot have nothing to begin with and then have the existence of something be based on chance. The existence of something rather than nothing is the expression of a Mystery that goes far beyond mechanical probability. Mechanical probability is only a concept that arises after many, many other things have appeared. And it is really just an argument that very mortal, poor, suffering little characters create, not only to account for everything but to feel that they have power over things through knowledge.

The motive of materialism is the motive of power, the motive of knowledge. The motive behind the motive to know is the motive toward power or control over what one can get to know. The materialist model is an expression of the lowest kind of orientation toward knowledge of which human beings are capable, which is to get something named and to achieve control over it. You cannot have control over everything if there is a big God out there or some sort of sublime Wisdom pervading everything. You cannot acquire control over That. The only way you acquire control, then, is to say that this is just inert stuff moving mechanically and by chance. Then when you find out its mechanics, you can get power over it and you can control it, you see. You do not have to yield yourself. You do not have to give yourself up.

DEVOTEE: Master, it seems that the same rule could also apply to the materialist version of death: "When you're dead, you're dead." And yet, it has been shown that nothing can really be destroyed physically.

MASTER DA FREE JOHN: Everything that is apparent, everything that is substantial—in other words, anything we could call matter—is changeable. Its present form can be destroyed, but because matter is energy, you cannot destroy anything. You can only transform everything. Everything that you are can only be transformed. It cannot be destroyed. This body is transformed at death into its elements. What you are at this level obviously can be destroyed, in the sense that it will no longer be you as an individual. But you are not reducible only to that material part. There are subtle material aspects to your self, and then there are most subtle aspects that are also part of you but that you could not even call material. Then there are supermaterial aspects to your self, and then there is the Transcendental Condition that you are ultimately. Therefore, what you are is not destructible. Many features of what you seem to be are changeable and can be destroyed in the sense that you can cease to be them as an individual, but you yourself cannot ultimately be destroyed. You yourself are That Which is Appearing as everything and is Indestructible.

Thus, you do survive death. In other words, you are, as an entity, subtler than this gross body. When it drops and is reduced to the elements, you still continue in a subtler form, partially but subtly material, and you may even return to a gross physical state at some point. But even though that is true, it is not conducive to ultimate Happiness. All that means is that you can continue to be transformed and troubled by conditional existence, even though you die.

The Great Truth is that you transcend all these forms—not that you merely exist separate from them, but that their arising does not bind you in any sense and that you are That out of Which everything is made and that you are eternally Free even in the context of manifestation. Being That out of Which everything is made, you can magnify your Realization of That to the point of Outshining all of Nature.

This is the Great Truth. Survival of death and reincarnation are only secondary truths in the mechanics of the cosmos. By simply standing as That, recognizing all, you become present as the Divine Player, but you also ultimately Outshine conditional existence. In other words, you do not merely possibly migrate to higher planes of existence, but you transcend the cosmic domain itself, the play of Nature itself, in all its planes, high and low. This is the Truth, and this Truth is Realized only in the seventh stage of life, although it may be thought about and in some sense intuitively appreciated by individuals in an earlier stage of life.

In some portion of your mind, you do not know that you survive death and that there are invisible planes to which you might migrate. You are simply fixed in or confined to the doctrines and dogmas of this world of gross egos who have not penetrated the Mystery of existence sufficiently even to know this fact.

DEVOTEE: Master, you have often said that we can only know about the mechanics of existence as we evolve through the stages of life, but we never will know exactly what they are.

MASTER DA FREE JOHN: Yes. You may have some intuitive sense of what they are, and that intuition drives you further through the various stages to the seventh stage. But the mechanics of the stages themselves are all limits on knowledge—perhaps advances on previous knowledge, but still limits on knowledge and limits on Realization. The seventh stage of life is associated with unlimited Realization and Free Knowledge, the Free capacity to inspect existence and to know what its laws, even its "matter of facts," are. Thus, it is tacitly and also experientially obvious, in the case of the Adept in the seventh stage of life, that people do not die when they die and that there are other planes to which people migrate and from which they come.

Not all Adepts have greatly expanded knowledge based on experience, but all Adepts in the seventh stage of life do enjoy perfect Realization. This Realization accounts for all of Nature even though the Realized beings may not experientially enter into the investigation of all the planes of Nature. Ramana Maharshi[3] is such an example. He did not have many visions of the dead and ghosts and so forth, although it was not hidden from him that you do not merely die when you die. Maybe he had an experience here and there, who knows? In any case, he was not a knower in any expanded sense. He was not experientially involved with all kinds of subtle and factual, expanded knowledge, even though he had basic presumptions about existence that are native to Realization itself.

You all create your own visibility. You dress and do things because you see and you know and notice that you are seen. How does the flower do it with the bee, then? It must somehow or other exist in the domain of seeing and knowing that it is seen. This implication is clear. Whether or not it is totally understandable and comprehensible is another matter. But the patterns and colorings of flowers are so complex, so profoundly well suited in discrete detail to the survival association with insects, that this whole process of the evolution of flowers and insects is a mystery beyond the capacity of the materialist's model to comprehend.

DEVOTEE: Master, it is often suggested that insects adapt their coloring and shapes to the trees and plants. What is to say that the trees and the plants did not adapt to protect the insects?

MASTER DA FREE JOHN: I think it is obvious that they adapted mutually. If evolution is in some sense factually true, then for everything that evolves in an already existing system there already exist many kinds of differences that cooperate with one another and modify themselves mutually.

Another interesting mystery in all of this is one I pointed out at the beginning of *The Knee of Listening*. It is curious, you see, that the flowers do not doubt. The ants do not doubt. The bees do not doubt. The bees do not wonder, "To be or not to be." (Laughter.) Why don't they? You cannot say, "Well, the individual bee or flower has not died yet, and therefore it does not doubt." Individual bees and ants, insects,

3. Sri Ramana Maharshi (1879-1950) was a God-Realized Sage who lived, taught, and radiated the Presence of God among devotees for more than fifty years at Tiruvannamalai, South India. After his own Awakening in September 1970, Da Free John found esoteric corroboration of his Realization in Maharshi's Teaching, and in 1973 he enjoyed a living Demonstration of Maharshi's Realized Presence when he visited the late Sage's tomb and former places of residence.

creatures of all kinds, flowers and plants are the product of an unending, unbroken history of a particular organic force and genetic impulse, in which not only the fact of death has been taken into account long ago but into which the motive of death has also been built. The flowers and plants do not merely die. They intend to die. They are programmed to die. In other words, in their most essential structure of existence, they are intending to die. They come into being not only with the fate of death before them, but with the intention of death at their very root. The same is true of us.

Why do we doubt, then? Why do the trees not doubt? Why do we? It is because of the capacity we have developed for abstraction or abstract thinking, this capacity to take up a position separate from ourselves and to think of ourselves as really being separate from ourselves, rather than existing in the participatory sense, as just identical to ourselves. And so we doubt because we lose sympathy with our root organization, our most fundamental organic motion or motive, as well as our ultimate Condition. Having lost sympathy with all that through thinking and self-abstraction, we also develop the capacity for chronic doubt and for our search for knowledge, then, on the basis of this same doubt. But the creatures and organisms in Nature in general do not exhibit any signs of doubt. Otherwise, you would imagine, they would have self-destructed long ago. But they persist, and each generation is as glorious as the last, if not more glorious.

The Force that is driving Nature, then, is undaunted. It is not subject to doubt. Neither are we when we fully participate in the Force of existence. Our doubt is an expression of our dissonance with Nature, our Narcissism, our self-contraction, our inability to be sympathetically related to existence, or to participate freely, without qualification, in the process and the fact of existence.

Doubt, then, is a peculiarly human phenomenon—if we can even call it human. It serves us in some sense by helping us to acquire knowledge. On the other hand, it also denies us Wisdom and disturbs our human existence.

DEVOTEE: Master, when you first started talking about the flowers and the bees, I was reminded of an experience at The Mountain of Attention when it became tacitly obvious to me that everything is Radiant Bliss-Consciousness. At that time I could feel the total relatedness of everything. That experience doesn't explain anything, but I could just feel the harmony of everything in that Consciousness.

MASTER DA FREE JOHN: There is an awesome interconnectedness to everything that is obvious only in a certain exalted state that may occur just for a moment sometimes. It may also become a permanent Realization.

We are being determined by our association with the body-mind. We feel ourselves to be inside it somehow. We are limited by its structure and therefore, in some profound sense, divorced from everything else. We see that we are related to things, that we need to cooperate with others and processes in Nature to survive, but we do so from the point of view of our individual existence as limited and defined by the structures of this brain and nervous system.

Even so, we do have the capacity for an exalted experience of Nature in a state of profound self-transcendence, wherein we are not being defined and limited by the brain and nervous system. Then, if only for a moment in a kind of satori, a flash of insight, not really thinking insight, but a tangible perception, we see that nobody is inside and that everything is existing in a universal Field simultaneously. Things are not merely interconnected via their functional life, as individuals related to one another, but things are simultaneous with one another, existing in a single Field of Energy or Force that is Conscious and that is somehow animating, controlling, and lawfully organizing everything.

There is a substance to this satori. It is a perception, not merely a thought. "Insight" is not really a good word for it because insight is generally associated with an act of thought. It suggests a phenomenon in which an individuated attention suddenly discovers something, whereas this Realization is free of individuation. In fact, such freedom from individuation is uniquely what this insight is all about. There is no individuated attention. There is no confinement to the brain-mind or the body-mind or the nervous system, but there is this direct Realization—not merely an intuition in the sense that it is in any way conditioned by something and hidden, but an even tangible perception of the universal Field. This Field is Energy and Consciousness, and it is perfectly obvious in a certain exalted state.

In fact, it is this exalted state that is advocated in particular in the Zen tradition. Zen practitioners seek to attain just this perception through their exercise. In general, for those who exercise themselves in that manner, it is just a moment, a flash of obviousness. Likewise, nirvikalpa samadhi,[4] which is pursued through yogic techniques, is a

4. The Sanskrit phrase *nirvikalpa samadhi* means "formless ecstasy." It refers to a state of total

kind of moment, a flash of insight, a breakthrough consciousness, wherein this same Field is grasped transcendentally, prior to all objects. Then when attention returns to the body-mind and conditional awareness, the residual effect of this condition makes something about all this arising world profoundly obvious, even though one perhaps cannot account for it through the mechanics of mind nor regain it in any perceptual sense once attention has returned to its bondage to the brain-mind and nervous system.

This very satori is sometimes called Enlightenment. It is Enlightening, a profound Awakening, but it is not precisely the same as Enlightenment, because it is only a moment of insight and not a constant, tangible Realization, whereas the seventh stage of life is associated with a constant, tangible Realization of the Obvious.

DEVOTEE: Master, I often feel this. Particularly when I lie down to go to sleep at night, I have an interesting feeling in which it becomes very obvious that there is no space between things.

MASTER DA FREE JOHN: Because everything is One.

DEVOTEE: Everything is the same. And my sense of everything is that I can feel it completely as myself and that I am that also. This feeling is not willed into being. It just occurs.

MASTER DA FREE JOHN: You say it is typically something you feel when you are going to sleep. When the usual restrictions of the nervous system and the brain-mind are relaxing, and before you go into dream states, which are also in some sense monitored and limited by the nervous system and the brain, there is this kind of exalted, free perception wherein something is glimpsed that you cannot quite grasp. But it is glimpsed. It is obvious. It is not an hallucination. It is self-verifying and associated with the ultimate Condition of Existence. It is simply not final Realization, but it is Enlightening. It is liberating in some sense. It is useful and it helps move us on, helps us grow, gives us distance from the things we take very seriously and that represent our confinement in ordinary life.

(but temporary) absorption, achieved through the ascent of attention beyond the possibility of the nervous system to condition awareness. This state transcends the ordinary subject-object consciousness. It represents the ultimate attainment of the fifth stage in Master Da Free John's schema of seven stages of life (see Appendix).

DEVOTEE: Master, in moments of feeling this great Happiness, this Oneness with everything, all beings and all speech always point to That, and every word that is spoken is a pointer, an indicator of that One Great Being. It all seems to indicate that in fact we are all this One Being, whether we know it or not. You speak the Truth of That, and you point to That One.

MASTER DA FREE JOHN: Who is living you now? Who is being you now? That One does not seem to speak. If you ask someone a question, someone else talks. A someone who is somehow presumed talks back to you, one who does not claim or prove to know very much and is not responsible for his or her own existence, did not create the body, does not know where he or she is, does not really know very much about what is going on, at most knows about some things and also has a great deal of false knowledge, false presumptions, and limited experience. This is the one we get to talk to most of the time.

On the other hand, even that one is nothing but the Great One, shown through a certain figure, a certain attitude, a certain limit. We really are talking to That One all the time. That One is the only One Who is talking all the time, but That One seems to be a fool, seems to be the ego or Narcissus. It is only when we have broken out of the mold of our own Narcissism, which confines our awareness and limits us to the persona of our own imagination, that we see the Great One everywhere and as ourselves. And that is what there is to Realize. That is what the Way is all about.

What is any of the rest of existence about, anyway? What is its purpose? What is important about any of it, except that? Nothing else is important! It is not that we should not pay any attention to the ordinary details of life, but they are ordinary, that is all. There is no reason to become salt-of-the-earth creatures dominated by materialist conceptions of life, limiting our possibilities all the time. Take care of the ordinary business of life, but be devoted to this Great Matter. Life not devoted to this Great Matter is without use for itself, and only in some conventional sense is it useful to anyone else. There is not any significance or purpose to existence unless it is devoted to this Realization.

How many people are so devoted, though? How many people would consciously confess that their life is devoted to this Realization? I mean devoted to it, absolutely <u>devoted</u> to it—how many people would tell you that? A handful of humanity! It is absurd. And that is why everything is so difficult, that is why human life is the way it is, that is why the present state of history is what it is. This devotion is absent, and all that is left over are all the illusions of mechanically oriented egos struggling to survive and somehow to achieve pleasure, not involved with any great impulse, getting more and more tired, and eventually dying after they trouble a whole lot of people for a lifetime. I mean, all that was offered to me in my childhood was the possibility of going into the window business!

CHAPTER 16

THE GAME
OF PERCEPTION

a talk by Da Free John
January 18, 1983

MASTER DA FREE JOHN: During lunch we considered briefly, but not conclusively, the question of whether you actually see mental images, as in dreams and mental pictures in the waking state, or merely presume to see them. The same question could be put in another form. Is there perception, or is there only conception?

We do not perceive on the surface of our bodies, you see. We receive perceptions, so-called, through the mysterious, electronic operation of the brain and nervous system. What is the actual status of perceptions at their point of cognition? Are they perceptions? Or are they conceptions, just presumptions? Is there such a thing as perception? Or is perception just a form of thought?

Consider your dreams. Dreams are self-originated, basically. If you see some scene in a dream, what portion of it do you see? Do you see the object at which you are immediately looking, or do you see the whole scene? If you are seeing only that portion of the scene on which your attention is focused, then what is the status of the rest of the scene? Does it exist? Or do you presume that it exists? What are its edges? Where does it come to an end? If you are looking at a room in a dream, are there other rooms simultaneous with the one you are seeing? How much of it is created? How much of a place is created in dreaming so that you may see the portion you presume you see? Must you create a total universe to have a room on which to focus? Do you actually perceive any of it? And if you create it, why must you perceive it to know it?

It would seem very likely that all you do in the dream is conceive the scene, and that you do not perceive it. Well, what is the answer?

DEVOTEE: Master, a group of people who are all looking at the same object do not all see the same thing.

MASTER DA FREE JOHN: If an image is self-originated, how can you have only a partial point of view toward it? In other words, how can you know only that portion you see if you had to create the whole thing to see it in the first place?

We all know that we do, in effect, perceive our mental images. There is no reason to argue against that fact. At times we know when we see images in color, for instance, rather than in black and white or some limited selection of the color spectrum. In effect, then, we at least often perceive mental or psychic images. But what is the status of these presumed perceptions? Are they actual perceptions or are they just conceptions? Are we only thinking that we are perceiving?

DEVOTEE: But isn't there a difference? When I am thinking about something and trying to create my own movie in thought, I know I can't see it quite as clearly as I can when it occurs spontaneously, as in a dream. The image is much more vivid in the dream.

MASTER DA FREE JOHN: Is there a significant distinction between dream images and mental images, and perceptions arising in the waking state via the senses? We tend to presume that our mental images are largely self-generated and that our sensory perceptions are generated by contact with an existing environment and are therefore not self-generated. At least in principle they are not self-generated, although we modify these perceptions mentally and thus we all appraise a situation differently or notice different things in every moment of perception. But is there any ultimate difference between our mental and dream images and sensory perceptions?

Can we make judgments about the gross phenomenon of perception based on what we can notice about the mechanism of conception? In other words, can we examine how we self-generate mental images in dreams and reverie and, on the basis of that consideration, justify the point of view that the gross world of sensory perception is merely a conception, is in fact self-generated, like mental images experienced at other times, in reverie, or in sleep, or in dreams?

Well, what is the answer to all these questions—or these variations on the same question?

DEVOTEE: Master, does this consideration have anything to do with synchronicity? You once said that our thoughts are actually synchronistic with what occurs, so that what seem to be merely images in our dreams are actually synchronistic with objects and spaces and people apparently outside us.

MASTER DA FREE JOHN: Yes, the perceived phenomena we generally call psychic—in other words, mental images or other forms of conception acquired psychically in the dream state and in reverie, wherein we notice something that is going to happen in the future, or see something occurring in some place where we are not physically present—these psychically acquired forms of knowledge are filtered through our mind and our nervous system and the brain, so that, at the point of our cognition, they have become transformed by our own mechanism. Thus psychics, for instance, who relate to such phenomena professionally or practice psychism intentionally, are very often wrong in their judgments. They see an image that apparently has to do with something outside their present space-time circumstance, but their vision or view of it has been so modified by the mechanism of the brain, even of the mind independent of the brain and the nervous system, that the information has been significantly transformed.

Some forms of psychically acquired knowledge or information are much more direct, clear, or unchanged than other forms. But when there is a psychic premonition, let us say, what have we contacted prior to its transformation by our mind and brain? What is it that we have contacted? What is its status? Is that contact a matter of our going to another time and space? Or is it some form of electronic cognition without any sensory accompaniment?

Further, when we receive the information, so-called, when we have it in the form of some certainty, some sensory structure or image, what is its precise status? Are we actually seeing an image? Is there actually some kind of sensory performance or phenomenon there? Or, even if there is, is it merely some sort of electronic cognition without sensory accompaniment? Is the sensory accompaniment, the plastic configuration of conscious events, merely a presumption? Or do we actually experience things in sensory or plastic form?

DEVOTEE: Master, you asked earlier if we needed to create an entire universe to view a specific object or a place in the realm of our vision, and I was wondering how you would know that the universe exists if this room is all we are capable of viewing at any particular time. How would we know there is something outside this room? It seems our presumption about the room and the world is just that—a presumption, but we do not really know.

MASTER DA FREE JOHN: Yes, we make the presumption largely because we have been outside the room in other places, so we have a complex sense of physical reality as a phenomenon extending beyond the room. If we all suddenly appeared in just this room, and it was a solid compartment so that we could not see beyond it and had no other, previous physical or psychic experience of anything outside it, we would have no reason to presume there is in fact anything outside this room. We might suggest to one another that maybe there is such an outside realm, but we would have no direct, experiential reason to presume it or to prove that the possibility is a fact.

DEVOTEE: Even now we do not know that an outside world really exists. We assume that it does, but except for the evidence that comes through our field of vision in this particular body-mind, we really have no evidence that that world exists.

MASTER DA FREE JOHN: Yes, we have no ability to prove its existence. So we cannot know about its existence. But we can know something about the fact of perception itself.

The same mechanism is involved in all perceptions. We need not, therefore, experience all perceptions to discover what basically is occurring in the whole affair of perception. Nothing is achieved by adding to this room an infinite number of other rooms. We can notice and examine basically the same process even under the most highly reduced phenomenal circumstances. If phenomenal awareness were reduced to the awareness of a point in space, the same fundamental circumstance would still exist that exists in the case of the infinitely projected, complex field of perception, present and possible.

What there is fundamentally to examine, then, is the process of perception itself. What is its status? Do we in fact see mental images? Or do we just think we see them? If we are only thinking we see them, you see, that fact does not change the experience. The experience is the same. But if we could come to a point of certainty about this matter one way or the other, we would know something about the status of what we are perceiving and of the process of perceiving and of ourselves in relation to what we perceive.

DEVOTEE: We must think it. If we looked at the wall with a microscope, for instance, it would appear perceptually different than it does to the human eye.

MASTER DA FREE JOHN: Yes, our perception is highly selective. It is determined by the mechanism. A completely different perceptual mechanism would see this so-called room in an entirely different fashion than we see it. To a certain visual mechanism, theoretically at any rate, the room could be transparent.

Our perception also depends on location. If you went up to that cabinet there and continued your visual exploration of it, even atomically, you would go far beyond the perception of the grainy wood. You would start seeing its molecular structure, first of all its highly magnified minuteness as a conventional solid object, but then its molecular, atomic structure, its electronic state. It would ultimately be visualized as nothing but light. So what is our perception of it anyway, then?

That which we are witnessing is conditioned by ourselves, at least by the psycho-physical mechanism we are by extension, so that what we are seeing is as much ourselves as it is the thing we are seeing. We are only seeing it in that mode in which it can be seen by us. It is not otherwise perceivable as we seem to perceive it unless we are present in the form of the psycho-physical mechanism that we are. Our perceptions themselves, then, even though we say they come from the environment, are determined by the mechanism that we are.

But we are also just viewing or witnessing the mechanism itself. Our dream states and reveries, insofar as we remember or acknowledge them in general, tend to conform to the model of perception that belongs to the waking state and sensory consciousness. We do tend to dream, to imagine, to make mental images, but along the same lines as our gross sensory perception. In other words, when we dream, we see things in a rather fluid state, but they do basically conform to the solidity that characterizes the waking state. We see people, we see things that basically conform to what we perceive in our sensory, waking-state consciousness.

But is that inner perception inherent and necessary? Are other forms of cognition, experience, even perception, available to us? Are they perhaps actually generated in all states? Not just in dreams, but also in the waking state, or in certain reveries in the waking state, are forms of association with phenomena generated that do not at all conform to the model of gross perception?

DEVOTEE: Obviously, the intuitive faculties in the scheme of the koshas[1] or subtle psycho-physical sheaths involve something other than ordinary perception and conception.

MASTER DA FREE JOHN: Yes, but how does this something take form as an experience? Do you perceive space, in other words, in some fashion that has no reference to sense perception? Are you aware of others, of objects, of space, even tangibly, but without sensory references?

In other words, you generally acknowledge that you are perceiving or thinking of a spatial form when you are seeing it represented in the mind in the likeness of gross perception. But do you otherwise also perceive space, even in the waking state, very directly and tangibly? Perhaps you are not generally acknowledging these other forms of awareness because of the convention of accepting gross sense perception as the basic model of awareness, of knowledge, of experience. But do you have any experience or any way to acknowledge that you do have contact with spatial forms beyond sensory perception?

DEVOTEE: Master, I was considering the different ways I know that we perceive you. Your body is sitting here, but I know at times of deep meditation or strong intuition, I have experienced seeing you as light.

MASTER DA FREE JOHN: But that is a perception, you see. It is like the perceptions you can have through the senses in the waking state apart

---

1. Vedanta philosophy identifies five *koshas* or functional "sheaths" that compose the human individual: the food sheath (*annamaya kosha*), the life-force sheath (*pranamaya kosha*), the mind sheath (*manomaya kosha*), the sheath of intellect and higher intuition (*vijnanamaya kosha*), and the bliss sheath (*anandamaya kosha*). Beyond all these sheaths abides the omnipresent Transcendental Self or Reality.

from such experience. The sun is just light. You can see a flash of
light, and so you may have an experience of seeing me as light, but
that experience is a mode of sensation. Do you have actual cognition
or tangible awareness of objects, spaces, and the like without any
sensory reference whatsoever? If you do, how do you acknowledge it?
What substantial form does that cognition take that we could talk
about?

DEVOTEE: Master, I was thinking that even though there is apparently
individuated consciousness, or perception, we all tend to agree in
general about what is arising. If we did not presume individuated
consciousness as separate beings perceiving everything, things would
still continue to arise, but our relationship to them would be different.

MASTER DA FREE JOHN: We communicate with one another. We
make language. We have all kinds of signals, and we come to a kind of
consensus about experience in general. This is how we are able to live
with one another. But if we did not bother to achieve consensus and to
communicate with one another, we would all still be having experiences
of some kind. We just would have no basis of agreement about it all,
nor any mutual communication about it. These phenomena would still
arise, presumably even apparently individuated up to a point.

DEVOTEE: But would they still arise even if we did not presume our
individuation?

MASTER DA FREE JOHN: Insofar as they arose within the context of
an individual mechanism, we would tend to acknowledge their arising
in relation to an individuated "I."
    The question is not whether there is anything arising, or whether
it is merely our thinking that makes it so. That is the kind of question
that gets asked in academic philosophy, you see. If there is no one
there to perceive it, does the world exist? If a tree falls in the forest but
nobody is there to see it or to hear it, does it actually fall? That is not
the question I asked. Apparently, in effect, we see mental images in
dreams and reverie, and I am asking not whether we have that
experience—we obviously do. We all agree about that, right? But what
is the status of that experience? Do we actually have a perception in
dreams, or do we merely think we are having a perception, so that our
thought takes on the form of an apparent perception? It may be that

we are not in fact even having a perception, that when we dream, we are not actually seeing anything but are only thinking we are seeing something.

In other words, is dreaming purely an act in consciousness? Are there no visual or other sensory relations associated with it except that you, by thought, superimpose the presumption that you are having such a sensory perception? Dreams, then, could be nothing but electronic states of consciousness without any sensory attributes. But consciousness in the form of mind could be functioning in the dream-state such that we think we are perceiving. But are we actually perceiving? Or are we just thinking we are perceiving? Is that thinking just a habit of thinking based upon the phenomena of the waking state?

It may very well also be that sensory perception in the waking state is nothing but a form of cognition, an electronic state of consciousness without any reference that we could call perceptual. But we transform this electronic state of cognition into the presumption of perception. In other words, this waking state could be nothing but a state of consciousness without any substantial attributes at all. What we call substantial attributes—perception, sensations, forms, and the like—are nothing but conception effective as objects, forms, and so on, or being made to seem as such. In other words, this experiential world could be nothing but consciousness modifying itself in the form of apparent perception.

DEVOTEE: Master, you answered this question very directly in *The Liberator (Eleutherios)*.

MASTER DA FREE JOHN: Oh yes?

DEVOTEE: At the end of your proofs of the Divine Reality, you say that in fact there are no objects, only Consciousness.

MASTER DA FREE JOHN: Well, I may have said that, but is it true? (Laughter.)

DEVOTEE: Is it not true? There are objects?

MASTER DA FREE JOHN: Well, I did not say it merely so that you would believe it, you see. It is an argument. It is a consideration. So, I

am asking you this question again for you to consider this matter in
the present.

We are talking about the functional status of things like mental
images. Now, we could discuss mental images, such as the dreams we
had last night, perhaps. In general, in discussing them, we would say,
"Well, I saw this, I saw that, this happened, that happened," and so on.
This conversation amounts to a consideration of the status of those
things we could otherwise discuss in rather conventional terms. We
could talk about our dreams in ordinary terms, just as we could talk
about our memories, or what happened earlier today or yesterday, you
see. But what is the status of those experiences? When you describe a
dream you had last night in which you saw somebody or other and this
and that happened, what is the status of that experience? Was it in
fact a perception, a visual experience, an experience in other sensory
terms as well, or not? Was it something else? Was it merely a
conception of visualizing, a presumption of phenomenal awareness?

DEVOTEE: It definitely has to be the latter, because we would show the
signs on the body. For instance, if I saw myself losing a finger in a
dream, and if that experience had a perceptual basis, then I would
wake up with a finger missing. But in fact, I can go through all kinds
of dramatic events in the dream state that do not affect the body or the
environment in the waking state.

MASTER DA FREE JOHN: They may not affect your gross body. But
that does not necessarily mean that the experience itself was not a
perceptual or visual form.

DEVOTEE: Yes, Master, but it seems obvious that it must be thought
and the thinking process that are somehow generating the perception.
If someone looks at a wall, what he is thinking determines what he is
seeing ultimately. I mean, if five people look at the wall, they all see
something different, even though they are all still looking at the same
wall.

MASTER DA FREE JOHN: Yes, but how does that relate to the dream
experience? Presumably the images in the dream state are not
reflections on something that otherwise exists and that someone else
could also perceive. Sitting in this room, we could all look at this
cabinet and each come up with our own independent description of it.

But when you are dreaming, no cabinet exists apart from your perception of it. There is just a perceived cabinet. Apart from your perceiving it, presumably, at any rate, it does not exist. It is just a presumption.

I am asking you, what is the status of that experience? It is a presumption, that is to say, it is self-generated. But is it actually a perception? Does it have actual, perceptual form, or do you just think it has perceptual form? In other words, is there anything going on in the dreaming other than an activity in consciousness, completely independent of perceptual relations?

DEVOTEE: It seems so.

MASTER DA FREE JOHN: Are you saying that there is such a thing? That apart from a transformation of consciousness itself without sensory relations there is, in fact, another process going on in dreams that is sensory in nature? Is that what you are saying?

DEVOTEE: No.

DEVOTEE: Master, what about premonitory dreams?

MASTER DA FREE JOHN: Well, my own premonitory dreams, which occur constantly in the form of "future junk" about movies I will watch later and other coming events, could be a mental sensory creation that in some sense reflects a non-sensual, even non-perceptual contact with something outside my present moment of time and space. Psychism, you see, does not seem to have anything to do with a direct awareness of time and space.

When we are having psychic awareness of the future, for instance, we do not have sensory contact with a future moment in time and space with all its physical, sensory characteristics. Apparently we contact it in some other manner, but then we become aware of it by reflection, through the medium of our own mind, brain, and nervous system, even our memory. Out of this we fashion a knowable, perceptual form, and we read that form in psychic experiences. But to have mocked up that form, which is the information we then try to interpret, what was it with which we came into contact? What in fact is the original form of our contact with the future after which we make this image, which is a relatively confused version of the future?

It seems that we must have direct contact with it in some form, though not of the sensory kind, and then we construct a confused version of it, on the basis of which we try to predict the future. Let us say that a psychic determines there will be a plane crash next Thursday. What happens? He or she sees a plane crashing, perhaps, or some similar image, and from that perception derives the information that there will be an accident, a plane crash. In addition, perhaps, he or she sees two women dying. But then it turns out that a man dies in a plane crash on Thursday. Thus, there can be variations on the predicted event. It may not even be a plane crash. Maybe there will be a plane crash on Thursday, but what the psychic sees is a toy boat burning in a bathtub, combined with a sense that the incident is associated with Thursday.

In other words, when we have psychic awareness of the future, the mind-body mechanism creates a confused, or at least confusing, version of the future. What we then regard in order to tell others about this possible future event is the image we make. Now, in order to make that image, we must pass from a pure contact to a stepped-down, modified version of that with which we have had contact. And this stepped-down or modified version is somewhat confused or not altogether true to the facts. Some premonitory visions are very clear and straightforward, but for the most part, our premonitory awareness takes the form of a confused, plastic version of the future event.

First of all, if we have the capacity at least under some circumstances to know the future, why would we not simply know the future and bypass the mechanism of mind and body that creates a kindergarten picture of it? Just so, in the waking state of our perceptual life do we not do something similar? There is perhaps a very direct awareness of everything transpiring in the present. But we employ a perceptual model acquired through the mechanism of the body and transformed in various ways by our psychic apparatus, or our mind, and we know the present only through this model. Therefore, we do not know very much.

Perhaps in some way we may come to have very direct contact with the present. Then everything about it is totally obvious. Then there is not the slightest bit of confusion, but only perfect Wisdom, absolute God-Realization, total Consciousness, the most full and clear Realization of every possible fraction of the present moment without the least confusion, without the slightest limitation represented by self. Yet, in our ordinary state what we end up knowing about the present is determined by the filtering mechanism of mind and body.

If we already have this larger, full, complete, perfect, and direct rendering or awareness of everything, why do we introduce or at least take into account the mind-body mechanism? It is only a limit on That Which we otherwise know perfectly. And if we do know It perfectly, why do we not simply know It? Premonitory dreams demonstrate that we at least can know the future. Yet, premonitory dreams show all the evidence of the same kind of process that occurs in the ordinary waking state of perception as well. In premonitory dreams we introduce a model—a plastic, a vision—between the direct form of awareness and our attention or cognition, and then we try to read the future by looking at this model.

The process is like throwing bones or looking at tea leaves. It seems very primitive, does it not? Nevertheless, we must, it seems, have a perceptual dream model of the future to be psychic about the future. But if we have the ability to know the future, why do we not just simply know the future? Why are we introducing this stepped-down, kindergarten version of it and then confusing ourselves with that, or losing our full awareness of what the future is?

Do we actually have these perceptions? Is there really a perceptual world in fact, not just in effect? We know that in effect there is a perceptual world, because we have experiences. But does the perceptual world in fact exist or is it merely a function of consciousness, a kind of blind spot, an habitual presumption based on fear, or suffering, however you may account for it? Is it just a mechanism of presumption whereby we limit our eternally perfect Condition? And does it in fact exist as perception, or is that which we are calling perception nothing but an electronic modification of infinite Consciousness, a way of blinding ourselves?

DEVOTEE: I think you've got it, Master!

MASTER DA FREE JOHN: It sounds like a good idea to you, does it? It sounds like this could be the way it is? Could be, could be! Something like this certainly seems to be the case in terms of premonitory dreams.

DEVOTEE: And the present.

MASTER DA FREE JOHN: If a person can know the future—and we know there are premonitory dreams—there must be some sort of pre-perceptual contact with the future. But the form by which the psychic knows future events is this kindergarten drawing, this childish, dreamlike perceptual version or model of the future. For this reason psychics are frequently wrong. They do not know what they are looking at. A psychic may have an unusual dream and know it relates to some event. Then an event finally happens, and the psychic knows tacitly that the dream was a symbol for that occurrence. But the dream somehow was an after-effect of a direct contact with that event.

Why did the dream intervene, if he or she already had direct awareness of the future?

DEVOTEE: What is the dream ultimately? The dream is the individuated consciousness getting in the way of or modifying that pure awareness, that direct knowledge.

MASTER DA FREE JOHN: Yes, but why is it there? And what is its ultimate status?

DEVOTEE: It is the ego, the dreamer.

MASTER DA FREE JOHN: Yes, well, that is a name for it.

DEVOTEE: It seems that we just allow certain conditions, such as the dream state, to be the media of an intuition that was originally profound.

MASTER DA FREE JOHN: As soon as people think of becoming spiritual or religious, right away they want to start having visions. You think that you do not know God or the Transcendental Condition. Thus, you think that in order to get to know God, you must have a vision. Traditionally, it is recommended that, through meditative exercises, you should get into something like the dream state while you are awake so that you begin to see things that are not obvious from the point of view of bodily perception. It is a common presumption in the traditions that if you could do that, you would be getting in touch with God or with Reality as It really is, whereas what you are actually perceiving through the sensory mechanism of the body is a falsification of or at least a limitation on That.

I suggest to you that such visionary dreaming is not the way to contact Reality at all. Perhaps, you see, you are already perfectly coincident with God, perfectly Full, perfectly Realized, perfectly established in the Truth of Transcendental Existence, and in fact all your visionings, your gross or subtle perceptions, are kindergarten versions of That, models you place before yourself that are really only confused, stepped-down, highly transformed versions of That Which you hope to Realize. As long as you persist in creating such models as your means of knowledge, you are only confusing and blinding yourself to That Which is tacitly Obvious.

Therefore, it seems that we are involved in an effort to dream and to perceive. We are habitually oriented to this effort, but it is something that we are adding to a Condition that is already Perfect. And because of this, we are always being imperfect, always falling short of That with Which we are already perfectly coincident.

Hence my constant criticism of attachment to visions and other subtle, religious phenomena. It is not that you cannot have such experiences, or that they are not real in some conventional sense. But they are part of the mechanism whereby we fall short of That Which is already the case, already obvious, already the Truth. By persisting in that effort, we are only continuing to bind ourselves. We do not actually grow by attaining more subtle visions. We are merely expanding our visionary life in that way, but we are not growing in the spiritual sense. In other words, we are not really transcending that which must be transcended if we are to be in direct contact with That Which ultimately Is, That Which Is naturally.

Perhaps, this whole game of perception—this effort whereby we come into association with physical bodies, for instance, through reincarnation—is just a mechanical effort based on fear or self-contraction. We think we need this effort. We presume we are gaining something by it or getting close to what we want ultimately. But that effort is, in fact, the very process whereby we forget or fall out of conscious contact with the Real, the Obvious. Perhaps it is not necessary to indulge in perception at all in any form, internal or external, or even to have tangible association with time and space.

DEVOTEE: And still be active and bodily present?

MASTER DA FREE JOHN: Not necessarily bodily present. Perhaps one could be bodily present at the same time, but that presence would not function as an impediment. In the case of the Adept, for instance, the body-mind is present, and it is generating all the usual phenomena of conception and perception. But these phenomena are no longer binding, they are no longer acting as impediments, they are no longer needed. They are just there. They are a convention.

DEVOTEE: Master, there was a day a few years ago when the principle of this consideration was completely obvious to me. It was also the day when the principle of Divine Ignorance became completely obvious to me. I saw you walking across the Sanctuary, and your Form was greatly expanded. I realized that all you were doing was seeing what was right in front of you. No machine of perception or motor activity was operative. You were so amazingly present that the whole activity of perceiving was completely exposed to me. I do not know how else to say it.

MASTER DA FREE JOHN: That is a kind of satori, a glimpse, in which you are at least for a flash of an instant tacitly free of the mechanism of mind, body, brain, nervous system, and self. At any rate, at the moment something about the Status of existence is tacitly obvious. The Revelation did not take the form of a thought necessarily. You might not have begun to think about it until afterwards, in which case you would by then have also lost the Realization.

There is a difference between this moment of Obviousness and the moments that might follow from it. And the Condition in which such Realization is tacitly Obvious—without cause, without impediment, without change, never ever limited by the body-mind or by any state, waking, dreaming, or sleeping—is the Enlightened Condition. Apart from Enlightenment there are glimpses, perhaps—satoris—but there is also a kind of nagging, gnawing sense underneath all our troubles and our mind. That nagging sense is part of the motive toward release that is behind our seeking. However we may justify our seeking, that sense is somehow behind it because it unsettles us, it makes the conventions of life non-ultimate, ordinary, and therefore not ultimately satisfactory.

If what I have begun to suggest through this conversation is true, then, you see, at this very moment it is already tacitly, directly obvious in your case that there is only Radiant Transcendental Being. You are in a Condition of absolute Freedom, Bliss, Consciousness without impediment. Yet all space-time is also inherently obvious in terms of its ultimate Condition and even obvious to awareness, knowable prior to perception, prior to the assumption of a point in space, a mechanism of perception. All of that is inherently so, inherently true. It is the Truth.

But in every present moment you are functioning as the subject, the "I" made of the body-mind, generating perception in response to everything. You generate perception in dreams, you generate perception in the waking state, perhaps in some subtle sense you generate a tangible, objective, or phenomenal state even in the deep sleep state. Thus, as a matter of conventional experience, you are always present as this "I," this subject, and you are experiencing a perceptual model or a kind of kindergarten duplicate of this Real Condition, highly modified, limited, and transformed by your own "I" mechanism.

Therefore, you live in terms of limitation, and you are striving to break out of what appears and feels to be a shell or confinement, within and beyond which is this certainty of the Absolute. But because you confine yourself to this apparatus, this model or revision of Reality, your actual, out-front knowledge and experience is always a version of limitation. It is always an expression of this shell consciousness, you see. Therefore, you do not know what your own Status is, ultimately, and you do not know what the Status of these objects is. You do not know what anything is. You live in this mysterious, driven state, confused by your own presumption. And what is there to discover ultimately but only That Which is Prior to your own presumption—in other words, That Which is already the case, the Obvious.

Ah, but none of this may be true. This may all be just fancy.

DEVOTEE: No, it is definitely true.

MASTER DA FREE JOHN: In the waking state we make a casual presumption that we perceive occurrences and other beings, and then, having perceived them, we begin to think about them. Now, this may not be exactly the sequence, except as a matter of convention. We may actually be profoundly involved in a totally different process than perception to begin with, and we may enjoy a direct awareness of all space-time, including everything that is coincident with the present sphere of our attention, entirely apart from exploitation of the perceptual mechanism. And all of that activity may itself be a process in consciousness, a most subtle form of thought. This whole affair of perception may be a very secondary event or process to which we are, however, habituated, such that we even discount the higher and original mode of our contact with everything. Our thoughts, therefore, even less than our perceptions, or our rather gross wanderings, may be based on a sense of frustration and complication.

Examine the dream state, for instance. The dream state is very similar to the waking state in that we are perceiving events, reacting to them, and even thinking about them in various ways. But you could not say that thought began only after the perception in the dream state, because you yourself are generating the perception. You have invented the whole thing. Not only have you invented that which you are perceiving, but you are even inventing your play within it.

Having invented it, you then enter into the process of perceiving it and presuming yourself to be caught up in it. You invent the scene wherein you are being chased by the gorilla or some other terrible event is happening, and then you inject yourself into it and play the one who is being chased. But you have made both the gorilla and yourself, and you have made yourself be the one who is being chased. Somehow you have chosen to play out the event that way. It would seem that you had an option not to play it that way, at least originally, because you made the whole scene and played out that option to begin with.

It may very well be, then, that in the waking state you are likewise not merely a perceiver and then a thinker and then a self, or an awareness, in the midst of all this. The whole affair of perception and thinking that commonly occupies us may be unnecessary, or at any rate it may be a very secondary and generally confusing exercise. We may originally, tacitly, and basically in every moment be involved in a greater Event, a greater Association even with phenomenal existence, than the one shown to us through the mechanism of perception, thinking, and the sense of being "me" involved in an event. This certainly seems to be true in the case of dreams. It may also be true in the waking state.

How can we know whether it is true or not? Well, I am certain that you cannot merely think this out logically and come to a conclusive opinion about it. You must enter into the phenomena of self and object. You must discover the condition of self by discovering the source of the primary mechanism of self, which is attention. Having realized that condition, then, perceiving events, or being aware of conditional existence, you may also be tacitly aware of or able to recognize the ultimate Condition of those events and thereby Realize a Condition that transcends self and objects and involves not only Transcendental Existence, prior to space and time, but a kind of participation in space and time that is prior to self and perception.

That Condition manifests itself through various kinds of Siddhis that have spiritual significance, as well as secondary siddhis that use the duplicating, sensory mechanism of mind and body as part of the process of the magic of these apparent powers. Relative to psychic perception of the future, for instance, premonitions ordinarily take the form of vision or some perceptual model that has been transformed by the body-mind of the psychic. It is not always readily obvious, then, just what is the future event being modeled or shown. Even if the psychic experiences of the future are very clear in vision, you are still only seeing a model of this future event. Because the future event has not happened yet, in some sense you could not be perceiving it, at least from the point of view of the body. However, in another sense it has happened—if all of time and space is coincident, and there is good reason to presume that such coincidence is the case, based on the discoveries of contemporary physics.

Is all time and space simultaneously existing in an objective, perceptual form? Not necessarily. In any case, our contact with the future is obviously not necessarily involved with a perceptual contact with it. It can be a contact with the future that has no perceptual references. That contact is part of the higher physics or electronics of manifest existence and takes on a perceptual form only afterwards, in some reflection or retreat from the intuited event. This reflected model can more or less conform to the future event, or it can be so confused that we cannot even tell we are seeing a future event. You may in fact be having future dreams all the time, but the dreams are not recognizable as such because they are so profoundly transformed that you cannot notice the intuition involved in their arising.

Likewise, in the waking state our perception is a model of what we think we are perceiving to be objective to us. As I pointed out earlier, we are not existing at the surface of the body, and we are therefore not at the surface of the eyeball so that we are just seeing the room as it is. Our awareness of the room is not at the eyeball level. It is very difficult even to say where it is at all. In fact, it is ultimately impossible to say where it is except to locate it in the transcendental sense. But in terms of the general mechanics of perception, we do not merely see the room. Rather, there is a kind of camera-like mechanism of the eyeball that transfers what is reflected against its rear surface through a strange combination of nerve endings. That reflection is translated in the occipital region of the brain into a mass of electronic impulses and then—where?—somewhere central to the Life-impulse itself, the Current of Life Itself, or in the mind even beyond the body, or in Transcendental Consciousness, transcending space and time altogether, all of that is recomposed into the form of a concrete image.

We do not merely see a bunch of electronic blips. We see what looks like this solid place with all these solid bodies and objects. The event is retranslated, you see. First it is perhaps this solid room and these solid bodies, then it is changed into electronic impulses, and then it is translated again into a solid image. Thus, perception is something like what we can imagine goes on with television transmission. A camera is set up in front of a scene or some people acting out a drama. The image received by the camera is translated into electronic impulses, and those electronic impulses are projected into the space of the Earth and received by antennae that convey them to TV receivers. Then the TV receivers translate the electronic impulses into an image on the screen that looks very much like the concrete, objective, solid, physical scene in front of the camera way back at the origination of the process. The scene does not even necessarily exist in the present—it could have been put on tape, you see.

Our own act of perception in general would seem, therefore, to be something like the transmission of television impulses. Although this analogy cannot account for its ultimate features, it does, however, account for its mechanical features in a way that seems reasonable to us. Our perception of this concrete room, then, is a retranslation of an electronic pattern that perhaps was received by something like the eye of a camera in our own eyeballs in relation to a solid, physical environment.

But perhaps this solid, physical environment at the other end of the camera, or on the other side of the eyeballs, is nothing like what we perceive it to be. At least it is not ultimately what we conventionally perceive it to be. Again, on the basis of the physical considerations of modern science, we must presume that all this solidity is just an apparition made of light-energy that goes through a process of translation in the medium of the elements of Nature and comes out at the other end looking like or seeming to be bodies in space.

In other words, in order for this room to appear as solid bodies in space, space itself must be transformed through a mechanism that not only exists in us, in the process of our perceiving, but in time and space itself. In order for these solid bodies and solid rooms to exist in any sense to begin with, light, or energy, which is nearly intangible, must take the form of atoms, molecules, and biological materials and go through a process of transformation or translation into solidity.

Even that solidity is perceptible in all kinds of ways, depending on the mechanism or the camera. Use an X-ray camera, and what you see looks a lot different than it appears to your eyeball or to a regular camera. Throw different kinds of light on it, and it looks different still. Come up close to it, magnify it, view it electronically—how it seems to be will depend utterly on the mechanism you bring to the perception. But then, in order to perceive it at the other end, you must pass through a similar process of first reconverting it into light and electronic impulses and then reconstructing it at the perceiver's end into this apparent, selected, solid, recognizable form.

So what is going on here, exactly?

DEVOTEE: As you have said, Master, "This Maya is great!" (Laughter.)

MASTER DA FREE JOHN: This Maya cannot be comprehended!

But all of this is so, is it not? It is not really a matter of conjecture. If we bring imagination to the moment, all of what we have just considered is so. Actually, you see, we with our troubles and all our seeking are busying ourselves with conventions of perception. We are all engaging in a studied exercise of compulsive attention to models of Reality, translations of ultimate Reality, modifications of Transcendental Existence. We are compulsively involved with these models, troubled by them because they are all representations of a limit. Therefore, we also react to them, and this reaction reinforces our trouble, dissociates us from the model itself, and causes us to superimpose a model of self on the model we presume of that which is objective to self.

Thus, our trouble is magnified even after the fact of this model. And the model itself is a magnification of trouble in some sense, unless we can enter into the affair of perceived reality totally Free, without the slightest trace of fear, self-contraction, or self-delusion.

DEVOTEE: Master, I was thinking this morning about this trouble, and how primitive is the sense of fear. Regardless of what is going on in the room—there could be nothing threatening happening in the room, and I might not be thinking or dreaming about anything negative in particular—and yet there is that trouble. Where does it come from? It seems to be the thing on which everything is built.

MASTER DA FREE JOHN: We could say it is simply a reaction to the model. In other words, that trouble is a reaction to perception, and perception is a conventional, miniaturized version of a portion of Reality in only one of its potential states and, in fact, only one of its actual states. We are troubled by that. How miniature is our trouble, then? Our trouble itself is miniaturized Being!

We are like children looking at clay models of the world, you see, and taking it all very seriously. We are taking the perceptual model of existence and the mechanism of our perception or our modeling very seriously. We are even taking the mechanism in Nature that models appearances very seriously. And being very serious, we are very serious! (Laughter.) It is very difficult to recapture a sense of humor in the midst of all of that because the real sense of humor depends on Freedom, transcendence of self, transcendence of the model, and transcendence of the mechanisms of convention and of appearance.

DEVOTEE: Master, that transcendence is the source of humor. It is what you communicate, even in the first moment of our contact with you. It was the intuition that came alive for me in hearing you laugh. Your laughter communicated absolute freedom from that limitation and that model of existence. You gave it no quarter. It had no relevance to your own Condition, and that is what attracted me.

MASTER DA FREE JOHN: Nor is it of any relevance to your Condition.

DEVOTEE: Yes, and that also was communicated.

MASTER DA FREE JOHN: It would not be so funny if that humor had everything to do with me but had nothing to do with you. (Laughter.) I mean, I might chuckle a little bit here and there, but if the trouble were very real and actual for everyone else and not at all real for me, that would be good in some sense for me, but it would not be totally true. It would not be the Truth, it would not be a laughing matter yet.

Thus, if you notice me laughing, or if I really do enjoy a true sense of humor, it is because I notice something that is also true in your case and is also presently the Truth in your case, really, presently the Truth in your case.

That Truth does not seem obvious to you only in the superficial aspect of your being. Your own being is a great Realm, most of which is absolutely and eternally Free. A portion of it, however, is devoted through the mechanism of attention to the seriousness of this apparition, the seriousness of being an independent self confronted with objective conditions, or objects that are merely as they seem to be. But that occupation really occupies only a minute and most superficial fraction of your being. Thus, it can be laughed at. Even though you are still involved in working through the process of self-transcendence, you can enjoy a sense of humor, because in any moment you can appeal to your fundamental Being—that Force of Energy and Consciousness in you Which is a great Resource and Which in any moment need not feel bound by what it perceives. Even though that One does not cognize at the level of the mind everything about the ultimate condition of this existence, there still is this free Resource. You can Locate It. In fact, you Locate It in every moment in which you are Happy.

CHAPTER 17

HOW DOES THIS ROOM APPEAR WHEN SEEN FROM ALL POSSIBLE POINTS OF VIEW?

a talk by Da Free John
August 28, 1982

MASTER DA FREE JOHN: Consciousness is not in the body. Consciousness is not identical to the brain or the nervous system. Consciousness is an utterly Free Location or Disposition of Being. It seems to be associated and bound up with the body-mind, and therefore we tend to become full of ideas that are expressions of doubt. We tend to wonder, "Well, perhaps this Consciousness is just a secondary result of some kind of molecular activity in the nervous system. It's really brain-based. It's just naive to think that Consciousness is some kind of immortal principle." From our conventional position that kind of thinking could be true, but to dwell upon it is merely to magnify our doubt. What we must do is investigate Consciousness and see how Consciousness is related to all the other kinds of phenomena.

If we do that, we find that Consciousness is related in precisely the same way to the stomach as it is to the brain, to the bird in the yard as it is to the hair on the head, to the eye as it is to the toes, to the outer form of the body as it is to the inner. It is related equally or in the same manner to all of these. It is unique even in the context of psycho-physical existence. It is obviously the primary Principle, not

some secondary effect, of our real, psycho-physical existence. It is the
reason for that existence, the import of it, the significance of it. If only
some secondary result or something mechanical were our Real
Condition, then how could it have such primary significance in the
context of the body-mind? You would think, therefore, that the fleshy
body would have more importance than Consciousness. In that case,
you would be the fleshy body and observe the Consciousness just as
you now observe your toes.

At any rate, this Consciousness is your Position, so you have no
option but to investigate It, to see Its importance. Just to begin that
consideration is to be relieved of some of the doubts associated with
mechanical interpretations by seeing the importance of Consciousness
in the context of the body-mind. But as you come into a position of
equanimity in which attention is free, your recollection of the Position
of Consciousness becomes naturally more profound, and the investigation and exploration or intuitional inherence in Consciousness
becomes a profound activity or disposition. In that disposition the
Ultimate or Transcendental Status of Consciousness becomes suddenly
and absolutely clear. That is the moment of supreme maturity in the
case of this Self-Magnified, Free, or Enlightened Disposition.

In my description of the event in the Vedanta Temple,[1] I am not
merely describing a moment that corresponds to the first stage of the
Perfect Practice, when I realized that Consciousness was my Position
as an individual being over against all its relations. Rather, the
incident in the Vedanta Temple is associated with the absolute
Awakening to the Transcendental Status of that same Consciousness,
prior to any act of inversion. Therefore, in that Awakening the precise
Status of all the apparent relations of that same Consciousness is also
tacitly and absolutely clear. It is thus an incomparable Awakening, not
a conventional awakening or the beginner's recollection or location of
the Principle of Consciousness. In the terms of the Way that I Teach,
it corresponds to the Awakening of "open eyes," or the most absolute,
profound, and unqualified Awakening in the seventh stage of life.

All who hear me Argue this consideration may also immediately
enjoy intelligent and intuitional recollection of Consciousness and its

1. The spiritual transformation of Master Da Free John was spontaneously perfected by Grace
while he was sitting in meditation in a small temple on the grounds of the Vedanta Society in
Hollywood, California, on September 10, 1970. For a full discussion of this event and its
significance, see *The Knee of Listening* and part 1 of *The Enlightenment of the Whole Body.*

Condition. And to enter into this consideration in Communion with me, in Spiritual Intimacy with me, is also to enjoy the Transmission of Awakening to the Status of this Consciousness or prior Being. The Argument is one aspect of the Force of my imposition in your lives. It relates to the process of "hearing" (or understanding). The other aspect is the imposition of this Awakening Force. That relates to the process of "seeing" (or awakening to the intuition of the Location and Status of Being). These two aids or forms of my Agency, Help, or Siddhi are the primary means whereby individuals may enter into this Enlightenment and practice its Way.

The capacity to "hear" and to "see" will vary from individual to individual in any moment in time. Those who cannot hear or see should listen and watch. They should involve themselves with me via this Argument and this culture of Agency, and let the Revelation become obvious.

A good number of you are involved in at least a somewhat advanced stage of the progressive demonstration of this Way. Therefore, it should rightly be presumed that you have indeed heard and seen, that this Disposition, this Condition prior to the modifying force of all relations and all the acts of attention, has been intuitively realized in your case in the process of your association with me. That realization makes you useful to other practitioners, beginners as well as all others at your level of demonstration of the Way, because you are able to serve the Remembrance of this realization in others. You are able to confess the Truth of my Confession and of this Way and of this Transmission.

A profoundly important aspect of the community of devotees is that it not merely be a gathering of those who are listening but rather a gathering of beginners and mature practitioners alike, so that within that gathering are at least a significant number whose hearing and seeing are profound and mature. Apart from the Spiritual Master personally, they represent the greatest aid within the community of devotees for this Remembrance. Therefore, to be of such aid is to fulfill a priestly function of the highest kind.

The sacrament of Remembrance is the great Sacrament, the "Mass" in our Way. It is not merely Remembrance in the conventional sense of remembering a God-idea, a God-image, a Divine personality. Remembrance is not merely the resurrection of structures of belief. It is the intuitive Recollection of the Position of Transcendental Being, the Free Position in which we always inhere.

In what sense are you all not Enlightened at the present time? In no sense whatsoever? Well, that is just a lot of foolishness, nonsense itself. Enlightenment is true only if you Remember Enlightenment Itself. Otherwise, to say there is no sense in which you are not Enlightened is more nonsense. Then you are un-Enlightened in every sense and in all the senses!

The word "nonsense" is interesting. It means to be not associated with the senses or sensation or common sense. Two conventions of awareness are established even in the structures of our mechanical being. They relate in some general way also to the two hemispheres of the brain.

The first convention of awareness is the convention of sense or common sense, or the linear conception of existence: being a body aware through the senses, existing and moving in space, and living in time, enjoying or suffering experiences in moments that move progressively from a beginning established at birth until an ending established at death. We who are born also die. This commonsense point of view is therefore appropriate or real enough in the context of ordinary life. However, it is not the absolute Principle of our functional existence.

Along with that first convention, which tends to be pushed to the background and is often not acknowledged because of the social conventions in which we live, exists another organ of conception or awareness that is not linear, not structured relative to the senses or time and space. If the first or more sense-based form of awareness and conception may be said to be associated in general with the functions of the left hemisphere of the brain, we could say that this other functional disposition is generally associated with the right hemisphere of the brain. Rather than conceiving things in terms of time and space, linear occasions, the linear progression of time, this other organ sees all of phenomenal existence in terms of a single Field. In fact, in that Field all time and space exist simultaneously.

In the science of physics in the twentieth century, this way of conceiving reality has been legitimized through the work of such scientists as Albert Einstein. The other way of thinking, the more linear way of organizing the conception of so-called reality, was previously legitimized in the domain of science by scientists such as Isaac Newton. Neither the one nor the other of these two ways of conceiving of existence is superior. Neither is to be regarded as the only legitimate way of conceiving reality. In fact, both of them are functioning simultaneously, and we constantly move through different kinds of conditional or manifest awareness corresponding to these two great divisions, these two great dynamic halves, of our apparatus. One aspect of us sees everything in terms of a single unified Field wherein all events exist simultaneously, and wherein there is really no beginning, no ending, and no death. The other aspect sees things in terms of birth, linear progression through time, cessation, and death. Obviously, from a certain point of view relative to experience, both these orientations have their right moment.

The tradition of science has produced two great visions of manifest existence, one that corresponds more or less to the linear, left-brained view and another that corresponds in general to the "Field conception" of existence. The first of these corresponds to the classical conceptions of physics, and the second corresponds to the modern conceptions of physics. The ultimate conceptions of a spiritualized consciousness may be said to relate to the domain of the right hemispheric, Field conception of existence. The limiting conventions taken very seriously from the commonsense point of view are transcended or humorously regarded from the right hemispheric view, the unified or Field view of phenomenal existence. The intuitional view of existence has its champion in the right hemisphere, and the commonsense view of existence has its champion in the left hemisphere.

Obviously, in the exchanges of daily society, the left hemispheric, linear, commonsense view is dominant and wants to command our allegiance to the absolute degree. It does deserve our allegiance in terms of the ordinary working out of our ordinary life, but it certainly does not deserve our allegiance in the absolute sense. Indeed, we must demand the freedom to grant ultimate significance to the intuitional point of view, which has a kind of functional presence through our right hemispheric activities but which ultimately transcends the dualities of the body-mind and the structures of conception.

A movement exists even in the domain of science that is ultimately legitimizing the point of view of great Realizers, Adepts, mystics, and saints. There exists the possibility of a conjunction between the great culture of intuition, or the Great Tradition of spirituality, and the tradition of science as it is projected in modern physics and disciplines that are perhaps scientific but that are building themselves on the base of modern scientific conceptions of physical reality.

Common sense is a good thing for your ordinary life. It is a good thing to know how to walk, talk, and work, and how to avoid touching a red-hot stove. But you cannot make absolute philosophy, you cannot construct true conceptions of Truth or Reality, on the basis even of the dreams of common sense! The Truth is intuited in the domain of nonsense—not stupidity, but the regard that transcends the common sense of the linear occupations of the bodily based personality.

You see, we are all naturally present here with one another through these human vehicles. What we are perceiving in this moment is commanded by the nervous system and the structures of the brain, whereas we think that what we are now perceiving is what is actually here. It is here only within the framework of the conventions of the structure whereby we become conscious of the world. If this brain-mind were not functioning, if this nervous system were not limiting consciousness at this moment, if no one's brain-mind and nervous system were structuring the awareness or comprehension of what is the case now, so-called "here"—what do you think this place would look like? How does this room actually appear without the mediation of these brains and nervous systems? And what does the room look like anyway?

Again, because we are confined to the point of view of this particular kind of body, we not only see things in a peculiar fashion, through the mediation of this structure, but we also always conceive of reality from a point in space. You can move around in space, but at every moment you are only at one point in space. When you think of this room, you can develop an image of the room in your picturing mind for yourself. And that image will look more or less like the room appears to the eyes located in a certain position in this room. But the room, as it is, is seen in Truth only when perceived from all possible positions in space.

DEVOTEE: We never see it.

MASTER DA FREE JOHN: No one ever sees it. How could it be seen? What would it seem to be if it could be viewed from all positions in space simultaneously, and by a manifest form of Consciousness that is not limited by our particular kind of nervous system, brain, and body? The room already does exist as such. And none of us, in the terms of being bodily present here, is aware of it as such. What does this room look like when it is viewed from all possible points in space?

DEVOTEE: Even from one point in space, it is different for each person.

MASTER DA FREE JOHN: Yes, there are subtle differences, particularly in how we describe it. We think we can get a realistic view of this room if we put a camera over here. There would be no psychology behind the camera—it just snaps the shot, right? But to get a view of what the room looks like to the eye as the room actually is would require you to set up an infinite number of cameras in an infinite number of positions within this room, all of them not only fixed in one position but rotating in a sphere three hundred and sixty degrees in circumference, in all directions and simultaneously. The photograph of the room, then, would be an image of this room as it appears from all possible points of view rotated in all possible directions.

If you could place an infinite number of cameras in here, and take an infinite number of pictures, and superimpose them on one another—would you make a composite, or what? (Laughter.) How would you actually make this picture? What would it look like? A cubist painting? A hologram? Or would it look just like white light?

DEVOTEE: Ultimately you could not get a picture of the room because even the room is changing in time.

MASTER DA FREE JOHN: Yes, in the course of time there are changes of light. So you must also view the room at all possible times, under all possible conditions of light.

We take for granted that the room here is a very simple, objective something or other, which we all know very well and therefore do not need to investigate further. But, as a matter of fact, no one has ever experienced this room, not even once.

DEVOTEE: Master, different cameras also have different lenses, which are man-made and therefore mediate particular points of view.

MASTER DA FREE JOHN: Yes. The eye is a lens, too, and it distorts to one or another degree. So—we have an infinite number of perfect cameras. Perhaps an infinite number of imperfect cameras as well, with an infinite number of imperfections! (Laughter.)

DEVOTEE: Also, to different individuals, any one object can appear

different. The color of this pillow is beige, but it may appear to be a
different color, such as blue, to some people.

MASTER DA FREE JOHN: We all probably agree that it is beige or tan,
but some people may actually see it as blue based on a certain
mechanism of their own. We may say, "Well, they represent an
aberration—the thing really is beige." Nonetheless, all they represent
is a particular mechanism for seeing that pillow. And to that
mechanism for seeing that pillow, the pillow appears blue.

The same is true of the mechanisms of different cameras, and
therefore to get a complete picture of this room, we would have to use
infinite numbers of perfect and imperfect cameras, rotating in all
directions at every possible point in space at all possible times, and
perhaps from all possible positions in space both within and without
the room.

Now, every possible mechanism has a certain possible perception
as well as a certain possible location. We know intuitively, and we are
also assured by the disciplines of modern science, that matter is
nothing but a transformation of light or energy. Thus, all this is an
appearance made concrete through a particular mechanism of perception with which we are each individually associated. But actually all
that is here is light.

We are made to believe or to presume that certain conditions
objectively exist by virtue of our sensory apparatus, including physical
feeling, physical impression of hardness, solidity, and the like. But all
of that is simply a convention of our nervous system. From the most
subtle point of view of this location, there is actually light here. There
is no density to this place, there are no edges, there is no size.

What is actually the case, then? Is it not absurd for people to be
so matter-of-factly claiming we are simply mortal beings, materially
definable? We participate in our actual Being, in the physics of light,
the physics of energy, the physics of space, time, conditional existence
in all forms, and absolute Existence. We participate in all of that
presently. That Totality, then, ought to be the basis on which we make
reasonable and intuitive judgments about the nature of existence. It is
only the linear, left-brained, street philosophy, with all its fears and
forms of self-possession, that propagandizes this mortalist and
materialist doctrine. There is no justification for it. It has no leg to
stand on.

This is not to say that there is a leg to stand on from any point of view! We exist in Mystery, associated with apparent limitations at the present time. But we are not defined nor ultimately or absolutely limited by what is apparent in the apparent present. We exist in a Condition of Mystery, of Ultimate Ignorance—the Ignorance that is Transcendental Being, Ultimate Consciousness Itself.

To be completely sane, we must establish ourselves very consciously in that Great Mystery and Ignorance and all the processes of real intuition inherent in that Position. To do anything else is to be a monotonous and foolish character who wants to prove the linear point of view by kicking his foot against the post, saying, "See, I hurt my foot." That seems to mean, "All men are mortal to the ultimate extreme." That is not what it means at all. It is a joke. If we think more largely and clearly, we see there is no justification for the absolute pronouncements of mortalist and materialist philosophies. These philosophies are simply extensions of the linear practicality of mankind. When they begin to become absolute doctrines, enforcing the condition of humanity absolutely along their own lines, then mankind is threatened, you see.

Perhaps mankind always exists in the circumstance of being threatened until a perfectly Enlightened age, if there ever could be such a thing. Therefore, in every age we are obliged to be supremely intelligent and Awakened beyond the conventions of our own apparent physical mortality and all the street philosophies and sophisticated, mortalizing, materialistic arguments that stem from that apparent mortality and pervade our common culture.

DEVOTEE: Master, it just occurred to me that to get the complete picture of the room, we must also have an infinite number of shutter speeds.

MASTER DA FREE JOHN: Yes. It ultimately becomes completely impossible to get a direct comprehension of the nature and status and quality of this room. There is no such thing. Nor could we have such a total comprehension, therefore, of anything whatsoever, including ourselves or anyone else.

What do you look like? Just consider yourself in individual terms. You exist in your Totality right now, but no one in this room is in a position to see you in your Totality. And the only way you could be visually seen in your Totality is to be viewed from an infinite number

How Does This Room Appear When Seen
from All Possible Points of View?

307

of locations, from all directions in relation to you, at all possible distances from you, under all possible conditions, in every moment, in all time. You would have to be viewed from every position in space and time, therefore, to be seen as you are, at this moment.

Even from the most ordinary perceptual point of view you exist already in a totally mysterious, remarkable, even infinite Condition. Yet, this is not acknowledged by us. People cannot live by this Mystery. They live by the linear conventions of ordinary habits of speech and communication, and they want to make all philosophy out of this simplistic orientation, as if Truth were contained in the conventions of ordinary intercourse between people. Instead, the ordinary intercourse or relational activities between people are simply that. In themselves, they have nothing to do with the Truth. They are just an ordinary play of conventions of association. If the Truth is your concern or interest, then you must expand your consideration far beyond this commonsense application of the ego.

DEVOTEE: I was thinking, Master, that this argument undermines the Western formula of ego-based, objectivist philosophies.

MASTER DA FREE JOHN: Kant argued that we never see the thing itself, that we never know anything itself, because all our perceptions and conceptions are themselves determined by the mechanism of thinking and perceiving. Perhaps we could say that his philosophy is something along the lines of the argument I was just giving you, although Kant developed this consideration within the limited terms of the mind, was not a spiritual philosopher or an Adept, and therefore did not go beyond the activities of considering things in the conventional terms of perceiving and thinking. At least he did not do so in the Transcendental manner of an Adept.

Space and time are categories of our own apparatus and do not really exist "out there." And the perceptibility, the colors and contours and formal appearances we seem to perceive through the senses are not actually qualities that inhere in what we are seeing. They are, rather, the qualities inherent in our own mechanism. Therefore, we never perceive or contact anything else directly or even, perhaps, indirectly. We project the phenomena of our own mechanism on what is. Therefore, when we are talking about our relations and the world and others, we are simply describing ourselves, our own mechanism of manifest being.

This same kind of argumentation, however, is used to support certain kinds of materialist or conventional realism that deny the possibility of ultimate Knowledge and, therefore, of Transcendental Realization. We are not actually limited, of course, to the mechanism, nor to the linear habits, of perception and conception. Even in the mechanism, as I have indicated, there is another conventional conception that sees all things arising in or as a single Field. Beyond that are subtler organs of manifest being that go beyond the mechanics of the gross being. And there are ultimate features of our condition that are Transcendental in nature, if we will enter into them fully and Realize their Status.

Even so, it would seem to be true from the point of view of the mechanism, the mechanical personality, that no thing is ever actually known as itself. You cannot even know your self as yourself, because if you try to know your self through the mechanism of what you presume to be yourself, the mechanism projects itself on yourself, and thus you are seeing the mechanism. The mechanism is seeing the mechanism.

Who is the self, prior to the mechanism? What does it know or realize? What is its destiny? Such consideration belongs to the domain of spiritual philosophy, not materialistic philosophy. And of course materialistic philosophy is nihilistic, and the culture based on scientism is tending to be nihilistic. Superior individuals try to help overcome that trend, but in general the purely materialistic tendencies and commonsense motives of life and society tend to become destructive and nihilistic, strictly limiting Reality to the perceptual bind of life and suffering and death.

DEVOTEE: Isn't that basically where Western philosophy has wound up?

MASTER DA FREE JOHN: Yes, that seems to be the basic or general consensus of twentieth-century philosophy. Of course there are spiritual philosophers of a kind in Western history as well.

DEVOTEE: Master, I remember that when I took courses on philosophy in college, I expected to have my sense of things somehow expanded. But the field of philosophy seemed to be nothing but semantics, a dead end.

MASTER DA FREE JOHN: This was my experience, too. I was involved in philosophy at Columbia.[2] I have mentioned to you all that in the first week, during the introduction to life at Columbia, Grayson Kirk, the president, gave a speech in which he said, "We cannot make you happy, but we will teach you how to think." What he did not say, and what also turned out to be true, is that not only did they teach me how to think, or how to apply the mind to things or to be applied as the mind to things, and not only were they not able to make me Happy, but also they made me very, very un-Happy (laughter) as a result, because the whole consideration became more and more desperate and ultimately nihilistic, hopeless.

All that philosophizing, then, eventually became totally useless to me. Eventually I examined it all, I went through it very rigorously, and it was not about anything significant. It had nothing to do with what I was personally investigating. I then went on to develop my own experiment, without knowing there was really a tradition for what I was doing. Eventually I did locate that tradition, which I call the "Great Tradition," but I was not aware of it as it really is during the earlier phases of my own experiment.

DEVOTEE: Master, I once took a course in philosophy and logic. On the last day of the course, when examinations were over, I told the instructor, "You've given us all this philosophy, but all this critical thinking has not made you happy." It completely stopped him.

MASTER DA FREE JOHN: I had to take a certain number of courses in logic and mathematics at Columbia, and I can remember being impressed by theoretical, formal logic. But there is probably no other subject I ever studied that seemed more irrational and useless to me. I could follow all the trains of systematic thinking, but I never believed logic. It never convinced me of anything. The propositions one would have to affirm on the basis of conventional, realistic logic were not propositions I could believe, apart from the ordinary conventions of commonsense thinking.

But you do not need such profound logic to engage in common-sense thinking. Such thinking is a simpler affair. Classical, formal logic is based on commonsense thinking. It is a way of analyzing common sense, ultimately analyzing language itself, and becoming involved in a

2. For an account of this period in Master Da Free John's life, see *The Knee of Listening*, pp. 11-15.

reductionist and therefore un-Happy view of reality, without great options. For me such logic had no ultimate significance. Although it seemed to be an exercise that was somehow supposed to become involved in ultimate significances, it only reduced itself to banal significances, more banal still than commonsense reality. Thus, what I encountered at Columbia was the whole culture of commonsense reality, conventional thinking, reductionist logic, materialism, and humanism. I passed through that great trial and went on to continue to pursue my own experiment.

Among the elements of human culture that were reduced to non-significance for me was religion, not religion in any ultimate sense— ultimate religion was not really being discussed or considered in that academic environment—but conventional religion, the religious options. Upon direct examination and thorough, scholarly study, the great religions all prove themselves to be basically the products of ordinary human conception. They have no claim upon us if we thoroughly examine them. But they do relate to a Great Tradition of spiritual, esoteric, and Transcendental Realization. I contacted that Tradition only later. After my own experiment had begun to become fruitful, I began to locate this Tradition in various forms. I eventually developed a sense of that other Tradition, that other culture, which was not really given its proper voice in the academic world of Columbia, disposed as it was to affirm the reductionist, commonsense, realistic views of materialism.

I also went on to investigate these great religious traditions and to practice within them. I investigated their various propositions and discovered their failings, their absurdities, and their lack of ultimate significance in many cases. On the basis of all that consideration, I developed my understanding of the Great Tradition, the seven stages of life, and the ultimate process of Spiritual or Transcendental Realization.

If Wisdom is your goal, or the substance of your pursuit, you will not find it in the conventional schools or universities. If you are established in the Wisdom-school of a true spiritual culture, however, then you might go to these mind factories in order to be of service to this world. Such is a possible and viable orientation for certain people. But for most people going to college or university is part of the drill of becoming a useful citizen. We are all being constantly drilled in this commonsense view and made malleable. We are forced to adapt to a certain kind of commonsense view so that we will remain useful and nonthreatening.

To some degree this is an appropriate enough indoctrination, at the ordinary social level, yet it must not be made an instrument for governing our Consciousness altogether. We must be free to expand our consideration and be in touch with the features of our being in all terms possible.

Perhaps most people are not so adventurous. They are afraid and want to be comfortable. They want to live by common sense and to try to be as easeful and pleasurized as possible while they are alive. That approach is fine for them, but it is not a tendency or point of view I have ever thought anybody could really take seriously. There would have to be a great deal of fear behind it somewhere. How could anyone permit his or her existence to be determined by the workaday conventions of ordinary social life? Ordinary life never seemed to me to be a reasonable alternative although I have seen people choosing just that all my life. For me it has never been an option. It has always been totally absurd to me that from birth one could become devoted merely to things as they seem. Such a pursuit never interested me.

DEVOTEE: In meditation, Master, I have often experienced the mechanism of the ego as a desire to make sense of the spiritual process, which is really a confrontation with the obliteration of that very mechanism. There is no way to make sense of it. The process is the transcendence of that impulse. It is a death.

MASTER DA FREE JOHN: Meditation is death. If you enter into it most profoundly, you must let what you fear happen. You must be willing to move into the shuddering that you know represents the last moment of life and the loss of consciousness in this particular form. Ultimately, you must be able to let meditation be that profound. Individuals within the Great Tradition have therefore often stated that religious or spiritual life is a matter of dying daily, dying constantly, going to death deliberately, sacrificing yourself to the absolute degree, to the point of death, in every moment—dying to the past, dying to the future, dying to the present.

What do they mean by all of that? They are not nihilists, but they are talking about a transformation of existence of which we become capable only in the voluntary act of surrender. We are not capable of it otherwise, by tendency. We want to hold on and continue as we seem to be, because presently we are continuing.

But in meditation you must go beyond the motives of fear. When you have thoroughly gone beyond that fear, that is Samadhi,[3] you see. There is no restriction on meditation. Then there is only That Which meditation Realizes. There is no meditative act anymore. And there is no birth. What seems to be born is observed. There is no further identification with it in any ultimate sense.

---

3. When capitalized, the term "Samadhi" refers to the permanent condition of Enlightenment or God-Realization, while "samadhi" (in lower case) refers to the various temporary yogic states. See p. 136, n. 10, for a description of this distinction.

CHAPTER 18

THE BODY AS ENERGY AND THE UNIVERSAL FIELD OF CONSCIOUSNESS

a talk by Da Free John
February 28, 1983

MASTER DA FREE JOHN: The taboo against subtle phenomenal existence originated in conventional religion, which anciently taught that practitioners should not associate with negative spirits. With the development of scientism, a new taboo has replaced the religious one, based on the doctrine that material existence is the limit of life and there is no such thing as a subtle world or a subtle dimension of existence. This doctrine is a misconception—a lie—yet because of these taboos, millions of human beings have gone on for centuries presuming that subtle phenomena do not exist.

As a result, people have become more and more degraded by the subtle—as well as gross—effects of their interaction with one another. These degrading effects inevitably occur when we remain ignorant of the fact that subtle phenomena exist and when we fail to become responsible for them. The mere taboo against interaction with such phenomena simply because they can have negative qualities is not sufficient. We must come to real self-understanding, an understanding of the kind of mechanism we are, of how we function altogether, what effects we can create, and how effects are created in us. Then we will be in a position to avoid, through right spiritualized action, either

313

creating or being affected by what is, in effect, "black" or negative
magic.

Lack of self-understanding, coupled with taboos against observing
the existence of subtle phenomena, puts us in a difficult, even
dangerous, position. Thus, humanity finds itself in the vulnerable
situation where it can destroy itself, and where individuals can destroy
or limit others profoundly without understanding how they are doing
it.

Because of the scientific, materialistic ideal, we tend to think that
we are just material entities and that therefore we function only in the
gross material sense. This is absolutely a lie. In fact, we exist in much
larger terms than are even imaginable, but we do not function
consciously except in rather limited terms. The taboos represented by
scientism tend to limit our functional existence to the gross physical
domain of materiality. We are only permitted by scientism to be
conscious within the gross physical domain and we are obliged
therefore to be unconscious in every dimension beyond that. We are
naturally involved in some of the dimensions very close to our
material existence, but ultimately we must take all dimensions into
account. To do so obliges us to enter into the dimension or domain of
Enlightenment.

We must begin by understanding ourselves in most immediate
terms and becoming responsible for the dimensions of our functioning
that are very close to gross personal existence in this world. That is the
first stage of our learning. Thus, it is important for us, even at the
beginning of this spiritual Way of life, to observe and understand and
become responsible for ourselves as energy, as spirits.

We are grossly manifested—there is no doubt about that—but
we are not only grossly manifested. Our physical body is of a certain
size, five or six feet long, with two arms, two legs, a head, a trunk in
the middle, and various other features. The physical body is one aspect
of ourselves. So long as our senses are functioning rightly, they
provide us with information about ourselves and others quite readily.
But we actually exist in another form as well, which is also quite
tangible and personal, and that is the dimension of our etheric being
or etheric sheath. This sheath pervades and envelops the gross food
sheath and extends for some distance outside the body. How far it
extends depends on the qualities of each individual.

Everyone is present, then, not merely as a gross material entity,
but also as a subtle material or etheric entity. We are actually extended

even beyond that etheric envelope into the astral domain, and ultimately we are inserted into the infinite Field of forces and into the Ultimate Transcendental Force. We must discover that we live in the Infinite Domain of God, and we must be able to function consciously in that Domain and in every finite dimension within which we are manifest in that Infinite Domain.

The first stage of learning relates to our gross functioning personality, but we cannot really even pass through this stage, and certainly we cannot fulfill it, if we do not take into account the etheric dimension. Yet, it is relatively easy to discover that this dimension of yourself and others exists. It is not a matter of becoming capable of visualizing it or seeing auras, though some people can do so. In fact, almost anyone might be able to develop visual sensitivity to the etheric aura. But the etheric dimension is very tangible to everyone at the level of feeling.

We have several senses, most of them localized through a specific organ. We see, but seeing is in general localized through the eyes. We hear through the ears, we smell through the nose, we taste through the mouth, and the entire body is an organ of touch. In terms of its comprehensiveness, then, the body is the senior sense organ, and the sense of touch is the means whereby just about anyone can very quickly become aware of the aura or the etheric energy field of the body.

A few minutes ago, you conducted the experiment here of moving your hands back and forth in front of one another without letting them touch. Soon you begin to feel a kind of tingling force, almost like a fluid, that you feel squashing up between your hands as you move them back and forth. Once you begin to feel that tingling, rotate the hands circularly and you can feel the breaking of what seem to be tangible rays of force. Anyone can feel this force, which is clearly energy emanating from the body.

The Eeman screen[1] is another way of discovering this force. When you use an Eeman screen, you can feel a tangible, changing field of energy as well as various effects from the changes. Thus, through

---

1. Eeman screens, named for their inventor L. E. Eeman, are simple metal screens about ten by fifteen inches in size with metal handles. They are used to realign and energize the etheric circuitry (or natural energy field) of the body. See Bubba [Da] Free John, *The Eating Gorilla Comes in Peace*, pp. 412–14, for a more detailed explanation of their use. *The Eating Gorilla Comes in Peace* is a comprehensive manual of health practice that affirms Love, or the feeling-connection to Infinite Life, to be the true principle of well-being.

the subtle development of the sense of touch we can become sensitive to this field of energy and know then that we are energy, that we are manifested as an etheric personality, just as we are manifested as a gross physical personality.

The etheric field of energy basically conforms its shape to the physical body as long as we live in the physical sheath, but it also participates in the astral forces or the finer material energies. On the one hand our etheric field of energy conforms in general to the shape of the physical body, but on the other hand it surrounds the physical body as a kind of bulb or egg-shape. Where it is rather shapeless or curved or egg-shaped, the etheric is bleeding into or connected to the astral. Even this etheric aspect of ourselves is something we could call the lower astral dimension. In some literatures it is simply referred to as part of the astral dimension.

DEVOTEE: Master, are there two different bodies then, one that is similar to the gross physical, but made of energy, and one that is curved or egg-shaped?

MASTER DA FREE JOHN: The right way to think of it is that we are just energy. At one end of the scale that energy is infinite, nothing but the Radiance of the Transcendental Self, the Divine Being, and it pervades all the cosmos. This energy is stepped down by degrees. At each major step this energy becomes more gross, and different functions, activities, and qualities are associated with each step. By the time this energy reaches the physical level, it exists in its most gross or most dense form. The etheric is simply the next subtler aspect of the continuous spectrum of energy. Thus, there are not really two separate bodies; they are just different degrees or levels of the same force.

The physical body is a discrete or particularized form. While we live in association with the physical body, the etheric body, as I have already said, extends out some distance from the body but basically conforms to the gross physical shape. Beyond that immediate range of energy we begin to enter into subtler dimensions of energy we can begin calling the astral field. The astral field itself comprises a number of increasingly subtler levels. There are really no absolute breaks in energy but only different qualities of one great Energy, one great Force-Field, becoming more and more particularized, and the closer this Energy is to the physical, the more It conforms to the physical in shape and appearance.

First there is a kind of emanation that conforms basically to the shape of the physical. Then at a certain distance it begins to become a kind of radiance or sphere. There are many levels of spheres. As we get deeper and deeper into the domain of Energy or Being Itself, we develop the capacity to be sensitive to and observe the qualities inherent in these different levels.

At the level of ordinary human learning, we must become sensitive to the gross personality and its functional aspects, its nervous system, its right and left halves, and the processes that keep it in balance. We must also become sensitive to our etheric aspect, the energies that are very intimate with our gross physical personality, and to some degree we must become sensitive to our lower astral personality, the dimension of our existence that includes our higher psyche. Ultimately, we must go beyond all three of these levels in our Awakening, but at least these three—the gross, the etheric, and the lower astral or psychic dimensions—must become part of ordinary human self-knowledge at a relatively early stage in life. Basically, they should be part of our equipment by the end of the first three stages of life.[2] It is from there that we can begin to grow in spiritual terms and to go beyond the astral level.

We begin to grow spiritually through the vehicle of the fourth stage of life. In the fifth stage of life, we expand into the higher astral or super-personal domain of the universal cosmic field. Then, in the sixth stage of life, we "break the causal seed" of the manifest personality, which is the root of the astral, etheric, and gross aspects of our manifest existence. When this seed, which is in the heart, is penetrated or transcended, then we Awaken into our Real Existence as the Transcendental Self and we are, by virtue of that Realization, made Infinitely Radiant. Then we participate in the Infinite Field of Being, which transcends the cosmos. We are projected into the realm or process of Translation, which ultimately goes beyond cosmic existence altogether. But as a matter of basic human learning, we must first come to the point that our astral or psychic life is legitimized and not suppressed by the taboos associated with materialistic philosophy.

Earlier this evening I talked about Carl Jung, who in some circles is regarded to be the equivalent of a great religious figure, something like an Adept. In fact, his work was in the three dimensions I have just

---

2. For a fuller treatment of education in the first three stages of life, see Da Free John, *Look at the Sunlight on the Water: Educating Children for a Life of Self-Transcending Love and Happiness.*

described, and the limit of his investigation was the lower astral or psychic dimension. Nevertheless, the significance of his work lies in his legitimization of the psyche.

As Western Man became more and more dominated by the ideology of traditional scientism or materialism, the psyche began to lose its legitimacy. The process of the delegitimization of the psyche reached its conclusion with the work of Sigmund Freud. Freud obviously made some positive, valuable contributions, but among other things, he simply advanced the view of materialistic scientism into the domain of the psyche. For Freud and his followers, the psyche or the unconscious is an organ of material existence, and the contents of the unconscious are really repressed urges and complications of our material existence, the product of sexual and basic frustrations in life. Thus, from Freud's point of view psychiatry is designed to recapture these contents using techniques such as dream therapy, so that a person can inspect these contents and stop repressing the material energies associated with gross physical existence. The goal of this work is to re-achieve a state of sanity of gross personal as well as social living.

Jung's work involves a fundamental criticism not only of Freud's orientation but of the doctrine that is basically a development of materialistic idealism. Jung re-legitimized the psyche. His point of view was that the psyche was not just the unconscious, not just something full of repressed contents. By examining himself and others, he discovered a much bigger psyche and a much bigger unconscious than the unconscious represented by repressed instincts.

Jung's conception of the psyche is that it is ultimately a universal phenomenon, a collective unconscious, and that it is also a kind of objective domain. Just as the natural world that appears externally to the senses is apparently an objective domain, the psyche or internal world is, from his point of view, a kind of other universe, equally as important as the objective gross world. He also believed that the contents of the psyche are not merely created by us, but rather we participate in them. They are just there, in the same way that stars and mountains are just there.

Thus, from Jung's point of view, well-being is not merely a matter of getting in touch with repressed contents, repressed instincts, and so forth, but a matter of getting in contact with the psyche itself. This includes contacting the level of the personal psyche represented by associations in dreams and archetypal contents that are rather personal, but it also includes contacting the domain of the psyche that is universal and that contains images duplicated by all dreamers in all cultures. Jung regards well-being to be not merely the struggle of the gross personality with his or her instincts, but also contact with the psyche itself for the sake of being in touch with it and participating in it. It was his point of view that the psyche is a real dimension of our existence and that we must live consciously as the psyche. The unconscious must become available to consciousness, not merely to liberate repressed instincts so that we can stop being emotionally aberrated, but to be in touch with reality. The psyche for Jung was simply reality, and if we are not in touch with reality, we are not merely repressing instincts and bad memories and so on but we are repressing reality.

Jung's work obviously has legitimacy, but it concerns the lesser domain of human growth. It is not really about religion in the highest sense, or spirituality. It is about the psyche. In our language, Jung conceived of human normalcy in terms of the gross, the etheric, and the astral dimensions. He conceived of normalcy in terms of a balance of these contents, particularly in terms of the relationship between the gross personality and the psyche. Thus, he conceived of normalcy in rather traditional terms, and at the limits of what I have just described as the basic education we should enjoy by the time we have fulfilled the third stage of life. He did not really understand the process that goes beyond the psyche and its contents. He did not understand the spiritual process, or the higher stages of life, although he often commented on them. Not being a practitioner of the spiritual process, but rather being an investigator of the psyche's contents, he did not really understand what he was talking about.

Jung was operating in the domain of shamanism, of the magical culture of the old world, not the world of spirituality but the world of human beings as spirits, individual spirits, psychic personalities, beings of energy. He did not understand the higher astral dimension or the ultimate Spiritual Dimension, although he was becoming sympathetic to them. He felt something about them, but he did not quite know how to instruct people about these dimensions. He in fact communicated some ideas about spirituality that are suppressive of the spiritual process and possibility. Thus, the Jungians tend to confine people to this so-called Western mode of existence, which is concerned with individuation and ego-development and psychic self-knowledge, by communicating a number of taboos that actually work against people's becoming involved in the higher spiritual processes. These taboos state rather baldly that Westerners should not become involved in the higher spiritual processes, and these taboos therefore represent Jung's limit.

DEVOTEE: Master, your discussion reminds me of a dream in which I was attracting faraway objects to myself. I specifically sensed that there was no distance between the objects, that the space between them was just energy, and that I could simply use this force or energy to attract anything far away to me. I had the sense that if I woke up, I could actually do this! But when I did wake up, I was overwhelmed with fear, and I felt that it is fear that I must transcend altogether.

MASTER DA FREE JOHN: Because of our material view of existence, we tend to think that space is empty, that it is just the distance between objects and is not itself a positive substance. The most we may think is that some chemicals may be floating around in space, because we know we breathe, but without a subtler awareness, a subtler sensitivity to phenomenal existence, we tend to discount the fact that space is pervaded by energy. Space is continuous. It is not just the distance between objects. Rather it is that within which objects appear. In fact, objects are space. Space is energy. We are energy. And we participate in infinite space because we are extended into infinite space.

We exist at one level as a specific physical entity but dependent on all kinds of physical processes for its birth and its survival. We are also a personal field of energy that is rather limited, shaped like the physical, and very intimately associated with our physical existence. That energy is not only outside the body, but it pervades the body as well. It is the energy of the nervous system, and it is to some degree dependent on the state of the physical body.

The food taken by the body and our general environment support a kind of chemical process that produces the etheric dimension. But this etheric dimension is not merely created by chemical, electric forces. It also derives from the astral dimension. Our etheric sheath, then, is a limited personal field of energy that on the one hand is arising from and supplied by the universal field coming out of the astral dimension, but on the other hand is supplied by the physical body. Thus, to treat the physical body wrongly will decrease nerve force and weaken the etheric envelope, will even have some effect on the astral, because the astral is the psychic part of you.

You can also get in touch with your astral dimension through various kinds of reverie and dreams wherein the deep psychic content, both personal and transpersonal, begins to appear. In that dimension you can sometimes see future events, see places in the present moment that are outside your physical locality, and so on. We can therefore locate our astral dimension through reverie just as we can locate the etheric through touch or sensitivity to the field of energy.

Etheric and astral dimensions clearly exist in ourselves, but we tend to discount them because of the way we think. Our thinking is determined by the current popular, official, dogmatized concepts of reality. In our time, the dogma is fundamentally materialistic, and all other doctrines that may have had force in the past are sort of hanging on by their fingertips because of the religious institutionalization of culture. Those doctrines can no longer really justify their point of view. They continue to try, but in our time religious doctrine more or less accommodates the scientific point of view and thus represents a religionized version of materialism. The popular doctrines that tend to enforce our thinking limit our sensitivity to the dimensions of our existence and limit our participation in existence altogether.

These doctrines are superimposed on us, and not merely through verbal indoctrination. We are taught these doctrines under circumstances where we are vulnerable to believing they are true. Beginning in our youth we are indoctrinated into thinking like materialists through the educational process of our society. Many stimulus-response mechanisms are involved in receiving the implant of this materialistic notion. In effect, we are brainwashed into becoming materialists. The final effect of this indoctrination is that we tend to discount or doubt the possibility that we are anything other than gross physical beings.

Therefore, we become subject to the rest of the doctrine. First there is the materialist doctrine that constructs our view of reality. Then there is the offshoot of that doctrine that tells us we should work, consume the goods produced, be socially productive, and be sane, since sanity is highly regarded in our time. On some level it is of course appropriate and good to serve the social purpose of our time, to help others and be part of the process whereby humanity survives. But on another level we must not allow ourselves to be confined by that point of view. Our life must be greater than that. We should serve the social purpose in some basic positive sense, but our life must not be limited to it.

To grow beyond confinement to being just salt-of-the-earth, gross personalities—living sixty or seventy years or so, and working within the context of social ideas—we must deal with the materialistic doctrine that prevents us from exercising our sensitivity to dimensions of existence that extend beyond the gross physical. And really, it is religion's job to help human beings become sensitive to what is greater than mere material existence, and not merely to pass on a bunch of myths that make us feel better as grossly confined personalities. Only by being sensitive to what is greater can we even function in the material domain with anything like sanity and be happy at the same time. Thus, we must transcend the doctrines of our time that are propagated through the means of scientism, political propaganda, and many ordinary social mechanisms, including TV.

Part of my Work, part of this Teaching, is an effort to help you break out of this enforced model of Reality that is preventing you from being sensitive to your actual Condition and to dimensions of your existence that go beyond and ultimately even transcend material existence and all forms of limited, egoic, conditional existence. But in that process, the first thing you must do is complete your ordinary learning and break the spell of the materialistic model. You must become sensitive to yourself and understand yourself, and through your sensitivity observe your physical existence fully. Then you must observe your etheric existence, your existence as energy, and begin to function consciously as energy in relation to others.

Be useful to others, but also be alive as energy. Be free. Be balanced. Be sensitive to your psyche in the lower astral realm. Be sensitive to the contents of your consciousness. Permit yourself to experience the contents of consciousness. Do not shut them off. Become capable of dreams, of reverie, and of being psychic. Be sensitive to your archetypes, the poetry and metaphors of your consciousness. Allow them to be legitimized. In other words, legitimize subjective existence. You must legitimize it before you can transcend it, you see.

You must become sensitive to yourself not just as a physical being, but as an etheric and astral being. To become so sensitive is a matter of ordinary human learning. Even someone who has fully learned all this has not begun the spiritual process. It is just the ordinary equipment of human beings. But when human beings become responsible for this ordinary equipment, then they can grow beyond it, transform it, and make it usable in a higher sense. We are not here merely to grow wheat and make computers! To be socially productive is just one aspect of our existence, and we have no business being devoted to it exclusively.

We must evolve a free human existence and be free to grow in dimensional terms. We live as energy. We live as light. We live in the Infinite Domain of God. This is self-evident when we become sensitive enough to break out of our mind-set. And only when we begin to grow into and participate in that greater Dimension are we becoming truly religious and spiritualized.

DEVOTEE: Master, I recently had an experience that was somewhat dreamlike, but it was clearly not a dream. I had been awake, writing in my journal, for about two hours when I suddenly entered a state where I experienced one scene after another, just as in a dream. But I was fully conscious, completely awake.

MASTER DA FREE JOHN: Such experiences are not altogether like dreams because they are super-real. They are so clear to you, and you are so clearly awake in them. You are not busy sitting down trying to imagine something. You are not sleepy or asleep. These experiences therefore have a kind of objective or self-verifying force about them. But one of the things that makes people discount such an experience is that when they return to their ordinary state of consciousness, when they come back into association with the physical and begin to remember the experience, it seems somewhat like a dream. It seems to have been somehow fabricated, or at least produced, by their own consciousness or their mental disposition. Once they have entered into the gross state again, they tend to discount the experience. But the tendency to discount such experiences on the basis that they are somewhat dreamlike is itself a product of our indoctrination.

The astral world is a dream. So is this gross physical world in the sense that it is simply a play on Consciousness. Astral experiences, like gross physical phenomena, seem to be different from dreams because they are so concrete. They do not seem to be coming out of the psyche, and they are in no sense willfully created by us. Astral and gross phenomena seem to be out of our creative control, just as the tree in the yard may seem to be. Yet, we participate in all phenomena via Consciousness. Therefore everything, even natural forms in the gross plane, is a psychic or mental phenomenon, a phenomenon of Consciousness. On the one hand, objective laws are associated with these phenomena, with their appearance as something external to us. But on the other hand subjective laws, or the laws of Consciousness, are also associated with them.

We tend to think, based on our material view, that if Consciousness is somehow causing something to exist, we should regard that something to be like an hallucination—in other words, we should discount it as Reality. We tend to think like this because we do not understand and participate in Reality. We are dissociated or divorced from It through various kinds of presumptions. But conditional reality is, in fact, Consciousness. It is a phenomenon in Consciousness. And it is only by entering fully into Consciousness and all its laws and aspects that we can understand our situation in any moment of awareness. Thus, the fact that astral perceptions have the quality of a dream or hallucination or something brought into being because of Consciousness does not mean these perceptions are unreal or should be treated arbitrarily as hallucinations or psychotic phenomena. Rather, we must simply change our view of Reality, based on our thorough investigation of experience, including astral experience.

Yet the mood of science or materialistic thinking does not permit us that investigation. It wants us to regard the phenomena of Consciousness as alien to or a secondary manifestation of what we must understand to be material existence only. But this is an arbitrary and rather ritualistic point of view, a completely false doctrine of egos. There is not the slightest trace of Truth in it.

We exist in the Infinite Domain of Consciousness, the Infinite Domain of Mind, the Infinite Domain of Energy, and everything and everyone is Consciousness, Mind, and Energy. There is no thing that is not That. We are That, Nature is That, everything objective is That, everything subjective is That. Everything is a modification of Conscious Energy. Therefore, we must ultimately Realize that by recognizing that everything and everyone is Consciousness, Mind, and Energy, we Outshine or transcend conditional existence and enter into the Plane or Domain of Being Itself, Consciousness without qualification, Energy without limitation, Mind without contraction or falsification or stepping down from the perfectly Free State.

Everything is a psychic phenomenon, a phenomenon of Consciousness. And Consciousness is not merely that which Witnesses everything. Rather, Consciousness is the Substance of everything. Therefore, Consciousness is not only awareness. Consciousness is Energy. Consciousness is Self-Radiant, and everything that arises is a modification of That. Everything that appears as objective Nature is a form of energy, but a form or modification of the Energy that is Transcendental Consciousness or Being Itself. The recognition of everything as Consciousness breaks the spell or enchantment associated with modified existence.

Modified existence thinks and wonders and explores and tries to figure everything out, tries to win and tries to survive. As egos we are busy being already modified versions of That Which is Transcendental and Infinite. As egos we explore reality from that modified point of view. The Realization of Truth comes when we understand and transcend that limit, that already modified state, and, through real sensitivity, observe and ultimately comprehend or Realize the Condition of conditional existence. We Realize the Truth when we transcend this already conditioned position. None of our searches as conditioned or limited beings result in Truth. They are an enchanted adventure.

Human beings are all enchanted. We are already modifications of the Real, and we explore existence as modifications. We do not see how modifications arise. We do not see That in which modifications arise. We are limited to modification itself, to what we simply appear to be. And we break this spell only if we are free enough to thoroughly investigate our circumstance, our condition, our functioning being, all our parts, all our aspects, and begin to know reality in an expanded sense, beyond what we presently appear to be. The more we go beyond these limits, or the point of view of contracted being, the more directly we can intuit the Condition of conditions.

When we can most perfectly and directly Know the Condition of conditions, that is Enlightenment. Nothing else is Enlightenment. And in the Enlightened Condition, everything is recognizable. We no longer view things from the point of view of an already contracted state. We view everything from the Self-Position, the Transcendental Position. Everything is recognizable, then, as just a modification of That. There is no bondage, no enchantment. There is only Freedom and Bliss, the Disposition in the seventh stage of life.

Prior to the seventh stage of life, we must understand ourselves and expand beyond our shell of contraction and individuation. We must see beyond our apparently modified state, beyond the body-mind, and enter into the field of dimensions or the planes in which the body-mind and all fractions of our ultimate Personality are arising. In the first levels of our investigation we learn about ourselves physically, emotionally, mentally, etherically, and psychically in the lower astral sense. Ultimately, though, in the higher stages of the spiritual process, we begin to go beyond this lower vehicle. We enter into the cosmic domain, and then into the Infinite or Transcendental Domain of manifestation. The fourth stage of life is the passageway between these two basic stages of learning.

Because the fourth stage of life is the transitional stage between ordinary human learning and ultimate expansion and transcendence, it is a very important stage. Before people can come to that point of transition, however, they must first at least learn about themselves functionally, not just in gross physical terms and ordinary mental and emotional terms, but also in etheric and lower astral terms. They must find out that they exist as beings who are energy, and they must function as such freely and in a balanced state while being helpful to others. They must learn about themselves astrally or psychically and achieve a state of legitimacy, allowing themselves to exist as psychic personalities or beings who exist in an expanded psychic domain.

You really must do this before you can truly enter into the spiritual process. You can practice some rudimentary or superficial aspects of spiritual discipline, but you cannot really enter into the spiritual process until you enjoy this kind of ordinary learning that epitomizes the learning of the first three stages of life.

It is possible that some people may enter into spiritual exercises based on minimal self-observation and a minimal conscious capacity in terms of the lower astral, the etheric, and the physical being. Therefore, the original stages of their discipline leading toward spiritual maturity will involve their gradual observation of and adaptation to these more expanded aspects of their personal existence. Through meditation, life-exercise, and various other disciplines, and through visions, dreams, and so forth, they will gradually begin to become familiar with their more expanded or higher dimensional existence—which is still just part of their ordinary personality, but which they must necessarily understand and become conscious of, and conscious participants in, before the spiritual process can begin to flower.

Initially, you must of course use the Teaching to the point of self-understanding, and that self-understanding must become sufficient for you to become intimate with and to participate in the Universal Current of Divine Blessing. But it may take you some time after that to begin to become practically familiar with the etheric and lower astral aspects of your existence. And you must pass through that kind of learning before you can legitimately practice the second stage of the Perfect Practice.[3] Your life-discipline and your meditation must have familiarized you with the etheric and lower astral aspects of your personal existence sufficient for energy and attention, which are unconsciously trapped in these aspects, to become consciously available for the great and ultimate exercise of self-transcending intuition of the Transcendental Condition.

Thus, learning about the etheric and lower astral aspects of your existence should not be taboo. On the contrary, you must find out about them. This does not mean you should become a sorcerer. Only by exploring yourself and really becoming responsible on every level of your being can you avoid doing "black magic"—because everybody is unconsciously doing "black magic" now. Only the rare and strangely acculturated individual becomes conscious of these dimensions and then does black magic. This generally occurs in societies—shamanistic societies for example—that are founded on rituals of self-protection, self-survival, and killing of the enemy.

True self-awakening to the etheric and lower astral aspects of yourself is associated with spiritual acculturation, with real religious and spiritual processes. Then when you learn about these dimensions of yourself, you begin to enter consciously into a state of participation in them, and you actually eliminate the imbalances, the negativities, the unconscious "black magic" and become a positive, benign, and human presence. It is not by making this kind of learning taboo, but by making it in effect obligatory, necessary, real, and truly available in a fully human and spiritual context, that human beings will stop destroying one another, stop undermining the process of existence in this plane, and allow humanity to devote itself to its right evolutionary course.

Human beings are naturally involved in two streams of evolution—one horizontal and one vertical. We can picture it in this way. On the one hand, because we are grossly manifested we are involved in a sequence of evolutionary changes that will ultimately produce different kinds of human beings. We are all part of the horizontal or gross evolutionary process that will go on for aeons, for as long as the gross universe exists. On another level, because we are not only grossly manifest but are manifest dimensionally in many other subtle planes

3. The Perfect Practice is described on p. 173, n. 9.

of existence as well, we are involved in another kind of evolution, a vertical evolution, that would ultimately lift us out of human birth and even birth in the gross material universe, into higher or subtler planes of cosmic existence.

But, in Truth, we are involved or should be involved in a third or great process, which is the process whereby we transcend all evolutionary courses and are directly lifted out of both the horizontal and the vertical planes of evolution or courses of manifest adventure, of activity and rebirth and so forth, into the Transcendental Domain that is prior to cosmic existence.

Thus, there are really three alternatives for any being in the cosmos. You can just live and die and be manipulated by the trends of your time or your own idiosyncracies and be reborn in some other time and place, in this world or in some other world, but within the gross material universe. You can go on and on and on in that arbitrary sense, sometimes advancing, sometimes falling back, caught up in the horizontal world of evolution. Another alternative is to enter into the stream of vertical evolution and, through various kinds of exercise and self-discipline, move into the astral worlds, never again being reborn into the gross physical universe, but born instead into subtler cosmic planes, gradually moving through them during aeons of time or timelessness in the play of vertical evolution. The third alternative is to observe yourself, make contact with the Transcendental Adept, make use of the Transcendental Teaching, and, through the ultimate exercise, transcend both the horizontal and vertical planes of evolution.

We can utterly transcend all progressions—and they are by no means linear. Whether we are in the horizontal or the vertical planes of manifestation, we move up and down, forward and back in both time and space. There is no simple linear act. Our tendencies at any time govern our destiny, our movement up and down, forward and back, in space or time. But all of this can be utterly transcended if we will understand ourselves completely, investigate ourselves not merely in gross personal terms or in etheric and lower astral terms, but investigate our existence utterly, horizontally and vertically. We must observe and understand the whole field of our participatory existence and exercise ourselves in the Truth. We must become intimate with and devoted to the Truth. In that case, the process is fulfilled not in horizontal or vertical transitting in space and time, but in Translation beyond space and time or stepped-down, conditional existence.

You see, a lot of the drama that is occurring in this world is just a reflection of what is going on in the subtle worlds. Wars there become wars here. Conflicts there become conflicts here. The same kind of gaming between egos goes on in all the planes of Nature, and the subtler dimensions are expressed in the grosser dimensions. In the gross world human beings create complications apparently on their own. In other words, they create complications based on the evidence in the gross world alone, but they are also informed and controlled not only by the archetypes of the subtler worlds, but also by the phenomenal beings associated with those invisible realms. Therefore, human beings need to become just as responsible in the invisible worlds as they do in the physical world. In fact, responsibility is even more urgent in the invisible worlds, because if things were straightened out in the subtler realms of the cosmos, they would work out much more easily here.

Human beings are unconsciously under the control of all kinds of forces. They are not merely controlled by the reactions and phenomenal play of this Earth. We human beings are not merely controlled by what we notice and do with one another. We are being unconsciously controlled by all kinds of forces that we could contact through the deep psyche and higher awareness, but that now remain relatively unconscious. Even so, the processes that duplicate what is in our unconscious, in our higher or invisible psyche, go on whether we are aware of the origin or not.

Thus, merely to die, merely to go to another world, simply to get out of this place, is not to go to heaven. It is simply to move, either vertically or horizontally, in the planes of the cosmos, all of which are planes of egoic conflict. And if there is conflict in the higher worlds, it is unlikely that there will be peace in the lower worlds. Those who fill the higher worlds are beings who at one time or another inhabited the lower worlds and learned their conflicts here as well as there. Thus, if you are to live a free human life, you must become sensitive to what is controlling you at the subtle level. You must become not less conscious but more and more fully conscious.

We allow so much to be unconscious because life is already so difficult. We would just as soon not investigate that of which we are unaware. But we are controlled by the unconscious whether we are aware of it or not. This is evident even within the framework of modern psychology with its materialistic bias. The unconscious controls conscious life. If we become aware of the unconscious, it still controls conscious life, but then we have the possibility of breaking the enchantment, the spell, and of permitting the higher disposition of existence to animate gross existence.

I do not really have an unconscious, except insofar as I am associated with other beings, and in that sense I have an immense unconscious! But for me it is conscious, something I can be fully aware of, something I can deal with. If I have anything like a dream, it is always someone else's content. Whatever I am experiencing in life is your creation, the creation of other people. Whatever occurs in this body is your creation. I am just aware of it. And when I lie down to sleep at night, I do not become unconscious. Rather I move through different forms of conscious awareness, inspect different kinds of things. And what I see does not arise from my repressed life or my unconscious life. It arises from the domain of unconsciousness that pervades all of Nature. If I have my attention on anyone, or if they have profound attention on me, I will see their images. I see the future when I sleep, even the petty future of what I might perhaps watch on television the next day.

In other words, I do not, as people generally do, experience the contents of a personal psyche. When most people dream, they actually do experience the ordinary repressed consciousness of their daily life, the results of their stresses. They experience all kinds of personal dreams. But I do not have any personal dreams. If I experience anything like a dream, I am simply fully conscious of it. I do not lose the awareness of my state, my Real Condition. These "dreams" are just "future junk" and the contents of the people around me who have their attention on me. It is an uncommon and extraordinary condition, and it has been true all my life, even though it has become particularly clarified since the event in the Vedanta Temple.

When I would sit for meditation after that event, I found I was not meditating anymore. There was no need to meditate. There was no depth to achieve. There was nothing to realize. I was not seeking for anything. In the first year or so after the event in the Vedanta Temple, I would meditate as a matter of routine, particularly because my household was meditating. But, from the moment of that event, there was no personal content. If I sat down to meditate, I would see other people, see their contents, see whatever they were. If I dreamed, I would see the images from other minds, the unconscious of other people that began to invade my awareness. This has been true all my life and it has been true in a special sense since the event in the Vedanta Temple, because it was at that time that my Teaching Work was commanded and became spontaneously necessary.

Thus, I am still dealing with the unconscious and with egoic conditions, but they are not mine. They are never mine. I do not have this kind of experience. There is no inside, no inner depth. I never get involved in it, never experience it. It is a void, a void of personal existence. Where there was a personal existence before, now there is a void. To the degree there is personal existence, it is the personal existence of other people. This is what I see, what I meditate. It is that with which I work.

But I do not experience only the contents of other people, or the unconscious of the cosmos, or the void of ego, or the void where the ego was. Prior to all that there is Infinite Being, Infinite Consciousness, Illumination Infinitely Extended. Thus, I am void of personal existence, but I am Infinitely Full. There is no ego, no self-reference, no self-content, no repressed content, no unconscious, no ego-bond limiting the awareness of the Transcendental Condition. The contents of these other beings on all kinds of planes are arising, but at the same time there is this tacit, continuous sense of Infinite Being. And everything that arises is seen in a Field of Unqualified Illumination.

Just as you might become aware in a dream that what you see are your own mind forms, parts of your own psyche, and know therefore that your consciousness pervades them, that they are just an animation of your own energy, that is my sense of this moment, right here. A higher physics is involved in it, but it is very much like your becoming aware in one of your dreams. I do not experience myself as an independent consciousness. I am just Consciousness Itself, and I am completely, immediately aware that I am the same Consciousness That is you, Witnessing your mental and physical states. I am exactly that One—not merely like It, not merely the same in essence, but precisely that Consciousness. And all these mental and physical forms you call yours, all these environments, everything that can be seen, I am tacitly, directly, immediately, and without qualification aware that this is just Me,[4] My own Radiance, My own Energy, the Transcendental Self modified as forms.

Everything is obviously pervaded by this Energy. This Force is tangible to me—it never leaves. It is just so. There is just that Force. Everything that is arising as an appearance, mental or physical, is

4. The capitalized "Me" does not refer to the individual identity. Rather, it is an Ecstatic expression of the free consciousness of the Adept, who is identical with the Divine Being, not in any exclusive sense but because the Divine occupies his total vision.

pervaded by that Force. I immediately see anything simply as that Force modified in one form or another. All of this is Illuminated, pervaded by this Energy, and all beings are My own Consciousness. This is simply so, and I do not have to think about it for it to be so. I am in that State wherein it is just obviously so, just as it might be obviously so to you in a dream that people and the images occurring in it are the products of your own psychic self-consciousness. If you entered deeply into that awareness, you would Outshine the dream. You would simply be Self-Aware, and all these characters would be sublimed into a state of unification with your own consciousness. And then you would probably wake up.

I have just described to you some of the phenomenal aspects of the Enlightened Condition, in which there is just One Consciousness, and It is literally the same as all other consciousnesses. There are not in fact other consciousnesses. There is only Consciousness. And Consciousness is Infinite, Transcendental, and Self-Radiant. Its own Radiance is Chit-Shakti,[5] Infinite Force of Being. And everything that arises, in the form of all kinds of individuals, discrete events, objects, worlds, phenomena of all kinds, is just that Force. Just That. Nothing else. Just That. It is Self-Evident that this is so in the Awakened state. But for the conditional personality that has not become sensitive to its Real Condition, or even to dimensional aspects of its mechanical condition or functional existence, this is not self-evident.

The conditional personality thinks that he or she is a specific consciousness and feels separated somehow from other beings, other consciousnesses. He or she feels perhaps somehow essentially like other human beings, but not identical, not literally the same. There is no feeling of Identity or Equation in the perfect sense. Similarly, his or her own body seems entirely different from other bodies, and the objective world seems full of independent, separate objects. Thus, the usual individual does not feel, does not observe or literally know, that all these discrete phenomena are arising in a single Field, and that that Field is the Field of Consciousness Itself, and that Consciousness is just One Being. This is not obvious from the egoic point of view. But from the Enlightened point of view, it is simply Obvious. According to tradition, when Gautama the Buddha apparently was asked what he had Realized, he said, "A tacit understanding. Nothing more."

5. The Sanskrit compound *cit shakti* (often spelled *chit shakti*) means literally the "Power of Consciousness." See p. 266, n. 2.

There are profound experiential differences between an Enlightened personality and ordinary egoic personalities, and we should not
make light of this fact. But in some basic sense, phenomenal
experience is exactly the same in the Enlightened case as it is in the
ordinary case. There are still apparent individuals, the world, functions,
experiences, and states of all kinds. But the difference between the
Enlightened case and the egoic case is that in the egoic case everything
is seen in separation and individuated terms, and the Unity, the
Universal Field wherein everything is arising, is not obvious. In the
Enlightened case this Universal Field is Obvious. The One Consciousness that is all beings is tacitly Obvious, perfectly, directly Obvious. It is
a tacit, unspoken understanding. It does not depend on mind for Its
Realization. It is not a belief. It is a state. It is simply obviously so. And
nothing, nothing whatsoever, can limit or destroy that Realization.
Nothing touches it. Nothing has power to bind any longer. Whatever
arises is recognized to be a transparent or merely apparent, unnecessary,
and non-binding modification of Transcendental Being. It does not
have the power to bind, even though it exists just as it seems to exist
for everyone else. But it is not quite the same as it is for everyone else,
because it is tacitly Obvious that there is just the One Transcendental
Being, and all of this is a modification of Its Radiance. Whatever arises
is transparent in the Enlightened case. It is Self-evident as just a
modification of One Thing, and modifications do not have the power
to bind. They are merely apparent and have no necessity. Whether
they arise or not, there is still just the One, Infinitely Radiant, Self-
Radiant, Transcendental Being, the Love-Bliss of Infinite Existence.

Thus, there is no necessity to Nature, no necessity to birth, death,
or change. None of it has any necessity. It is all transparent and has no
power to bind. This is what Gautama meant when he said that what
he had Realized was just a tacit understanding, nothing else. In other
words, nothing was added at all. Nothing phenomenal is added in the
Enlightened case. Rather, everything simply becomes Obvious as it is.
But this is a great difference in some sense, you see—not a difference
in the conventional sense, not a phenomenal difference—but it is a
difference in the ultimate sense, in that What is perfectly Obvious
from the Enlightened point of view is not at all obvious from the egoic
point of view. Yet the same Truth pertains in both cases.

You are in this moment appearing in precisely the Condition
that is Obvious to me, except that what you think or presume to be
your condition is not the case. What is the case is simply not Obvious

to you. But you are still the result of the manifestation of That Which is the Truth. Enlightenment, then, is just this tacit Realization and nothing else. It is not a matter of adding anything to existence. It is just a matter of tacitly Realizing the Obvious Condition of existence.

CHAPTER 19

Going Beyond the Scientific Mind

by Ben Pierce

The household in which I was raised entertained the ambivalent attitudes about science that were common among middle-class Americans in the second quarter of the twentieth century. Science was considered to be a rather mysterious affair that had little to do with daily life. And scientists, though furtively held in awe because they dealt with the unknown, were nevertheless stereotyped as quaint eccentrics who were somewhat naive about the practical matters of the "real world."

Although I had a childhood interest in natural phenomena, and especially wondered about the origins of things, in the Catholic environment in which I grew up science was seen as a threat to religious dogma, and any serious study of it was discouraged. At best it was said to be a waste of time, and at worst it was considered sacrilegious. Even so, the first books I can remember buying for myself, and the ones that gave me the most pleasurable reading experience in my early youth, were science fiction. Certainly, a major motivation for such reading was escape from a dreary present into an exciting future, but there was also a genuine fascination with the marvelous technology projected for the future.

I attended Catholic schools from first grade through high school. The almost continuous round of negative experiences in these schools resulted in my developing an early but repressed resentment against any form of religious activity. The depth of my disaffection from religion in general and Catholicism in particular emerged into my consciousness when I was about twenty years of age. It was during World War II, and on the day before I was to go into a battle in which heavy casualties were expected, that I decided to attend Mass. I found everything about the ritual to be meaningless and intolerable. I walked out, preferring to face the fear of death on my own. A popular religious platitude of the time was, "There are no atheists in foxholes." The fact that I was an apparent exception to this made me doubt the authenticity of religion even more.

Because of the war I became professionally involved with engineering, aviation, and other aspects of technology. Such activities were attractive to me for two reasons. First, they worked: In contrast to my experiences with religion, technology had the very appealing qualities of making logical sense and having attainable goals. Second, both engineering and aviation allowed me to play the role of adventurer in exotic places, which apparently was an unconscious attempt to learn "the meaning of life" through exposure to the widest possible range of experience.

After four years of this enterprise the adventurous life began to wear thin. Imitating the Hollywood macho hero was not only highly dangerous—it was also very strenuous. Through my fatigue I saw that essentially I had accomplished nothing and was headed nowhere. Life began to appear meaningless.

Desperate for something to hang on to, I decided to give religion one more chance. I thought that maybe the problem had been with the popular and simplistic laymen's form of Catholicism with which I had been involved. I began to explore the more "esoteric" aspects of religion.

Now the search for meaning had begun to emerge as a conscious effort. First I lived for a short while in a Trappist monastery, and then even attended a Catholic college for a year and a half. Considering my background, the result was almost predictable: absolute rejection of anything even remotely religious. The philosophical and theological explanations of my teachers seemed to me no more than childish game-playing, which afforded neither intellectual certainty nor psychological solace.

It was at this point that the scientific approach became very attractive to me. Of course, my training and professional experience in engineering had already given me a background in science, but this tended to be limited to the practical applications of science to technology. What I was now interested in was "pure" science, or learning about Nature without concern for the "usefulness" of the information. Again I was eagerly seeking for meaning to life.

I began to explore various branches of science with a great passion, but I was particularly fascinated by research into the biological and cultural origins and development of mankind. This intense devotion to science, in one form or another, to the virtual exclusion of any religious or spiritual considerations, remained the primary focus of my life for some twenty-five years.

The first two decades or so of this period were a heady time. I had a voracious appetite for facts, and although it remained insatiable, within a few years my knowledge began to afford me some comfort. The world was starting to appear intelligible, and I happily joined the ranks of producers of knowledge. The exhilaration of understanding new contexts and complexities and the satisfaction of being able to contribute to the stock of discoveries about reality became my staple diet. The peak personal fulfillment, self-confidence, and pride coincided with my involvement with the Man-in-Space Project, which, at the time, appeared to be the very pinnacle of scientific endeavor.

Eventually, however, this state of left-brain satisfaction no longer sufficed. Gradually, the entertaining distractions of science and technology ceased to be capable of diverting my attention from my neurosis. Pain, fear, and anger, long repressed and hidden, began to surface with increasing frequency and intensity. Although I managed to maintain a reasonable facade of sanity, it seemed to me that my mind was becoming a veritable chaos.

It began to dawn on me that science did not have all the answers. Certainly, any "scientific" forms of therapy that I tried in order to alleviate my predicament either did little or no perceptible good, and in at least one instance actually exacerbated my difficulties.

By the mid-1970s, it had become clear to me that my love affair with science had proved barren. Science had utterly failed to satisfy whatever it was that I needed and was searching for. In a state of complete frustration with what had appeared to be the best way to a sane, happy life, I desperately turned once again to the exploration of the mystical or spiritual approach. A familiarity with oriental cultures had convinced me that people from such backgrounds tended to have a more serene outlook on life than was typical of occidentals. Moreover, it seemed that proportionately more people from the East had apparently attained some sort of spiritual fulfillment than was the case in the West. So, I thought that perhaps the Eastern religious approach might succeed for me where the Western one had failed.

I started my renewed quest in the domain of religion with an unsuspected burden: my left-brain habits of thought, cherished and multiply reinforced throughout my long years as a scientist and engineer. Thus, the major criterion by which I judged a spiritual method to be acceptable was that it did not directly conflict with scientific doctrine in any major way. For this reason I immediately felt attracted to Zen: It kept spiritual tenets to a minimum, and its simple, matter-of-fact approach came across as little more than a form of psychological discipline. I also began to delve into the works of reputable scientists, such as William James, and a number of modern physicists who were favorably disposed towards spirituality or a nonmaterialistic perspective on reality. Later I became an avid follower of iconoclastic but intellectual gurus, notably Krishnamurti.

Now I was convinced that I was on the right track, and my spiritual search grew in intensity until it became the all-consuming, number-one priority of my life. My daughter was grown and financially independent, and I had an independent income that secured my wife's future—which meant I could turn my obsession into a full-time occupation: I went on the road. Yet, to my chagrin I discovered that the more intensely I pursued my search the more frustrated I became, because I could see that beneath the minor surface changes I had been able to initiate in my life, I was still the same old confused, suffering, sick neurotic. I had to admit defeat: After all my efforts and troubles, nothing had substantially changed.

Eventually, the strain of this inner conflict caused me to fall seriously ill, and I was forced to reconsider my situation. At the time the only real alternatives left to me appeared to be insanity or suicide. I settled for an in-between solution of passive toleration of my dilemma. Perhaps, I was halfheartedly waiting for an even break, a ray of light.

The hoped-for turnabout occurred in mid-1982. My wife (with whom I was reunited) suggested we attend a movie on Buddhism that was being shown at the local Dawn Horse Bookstore. This was my first contact with anything associated with the Adept Da Free John.

Once again I entered into the spiritual search with new hope and enthusiasm, if only because this seemed preferable to the other two extreme alternatives. Once again the attraction was primarily intellectual. Master Da Free John spoke eloquently and in convincing detail about the problems of our modern life-style. He covered a wide range of topics—from science to diet, to sex, to living in community, to mysticism—and I found myself in surprising agreement with his thoughts and arguments.

But, once again I experienced frustration and despair. I knew what the Adept was saying was "right," and still I found myself unchanged by it. But this time I was given an explanation for this fact. I, indeed, could not change, since my ego-self alone was the problem, and the ego was not about to "cure" itself. Rather, as Master Da Free John explains in his writings, the ego can only be transcended by way of a transcendental process—of "Grace"—as it is initiated and cultivated in relationship to the Adept. I understood this message, and so I tried not to try, and even tried not to try not to try. There was nothing else for the "I" to do but engage in such absurd, self-defeating, and futile behavior. I had long been aware that I was incapable of love. I was now learning that I was also incapable of the kind of surrender that lies at the core of all authentic spirituality and without which no real change could be possible.

Although my apparent inaptitude for spiritual life pained me immensely, and became increasingly painful as it revealed itself more and more, still, I could see a way now of doing the impossible. After more than a year of studying the Adept's Teaching, while on retreat recently at The Mountain of Attention Sanctuary, I was suddenly overcome with a beautiful whole-bodily experience of release, in which surrender appeared to be the only natural way of life. At that moment, I felt I had been touched by God, and for the first time I sensed a palpable spiritual connection with Master Da Free John.

Nevertheless, I am still the same confused, suffering neurotic! But now this observation no longer devastates me. There has been the very modest beginning of acceptance, of surrender, even of love. All this feels quite new to me, and I tend to slip back to my previous disposition. *But* I am beginning to see more clearly the many manifestations of my unlove and lack of surrender, and I am being opened to the possibility of change.

Since the first moment of coming upon the Teaching of Master Da Free John, I have been grateful for this incredible gift that he has bestowed on the world. Now, having been given the Grace to see that surrender and therefore spiritual life are not impossible for me, my gratitude has grown most profound. Being able to feel gratitude toward Master Da Free John as the Source of the Teaching has had the miraculous effect of opening my long-occluded feelings toward the Divine.

The spiritual experience I had at the Sanctuary might have been seen as completely out of character for me. Certainly, nothing like it had ever happened before I began to study the Teaching of Master Da Free John. But in the year preceding this event, gradual changes in my attitudes were occurring. For example, formerly even the use of the word "God" was embarrassing to me (except for cursing). But as I began to see God as the Great Mystery, I began to relax into the acceptance of the Divine Unknowable.

Science remains one of my foremost secular interests. I simply enjoy being engaged in scientific activity. As it has for many scientists, science well done has an aesthetic appeal to me. But science no longer serves as the basis for my philosophy of life, nor do I look for ultimate answers in it any longer. It is the best method we have for learning about aspects of the phenomenal universe. But for understanding the true purpose and meaning of life, it is no more relevant than sports, drama, music, or any other cultural activity.

For that we must turn, with an unprejudiced mind, to the magnificent Teaching of the great Adepts of mankind. Here we will find more than gray theory—an actual Way that leads to transcendence of the phenomenal universe and into Enlightenment or Transcendental Realization. Master Da Free John's Way of Radical Understanding or Divine Ignorance has opened up for me this greatest of all possibilities.

Thank you, Master Da.

Postscript

Four months or so have elapsed since writing the above account. During that short span of time my life has undergone a remarkable change.

My wife and I have been married for thirty years. Within a few years after our marriage, I made the horrifying discovery that I was incapable of loving her, and I eventually confessed this to her. I truly appreciated her many fine qualities, and she was dearer to me than anyone else, but loving her, or anybody, was quite beyond my ability.

Recently I went on another retreat at The Mountain of Attention during which I passed through a graceful process of emotional opening-up. It felt as if I were being given a taste of the Happiness or Love that is our native Condition. The energies in my body flowed freely, and I was unwittingly introduced to a new perspective on life. I suddenly realized that my incapacity to love was not something I had to passively endure or bemoan, but that it was actually an activity on my part of withholding love.

This led me to the most uncharacteristic resolution that I must cease withholding love from my wife and instead embody the Love that clearly was always accessible to me. I realized that I simply had to show my wife love. The force of this insight, luckily, left me no option. Immediately upon returning home from the retreat, I said "I love you" to my wife—for the first time in a quarter of a century. And I meant it. It was the first step in my incarnation of this profound relational gesture. We have never been so intimate, sharing, or happy together as we are now. And this newfound emotional openness is creating beneficial effects beyond my marital life.

I am aware, of course, that this is no great spiritual attainment, but merely the humanization of a spiritual tyro's life. But it is on the very simple level of our day-to-day relationships and activities that the spiritual process of self-transformation and ultimate self-transcendence begins. As Master Da Free John writes in *The Knee of Listening:* "This moment is the moment of Reality, of Union, of Truth." Reality is our everyday circumstance, and that is where the field of our spiritual practice is. I count myself so fortunate to have been granted this recognition.

A year ago I wrote a letter to Master Da Free John in which I attempted to express my deep and heartfelt gratitude for his compassion and for the Teaching. Nevertheless, I felt constrained to say, "If I were able to love, I would love you." I was even incapable of loving the one person who, I intuited, was never wavering in his love for all beings.

Now I feel free to say: Master Da, I love you.

During the 1940s Ben Pierce flew planes for the Navy and a commercial airline. He was also an engineering officer in the Navy and the Merchant Marine.

In the 1950s and 1960s he did research-and-development work in various aerospace activities, and became Senior Research Engineer for a large corporation in a program associated with the Man-in-Space Project.

He later became Manager of Research for two companies, in one case developing and testing safety equipment for automobiles, and in the other evaluating technical training programs at oil refineries and for the Job Corps.

He has taught and done research in the behavioral sciences at several universities in the United States and overseas. He holds four academic degrees, including a Ph.D. in anthropology and a B.S. in engineering.

PART FOUR

THE PARADOX
OF BEING–
CONSCIOUSNESS

The mechanism of attention is a mechanical structure, binding on Consciousness, and what you know in the plane of the mind is not sufficient to enable you to transcend the mechanisms of attention. Many people, on the basis of a religious or spiritual point of view, entertain some level of presumption about such mechanisms and the after-death process, but they have not the ability to enter into a higher destiny or the Transcendental Condition of Perfect Freedom, Liberation, and Eternal Existence in the Divine Domain. Thus, humanity needs more than science. In addition to some higher or esoteric knowledge about the circumstance of our existence, humanity needs the Wisdom of Transcendental Teaching and the Wisdom of practice.

Da Free John
Easy Death, *p. 264–65*

INTRODUCTION TO PART FOUR

Through the talks and essays of the previous part, which argued for a participatory mode of existence, we followed the Adept Da Free John into the "twilight" of the psychic dimension where the laws of logic and the analytical sharpness of rationality are challenged. The rational mind experiences this adventure as a threat and a loss of clarity. Yet, the apparent lucidity of rational life is gained by freezing the "rheomode"[1] or flow of existence into a static representation, a mental icon. Thus, rational focusedness is achieved at the expense of spontaneous life itself. One has to abstract oneself from the flow of things in order to observe and analyze—and, undoubtedly, to feel immune from—life. Looked at from a larger perspective, however, the abstract-material dimension that is our familiar universe is less luminous than the seeming "twilight zone" of the psyche. A photograph never captures the luminosity of the real landscape. Abstraction, like the chemical translation process of photography, entails a diminution of light. Perhaps this metaphor helps one to understand how a sorcerer like Carlos Castaneda's Don Juan[2] can regard the "other" dimension to be as real as the material world—if not more so—and also why otherwise fairly ordinary trance mediums can display astonishing intelligence and knowledge.

But, as was explained in the introduction to part 3, the psychic dimension must not be confused with the Ultimate Reality Itself. It is merely an intermediate space, lit up, as it were, both by the Transcendental Source of all light and by its refractions in the "atmosphere" of the material realm—hence the label "twilight" dimension. The psychic realm is perplexing enough to the rational mind with its penchant for sharply defined categories. But the Ultimate Reality, or what Master Da Free John calls the Radiant

---

1. This phrase is borrowed from David Bohm, *Wholeness and the Implicate Order* (London: Routledge & Kegan Paul, 1980), pp. 27ff.

2. See C. Castaneda, *The Teachings of Don Juan* (Harmondsworth, England: Penguin Books, 1968).

Transcendental Being, is a perfect Mystery.[3] It is the ultimate Paradox:
It goes against (*para*) all opinion (*doxa*), all commonsense notions. It
is not merely an objective puzzle that could be solved given sufficient
time and ingenuity, but it is irreducible and unfathomable.

In his book *The New Consciousness in Science and Religion*,
Harold K. Schilling, an emeritus professor of physics, has devoted a
special appendix to defining the concept of "mystery."[4] He starts out
by rejecting the common usages of the term, which equate it with the
problematic, the as-yet-unexplained, the forbidden secret, the worthless
or to-be-disregarded. The genuine Mystery, he argues, is inexplicable,
unknowable, and even imperceptible and inscrutable. Beyond this, it
has the quality of being limitless, inexhaustible, infinite. Schilling
speaks of "the *ever-receding-horizon* of our knowledge and understanding; no matter how far we press the analysis of the known, the
end of it remains out of sight."[5]

The Mystery is the inexhaustible Fullness, the bottomless Depth
of existence. We exist in that Mystery, and our individual lives are
unthinkable without that ultimate Paradox. Indeed, we live out our
self-enclosed lives in reaction to that Mystery. As Master Da Free John
explains:

> *The usual man or woman recoils from the Mystery of the Infinite
> by absorption in the reaction of mortal fear. Thus, fear produces self-
> possession and loss of Communion with the Divine. Such recoil
> produces psycho-physical adaptation of a reactive kind, and every
> function, every relationship, every condition of experience, high or low
> in the structure of the body-mind, becomes a reflection of the primal
> recoil toward self, away from relations, and away from Communion
> with the Living Mystery that is Divine. The self-possessed individual
> is wound up in self-recoil, and every part demonstrates the reactive
> drama of relational avoidance, subjective bondage, and bodily dis-ease.[6]*

3. In its understandable eagerness to legitimize itself, the still young science of parapsychology is
particularly mindful of the canons of science. With the help of the respectable theory of
probability, it endeavors to accomplish the impossible: to rationally penetrate the irrational. This
is tantamount to casting brightest light onto twilight—an act that surely makes the latter vanish
at once. To the degree that parapsychology is successful in this almost quixotic undertaking, it can
be considered "shady," that is, it can be deemed as participating in the twilight of its subject
matter. And this is precisely the accusation made by the antagonists of parapsychological
research, though evidently for the wrong reasons.

4. H. K. Schilling, *The New Consciousness in Science and Religion* (London: SCM Press, 1973),
pp. 267–76.

5. Ibid., p. 269.

6. Bubba [Da] Free John, *The Enlightenment of the Whole Body*, p. 268.

It is difficult for the consciousness in recoil to recognize its reactivity and to sense itself as being immersed in an inalienable Mystery, precisely because the repression of that Mystery is the basis for the individuated consciousness. In order to sense or feel the Mystery in which everyone and everything inheres, one must surrender one's self-position by discontinuing the habit of externalizing the Real. The Mystery cannot be confronted, it can only be lived—or, more accurately, one can only allow oneself to be lived by It. Master Da Free John suggests two practical exercises that might help the reader to come to an intuitive appreciation of all this.

First, set aside for a moment all of your knowledge about the universe and all your religious or scientific presumptions about how it all developed to this point in time. Simply consider this: Even if all processes and all beings evolved or appear to have evolved mechanically and by accidents of association, rather than Mysteriously, as an expression of an eternal Divine Radiation of events, then why does anything or anyone exist at all? How does the existence of anything and everything come about as an accident? Where did that accident occur? Within what is it all occurring? Where is space?

I cannot consider the very existence of anything and everything without developing a thrill in my back and head, so that it feels as if my hair is about to stand on end. We do not know what even a single thing is, or why it is, or where it is, or when it is, or how it came to be. We are confronted by an irreducible Mystery, and that Mystery is profound. If you will truly consider, even for a moment, the matter of the paradox of the existence of anything whatsoever, you will feel intuitively in touch with the Mystery that is Reality Itself. The mind falls away in that moment, and even though you will not have come up with any "knowing" explanations for the world, you will enjoy a tacit sense of Communion with the Living Reality of the world and of your own mind and body.

As a second exercise, examine yourself for a moment and feel any and all forms of bodily contraction, emotional reactivity, and mental concern that possess you. If you will do this deeply and truly, even for a moment, you will become aware of your chronic state. We are, except in the attitude of total psycho-physical Communion with the Living Divine Reality, in a chronic state of reactive contraction or tension, simultaneously in mind, emotion, and body. If you can observe and feel this for a moment, you will sense how it is all a single gesture—a withdrawal or contraction from release into the condition of unqualified relationship. And once this becomes clear, on the basis of a moment of insight, you will be able to relax and feel, beyond thought and reactive emotion and bodily tension, into a sense of self-releasing intimacy with all the conditions of the world. And that release will establish you, at least for a moment, in the wordless experiential sense of Communion with Life, or the Nameless Radiance that pervades the world and the body of Man.

These two considerations or exercises are a moment's cure for too much knowledge about things and too much self-possessed reacting to things. In the moment in which we stand free of the self-defining contractions of mere knowledge and mere reaction to experience, we stand in direct experiential intuition of the Divine Mystery or Living Reality that is the Truth of the world, and that is the very and eternal Urge to religious consciousness and the higher evolution of Man.[7]

Perhaps Albert Einstein, a deeply religious man, expressed this sense of intuitive apprehension of the Real when he wrote:

The fairest thing we can experience is the mysterious. It is the fundamental emotion which stands at the cradle of true art and true science. He who knows it not and can no longer wonder, no longer feel amazement, is as good as dead, a snuffed-out candle.[8]

However, Einstein brought to this feeling at least some excess baggage: his conviction that reason can have access to Reality. Hence his lifelong struggle to conceptualize the (mathematical) beauty of the Mystery as It reveals Itself in the (apparent) laws of Nature. For this reason it was also difficult for this great genius to accept Heisenberg's uncertainty principle, which has become the cornerstone of modern quantum physics. For Einstein, God simply did not play dice. Yet, quantum physics has restored the idea of the ultimate Mystery of existence to respectability. There is room again for unconditional awe at the awesome, unknowable immensity of Reality.

With his famous equation $E=mc^2$,[9] Einstein has not only topsy-turvyed physics and cosmology, he has also started a chain reaction of

---

7. Da Free John, *Scientific Proof of the Existence of God Will Soon Be Announced by the White House!* pp. 20–21.

8. A. Einstein, *The World As I See It*, p. 5.

9. $E=mc^2$ is the mathematical equation formulated by Albert Einstein in 1905 to express the

paradoxical formulations without which modern physics is impossible but which at the same time render futile the very program of rational science, which is geared to assemble a complete, coherent, intelligible, and perfectly predictable pattern that is supposedly a faithful replica of reality.

In his talk "CHRIST=mc²," forming chapter 20, Master Da Free John suggests that the real significance of Einstein's equation (and, by extension, of all the other paradoxes of modern physics) has still not been understood. For, if the material world is really not material at all but a transformation of energy, then one would expect this to profoundly change Man's psychological life, not only his physical environment, through the technological advances that have been made possible on account of Einstein's equation. There *are* personal consequences from the fact that the physical cosmos is, as the Adept puts it, "a speck floating in a Realm of Light-Energy that is neither visible nor comprehensible to Man in his subhuman, unevolved, and un-Enlightened state" (p. 364).

Master Da Free John compares the formula $E=mc^2$ to the more ancient one of "Christ is risen from the dead." Both formulas are inaccessible to the conventional mind, whether it runs in the grooves of science or exoteric religion, because both are indicative of a nonmaterial truth. Master Da Free John is here not considering whether or not, or in what manner, Jesus of Nazareth actually rose from the dead, but he focuses on the communicative value of this Christian credo in terms of Man's evolutionary capacity and in light of the nonmateriality of existence.[10]

Apparently the Adept Jesus had his own difficulties with the materialistic mentality of his age. The *New Testament* has preserved the following biographical fragment, which is pertinent in the present context:

---

ultimate equivalence of matter and energy. "E" stands for energy, "m" for mass or quantity of matter, and "c²" for the speed of light (186,000 miles per second) multiplied by itself. This formula shows that the amount of energy represented by any given material object can be determined by multiplying its mass by the speed of light squared. Thus, the formula represents the actual conversion of matter into energy. This conversion takes place in the nuclear reactions that produce light-energy in all stars and in man-made atomic or nuclear weapons.

10. For a succinct and critical treatment of the traditional belief in Jesus' survival after death, the reader is referred to Da Free John, *A Call for the Radical Reformation of Christianity*, especially pp. 8–9.

And Jesus went out, and his disciples, into the towns of Caesarea Philippi: and by the way he asked his disciples, saying unto them, Whom do men say that I am?

And they answered, John the Baptist: but some say, Elias; and others, One of the prophets.

And he saith unto them, But whom say ye that I am? And Peter answereth and saith unto him, Thou art the Christ.

And he charged them that they should tell no man of him.

And he began to teach them, that the Son of man must suffer many things, and be rejected of the elders, and of the chief priests, and scribes, and be killed, and after three days rise again. (Mark 8:27–31) [11]

Who the Christ, "the Lord," was has kept many generations of theologians busy, and the debate has still not come to a close. Whoever Jesus of Nazareth may have been—historically and in metaphysical terms—he was to all intents and purposes intimate with the energetic nature of the cosmos, as are all the Adepts of mankind. St. Matthew in his gospel (17:1–2) tells us of an incident in which Jesus took three of his disciples to the top of a high mountain where he "was transfigured before them: and his face did shine as the sun, and his raiment was white as the light." [12] Those acquainted with the tradition of the Adepts readily recognize this to be a literal description that does not need to be demythologized or turned into a mere symbolic statement. Jesus' Transfiguration before his disciples can be interpreted as a compassionate gesture of demonstrating to them not his personal superiority but the nonmaterial nature of this seemingly solid physical realm. Simultaneously, it can be understood as an initiatory event whose momentum would inexorably move his disciples closer and closer to God-Realization. Many similar Transfiguration phenomena are reported of the Adept Da Free John, who has, moreover, granted all kinds of firsthand experiences of the energetic dimension of reality to numerous spiritual practitioners as part of his Teaching Demonstrations. [13]

11. *The Holy Bible*, Authorized King James Version (Oxford: Oxford Univ. Press, n.d.).

12. Ibid.

13. The most memorable Teaching Demonstration, extending over four months, is the "Garbage and the Goddess" period (from March to July, 1974). During this period, Master Da Free John induced, by way of Transmission, in individuals and even in large gatherings all kinds of psychic and mystical states, including temporary immersion in the Transcendental Reality.

In themselves such experiences, even if they take the practitioner to the very heights of mysticism, have no more value than any other type of experience. Their significance lies in their power to transform the individual by making him available for the spiritual task of conscious self-transcendence in the face of the all-engulfing Mystery. This is the point of chapter 21, which is the abbreviated version of a much more detailed autobiographical account by a longtime practitioner of the Way of Radical Understanding or Divine Ignorance. Joanne Mied, a former systems analyst, describes how her left-brained approach to life had hampered her spiritual practice until, thanks to the graceful intervention of Master Da Free John, she was able to begin to appreciate the very real limitations of an abstract and materialist orientation to this psycho-physical universe.

In chapter 22, which is a talk entitled "Hardware, Software, and Transcendence," Master Da Free John avails himself of computer terminology to highlight a dualistic metaphor that is pervasive in human thought, but that is based on the illusion that Life comes in so many separate packages.

Nature, the World-Process, cannot be compressed into any simplistic schema of this type. Master Da Free John reaffirms the testimony of all the Adepts: that Nature cannot ultimately be comprehended, that the apparent regularities "discovered" by scientists are not necessarily descriptive of reality. Astrophysicists may speculate about cosmic creation and postulate a "Big Bang" where religious authorities once proclaimed a divine *fiat,* but they cannot truly account for the existence of the universe. One can still ask, Why is there something and not merely nothing?—a question Master Da Free John posed in a previous chapter. He does not, of course, expect an answer. There is none. The only possible "answer" is a nonverbal gesture: the direct transcendence of the one who phrases the question and expects an answer in the first place. And this response is always a personal matter.

If the whole multidimensional cosmos—whose surface structures are barely scratched by modern science—is a vast paradoxical process that arises as a mystery in the great Mystery of Being-Consciousness, what is the status of the ego in all this? Master Da Free John compares (not reduces!) the egoic consciousness, which creates the illusion of the fragmented world, to a TV program operating primarily on the basis of repetitiveness. He concedes that some dialogue (apparent self-understanding) can and does occur and that if this self-understanding is pursued radically (paradoxically) enough, the program starts to recognize its own ultimate irrelevance and illusoriness. It begins to glimpse its independence from the hardware with which it is associated. In that moment it becomes self-transcending. But there can be no full comprehension of this fact. For, perfect transcendence means perfect Ignorance. The Enlightened being is the one who has stepped out of this looped knowledge program. The program continues until the hardware itself (the body) breaks down, but all this is now recognized as being of no consequence for Consciousness Itself. The Self-Identity abides unaffected by the changes in the program and the hardware, and their final destruction is a wholly insignificant "quantum event" within the total Field of Being-Consciousness. The Transcendental Self always stands Free. Thus, the Adept lives *as* that Self-Identity but *through* the hardware-software of a particular localized modification or quantum wave function of the total Field.

The Adept's paradoxical status and function is further explained in chapter 23, called "M-Fields and the Work of the Adept." Again using a modern metaphor—in the form of Rupert Sheldrake's hypothesis of formative causation—Master Da Free John endeavors to elucidate the mysterious relationship that pertains between the Enlightened Adept and those who come into his sphere of Influence. It should have become clear by now that the Adept, or rather his Transmission, is crucial to the spiritual process: His Presence initiates (in some cases) and amplifies (in all cases) the self-transcending vector in others, providing there is a basic psychic openness or receptivity; otherwise, they will only suffer their native self-contraction more intensely.

The human Spiritual Master is an agent to the advantage of those in like form. When one enters into right relationship with a Spiritual Master, changes happen in the literal physics of one's existence. It is not just a matter of ideas. I am talking about transformations at the level of energy, at the level of the higher light of physics, at the level of mind beyond the physical limitations that people now presume, at the level of the absolute Speed of ultimate Light. The transforming process is enacted in devotees, duplicated in them in and through that Living Company. It is not a matter of conceptual symbolisms or emotional attachment to some extraordinary person. It is real physics.[14]

14. Da Free John, *Scientific Proof of the Existence of God Will Soon Be Announced by the White House!* p. 364.

The Spiritual Transmission of the Adept obviously presupposes a Sender and a receiver, and the quality of the reception depends on the latter's capacity for attunement to the Adept's "Presence," his "morphogenetic field." And that attunement is a matter of individual surrender. This is not a childish response of dependence on the Adept as a father substitute, but a mature gesture of self-transcending participation in the transformative Agency that the Adept represents. Thus, the devotee is not the cultic devotee of the personality of the Adept, but he is the devotee of the Ultimate Reality as It is made transparent through the perfect ego-surrender of the Enlightened being who functions as "Guru." [15]

This important difference is difficult to appreciate without a clear understanding of the phenomenon of self-transcendence, which is the alpha and omega of the spiritual process. It is often and wrongly presumed (and feared) that self-transcendence, or ego-death, is equivalent to the obliteration of individuality, the human personality. This misunderstanding arises as a direct result of the ontological condition of un-Enlightened existence itself: The "usual man," as Master Da Free John calls the un-Enlightened individual, experiences himself as identical with the phenomena of the seemingly solid and bounded body-mind, presuming the ego to be some kind of substantive actor. Upon Enlightenment, this myth is at once dispelled. The body-mind then reveals itself as a process (in quantum mechanical language: a wave function) that occurs spontaneously in the midst of countless other similar processes (or wave functions). The ego is simply the mysteriously and spontaneously arising *activity* of partial identification superimposed on Reality, thus producing the illusion of an internal subject confronting an external world (including the externalized body-mind "belonging" to that subject). As Master Da Free John explains:

The body-mind is our agent—a kind of mechanical or computerized receiver and transmitter, a space-time module that determines, defines, and limits every condition that is our experience and our knowledge. Whatever exists to be experienced or known is always mediated by this machine.

15. The true role of the Guru is indicated in an esoteric etymology of this Sanskrit word, according to which the two syllables—*gu* and *ru*—are interpreted as meaning "dispeller (*ru*) of darkness (*gu*)."

This machine is also what every individual regards to be his or her "self"—even though the body-mind is as much an object or relation of awareness as any of the objects or relations experienced or known via the agency of the body-mind. Truly, the self is the awareness that monitors the body-mind, the experiences and cognitions developed by the body-mind, and all of the objects presumed to exist in relation to the body-mind.

The actual status of our existence is that "I" is simple awareness associated with a body-mind-apparatus that is arising dependently (not independently) in relation to a great space-time field of energies and apparent forms. The field of energies and apparent forms is not experienced or cognized directly. Rather, it impresses itself upon the experiential and cognitive apparatus of the body-mind, and the body-mind conducts those impressions (in the form of electrical impulses) to the nervous system and brain, where those impulses are sorted out and presented to awareness in the form of facsimiles mysteriously made of the energy that is most intimate to the conscious self of awareness.[16]

And:

As we accumulate impressions over time, the field of our awareness comes to be felt as a threat. Thus, a protective reflex develops. It is a subtle contraction at the very root of the meeting between awareness and the body-mind. And that contraction is then effectively felt at every level, dimension, point, or state of the body-mind.

It is this protective reaction or reflexive contraction that is the most critical and significant factor in the development of human existence. On its basis, awareness conceives itself to be individual, separate, and dependent on the body-mind, such that awareness becomes relatively weak and passive. Thus, awareness begins to hide behind the body-mind, and it may even seek to hide or escape from the body-mind (in the case of certain kinds of ascetical or other-worldly spiritual strategies as well as in the case of various kinds of neurosis and psychosis). Just so, this same contraction, experienced as it is in terms of being limited by and dependent upon the body-mind, tends in general to produce the sense of egoic identification with the

---

16. From an unpublished essay dated March 24, 1981, by Da Free John, entitled "What Are You Always Doing?"

body-mind—so that "I" is felt and presumed to be the psycho-physical persona, an entity separate from, dependent upon, and threatened and bewildered by the phenomenal field of its apparent relations.[17]

When that ego-identification is discontinued in the event of Awakening to the Transcendental Condition, the apparent individual characteristics—the so-called personality traits—associated with the particular configuration of space-time (that is, a specific body-mind) continue to arise. The Enlightened being appears to behave like all other apparent individuals, but he "himself" lacks the experience of subjectivity. He has become the Identity of all beings and things, and he simply "recognizes" the arising of the bodily-mental conditions, including the continuing (and self-preserving) tendency of the body-mind to conceive of itself as an entity in its own right in an environment of other similarly individuated beings. But individuation no longer holds any personal implication for him. A mind-baffling paradox!

It is out of this paradoxical State that the Adept speaks with prophetic authority. The "Me" of his Ecstatic speech is not the "me" of the un-Enlightened ego, experiencing itself as lodged in a finite body-mind. As Master Da Free John asseverates in the Ecstatic manner of the great Adepts of the past:

I am not born. And I am not one who has been born. I am not a reincarnated individual. I am not even an <u>incarnated</u> individual. I am not one who has a future. I am not one who is in the worlds. I am not one whose consciousness is here or there. I have seen all things and they all exist in Me, so I can describe them to you. But I am not always meditating on them, so they are really beside the point for Me. And I, fundamentally, know nothing about them, except that I recognize them perfectly.

I am simply a Voice that instigates your own insight. Da Free John is not one who is like you, who is related, who is knowledgeable, who is informed, who is saved or relieved. Da Free John is not any such person. Da Free John is no person. At some point you may begin to realize this. Da Free John is like a movie on the screen. You do not suggest to yourself when you see a movie on the screen that there is consciousness in the screen. The play itself is the argument. And Da Free John is not anything other than the process of his appearance on

every level of being. There is no implication of an individual in him.
There is no individual in Da Free John—none![18]

This is a God-Realized Confession. But What or Who is the God
thus Realized? That God is evidently not the God of theistic religion.
It is not any conceived or conceivable deity, but the Living God, the
Ultimate Reality Itself. This is the sublime subject matter of Master
Da Free John's talk "God Is the One Who Is Being Modified as
Everything," forming chapter 24. The Adept's speech about that One
Reality, or Divine Being, is not an attempt at description or theolo-
gizing. Rather, it is a goad for others to Realize for themselves that
Ultimate Condition.

However, since the Adept not only Transmits that Condition
silently, but in his communication also operates on the intellectual-
verbal level, he necessarily employs concepts. And therefore many
parallels could be pointed out between his "concept" of Reality and the
theological concepts that are idiosyncratic of other traditions and
individual Adepts. To some extent, Master Da Free John has done this
himself in several of his works.[19] Yet, his reason for engaging such
comparisons has always been the *practical* one of clarifying the
spiritual process for practitioners. In fact, his conceptual analyses all
ultimately serve to disrupt the proclivity, especially in left-brained
individuals, of feeling comfortable with a surrogate abstract reality,
whilst the Real is transconceptual and Alive.

Now, God-Realization is not the prerogative of special geniuses.
It is the real Condition of every being and inanimate object in the
world. Man, whose self-awareness has reached a critical threshold, is
potentially capable of intuiting this Truth. As the Christian patriarchs
put it: He is *capax Dei* or capacitated to have the "vision" of God.
More than that, God-Realization is the probable evolutionary destiny
of mankind as a whole. Master Da Free John goes even further than
this when he considers the possibility of the "Translation" of the
universe into the Enlightened Condition. How this is to be understood
is made clear in chapter 25, entitled "What If the Universe Were to
Disappear in Light?"

Chapter 26 is an essay called "Space, Consciousness, and Enlightenment," which outlines, in almost aphoristic terseness, the relation-

18. Da Free John, "The Heart Is Not Wedded to the Face," *The Laughing Man*, vol. 3, no. 3
(1982), pp. 96-97.

19. See especially Da Free John, *Nirvanasara*.

ship between manifest reality and Transcendental Reality or Consciousness. The propositions of this essay are to be intuited and Realized rather than merely comprehended by the intellect. Even though we can understand the language and appreciate the pristine clarity of thought, this evocative description of Reality becomes Obvious to us only at the moment of Realization, beyond conventional thinking, knowing, and experiencing.

This grand theme is continued in the subsequent short essay entitled "The Continuum," which rounds off the consideration of part 4. It is an Adept's reminder to mankind of the Ultimacy of Consciousness and a passionate exhortation to move beyond the pernicious parodies of Reality that currently divide humanity into warring camps and are responsible for the psychic and spiritual asphyxiation of Man and his continuing subadaptation to Life.

May this book invoke in the reader an intuition of the Mystery of existence, of the inexhaustible and utterly paradoxical Fullness that perplexes the scientific mind, fills the religious mind with awe, and is simply Realized by the one who transcends body, mind, self, and world.

CHAPTER 20

CHRIST=mc²

a talk by Da Free John
April 19, 1979

1.

ASTER DA FREE JOHN: Scientists tend to be as obsessed with self as any other human beings. And, in the trend of their own traditional philosophy, they represent the same barbaric mentality as those who are, in the manner of the streets, more obviously committed to fleshly mortality. Scientists, too, seem to want to reduce existence to physical, elemental terms. They are obsessed with "matter" and death and cause-and-effect relations. Consider, for example, the now popular theory that the universe was caused by a giant explosion, the "Big Bang." This theory has been confirmed by a great deal of physical evidence, and thus it has become the generally accepted view of how our universe appeared. This cosmology, like the physical laws considered by Newton, will probably always remain true on some level of experience, even though the paradox of such a view may become more apparent in the future. Somehow, the idea of the universe as a one-dimensional or strictly material event that suddenly begins and ends is basic to the popular and traditional understanding of "civilized" Man.

Physicists are currently considering the implications of the paradoxical fact that the physical universe is apparently not eternal but began with an explosion. They are also confronting the unavoidable conclusion that everything that preceded the "Big Bang" can no longer be discovered and known. In other words, scientists cannot in this case find the ultimate material cause they are seeking, because any facts or information that existed prior to the explosion that created the material universe have been totally obliterated or transformed beyond recognition by that explosion.

You can understand how this reasoning offends the conventional scientific mind, which is disposed to a total understanding of the physical universe in terms of the material sequences of cause and effect. Our scientists cannot fulfill their passionate elemental urge to thoroughly know about the physical universe. Because everything that existed prior to the moment of the "Big Bang" was destroyed in the process, they cannot seek beyond it for physical evidence, it appears. Even more, some scientists have gone so far as to consider that the fact of the "Big Bang" is compatible with popular religious conceptions of the origin of the universe, such as that described in the *Old Testament* book of Genesis. Such a view proposes a necessary link between popular religion and popular science, or at least a point where science reaches the limit of knowledge and must either be silent or defer to the archaic poetry of exoteric religious conception.

The philosophical alternative to ultimate scientific knowledge proposed by popular theorists would seem to be either never to be able to know or else somehow to become religious in the manner of downtown, middle-class churchism. But true religion is a greater conception than any that such theorists conceive. They are still talking about the creation myths of the *Old Testament* as if those descriptions were originally intended to be an historical record of fact (rather than a cultic device, containing both esoteric and exoteric religious instruction). The *Old Testament* and other such popular Scriptures were originally intended to communicate many dimensions of esoteric and exoteric meaning (although "civilized" people continually approach the ancient holy writings as simplistic and literal descriptions of the one-dimensional or material world of modern conception), but true religion is even a greater conception than that offered by the ancient books of Jews and Christians. We must therefore conceive of religion, both true and ancient, in greater terms than the popular mind conceives. Within the framework of great and true esoteric religious and spiritual consideration there is ample room for our sufficient and comprehensive understanding of the physical universe, including the "Big Bang" and all the other illusions of "matter."

Nevertheless, truly to understand the universe of our experience is not a matter of tracing the pattern of material events back to some

absolute original physical Event or material Cause. There may not be
such an Event or Cause in any case. If we trace the one-dimensional
chain of material events (or apparent effects of causes) back far
enough, even if we could discover what existed before the "Big Bang,"
there still may be no End to apparent effects and causes. But if we
accept the factuality and the implications of the "Big Bang" itself, it
does seem that, at least with the ordinary, mental equipment of Man,
we will never be able to go beyond a certain point, and so our prideful
presumption of attaining complete knowledge about (and thus
superiority over) the universe in which we are appearing will, we
must admit, inevitably be frustrated. Today's scientists may be busy
discovering all kinds of things, but they are, by virtue of this
consideration, beginning to realize that they are all something like
plumbers now, you see. They are no longer in the business of
discovering and disseminating ultimate knowledge, and so their
priesthood is in doubt.

But let us consider whether a truly illuminating understanding is
possible for us. Perhaps there is a conceptual link between the highest
considerations of scientific inquiry and the highest considerations of
true and universal religious and spiritual Realization. Consider this:
While the present configuration of "matter," or the apparently
material universe, can be perceived as an effect of a chain of material
causes originating with the "Big Bang" (and what presumably was the
case even before it), the material universe itself and as a whole can also
be considered in every present moment to be the expression of a
dimension of existence that is subtler and greater than the material
universe itself. Therefore, we may also perceive and conceive the
physical universe to be arising within and in some sense as the effect
of another dimension that is hierarchically senior to it and yet perhaps
otherwise invisible or inconceivable from the materialistic point of
view of the conventional and one-dimensional position of perception
and conception. In fact, I am certain that we must realize just such a
perception and conception of the universe in order to have an
authentic science and an authentically human culture. And the formula
$E=mc^2$ is perhaps best understood as a specimen of the very
conception I am suggesting. When its true implications are taken into
account, Einstein's equation of energy and matter (expressed in the
formula $E=mc^2$) represents the possibility of a multidimensional
interpretation of the total universe, in which the so-called "material"
universe is realized to be a paradoxical entity or process.

The conventional philosophy of pre-Einsteinian physics considers the material universe in the very primitive terms of the medieval mind (against which science was supposed to have rebelled). If we would approach the "matter" of the universe as honest physicists, as scientists who are truly sensitive to the higher physics of things, we would realize that the "material" universe is energy, that it is light, that all "material" events are an expression of another dimension than what we call "matter," that "matter" is itself energy, that it behaves as energy, that "matter," and the universe, and, therefore, Man and every individual being, are, each and all, a paradoxical manifestation of infinite Energy and Being, and that the struggle to trace the chain of material causes and effects back to and even beyond the "Big Bang" is a very naive and unillumined approach to understanding the universe of our experience and contemplation. It is the multidimensional understanding in the present that is significant. E=mc² is the modern left-brained or verbal-analytical expression of that multidimensional thinking—a way of entering into the realization that the physical universe is a paradox of light. Thus, we must understand that the universe of our experience is not merely a sequence of physical events and a material effect of the past. The "material" universe is a present expression of light. Matter is light; matter, or the total Realm of Nature, emanates presently from the Matrix of Light.

The obsession with one-dimensional cause-and-effect relations and the materialistic ideal of tracing the configuration of the present moment back to the "Big Bang" or some other material Cause are motivations founded in the barbaric—or at least archaic!—mechanical principles of Newtonian physics and the medieval dreams of Aristotelian philosophy and not at all in the ecstatic and liberating Realization of the paradoxical Reality in which the total World and Man are appearing. The formula E=mc² and the theories of relativity,[1] on the other hand, are expressions of the intuition that the universe is an awesome paradox (not a cause-and-effect simplicity),

1. The theories of relativity, as originally presented by Albert Einstein and developed by many physicists during the course of this century, propose the relative rather than absolute character of motion, velocity, mass, and other principal factors in the physics of Nature and the interdependence of matter, time, and space as a four-dimensional continuum.

Einstein proposed the *special theory of relativity,* which is concerned principally with electromagnetic phenomena and the dynamics of their activity in time and space, and the *general theory of relativity,* which is principally concerned with the concept of gravitation and the equality of gravitational mass and inertial mass. He and many others refined these theories over the years and sought to develop a *unified field theory* that would account for all the paradoxical properties and interactions of all known phenomena of the universe.

and that the present conditions as well as the ultimate Condition of the apparent universe (analyzed by our senses) are never more than partially revealed to the lower-adapted conventional mentality of unevolved Man. Just so, one of the ultimate consequences of this paradoxical conception is the conviction that "matter" is <u>now</u> energy, an expression of energy, a process of energy. To realize perfect identification with that subtle force that is light itself, material forms must be converted, that is true, but even now, as whatever form it appears to be, "matter" is itself a form of light-energy. And, likewise, when Man begins to awaken to this conviction in his own case, he thereby enters into a Process of more and more perfect identity with Energy, or ultimate Translation into the Infinite Domain of Light.

DEVOTEE: Einstein once said that there is enough energy in just striking a match to lift off a mountain.

MASTER DA FREE JOHN: The amount of energy manifested or radiated by even the smallest piece of matter, if we were to convert it into light-energy, would be tremendous. "$E=mc^2$" means that the amount of energy that any piece of so-called "matter" represents, and into which it could be directly converted, is the amount of its mass (whatever measure you use to determine how much mass this chunk represents) multiplied by the square of the speed of light (that is, the speed of light multiplied by itself). In other words, if the physical universe is converted into radiant energy, we must all enter into a domain of energy that is many times greater than the physical universe itself. The physical universe, therefore, is actually a speck floating in a Realm of Light-Energy that is neither visible nor comprehensible to Man in his subhuman, unevolved, and un-Enlightened state. Well! That is exactly the spiritual conception of existence, you see, except that true or spiritual existence encompasses far more than mere energies, even more than higher physical energies, and even more than the mere light of higher psychic consciousness. The entire psycho-physical universe, including you as you now appear, is a superficial, unnecessary, and free or non-binding expression or apparent modification of the Absolute, All-Pervading, Radiant Divine Consciousness. This is the fundamental Realization: Every thing is merely a transparent modification of Consciousness, of the Radiant Love-Energy or Transcendental Bliss-Light that is literally All-Pervading Transcendental Consciousness.

Einstein felt some religious implication in what he was under-standing about the physical universe, but he was not a practitioner of true or esoteric religion. He was not a practicing devotee. He did not observe the human body-mind with the same intensity with which he observed the rest of the physical (or, really, psycho-physical) universe. Thus, he did not discover any higher personal implications in his scientific findings than the humanistic urge to be a good and intellectually serious man in the world. He did not enter truly into a higher religious consideration, involving the actual transformation of his own body-mind into light, but such is the obvious implication of his formula $E=mc^2$, if you are thinking clearly. What is true of the physical universe and the total world is also true of this human psycho-physical being. Energy is our condition already. The body-mind comes out of energy, as does the entire world. And all of this and us must ultimately and will inevitably return to the Realization of prior identification with energy and with the Radiant Transcendental Consciousness that is the Light and Truth and Self of the world.

Einstein's scientific considerations are basically a repetition of ancient esoteric and paradoxical descriptions of the universe. His work has legitimized, in the mathematical, scientific terms of the twentieth century, a certain level of higher consideration about material existence. We have, in both the popular and academic areas of our industrial societies, accepted the general and technical implications of this very sophisticated and elaborate understanding of the elemental world, but we have not realized what that understanding implies about the world and about Man altogether. We are still suffering the cultural limitations upon which our scientific civilization has always been based. Scientists continue merely to think and doubt and exploit the worldly powers of their own enterprise, and they have not yet supported the creation of a total human culture based on the implications of their own discoveries to date. "$E=mc^2$" actually and exactly means the same thing to us today, to our nervous systems, to the individual body-mind or being, that "Christ is risen from the dead" meant two thousand years ago. "$E=mc^2$" is exactly what "Christ is risen from the dead" means. $E=mc^2$ is good news! It proclaims that matter is energy—that the body-mind of every human being can be Realized to be energy, or light.

What does this communication mean in human terms? It means that you are energy. However you may be described altogether, you are not "matter." Matter is dead stuff, a dead end, a solid and separate and only mortal thing. But "matter" does not exist in any case! There is no such thing as "matter," in itself and distinct from light, or energy, or mind, or psyche, or ego, or God. It is not that there is no such thing as our apparent experience here, but all of it is <u>energy</u>, or a temporary form of light. There are many more subtle aspects of light than we see in our subhuman manner, and the entire manifest cosmos, including the body-mind of Man, is a spectrum of energy. Therefore, human beings must become acculturated to living <u>as</u> energy, or spirit-force, instead of struggling in the barbaric mentality of the "flesh." And we <u>must</u> develop a culture of men and women who are being light instead of merely being "matter" and that dark, simple, dreadfully mortal thing that "matter" implies. We must create a culture out of our identification, at this moment, with light, or energy, or the "Holy Spirit" that is Life and that is Alive as every thing and every being.

"E=mc²" is the principal contribution of theoretical physics to date. It is the premier archetypal scientific discovery of the twentieth century. We are just beginning to realize its cultural implications, and those cultural implications are vast. The idea legitimized by the formula E=mc² is the greatest scientific discovery of our time, because it has the most archetypal force. Yet, it is not new. The same idea has been part of the great tradition of esoteric spiritual society since the most ancient times. This formula is simply the modern scientific form or statement of the ancient Wisdom of Life. Because this formulated idea was developed within the domain of science, it has been legitimized by argument and demonstration within the acceptable framework of what is conceived to be knowledge in our time. E=mc² signifies that all matter is simply a form of energy. Therefore, there is no such <u>thing</u> as "matter." The fundamental conception of our existence and the state of our knowledge at the present time is that we and every thing are energy.

But who acts as if energy is the actual state of our existence? People are, in general, still living as if "matter" is the ultimate state of all existence. The masses of humanity, including their intellectual and political leaders, are living in an archaic state of mind and culture. Thus, there are many positive cultural implications in the archetypal formula or rediscovery communicated by Einstein. "E=mc²," like "Christ is risen from the dead," is not made of words, but of archetypal symbols, or pure significance. It is the way the ancient good news is communicated in the terms of twentieth century logic. "Christ is risen from the dead" and "E=mc²" are the same truth stated in the terms of two different epochs of human understanding. Yet, nearly everybody pretends that there is a vast difference between "Christ is risen from the dead" and "E=mc²."

Intellectual and dogmatic pretenses have generated a sophomoric debate between science and religion, as if they communicate two different kinds of information. In truth, popular or exoteric religion and conventional or exoteric science represent two specialized points of view toward the same information. Science represents the analytical point of view, the separate consciousness, the mood of doubt, always analyzing what it sees, not involved in what it is perceiving, or always trying to eliminate itself from such involvement. Such a point of view has some practical application, obviously, but it also has its own inherent limits. Religion fundamentally represents the point of view of unity with everything, rather than analytical separation. It expresses the right-brained mystical and intuitive consideration, rather than the left-brained or verbal consideration. At some point we must come to realize the hierarchical relationship beween these two points of view. We must understand that the mood of unity is the highest or most fundamental point of view, and therefore the most essential cultural orientation. Thus, humanity must devote itself to true religion, to spirituality in its truest, most esoteric sense.

A greater, even more primary archetypal discovery than E=mc² is also concealed in the "native state" of religion. The reason that higher truth is yet hidden is that the only religion people commonly know about is essentially a banal, poetic, fixed-mindedness. Popular religion is not a living inspiration full of Transcendental Wisdom, and esoteric religion is ultimately comprehensible only to Adepts. "E=mc²" is transcended by the Truth greater than "Christ is risen from the dead," greater than the fact that "matter" is a species of light, utterly capable of direct translation into light. It is certainly true that "matter" is light, but the Truth of existence is greater than that. Yes, the Realization of Truth does include a literal transformation wherein the body is Realized and demonstrated to be light (as it is popularly believed to have been the case with Jesus of Nazareth). Spiritual growth is indeed a matter of Man's entering into the Domain of Energy. It involves the repolarizing of the energy of the body (or nervous system) from toe to crown, while also maintaining the capacity to express that Current of energy from the crown to the toe, and thus to live the full circle of the human structure in peace. But the ultimate Realization is a Transcendental Awakening into the Domain in which even light, or space, or change, or energy, or "matter," or the body, or Nature itself, which is essentially the play of light, are all arising.

What is the Condition or ultimate Domain in which light exists? What is the Condition in which Nature exists? We tend to think of Nature in the archaic terms of material processes. But we now also presume that $E=mc^2$, that Nature is only light or energy. What, then, is the Condition or "Place" in which light-energy is arising? The Realization of that Condition is the ultimate religious, esoteric, and spiritual discovery. Truly, energy is arising in the Transcendental, Absolute, and Perfect Domain that is Consciousness. Consciousness is Absolute, Infinite, Radiant Bliss—Undifferentiated and All-Pervading. It is that Condition in which light and "matter" and "mind" and all of us are arising. It is that Condition which is called "God," even by those who have no direct Realization of the Truth. The play of energy, or light, is, therefore, also God. And the human body-mind is full of light, or the Energy of Life. Indeed, Man is only light, or Life, even bodily. And the body of Man is to be Realized as nothing but Radiant Consciousness, or Love, which is the Self that is God.

Thus, we are always already established in a Divine Paradox. That is how we must understand the entire Realm of Nature. We should not despair of understanding the universe simply because we cannot go beyond the "Big Bang" in tracing the material chain of causes and effects. We may be deprived, at least as Man, of a certain inspection of the mechanics of great material processes—or we may not. Perhaps everything can be intuited. If we can enter into the domain of the psyche, the higher mind, or the consciousness of light-energy in its subtler aspects, perhaps we can then discover even the causative processes of material existence that existed previous to the "Big Bang" and that are otherwise unavailable to inspection by bodily or gross physical investigation by Man. Like the higher Wisdom or Truth Itself, this intuitive capacity is also hidden in religion. It is simply not considered or utilized by the current scientific establishment and our conventions of knowing.

The conception of $E=mc^2$ is arising in the Transcendental Depth that is Consciousness, just as are the self-idea and the subjective consciousness of the individual. The subjective or egoic self or body-mind is realized in the seventh or perfect stage of life to be not other than energy. It is not merely self-contained or objectively experienced bliss, but it is Ecstasy, or a Realization founded on self-transcendence, or the perfect sacrifice of the body-mind of the individual. It is Love, Energy, Radiance, and Absolute Consciousness. Everything is Realized to be simply the modification of that One Self and Reality Who is Absolute Consciousness and Absolute Energy, Undifferentiated, Transcendental, and All-Pervading. That is God and the Truth of the individual self. That One may be Realized to be one's very Self in ecstasy, when one transcends the subjective or psycho-physical self-reference and enters into God-Consciousness truly. That One may also be felt in relationship, Pervading all experience. And that One may be felt as a Divine Personality, great beyond ordinary conception, but nonetheless a Person, not mere energy (like the rays of the sun), but Consciousness (like the sun itself), Alive, Pervading all, Transcending all, Existing as all.

Presently, in the cause-and-effect terms of time and space, you cannot go beyond the "Big Bang" to account for yourself. You can, however, enter into consideration of the super-dimensional realm in which "matter" truly exists. That is an altogether different consideration of physics. What is the Condition in which light arises? When that Condition can be conceptually presumed through mathematical and technological consideration of phenomena, then those who are presently bound to the subhuman limits of popular scientific conceptions may realize a much higher cultural stage of human life. That cultural realization will bridge the gap between religion and science, and, ultimately, between esoteric and exoteric knowledge. It must be presumed, deeply in the psyche, that matter is a form of energy, a modification of light. But we must also see that light, energy, change, arises within the Infinite Radiance of Transcendental Consciousness. And what that means is that matter (and, therefore, the human body) likewise arises in Consciousness, since matter can be rightly conceived only as a modification of light. This higher and practical consideration must be brought into the scientific realm of physics, so that the spiritual consideration of Truth can begin to be understood in its fullest sense. This is an exalted consideration. It is not a street-level salvation "gospel." It is available to ordinary people if they will be converted to true and esoteric spiritual practice, but the origin and the fulfillment of the consideration itself is founded in a most high and ultimate Realization that exceeds all the limits of the body-mind of Man.

The analytical description of the universe in which current scientific formulas like $E=mc^2$ are appearing should begin to be accepted and legitimized within the greater framework of spiritual understanding that I have proposed. How can we legitimize this

conception? How do we bring true religion and esoteric spirituality
out of the closet—or, really, the cultural concentration camp to which
they have been relegated by all the barbaric and absolutist propaganda
of scientific materialism? Religion is the cultural idiot of the modern
world, while science is the TV hero of all the News, but the traditional
and current popular state of science and the materialistic culture it
promotes does not permit a fully illumined or enlightened or peaceful,
happy life. The higher and spiritual implications of revolutionary
contemporary physics must be understood relative to Man, to the
individual. Our scientists must therefore move the frontiers of science
from theoretical physics to biophysics. What is the significance of
$E=mc^2$ for the human body-mind? How do we promote and establish
cultural ideals that enable all men and women to function and grow as
light or energy rather than as lifeless matter?

We must presume, based even on our present understanding and
application of theoretical physics, that matter is energy. Then what
about our understanding and application of biochemistry, biophysics,
human anatomy, human life, human culture? What will we do when
we take the discovery of the relationship between matter and energy
seriously? How do we make medicine out of the understanding that
the human body is energy? How do we practice ordinary diet,
sexuality, and social relations on that basis? How do we bring the
higher knowledge of physics and spiritual esotericism into the daily
practice of ordinary people? And then, how do we also bring mankind
into the greater conception and ultimate Realization of the Transcendental and Divine Consciousness, in which matter, energy, and light
are appearing? If you are serious about such questions, then I suggest
you study all of the literature I have written for just such a one as
yourself. Then choose what you will do.

The Divine understanding of the universe, with all of its
paradoxes and mysteries, must be restored to Man. Human beings
must be allowed the greater and truly human culture of self-
transcendence in God-Communion, wherein they may also enjoy the
benefits of cooperative life, peaceful human existence, perhaps even
some technological sophistication—since there is nothing inherently
evil about technology—or even whatever simplicity a person may
choose if he or she prefers to be very simple about the ordinary affair
of material existence. Every person must be permitted the higher
understanding and free spiritual practice of Life, even if he or she
chooses to live a lifetime in relative seclusion, or within the Sanctuary

of an autonomous religious community, rather than in the broad popular environment of mass politics and all the casual births and deaths of subhuman acculturation.

2.

MASTER DA FREE JOHN: Can you conceive of the madness of such a universe as this? First nothing—and then all this, this apparent world, seemingly mechanical, in which every individual element or entity is, in itself, mortal, a world that seems to afford no opportunity for any individual to know anything about what is beyond and prior to his or her own actual, physical form or process. What an absurdity to appear out of nothing! Why should anything appear at all? Why should such a joke appear out of nothing? Where has all of this happened?

All of this seems to me to be very important for us to consider to the point of certainty and self-surrender. The intensity of our understanding of these matters will most definitely determine the quality of our lives. And how do you intend to get to the foundation of this wondering?

If the universe is simply mad, and if there is no way to understand it, no way even to feel back beyond the appearance of your own nervous system and body, any more than you can feel back beyond the "Big Bang" and discover how the universe came to exist— if that is the nature of existence, you see, then there are at least two basic ways whereby you can respond: Either you can become so serious that you seem not to take anything seriously at all (and so just burn yourself out, destroying yourself in self-indulgence or whatever chaos you want to use to distract yourself) or, with equal seriousness, you can approach life as the conventional Buddhists do!

The classical or exoteric type of Buddhist (who should be distinguished from the esoteric or higher type of "Buddhist," examples of which have appeared, for instance, among the Adepts of Tibet)[2] is

2. Criticism of the secondary or conventional aspects of any or all existing traditions is one of the primary functions or services Adepts perform for the sake of mankind. Thus, Master Da Free John speaks sympathetically about many aspects of Buddhism in general while criticizing what belongs to conventional path-consciousness and cultic asceticism. The Teaching of Master Da Free John is aligned to the highest expression of the Transcendental Realization found in the literature of Buddhism, e.g., the *Lankavatara Sutra,* the *Diamond Sutra,* the *Platform Sutra,* and to the Realization of Adepts such as Nagarjuna, the Sixth Patriarch, Padmasambhava, Marpa, Milarepa, and others.

responding to the same conception of the universe as the person who
burns himself out. He has exactly the same motivation! The person
who burns himself out does so because he cannot handle the "truth"
that he seems to have discovered. The usual Buddhist, however,
although convinced of the same "truth," does not take up the way of
self-indulgence; in his intellectual view, that is only another form of
suffering. Instead, he yields all the tension in his being. He just gives
up all hold on himself. He becomes less and less subject to the stress of
living, and he ultimately renounces all motivation, so that he is neither
threatened nor threatening. He becomes so free of reactive stress that
he is no longer struggling with his inevitable mortality. Thus, he
conquers the awesome facts of Nature by giving up all striving in the
midst of a mortal life.

    If you were to come to this conclusion—that you are mortal, that
the universe is essentially chaotic, that in any case you cannot know
beyond your own nervous system, that you cannot find out the actual
nature of your situation—if all that were to become your own
conviction, I do not see how you could take the world unseriously
enough to quietly play out an orderly and productive ordinary life,
except perhaps to the degree that you were simply frightened. And, of
course, such fear is an important element of life for most of us. People
are essentially desperate. They do live lives of "quiet desperation."
They have discovered, at least in their superficial reflections and
feelings, that they are mortal and hopeless, that they cannot know
anything ultimately and are not congratulated by the universe. And
they are afraid, because they know that they can suffer terribly, so they
neither burn themselves out nor yield to their mortality by giving up
to the point of the Buddhists' passivity, or nonresistance to change and
death.

    Gautama, called the Buddha, did not believe in striving toward
heaven worlds. There is no traditional command in classical or
original Buddhism to make efforts to succeed in mystical matters.
Gautama simply ceased to be disturbed by the mortal facts of suffering.
By craving experience and entering into the whole affair of experience,
including psychic as well as physical phenomena, he found that
experience itself is deluding. Experience makes us feel as if we are
involved in some great importance, whereas if we really observe
ourselves, we will see that in a very few years we will start getting
terribly ill, and eventually we will die, losing everything and everyone
in the process. Gautama's point of view was very desperate, in that

sense. He saw clearly that we can have riches and visions and all kinds of material "blessings," but these things all become ridiculous when we remember that we are mortal. Gautama's ultimate philosophical mood of nonreaction was based on the observation of his present and inevitable mortality, not on the idea of eventual immortality. He simply came to the point of yielding, of nonresistance. He could accept the view that bodily life and everything that we can have in mind is temporary and mortal, but he also realized that this life could pass without being disturbing. While alive, he engaged in no disturbing efforts to fulfill motivations and desires. He became desireless through insight into desire.

Gautama did not create any program for going to heaven or for existing forever in any objective form. Yet, the older Indian tradition of the immortal soul, of higher or heavenly worlds, and of reincarnation or transmigration is also associated with Gautama's patterns of thought and presumption. Such traditional lore, whether fanciful or factual, does not seem to fit very well with Gautama's particularly fatalistic observation of the facts of Nature. That is why so much of traditional religious Buddhism is really based on accretions of popular nonsense, such as developed over time in the case of all ancient exoteric religious traditions. The glorious heavenly images of the Buddha that have appeared within the later traditions of Buddhism have nothing to do with the original root of inspired intuition that awakened in Gautama himself.

The root of exoteric Buddhism is a desperate or fatalistic observation of the facts of Nature, which justifies the conceptual understanding that <u>you</u> <u>are</u> <u>mortal</u>—not that you are an immortal soul, not that there are great cosmic possibilities, but, simply and only, that you are mortal. Once this principle is accepted, anything great that may come into your experience has to be understood from that point of view, or you will be deluded by it. Thus, any great desire, when satisfied, can delude you, by making you forget your actual situation. The more involved you become with experience, the more you crave experience; and the more you crave experience, the more you want to continue to exist, and, therefore, the more you fear death. Gautama's approach was to enjoy insight into this matter, to presume with absolute clarity simply that "I" am mortal. That was the great insight. It was not a metaphysical idea of some sort. It was a process of awakening to mortality and allowing the sheer fact of mortality to overwhelm him, so that he could be liberated from the game of fulfilling all the psycho-physical forms of mortal possibility.

We also see a variation on the mood of this fatalistic insight in our contemporary scientific, technological culture. We are all tending to be possessed by a conception of our life and world and destiny that is based exclusively on the observation of the material and mortal facts of Nature, such as the "Big Bang" of the birth of the physical universe, beyond which we cannot know. When we presume that we are merely and only mortal, we also begin logically to presume other things—for instance, we may observe (and negatively interpret) that much of what are considered religious, mystical, and other-worldly phenomena are simply expressions of the internal, subjective, and self-generated profusion of the brain and the total nervous system. How then can we avoid having to yield to the extremes of fatalistic self-abandonment (rather than ecstatic, self-transcending, Life-positive, loving, and relational intent) through either degenerative self-indulgence or else passive giving up in nonresistance to the mutability of the world? How can we avoid the conventional methods of either passive Buddhism or nihilistic libertinism in the face of our maturing observation of the world?

To enjoy spiritual insight means that one has realized what is truly Transcendental, not what is merely psychic and attractive and apparently non-physical. So much of ordinary yoga and mysticism merely distracts people with internal objects that are hyped to them as spiritual, soul-like, immortal, and even Divine phenomena. But internal objects are, in themselves, nothing more than reflections of the changes occurring in our own nervous systems and the self-centered expansions of our own bodies and minds. People imagine themselves to be spiritual because they are involved in yoga, mysticism, poetic religious beliefs, and the like, but, truly, they are, in the midst of their subjective fascinations, no more spiritual (or surrendered to the "Spirit" that contains, pervades, and transcends the psycho-physical self) than a typical Buddhist monk, or an atheistic nuclear physicist, or a self-indulgent man on the street. Such people are simply focusing their attention on subtler aspects of the manifest self, the mutable psycho-physical being, whereas real spirituality involves direct and ecstatic (or self-transcending) Communion with the Transcendental Reality. Mystics, yogis, ascetics, libertines, even ordinary religious people are merely playing with their own nervous systems, their own bodies and minds. They have not yet begun to associate with the Living Divine Personality through the self-sacrifice that is love.

How can you realize the Transcendental Spiritual Reality—not merely your psyche, your nervous system, your internal subjectivity, but the Divine and Transcendental Reality that is prior to you, that is prior to the event of your birth, that will continue after your death, and that is so intimately associated with you that it is you? How can you discover this Transcendental Reality that is to be Realized at the very point where your own consciousness originates, and that is greater than the manifest identity of your own psycho-physical mechanism? How can you transcend the limits of your own body-mind? How can you penetrate the deluding power of your own experience? If you observe Nature clearly, you will see, as Gautama did, that your experience itself can be accounted for entirely within the limits of a mortal psycho-physical description. How, then, will you escape the apparently nihilistic paths either of burning yourself out by exploiting experience or of analyzing yourself and yielding all cravings to the point of the annihilation of experience?

The Way of Life, or the Living Truth, is to enter into active self-sacrifice, or ecstasy, toward or into the Radiant Transcendental Person, Reality, or Self, rather than to exercise either the exploitation or the passive yielding of our own body-mind. This is the principle of true and esoteric religious life. The body-mind must be able to function in and as such God-Communion at all times. Therefore, we are inherently obliged to learn all about the functional capacities of our own body-mind, and we grow by stages, eventually comprehending and mastering even the highest psychic and superconscious aspects of ourselves. But we must always, in every present moment, return to the fundamental and ecstatic action that I have described, and that is generated from the root of the heart, the essential root-consciousness of the psyche, the epitome of the entire body-mind. True religious practice is always to enter directly into sacrifice of the total body-mind to the Transcendental Reality, through self-transcending love, or ecstasy. That is the fundamental practice—not to enter into exploitation of the body-mind in any experiential way, active or passive, but to learn all about what is merely the body-mind so that you can surrender all of it ever more profoundly (while neither exploiting nor prohibiting any of it). At some stage in such heart-practice you may think you are surrendering quite profoundly, since you will have come to enjoy great mystical and psychic powers in the Realm of Nature, but you will again realize that that into which you have been surrendering is merely another part of yourself, your own psycho-physical being.

Then you must surrender beyond even that into the Absolute, Living, Radiant Consciousness that is the Reality and Truth and God and Self of all.

In this great spiritual process you Realize that the Divine Reality is not only Transcendental Consciousness but also All-Pervading and Radiant Force or Love-Energy. That Force is conducted within the great Realm of Nature by all the circuitries within your body-mind and by those greater circuitries within which exist your body-mind, all its relations, and even the totality of the manifest universe. That great Life-Current can be felt or intuited directly as the Universal, All-Pervading, and Absolute Being, and It can also be felt constantly in all the specific exchanges of our experience. We can be confined or contracted upon ourselves in the midst of all of that, or we can be open, radiant, expanded, free of our reactivity, our lovelessness, our fatalistic nihilism, our self-possession.

You must transcend your emotional problem, your physical problem, your sexual problem, your mental problem, your psychic problem. You must transcend all the usual and uncommon problems of unillumined Man, through the heartfelt sympathy of the total body-mind with That in which it inheres, That in which it is arising, That on which it depends absolutely. Live in the intuitive ecstasy of that devotion, that feeling that radiates freely from the heart. It is feeling, it is an emotional matter, breathed, felt bodily, granted by Divine Grace. Abiding in that practice, we depend upon and are given the spiritual Revelation that transcends the body-mind. This Revelation is not accounted for in the conventionally ascetic and Life-denying point of view of classical exoteric Buddhism, nor in the mind-worshipping other-worldliness of conventional religious and mystical esotericism (East or West), nor in the self-centered, nihilistic, and Life-degrading point of view of the burnt-out man on the streets, nor in the frightened mediocrity and subhuman ordinariness of the mass populations surviving anywhere in the world.

All who profess religious or spiritual aspirations must understand the Life-negative and nihilistic tendency in themselves. It is not a spiritual tendency. It is in fact an extension of worldly reactivity, the worldly tendencies of the usual man. It is not based on the Transcendental Realization of Life. It is based on the presumption of certain obvious material facts in Nature that support a nihilistic view of life. It is based on the illusion of "matter" and despair in the face of death.

The truly religious and spiritual Way also does not involve

strategic development of the great soul within, or presuming that your inner being, if only it can be separated from the body, is a great, immortal individual. Rather, true spiritual understanding involves the recognition of all experience, even the most glorious mystical raptures of the inner "soul," as a limit upon the Infinite Expanse of the heart's natively ecstatic feeling. Even so, such recognition is not nihilistic and "matter-renouncing." Rather, it is founded on ecstatic and radical intuition of the Paradox that even the body is Consciousness, Light, Energy, Bliss, Love, and Transcendental Radiance, prior to all the seriousness of self and world. Such recognition occurs within the Condition of God-Communion, Transcendental Ecstasy, the truly spiritual state of awareness Awakened by the Grace of the Living God. The limited being is naturally moved to give itself up to what is truly Great. And, therefore, only what is Great is ultimately Realized to exist, whatever may arise as experience.

Religion must be founded upon the Living Truth. However, the so-called "great world religions" are, in their exclusive and exoteric forms, not founded on devotion to the highest and universal spiritual Truth. We have just considered classical or exoteric Buddhism, and we should understand that it is not, at its root, founded on a truly spiritual realization of life. It is founded on a serious or even desperate interpretation of certain observations about the mortal physics of Nature. Other religions, such as Christianity and popular Hinduism, which are founded on the doctrine of the inner soul and the idea of God as a separate Creator, are in fact based on illusions of the nervous system, or the internal, subjective, and apparently non-physical aspect of the body-mind, as well as the illusion of "matter." Thus, the real spiritual Revelation is still essentially hidden within if not absent from the so-called great religions (although it has been at least implied by the demonstrative lives of great Adepts, among whom, paradoxically, we should include Gautama, Jesus, Krishna, and countless others). But the spiritual Truth of the Living Reality must be the foundation and essential Revelation and core of practice of any true religion. If any religious or spiritual way is true, then it necessarily involves the disposition of ecstatic self-release into the Living Divine Personality that is the Condition and Self of all beings and worlds.

However, the mere verbal recommendation of such a disposition sounds like a conventional, downtown religious message. Therefore, you must enter into the thorough and total psycho-physical considera-tion of spiritual Truth, and you must come to understand the whole affair of your life, of religion, of emotion, and of consciousness before you can truly become the devotee of the Living Personality of God. Otherwise, to consider devoting yourself to God is nothing more than a superficial religious idea. You must be truly "serious" (and, therefore, profoundly and intensely free or "humorous") about this consideration, because you must discriminate between your own limited experience and the ecstatic intuition of the Transcendental Divine Reality. Otherwise, you will never find your way out of the maze of conventional awareness. You must find the spiritual Reality—the Living Spirit, Person, and Self. You must be devoted to the Truth that includes and transcends you. Therefore, you must thoroughly investigate, consider, and inquire into your actual circumstance, your born-situation, your fundamental existence, the whole event of your experience. And, ultimately, you must come to the certain understanding that your entire existence is only summarized in ecstatic love of the Living God. You must become committed to a life of active, practical, and esoteric devotion to God. There is no other way to live and be happy and peaceful and sane.

CHAPTER 21

ATHEISTIC "COMPUTER BRAIN" OR PARTICIPANT IN THE PLAY OF GOD?

by Joanne Mied

I have always had a particular aptitude for science and mathematics. Especially mathematics held a great fascination for me. The more abstract the mathematics the better. I enjoyed solving logical problems. Not surprisingly, therefore, I reached for and obtained a scholarship to the Case Institute of Technology, which, at that time, had some four thousand students, only forty of whom were women. However, I did not feel comfortable in my new environment. Suddenly I found myself surrounded by bookworm types with bottle-glasses and minds running only in abstract grooves, or so it seemed. Although I was fond of intellectual pursuits, I also had lively social interests that were now threatened with extinction. So, at the end of the school year I settled for a job as a systems analyst instead. A year later, to broaden my skills and improve my professional opportunities, I went to the University of Hartford, where I obtained a degree in mathematics. Subsequently, I resumed my career in systems analysis.

My mind was never idle. I found my work absorbing and
rewarding, and in my spare time I would ponder physics problems and
logical puzzles. So, when—after many years of studying and apparently
practicing the Teaching of Master Da Free John—I at last came into
prolonged personal contact with the Adept, I approached him with an
overdeveloped left brain—something he could not fail to notice and
work on. I received my Teaching lesson at the Tumomama Sanctuary[1]
in Hawaii, where I had moved in June of 1982 to be part of the
support group for that retreat Sanctuary. During the following
months, Master Da Free John would frequently gather with us to
consider the Way and our "problems."

At the end of October I presented Master Da with a small gift—a
copy of Albert Einstein's *My Views*, the Indian edition of a compilation
of his letters, notes, and conversations. I admired Einstein's genius—
not least because I have never been able to comprehend his theory of
relativity—and I was curious about his opinions on philosophy and
religion. I should have known that Master Da would use this
opportunity to make a Teaching point, because he had begun calling
me, often at the most unexpected moments, "computer brain." He
would speak well of my professional expertise and often remind my
fellow-practitioners that my highly paid work in the world was a form
of service to the Sanctuary and the support group, but he would do so
only when I was out of earshot. When I was in the room, however, he
was intent on serving my spiritual practice by obliging me to inspect
my left-brained tendencies. On that particular occasion he observed
about me: "She doesn't know the difference between Enlightened men
and successful men. She doesn't know the difference between the
objectivist, egoic point of view and the spiritual point of view. That's
why she can't cut it yet." He went on to explain that I had chosen my
profession because of my tendency to dramatize the form of egoity
characteristic of the scientific-objectivist standpoint, which is essentially
nonparticipatory. By contrast, the spiritual point of view, he remarked,
is intensely participatory.

I felt singed by the Adept's criticism, but at the same time I could
recognize and feel the truth of it. I suddenly remembered the
numerous times I had sat in meditation and felt an unrelenting doubt
about the immaterial dimension, the Divine. I also saw how I was

1. A Renunciate Sanctuary of The Johannine Daist Communion located in Hawaii on the island
of Kauai. The Sanctuary is named "Tumomama," meaning "fierce woman," because of the strong
Nature-Power or Goddess-force associated with that place.

waiting for the Divine to reveal Itself to me "out there." I recognized my lack of participatory commitment in my spiritual practice and in my life altogether. I knew I would have to make a different gesture: The Divine becomes Obvious only through actual ego-transcendence, actual whole-bodily surrender, and certainly not through standing back in the position of the observer.

I began to consider my job and how it related to my emotional adaptation. In college I had difficulty choosing between mathematics and science on the one hand and child psychology on the other. The turning point was a course in the psychology of adolescence. I had studied very carefully for the midterm final, intending to get a perfect score. Reviewing the results of the midterm final exam, I found that the professor had marked wrong a multiple-choice question that I was certain I had answered correctly. I quickly located my "evidence" in the text and challenged his answer. The professor acknowledged that indeed *both* answers were correct. That decided it for me. I continued to dabble in psychology but majored in mathematics. For, at least in mathematics the answer was always either right or wrong. I disliked ambiguity and uncertainty. I saw how all my life I had wanted the world to be black and white, how I had preferred order to life, perfection to spontaneity, knowledge to the Mystery that existence really is. I was deeply grateful to Master Da for these insights into my life. I literally felt that he was rousing me from a dream—the dream of the exclusivity of material existence. But I was as if drugged, failing to regain waking consciousness. So, over the next weeks Master Da patiently persisted in his compassionate attempt—until I began to "hear" [2] him.

Soon after this first encounter between the Adept and my reluctant ego, Master Da launched into a profound consideration about "Spirit-Baptism." [3]

After a few days Master Da noticed that while most people were following his consideration of the Spirit-Current and were actually beginning to be sensitive to it, a few of us had been left behind. I was amongst them. Despite years of membership in this spiritual com-

2. The term "hearing" has specific meaning in the Teaching of Da Free John, as described on p. 40, n. 3.

3. In the process of Spirit-Baptism, the esoteric Transmission of the "Spirit" or "Life-Force" of the Adept is received by the prepared aspirant. For a discussion of this process, see Da Free John, *The Fire Gospel: Essays and Talks on Spiritual Baptism.* This book was composed from talks and essays given by Master Da Free John during the months of Joanne's stay at Tumomama Sanctuary.

munity, despite our love for the Spiritual Master, and despite numerous experiences of extraordinary phenomena, we were not only insensitive to the Spiritual Reality he was trying to communicate to us, but we were, deep down, even doubtful of its existence. Master Da described our condition perfectly.

> *The atheism from which people are suffering is not merely non-theism, but a state of self-contraction or divorce from the Spiritual Reality. Thus, when you see conditions arising in the present, you do not see the Spiritual Reality, you see merely the conditions. You presume them to be separate from That. You do not presume yourself to be That. You even may presume that there is no That. Not only is It not evident in the conditions that seem to be arising presently, but you do not presume that It necessarily exists at all.*[4]

It was painful to have the Adept declare us atheists. The comment that affected me the most was his observation that we were constantly observing and responding to the most gross level of existence, while entirely disregarding the most profound level of existence. This remark cut me to the quick. The Master continued:

> *You could say that all egos are atheistic in some sense, because they do not see the Obvious. They are not suffering from the absence of God. They are suffering from a limitation on the Vision of God. Nothing you do to yourself, either to stimulate or distract your attention, really works to break the spell of this false vision. You must understand yourself truly, and in understanding and transcending yourself you see the Obvious. When the world becomes recognizable, then the world also falls away. But it is not by excluding the world that we find God. It is by seeing the world as God, seeing this moment of conditions as God.*
>
> *Atheism is just one of the forms of self-possession. It is not really a description of Reality based on intelligent consideration. It is just one of the ways of communicating to others the sense of separation and doubt inherent in the ego.*[5]

After years of spiritual practice I was really an atheist! I was

4. From an unpublished talk given by Da Free John on November 7, 1982.

5. Ibid.

shattered by Master Da's criticism and overwhelmed with self-doubt. I wanted to defend myself and describe the spiritual experiences I had had, but his words rang true at a much deeper level, and so I remained silent.

I was intent on changing, and I knew that this was possible, for all around me I could see the bright, truly Happy faces of those who had passed through this bottleneck and emerged as strong practitioners. Yet, somehow I suffered from the sense that I was holding on to something that I could not let go. Later I learned that this holding on is the contraction that is the ego itself.

You are afraid to dissolve. You think that you have to be in a position somehow, observing something, holding on to something, being held by something, whether it is in this gross form or in some subtle contemplation. You are afraid to feel, to release your consciousness to Infinity, because that means you will lose your point in space. You are going to lose your life—that is exactly true. Thus, only when the Happiness of Communion at Infinity becomes obvious to you will that dissolution be permitted to become perfect. Because it does involve the dissolution of everything, the dissolution of body, of all energy, all forms, all worlds, all that is mind, all concepts. It does involve that literally, you see. That is exactly what you are afraid will happen! (Laughter.) That is what you call death and try to prevent. And that is exactly what does happen in this Communion. Everything is given up, everything is dissolved at Infinity.

Infinity must become your pleasure. Then this world becomes humorous and livable. Then you can make something sacred out of it, without holding on to it. It will pass away. Everything passes away, everything is changing here. Everything is action. Everything you hold on to changes, because it is itself change. Therefore, holding on to a position obviously is not Truth. The surrender of all positions is true.[6]

I was not ready to surrender. I was not ready to be free of the bind of the ego, but seeing it—feeling this holding on—was the first step. Perhaps this gave the Adept enough of an opening to initiate me into the disposition of Divine Communion.

This happened on many different occasions—while participating in one of Master Da's Teaching considerations, or during meditation,

6. Da Free John, *The God in Every Body Book,* pp. 65–66.

while doing household chores or watching television. Thus, one evening, while I was explaining to him the peculiar mathematical properties of the number nine, on which I had done some research, he suddenly interrupted my presentation at the point where I was proposing that the decimal system was connected with the fact that our two hands have ten digits. He considered my justification arbitrary, saying that if any anatomical features had been involved in the development of our numeral system surely the face would have been given priority over the hands. He went into a detailed exposition. My mind raced to keep up with his argument, but to no avail.

Then he moved his hand as though he were tossing something over his shoulder. In that instant my mind dissolved. I literally felt as if my mind was breaking open and rolling off my shoulders. I saw that there was obviously no necessity for anything in the universe. There was just this great Mystery of Light and Sound and Form, merely an amusement, a play. There was no reason for anything or anyone. The prattle of my mind had stopped, and I felt Happy and full. The conversation continued, but I remained in this mindless mood established by the Adept's Grace of Transmission.

The following months were a juxtaposition of criticisms and mindless moments of Blessing. However, I was continuing to dramatize my basic mood of separation and of feeling unloved. At one point, Master Da remarked: "All I'm trying to do is to get you to wake up. Why won't you practice, woman? What's the matter with you? Why won't you practice?" I was disconsolate. Then I was asked to start again at the beginner's level of practice—a devastating blow to my already faltering self-confidence. Master Da explained to me compassionately that I had skipped over the preparatory stages of practice. So, I began to engage study of the Teaching Argument as a form of meditation. I studied an hour in the morning and an hour in the afternoon, and before long it became obvious to me that in the past I had always confronted the Teaching intellectually only. This time I began to *feel* the Argument, to allow myself to be penetrated by it. I began to "hear" the Teaching: I could always only *be* Happy, but no amount of seeking could *make* me Happy, because Happiness was my prior Condition. In particular one essay by the Adept's pen, entitled "The Need Connection,"[7] helped me enormously. Here Master Da

7. See *Love of the Two-Armed Form*, by Da Free John, pp. 138–45. *Love of the Two-Armed Form* is a unique and extensive consideration of the subject of human sexuality and love and describes the regenerative practice of sexual embrace as a process of whole-bodily God-Communion in which self and lover are ultimately transcended in the All-Pervading Reality.

describes our chronic disposition or gesture of "You don't love me"—
the sense of betrayal that is coessential with the ego.

I felt the truth of this so profoundly that I knew it would change
everything in my life immediately. And it did. This was the understanding that Master Da had been urging me toward all along. I
simply rested in this consideration. And I had a sense that Master Da
could feel my new disposition. We happened to be at a beach at the
time. As I sat there glancing at the Adept, I knew that this was the day
I would let it all go. I just felt like—to hell with computers, I'm going
for God. Master Da describes so perfectly what I was feeling then:

> There is ultimately nothing to protect about Man, about you. You
> must give yourself up. You are finished! (Laughter.) You are at the
> end of your rope in this spiritual matter, in this fundamental sense. All
> that avails is the leap of Enlightenment, Awakening, or literal, perfect
> surrender into the Transcendental Reality, not knowing what That is,
> you see. You have no capacity whatsoever to transcend your funda-
> mental Ignorance. You give up everything. It is the unknowability of
> God into which you surrender, not some idea of any Deity at all. You
> just give yourself up to the Reality of the world, because you cannot
> figure It out. You give yourself up to It. At last, you have to give
> yourself up to It completely.[8]

My whole life I had chosen everything but God. That day it was
God first, and I did not even care if there was any second choice. The
more I surrendered, the more it became obvious to me that the Adept
was more than just a person who made pleasant or unpleasant
comments to me. It was evident to me that he was merely a window to
the Great One. He was no one. There was only the quality and purity
of the Great One shining through this apparent person.

That was a great moment for me. I finally saw my own activity
and was actually able to let it go. At last, I had enough space to see that
my holding on to the mind was the way that I defended myself against
everything that I feared. I also realized that in doing this I simultaneously shielded myself against the Adept's Transmission, or Power
of spiritual transformation.

Whenever I felt separate or was suffering for any reason, I would
simply notice that I was defending myself, that I was in my head,
activating my "computer brain." I would simply feel whatever I was

8. Da Free John, *The God in Every Body Book*, p. 104.

feeling in the moment and relax into it. And within a short period of time (or sometimes immediately) I would feel my heart open. I would feel literally as if I were moving down into my body. Promptly I would feel the Master's Transmission at the heart. And there would be Happiness. I knew I had been inserted into the spiritual process. I was "Spirit-Baptized." It was obvious to me that I was not really separated from God or Reality. I merely had to understand—and I could do that in any moment—to be tangibly reconnected with the Presence.

But this was merely the beginning of the spiritual process that Master Da had initiated in my life. At the beginning of March 1983, my husband and I returned to California, and we began to serve and live at The Mountain of Attention. There I began to experience an intensification of the Adept's Transmission. It became more and more obvious that there was no limit to the Adept's Transmission and that the only limit was in my ability to remember to practice in every moment.

One day, while meditating in Plain Talk Chapel,[9] I felt suddenly overcome by the Spirit Presence. It was a tangible Force outside myself, pressing against me, embracing me, and combining with me. It filled me and overfilled me. I felt every cell in my body vibrating with this incredible Energy. Its sheer force made me sit bolt upright, and the intensity of it was almost painful. I felt suspended, pressed against the Divine Reality. My heart was open and joyful. I rested in this embrace with the Divine for what seemed like a long time.

I told only my husband and my closest friend about this experience. Basically, I tried to act like it never occurred. And yet, it had a profound effect on me, and I could think of nothing else for days. I literally felt as if I had *seen* God. But it was completely offensive to me to even have had such an experience, much less to feel so implicated by it. I could not possibly doubt God anymore. Still, I did everything I could to deny the whole event. Often I would recall a particular comment by Master Da that, when he first made it, had penetrated all my defenses:

You are the standard computer worker—the woman of the future. She understands everything but herself. The man or woman of the future will understand everything and comprehend nothing, be

9. Plain Talk Chapel is a Communion Hall, or place reserved for meditation and devotional activity, at The Mountain of Attention.

able to manipulate everything and see through nothing whatsoever, live as a totally mechanical person who can penetrate the universe with a single glance and a small formula, summarizing everything in a few abstract words or funny little symbols with curious curves beneath them, to represent the elegance that has died.[10]

My doubts and uncertainty continued for some weeks. Then one day, while I was writing up this account, I saw to my dismay that I had literally been granted the Vision of God and yet was still acting like an atheist. Then I understood that I did not have to fall into this pattern anymore. All of my doubt and denial of God was simply unnecessary. I was at last certain of God. And this is not a matter of belief or even intellectual understanding but of intuiting the tacitly Obvious.

I offer this short account as a testimony to the compassion, love, persistence, and "skillful means" of Master Da Free John. He showed me how I had become entrenched in a materialistic view of reality and of myself, which not only curtailed my enjoyment of life but actually artificially separated me from the sustaining Power of the Real. Through his Teaching and Spiritual Transmission I was cured of the psychosis of doubt—the chronic disease that is crippling the lives of all those who confine themselves to the intellect. I am deeply grateful to Master Da for demonstrating to me the actual existence of the Blissful Being-Consciousness-Energy that is the true Nature of all phenomena and that is not subject to doubt or mere belief.

Joanne Mied, who holds a degree in mathematics, has been troubleshooting as a systems analyst for several major corporations. She has been a practitioner of Master Da Free John's Way of Radical Understanding for the past eight years.

10. From an unpublished talk given by Da Free John on February 11, 1983.

CHAPTER 22

HARDWARE, SOFTWARE, AND TRANSCENDENCE

a talk by Da Free John
November 24, 1982

MASTER DA FREE JOHN: Our brain and nervous system are a very subtle, very complex system operating on a higher level than the most sophisticated computers yet devised by human beings. It is an admirable machine, just as the high-technology products of human beings themselves are admirable. It seems remarkable that the same people you meet every day are producing these supermachines and actually making them work. In the same way, it is remarkable that jet planes fly, because most of the evidence of human existence offers an altogether different kind of story, of life as suffering and disasters and bungling, inability to create order, inability to cooperate, inability to make right decisions. In other words, the general products of human life are all a product of the golem or an almost subhuman persona.

In fact, this very complex, highly sophisticated, "super-tech" nervous system–brain is being all these golems, these ordinary characters who are always bungling, failing, dying, suffering, and struggling. And a fraction of the human beings on Earth are involved in some sense in extending our own nervous system–brain into machines and high conceptions of how to use the laws of Nature, making these great technological products work in one fashion or another.

But somehow even all this high technology and high science

388

wind up being manipulated by golem-like characters, such as politicians, and the tradition of how things are supposed to be. Thus, even though we have a very sophisticated technology, it is basically devoted to maintaining the military and keeping track of bank accounts and credit cards and nonsensical information, or what would seem to be very low-level information systems.

Underneath our ordinary suffering life and habits, the persona that we seem to be, is actually a very sophisticated machine. Why, if this is so, if there is underneath us or underneath Nature a super-tech, high-level machine with apparently infinite capability and power, why is this supermachine showing itself only as all these golems, basically as these bungling human personas? There is a supermachine subtly behind or at the root of all processes in Nature, but the same supermachine is also behind every individual personality. Why, then, if underneath it all, really at the crux of everything, there is this supermachine—why, at the level of appearances, in other words, at the level of what is being done by this machine, do we see all the evidence of this golem-like existence?

DEVOTEE: Master, perhaps this can be explained in terms of the distinction between software and hardware. The "hardware" is the machinery itself, the computer. The "software" is the program that processes the information you feed it and gives you back a balance sheet or answers the equation or whatever. The term "GIGO" in computer language stands for "garbage in, garbage out" and it indicates that the computer only responds to what is put into it. If you put garbage in, you are going to get garbage out. If the program is poor or if the information is entered wrongly or if the information is incorrect—well, if you put garbage in, you are going to get garbage out.

MASTER DA FREE JOHN: If, underneath it all and to begin with, there is this supermachine, how did it wind up being manifested as the garbage softwares of ordinary human existence? Why does the great human machine produce babbling personas and golem babble?

DEVOTEE: Because garbage is put in.

MASTER DA FREE JOHN: But that explanation comes from the persona itself. How does this great machine produce such a golem to begin with?

DEVOTEE: The garbage comes into the machine from all kinds of sources.

MASTER DA FREE JOHN: But the machine is also the source of those sources! Why did it make such software? If it is so great, why did it not right off the bat, right from the very beginning, create a superuniverse that works well?

Is the great machine in charge, in other words, or is it not? How did it get to be "not in charge" if it is such a supermachine? Not merely the human individual computer behind the software of the golem-like, ordinary personality, but the total universe is built upon such a structure apparently, a supercomputer, a supermachine that is even beyond imagination.

DEVOTEE: That is the same kind of question as, "If there is a God alive, then why is everything so messed up?"

MASTER DA FREE JOHN: It is a similar kind of question, yes. And it is a good question! (Laughs.) But I want you to tell me the answer! I ask you for the answer, and you just tell me how it is again in another form.

DEVOTEE: I don't know.

MASTER DA FREE JOHN: All this talk about software and hardware, you see, is just another way of babbling. It is just another way of telling me how it is. I am asking you <u>why</u> it is.

DEVOTEE: You got me! (Master Da laughs.)

MASTER DA FREE JOHN: Well, does anybody have an answer? Is there a supermachine in charge and duplicating itself in the form of all kinds of entities, local stations, local entities? And if so, why are all these entities always just babbling and being software of a "garbagenous" kind? This discussion suggests that maybe there is a great universal machine, and that inside every human individual there is a great machine (the brain, nervous system, and so forth). But it also suggests that there is another kind of machine, a software machine created by the devil or some such thing, a wholly different principle that somehow exists along with this supercomputer. Maybe they both exist. And it does appear that in the struggle between the hardware and the software, the software, until now and at least in this world, is winning, or in charge, because the computer cannot do any more or any different than is dictated by what is fed into it.

If all this is so, how did this other, second dimension of existence come into being? Who created it? Who put the software into the hardware? Where did the software come from? Conceivably, the hardware could somehow come from a Super Being, because it is ultimately perfect. But where did the software originate if not from that same computer, that same structure, that same Super Being? Is there another being, another reality, another force, another machine, that is in the business of making golems, or software of a garbagenous kind? Is Something Perfect creating Perfection and something imperfect creating imperfection? And are these two always somehow in play with one another? And may they ultimately achieve a kind of Unity wherein the software is transformed and aligned to the business and the ultimate will of the hardware?

DEVOTEE: This sounds like the battle of light and darkness.

MASTER DA FREE JOHN: Yes, it sounds like that old myth of the battle of the good forces and the bad forces, Purusha and Prakriti,[1] God and Nature.

Well, what is the case?

DEVOTEE: Master, do you know about the machines that now appear in banks, the ones you can operate without getting out of your car? You can draw on your account, and the machine tabulates your records for you. I got one of these cards recently and I was explaining to my wife how it works. As we were driving away from the thing, I realized that while I was explaining it to her, she had the impression that someone inside the machine was working it! (Laughter.)

MASTER DA FREE JOHN: She probably has the same feeling about you! (Laughter.)

---

1. The Sanskrit terms *prakriti* and *purusha* denote "Nature" and "Self" respectively. The Prakriti is the total manifestation, including the nonmaterial dimensions of existence. By contrast, the Purusha (meaning literally "man") is the Principle of Consciousness, the Transcendental Self beyond all manifest realms.

DEVOTEE: It led to an interesting consideration because it became obvious to me that she lives by exactly the same principle you are now considering. She is just like everybody else in that respect, maybe even more exaggeratedly so. She used to think that clocks basically kind of felt out what time it was and adjusted themselves accordingly!

Anyway, the principles of hardware and software become really difficult to deal with when you are talking about people, because, as you pointed out, we assume that we are individuals, that we are somehow the hardware separate from software.

MASTER DA FREE JOHN: But we act as if we are the software separate from the hardware. It is true that we think we are hardware, but we are really software. We think we are in charge, but we are the program. We are not in charge. We are just the program! (Laughs.) We call the hardware "God," and on another level we call it "the soul," you see. But as a matter of fact we are not in charge. We never do identify with the hardware. We always function as the software. Therefore, we are always turning out repetitions of the same dilemma with which we began.

DEVOTEE: Master, that is interesting, because as you were speaking, I realized that I always conceive of God as the software and this body-mind as the hardware.

MASTER DA FREE JOHN: You are in charge and God is the program? (Laughs.) Sounds as if we are getting into conventional religion here! (More laughter.)

DEVOTEE: The machine is perfect, though. The software—but I don't know if this metaphor is going to work too well any more . . .

MASTER DA FREE JOHN: It is a good metaphor because it uses the language of our time, the babble of science, but it also reflects a timeless metaphor, a metaphor that has always been projected by human beings in the language of the time in which they produce their own descriptions. I gave you some examples already. The dichotomy between Purusha and Prakriti, God and Nature, flesh and spirit—these languages reflect the same archetype as the hardware/software dichotomy. Thus, it is not useless to consider things via that metaphor. To do so is really a way of carrying on a kind of discussion that has involved human beings since human beings began to create sophisticated thought in any form.

There is a perception, in the functional order of things at any rate, of difficulties and of things always turning out the same and not becoming perfect, and yet there is at the same time a sense that there is something perfect—not merely a vague sense, either. There is a sense that we can even enter into That Which is perfect, a higher order, a higher disposition, a higher Law behind Nature and behind our own mechanical personality. These dichotomies that we are discussing are reflections of our experience.

Thus, to have the discussion is worth our time. We can use the hardware/software language or the Purusha/Prakriti concept or the soul/body dichotomy. We can use any one of these languages for the sake of this discussion, which is a process of understanding what experience is about and what is going on here, you see. I do not think this analogy breaks down any more than any of the other metaphorical analogies break down. We do seem to function like software or programs that have already been created and that have built-in limitations. The software does not seem to possess the ultimate ability to change its own program. The program may seem to change, but it always winds up being the same program again. It seems almost at will to build in limitations that then continue to produce garbage or the same kinds of results.

Now, over against this software, which ultimately winds up being in charge of its own experience and destiny, is a supermachine. We know that the nervous system and brain are a kind of supermachine that we are hardly even using. Why should this supersophisticated brain–nervous system be appearing as the usual guy, babbling about the usual obsessions and desires and acting dumbly and repetitively? If, underneath this karmic persona, there really is a superior machine even at the level of the individual, and if there are greater machines in the broader scale of Nature—which is the way it seems to us experientially—then why is that so? How can we account for it?

We are not in charge, you see. When you say "I," you are not pointing to the hardware or That Which is in charge of moving the body and bringing it into being. You did not create yourself. You are not creating yourself now. The "you" who responds in conversation does not produce the chemical secretions in the body and multiply brain cells and control the chemistry or reproduction. You are not doing any of that stuff. When you say "I," you are referring to the software, the persona, and that one is not in charge. You are not the One Who is Living you. The one who responds in conversation is not the One in charge. He or she is the program responding, a form of identity, a persona that is perhaps being projected by the hardware or the ultimate machine, that perhaps has nothing to do with that ultimate machine except that it is playing on it somehow like a record on a record player. Perhaps, apart from that association or play, the ultimate machine does not affect the outcome of this program.

Now, this description suggests something like what you experience to be the case. You are this body, or at least this body is the base of your sense of "I," your personal identity, but you did not create the body. You are hardly doing anything the body is doing except some very gross mechanical things, and even they are not entirely your responsibility or within the framework of real options for you.

It is also true that, when you are conceiving of existence and your own destiny, you can point to the inner machine, the nervous system and brain that is behind your own apparatus, and say, "Look, this is a supermachine in here, and this software persona out there is a bit of babble, a bit of repetitive destiny," and you can fret over that mystery. On another level, however, the nervous system and the brain are a different form of software, as much a program as the babble of the golem personality.

Thus, a kind of separation or independence is reflected in this conventional persona. It seems to be a separate or separable program placed on the machine of the brain and nervous system, but the machine of the brain and nervous system is itself software. It is not the great Machine itself, not even a great machine. It seems superior to the persona but is itself another form of software, a form of conditional existence that presumably has all kinds of limitations built into it and that will repetitively reproduce those limitations. It is also software, then, to some other hardware. How far back into Nature must we go before we find the true hardware of the Ultimate Machine? Is there such a thing? Or is there just an apparently infinite universe of software programs and no Ultimate Machine?

From the point of view of the conventions of experience, we say that there are, in effect, software and hardware, an outer persona and an inner, superior machine. But if we truly analyze existence and do not merely talk from the point of view of "I," then we can see that the inner machine is as much software or a conditional apparatus as the persona. All of Nature, then, is just software, but it is a hierarchy of programs. It is a kind of political order of programs: outer ones not controlling the inner ones and the inner ones being superior to the outer ones, but every inner one having another one inner to it or subtler than it upon which it is turning or riding and whose energy it is using. But if we analyze all of Nature as it is, we see that it is not built upon some ultimate machine but is a hierarchy of different kinds of software that function like pairs of hardware and software. It is all software but it functions like pairs of hardware and software.

Ultimately, then, all of Nature is nothing but software, without a hardware entity or great machine that is in charge. It is ultimately built upon not a machine that is in charge but the Great One, a Great Condition, Which, once Realized, cancels out or Outshines or makes obsolete all the software, all these hierarchies, all these complications of conditional existence.

As I pointed out earlier, when we reverse the order of things and, instead of using the apparently inner hardware to supply the juice for the running of the outer software, we turn the software in upon the hardware and then go back further and further, even that gesture does not work to perfect the personality, not in any ultimate terms at any rate. As soon as energy and attention are granted to it, the inner hardware works to transcend itself and ultimately to transcend all the levels of the hierarchy behind it.

When this conversion comes about, changes even along the lines of some more positive programs may come of it, but it does not result in ultimate perfection. It leads to the transcendence of the total structure of Nature, which seems to be software built on hardware but is actually all software programmed in hierarchical divisions, so that there always seems to be an outer part or persona or conventional destiny and an inner structure superior to it. But there is no ultimate inner superior structure. What we call God from the conventional point of view is, in effect, ultimate hardware, an Ultimate Machine that should be in charge, you see, but never functions as if it were in charge any more than the hardware of a computer system functions as if it were in charge. Actually the software is in charge, determining its own destiny.

The God of conventional religion is a myth conceived on the basis of this conventional experiential dichotomy between the outer self and the inner machine or inner self. We describe God on the basis of this convention of experiencing and call God a Creator, the One in charge, the One we look to and Who we hope will somehow perfect everything, including our own personal destiny. But that God does not exist. That God is the myth of our psycho-babble, our software program. Such an idea expresses our lack of insight into the structure of things. It is a convention or limit of insight that settles at some point for a myth rather than further insight and ultimate transcendence.

God is not the ultimate hardware in this machine of Nature. Nor are we, the soul, the ultimate hardware inside a personal machine. God is the Condition of Nature, the Condition of all machines, of all softwares and of what appear to be hardwares, all of which are softwares, you see. And God is Realized, then, through transcendence, not through the connection of conventional belief that hopes for perfection at the manifest level, the software level.

Generally human beings manifest the reductionist tendency to acknowledge and resort to something behind appearances that is ultimately responsible and in charge. This conventional human effort expresses a kind of metaphor or myth of conventional consciousness. It is part of our program, part of our software, our karma, because we "I's," even though we identify with the body and even though the body provides our base of self-acknowledgment, are not really the body. If we really were the body, we would bring ourselves bodily into being with full intention and would be consciously operating as the body, such as carrying on even the subtle activities of brain chemistry interfacing with cells and microtransmitters.

But we are not doing anything of the kind. We are babbling along, eating, drinking, sexing, trying to survive, worrying, being driven. We somehow express something at the periphery of the superior machine, but the superior machine never speaks. If I speak to any one of you, you will respond as long as you have the capacity of speech. But the you who responds when questioned will be found out not to be the body, but a program of the body, a face somehow projected by the body.

The television set over there is a very sophisticated instrument, but what kind of stuff comes out of it? What are the images on the screen? A bunch of babble, a bunch of nonsense. It transmits a golem life on its face. And what is it inside? A supertechnological instrument, a piece of very sophisticated machinery. Why should it be babbling such crude images? Those images somehow are the machine but they do not represent it truly, you see.

Our government is another example. It is supposed to represent the people in some higher sense, but it is like the people. It reflects the program of the people. It is not the higher machine or the ultimate mechanism of human society.

We tend always to resort to some subtler mechanism, some inner structure, even in our cells. Within us are great capabilities, but as a general rule human beings never actually connect with a superior machine. They always connect with the programming that is the face of the machine. No matter how much fooling around you do with the dials on that TV set, it is not going to project images in its own likeness. It is going to produce images in your likeness. It is working for you. But where did the machine come from? Human beings made it.

These golems, these ordinary human beings, are also facing some very sophisticated machinery in the form of their own body-minds, just as they face the TV set. Even the machinery of the body-mind is ultimately a conditional apparatus, but upon examination it seems to be far superior to anything you are tending to be or anything you are. No matter how sophisticated your thinking becomes, you will never get to the point where you, the one who responds to me in conversation, is even the mechanism of the body. You will never be speaking for it. You will be speaking on it, playing on it, but you are like a TV movie, you see. The Entity, Structure, Process, or Machine that is actually producing the subtle chemistry, producing the body and operating it right now, never speaks. It will never say to you, "How are you? Yes, I am glad to see you. While I am talking to you I am producing some very subtle brain chemistry. Would you like to see me do it? There. Did you like that one?" That One will never talk to you. Who is talking to you all the time? Who is engaging the conversation here? Is anyone, really, or is our conversation just these software programs combining with one another? Is it an illusion, in fact, like a TV program?

Who are we? Or are we at all? (Laughs.) Are we ourselves when we are just silent and not being these personas? This machine does not talk. Who are we when we are not talking, not thinking, not expressing our motivated life, not carrying on our egoic adventure? Are we really the machine then? When is TV the TV set itself? While it is playing movies for us, it is an illusion, a persona, a face, you see. But when no movies are playing, it is just a TV set.

So who are you? You will never be the TV set. Even the TV set is not TV, you see. It only gets to be TV, rather than just something inert without process, when the Life-Current, the Light-Force, is flowing through it and being modified by its mechanism. Our nervous system and brain are something like the TV set. Apart from the Living Current that is modified by the nervous system, the nervous system has no independent life. It has no self-consciousness. Thus, there is this Life-Force, or Consciousness, and then there is this supercomputer nervous system–brain belonging to the physical body, and then there are these personas, the programs of TV.

You, the you who is talking, are the program, not merely a someone. It represents itself as a someone, but its face is actually a complex product of all kinds of apparent entities. We make singleness out of existence, but existence is really a complex multiple structure without entity. What is single in that structure is the One Force-Consciousness, but It is modified in the form of these inert machines, these hardwares that never speak and never represent themselves and never take over truly. That Living Consciousness is shown, evidenced, or played in the form of these personas, these golems, these programs who are one step removed even from the hardware of the inner structure, the nervous system and brain, the TV set, which is not in charge, but which is an inert structure controlling the flow of energy in a particular way. It has no separate consciousness or separate existence. Behind it is the Current that gives it the possibility of animation but that never animates Itself.

Who, then, is represented? Who are these personas? Who are these programs? What kind of reality do they really have? Where do they come from? The Life-Current is not making them, because it does not say, "I am I." It is behind all these "I's." The hardware does not make them. The software determines its own destiny. How did these illusory personas come into being, and what is their present status? We are very concerned about them—we who are nothing but images, illusions on the face of the hardware that is a structure for using an ultimate Energy or Consciousness that neither speaks nor acts and does not take over.

Although we personas, we golems, would like the machine or the hardware or whatever is behind us to take over, nothing takes over. The programs are always in charge. Different programs come into association with one another somehow in this hierarchical world of machines that control energy. The programs interface with one another and modify one another and create different stories, different TV pictures, all filled with beings calling themselves "I" who say they are the body but have nothing to do with operating the body or bringing it into being. Someone's appearing on the TV set and saying, "I am the TV set," would be like your saying, "I am the body." That person is obviously not the TV set. Neither are you the body.

Well, who are you? If you had a real perception or understanding of your status, you would no longer be able to say that you are the body. You are somehow related to it. If the body were not there, you would not be there to say you are the body. But you are not the body. You are playing on the body, and the body itself is playing on a Universal, Transcendental Force or Consciousness. If that Consciousness were not there, the body would not be there.

But neither the body nor What is ultimately behind the body is in charge. It is not controlling or apparently even bringing these personas or programs into being through any kind of decision-making process or any will to perfect them. The personas are continuing on their own, it seems, although apparently they could not persist if there were not bodies or hardware structures and if there were not the ultimate Current and Living Consciousness. Those personas are their own destiny, and they are just going on. You are just going on. What kind of reality do you have, therefore?

More than evolution or the creation of advanced adaptations, the power of repetition would seem to be the superior or basic motion behind conditions in time. There are changes, some of which we could call evolutionary, but they are not primarily what is happening. Repetition is primarily what is happening. And, because the programs are not real, because they have no ultimate independent existence and are not even what they say they are, wisdom is not about finding out who you are in independent or entified terms. The real question is not "Who are you?" but "What is it?" "Who is it?" What is the ultimate Status of all this, not merely of you?

You are not a soul or entity that can be discovered inwardly and separately. What is the Condition of all these illusions and all the apparatus on which the illusions are riding? What is That? What is It? That is What must be Realized. It is Realized through the transcendence of the programs, not through their becoming inverted and full of self-knowledge in the conventional sense, in terms of extensive technical awareness of our own parts and structures. That awareness is a secondary form of knowledge. Ultimate knowledge, if we can call it

knowledge at all—and Ignorance is a better term for it—transcends
this program and also transcends the hardware, the mechanism
underneath the program.

Transcendental Realization has nothing whatever to do with
evolution. Evolution is about the continuation and development of the
programs. Transcendental Realization is about transcending the
programs, the mechanisms, all of Nature. Thus, Transcendental
Realization is not something that appears through evolution or that
has anything fundamentally to do with these programs or with Nature
as a whole. It has nothing to do with any of that. It is about
transcending all of it. As soon as you enter into the stream of
transcendence or Transcendental Realization, you are going beyond
the illusion of Nature altogether, not merely improving your program,
you see.

Can Nature be accounted for? In the Hindu tradition it is said
that this Maya can never be comprehended. Such is the Confession of
some Adepts. It is also my own Confession. Ignorance is the Principle.
You cannot ultimately comprehend what appears. You can carry on a
discussion such as the one we are having, you can engage in analysis
and see certain features about the process of things, but you cannot
know enough about it to account for it specifically and altogether. In
other words, how can you answer the question, "How does the
software come into existence?" or "How does the hardware come into
existence?" when all there is is the Transcendental Condition, prior to
will and activity?

Can you answer the question? We think we are supposed to be
able to answer every question, you see. We can perhaps break the spell
of our minds by contemplating this question, but it is more a koan[2]
than a question or problem that can ultimately be solved. We can
develop answers, but they will be conventional—in other words, they
will be part of the program itself and will ultimately have the status of
a kind of myth rather than the force of Truth. Can we comprehend
how all of this happens in God? We can comprehend something
about it, but we cannot grasp it ultimately. In our effort to grasp it

2. Master Da Free John has described the term "koan" in his writings: "What the Japanese call
the 'ko-an' is an apparent question—that is, we tend to try to answer it via the usual operations
of the mind. But the 'question' itself works to undermine the mental process. It is actually a form
of meditation on doubt, or failed mind. Therefore, the 'ko-an' is 'answered' only when it is
transcended as a motivator of thought. When its power to initiate doubt and confine us to doubt
is understood and transcended, then there is a sudden rush of joy, freedom, and tacit Intuition of
Transcendental Being" (The God in Every Body Book, p. 34).

"Ha! Webster's blown his cerebral cortex."

ultimately, we go beyond ourselves and beyond grasping, beyond knowing.

DEVOTEE: Master, I love how you say that you treat the body-mind as one of your relations. That approach seems to embody the form of the koan, or the paradoxical perspective, you are now describing.

MASTER DA FREE JOHN: "I" is a koan. It is not an entity. "I" is a koan, like "Mu"[3] or "What is the sound of one hand clapping?" or "Imagine a circle. Now imagine a square. Now imagine a circle that is a square." Those considerations are koans. The "I" is likewise a koan. Really to investigate it breaks the spell. It does not produce ultimate information, the perfect figuring out of everything, but it is a process sufficient for transcendence, or the breaking of the spell. It somehow interferes with the programming to enable us to consider the program as a whole and as it is.

All we are or seem to be is this program. We are like a TV program right now, just images. Somehow, because we are played upon That Which is Consciousness and Energy, we are involved in Consciousness and Energy just as we are involved in the hardware, the machine behind the persona. This makes it possible for us to consider ourselves, experience a dilemma, and be motivated by a desire for release or transcendence, because we are played upon and are ultimately Identical to That Which transcends everything.

Even though we are just a movie, just light forms seeming solid to one another, we are Consciousness, we are Energy. Thus, we can consider ourselves, even though we are an illusion. The "I" is an illusion, but it is played upon That Which is Transcendental and Ultimate. Therefore, even in the framework of this illusory program, the great consideration can take place, but it involves considering this program or yourself in much the same sense that a Zen practitioner considers a koan. The consideration in the end breaks the spell and vanishes this illusion.

These "I's" know that they depend upon the body and identify with the body, and so they are trying to persist through time. They do not want the TV set to break down, they do not want to die. But such craving and fear are the product of identification with the persona and

3. The Japanese expletive *mu* expresses negation and is used in Zen Buddhism as a principal koan, intended to lead the practitioner beyond all affirmative *and* negative responses—in other words, beyond the mind itself.

dependence on the machine rather than insight into and intuitive Identification with That Which precedes the persona and the machine. Once we identify with That, then the spell of fear and the effort of survival are broken. We are flashed beyond the persona and the machine and all the hierarchies of machines and programs in Nature. We break the spell. But as "I," as personas, we are in fear—which is as absurd as someone's appearing on the television set screaming with fear that the TV set will break down or that you will turn it off or that there will be a power failure! (Laughter.)

Perhaps there is a certain kind of self-consciousness in this persona that reflects its dependence on a machine that is out of its control. It senses that the machine is not immortal, even though the machine is extraordinary, very complex, and senior to its own apparition. But the persona knows that it cannot survive if the machine breaks down.

Well, what ceases to survive? The program ceases to survive. If all of Nature dissolved, the machines would disappear, but what would continue? The same Transcendental Condition would still continue wherein there is no fear and no delusion. We are fretfully seeking to accomplish something in the name of this illusion, in the name of this program, and therefore we assign great importance to its continuation and are very attached to the various features of this apparition or this TV vision. But it does not have any ultimate importance, although it certainly has conventional importance until we can break this spell and Stand Free.

I speak within the program, but I am not the machine talking. I am That Which is prior to the machine, Which has acquired Agency through the breaking of the spell in the case of a particular entity. That Which is prior to the total machine of Nature is then temporarily given voice through this mechanism. It is That Which is speaking to you. Neither the machine in between nor this personality apparently talking to you is actually talking to you. The mechanism has not taken over. In fact, it still has many limited tendencies of its own, as does this persona.

This mechanism is going to die. It is not the One talking except in the sense that it is the Agency of That One. This particular Agency comes to an end with the ending of this persona and its machine. Agency itself will not necessarily come to an end. The Agency will be extended into places, into the Teaching, and into other human beings, when the spell is broken in their own cases. I can extend the possibility of the Agency of That One through the activities of this persona and the machine upon which it depends. But I am not speaking for perfection, for some higher possibility in Nature. I am not the machine behind this persona nor some other, greater machine in Nature giving you an evolutionary message.

Certain aspects of what I communicate to you may have evolutionary force, of course, or even the force to change the programs. But fundamentally What is communicating Itself to you is That Which is prior to Nature, breaking through or simply Standing Free, and while Standing Free, That One is associated with a persona that came into being just as its machine came into being, through the normal route of structures and apparitions in Nature.

When the spell is broken, then the Transcendental or Great One has Agency—but only if the spell is broken. Otherwise, programmed entities are simply talking and acting, and machines of one or another capacity within the hierarchical scale of Nature are providing a functional base for these apparitions. Only when the spell is broken does the Transcendental Reality have Agency. Superior personas and superior machines exist, but their voices are part of Nature, part of evolution's expression of the disposition of the lesser stages of life, not the Truth of the Transcendental Condition.

DEVOTEE: Master, I was thinking how completely humorous it would be to us if somebody on television actually did scream in real terror, "Don't turn off the TV!" It is true, we are in exactly such a position.

MASTER DA FREE JOHN: Yes. You are all trying to stay calm, get along, and feel good. But in fact you are very uncomfortable, very, very uncomfortable. Aren't you?

DEVOTEE: Not in your Presence, Master.

MASTER DA FREE JOHN: You can associate with many kinds of useful company that serve your motivations as conditional personas, that give you hope, help you relax, improve your circumstance, and change your conditions in a positive direction. Certainly an aspect of my Influence in your life works in that direction. But my fundamental Force or Transmission in your life is a radical motion or impulse that would break the spell of conditional existence altogether, that would break the spell of your association with this software program of personality as well as with all the machinery or the hardware of Nature.

Thus, I do not merely work in the conventional sense to help you create order and evolve or change your program positively. At most that is a secondary aspect of my Influence. I am Wilder than that.[4] I Work spontaneously, without any self-conscious purpose, in some sense even chaotically. This is just how I function, you see. I notice it just as you do on an ordinary human level, because this body-mind is fitted to an Awakening Impulse. It is Free already of the program and the machinery, Free already of Nature. It is humorous. It is here to break spells. It is Crazy, therefore. Something like those secondary effects may also develop in my Company, but they have nothing to do with the primary Impulse or significance of my Appearance in your life.

And, as I mentioned already, as conditional personas you are all very uncomfortable. You can acquire, through improvement of habits and circumstances, at least a temporary sense of balance and generalized well-being as a conditional entity. You can make the television set function well temporarily. "Only put on pleasant programs. Do not put on any horror shows, psychotic killer shows, world news, and so forth. Stay spiritual. Stay easy." You can do all of that, but even if you do, and you cannot even do that to the point of complete freedom from possible interferences or limits on your conditions so that they always turn out well, still, underneath it all you are uncomfortable.

You know very well right now that, even though you can be relaxed and sit and enjoy my Company and one another's company,

---

4. Master Da Free John refers to his Teaching function in the manner of what is traditionally known as a "Crazy Adept." He explains this unique role in the following essay entitled "The Way I Teach":

"What I do is not the way I am, but the Way I Teach.

"What I speak is not a reflection of me, but of you.

"People do well to be offended or even outraged by me. This is my purpose. But their reaction must turn upon themselves, for I have not shown them myself by all of this. All that I do and speak only reveals men to themselves.

"I have become willing to Teach in this uncommon way because I have known my friends and they are what I can seem to be. By retaining all qualities in their company, I gradually wean them of all reactions, all sympathies, all alternatives, fixed assumptions, false teachings, dualities, searches, and dilemma. This is my way of working for a time. Those who remain confounded by me, critical of me, have yet to see themselves. When their mediocrity is broken, when they yield their righteous reactions and their strife toward all the consolations of the manifest self, they may see my purity.

"Freedom is the only purity. There is no Teaching but Consciousness Itself. Da Free John as he appears is not other than the possibilities of men" (*The Enlightenment of the Whole Body*, p. 53).

you are going to die, and you are likely to experience all kinds of
suffering and even derangement. Because you know that this machine
is not a god. It is not perfect. The machine behind your persona is
temporary and is itself mortal. You are profoundly uncomfortable
with your situation, and you should be. Not to the point of literally
deranging yourself with your discomfort, but that discomfort does
make you turn about from the mere pursuit of contentment, consolation, and improvement of conditions. Even though on some level
you may be devoted to those ends as a practical matter of daily living,
fundamentally you must be devoted to the transcendence of them,
because you will always be uncomfortable—and you should be.

This discomfort is not merely fear. It is a motion toward release.
It is a sane motivation rather than an insane one. Fear is an insane
motivation, or it can lead to insanity. But more fundamental or subtler
than fear is the simple discomfort or freedom from naiveté, a
fundamental sense that this persona to which you could devote
yourself is going to come to an end and is never perfect and is, in fact,
riding on a machine that will self-destruct one day. It will self-destruct
in any event, if in the meantime it is not destroyed by some other
machine or some complication of this program here, this drama that
is going on.

Therefore, even though as an ordinary matter you should
basically function so that you maintain a level of equanimity and help
others to do likewise, if you are intelligent, your fundamental
motivation will be riding on this sense of discomfort and will be
moving in the direction of release. This impulse makes it possible for
you to be sensitive to me and to this consideration. It makes it possible,
therefore, for you to practice the Way in the real terms of this
consideration, not merely to practice as an extension of your general
will to feel good, to have things turn out well, and to improve your
conditions.

Some people become conventionally religious. They are basically
seeking to make the program survive, and survive well. You can use
my Company in such religious fashion. You can use this Teaching for
the sake of the conventional will to survival and well-being. But true
religion or the real use of my Company is a matter of coming to meet
me on the basis of this impulse toward release, this lack of satisfaction.
If you are already more or less self-satisfied and do not understand
your position, if you do not even appreciate your fundamental motives,
then you will tend to use me for the sake of consolation, generally

finding out what you have to do to feel best while you live and to get along as well as possible. You can use me to help you understand something about right diet and then devote yourself to that—there are all kinds of other possible programs you can follow. But I do not communicate these considerations to you as programs merely for the sake of well-being. They are simply appropriate programs, if you will, which keep energy and attention loosed from the program of the persona so that they are available for this primal impulse to release, to transcendence. This is the significance even of the disciplines given to you in my Company. They do not have a conventional purpose, although secondarily they may serve such a purpose in some sense. Their fundamental purpose is to serve the possibility of release or transcendence by freeing energy and attention. But if you have not come into touch with your dissatisfaction, with this primal motive to release, then you will not use me or this Teaching or this Company for the purposes that are at its heart.

You must realize that you truly are uncomfortable and will never be comfortable as long as you are merely a conditional persona. No matter how grand the program may ultimately become, no matter into what plane you may be born, you will always be looking at this strange apparatus. I have always been sensitive to this fact. Yogic phenomena and mystical phenomena have therefore never bound me. I have had all these experiences—but when I have the experiences, I also see this weirdo machine. I do not just see the images on the TV set. I see all these wheels revolving and resistors, capacitors, strange waves, and all the rest of it—the whole insanity of that projection. I see the machine in its futility. But as an effect or as an appearance I see also the suffering inherent in its continuation.

Thus, for me there is no delight, no great solution involved in going in and up and entering the realms of mind. I see the wheels turning there, I see all the craziness out of which these images develop. I do not just see them congeal into the discrete images on the screen. I see them just before they become that, before the brain makes sense out of them. I see this psychotic wheel of lights, the infinite fractions, its cellular parts just about to show a discrete image.

When you can see that, you feel profoundly uncomfortable and are never comfortable even with the discrete image. Because I was incapable of being consoled by software or hardware, the spell was broken in my case. This Awakening demonstrates the ultimate virtue of discomfort or the inability to be consoled. It is the ultimate means, or that which puts us into intimate association with the ultimate means.

Therefore, the force of this Teaching is not merely to send you to a better world after death or to give you a better circumstance in your next lifetime. It is the understanding that even now you are in an in-between state, a "bardo," [5] and that you can completely understand your present condition to the point of transcending it. You can drop out of the program. You can Outshine it. God-Realization is not a matter of separating from the program, however. It is a matter of clearly understanding it and Outshining it by Standing Free, Standing in the Position in Which we eternally and therefore presently exist, the Condition that is being flowed in the inert machines and animated in the programs. It is possible to be completely Awake in the Transcendental State even in a moment such as this, even in this bardo.

It is the function of the Adepts to be thus Awake and to be able to communicate the Source as the Source, to Awaken others to the Source, to jiggle them out of their comforts, their programming, their commitment to the programming and to the destiny of the ego. Much of what I must do, therefore, is to interfere with you—not merely to console you, but to play all your games, and games you cannot even think of, to create bizarre slices of experience, to interrupt the programming. You are watching the set, and I zip little messages under the screen and make chaos out of the movie. Suddenly there is an off-the-air special report. 'Zap! Your favorite movie is suddenly interfered with, your football game is broken into. Much of that is what I must do. A word from the sponsor—everything—I interfere with it.

Part of my function, you could say, is to be a subliminal image. "Always remember Me." [6] Part of this Remembrance of Me includes remembering me just as I look to you right now. Having seen me personally, you remember me, you use my pictures and associate with my lifetime on some conscious level. You are using me as a subliminal message underneath all the ads and all the dramas of ordinary living. That message is a way out. Just to keep your attention with me breaks

5. *Bardo* is the Tibetan term for any of the intermediate or astral states of the soul after death and before rebirth. It can also refer to any kind of transitional or intermediate state or stage of life, and this is the sense in which Master Da Free John uses the term here.

6. Capitalization of "Me" as an expression of Identification with the Divine is described on p. 331, n. 4.

the spell. Of course attention to me personally is not the whole of this Remembrance but just a fractional part of it. Your attention to me is attention to the Spiritual Reality, not merely to this persona or to the machine on which this persona is riding.

Part of this Remembrance involves association with me as I seem, as a human person and so forth. But then you begin to see my image and my messages in the midst of all kinds of events. It is like subliminal advertising. There is an ad featuring a whiskey glass with ice in it, the bottle next to it, and a message saying "Drink Socko" or whatever it is. That is the way the ad seems at an ordinary glance. But if you examine these images, very often they have little words carefully worked into the design of the ice cube, perhaps, which say "Sex, Love, Happy," or other things.

You begin this Way, in other words, by living your ordinary events. But then somehow you see the words and images that are hidden in the picture, and you get the feeling that I am everywhere, that I am operating to make all this happen, that the Divine is making it all happen, that the Divine is controlling your life somehow or making things happen to your benefit, to wake you up, to help you out. That is true, but it is spontaneous Magic, and its importance is to break the spell, not to give you new spells that are more dramatic or unusual or consoling.

The best thing to do, then, is to be uncomfortable. That is the one thing you do not want, though. Bottom line, nobody wants to be uncomfortable. Everybody wants to be comfortable. You do not want to use your greatest virtue, which is the virtue of discomfort and the capacity to transcend the spell. Instead of doing that you try to maintain a level of consolation and involvement with all this hardware and software so that you will not feel uncomfortable.

You cannot avoid that discomfort. It is essential to your conditional life. You must find it, locate it, and really use it. That is the best thing to do. Do not be angry and sorrowful and guilty and fearful. Rather, be uncomfortable—in other words not satisfied and not satisfiable—in the framework of ordinary living, and you will find me, you will hear me, you will practice. You will have the will to practice transcendence, and you will do it in your daily life and in meditation. But you will not have any energy and attention for that practice if you are not uncomfortable, if you are not dissatisfied. You will tend to settle for the dissatisfaction in the form of neurotic emotion, which is not a sufficient basis for practice.

At least this is the way it seems to me, but you know how Crazy I am! All I can tell you is the way it seems to me. The real import of all of this is not whether or not there is some order underneath it all, evil or good, whether there is some conspiracy or some creative cause. The real importance to be observed is the non-necessity of this experience and, from the conventional point of view, the binding power of this non-necessary experience. The real import of life is not to discover its hidden secrets, the secrets of its working, but to transcend it, to break its spell altogether.

Even though, as people in the world, we work to generally serve the well-being of others in this confinement and even to find out some of the secret workings behind it, even though we may do all of that as an ordinary matter, the fundamental motion of our proceedings, our energy, our consciousness, our attention should be founded in our essential discomfort and our will to transcendence. Therefore, whatever we may be doing, if we understand, we will be renunciates and practice Samadhi moment to moment and not be fools. Above all we will not be fools to ourselves. Whatever conspirators there may be elsewhere, we fool ourselves by becoming overserious about our apparition.

So, it is appropriate to have had this discussion on an evening on which we have all gathered together to watch TV!

CHAPTER 23

M-FIELDS AND THE WORK OF THE ADEPT

a talk by Da Free John
September 9, 1982

MASTER DA FREE JOHN: A scientist in England named Rupert Sheldrake has, through experimentation, developed the hypothesis that all living things are associated with what he calls morphogenetic fields, or M-fields, which are not the same as the energy fields or auras that surround every living entity.

Sheldrake's hypothesis is that all like entities are tuned in to a primal, original M-field. He uses this particular theory, which has some experimental support already, although it is not yet generally accepted, to account for a phenomenon in experiments with animals where one generation of animals is trained to do a particular task and the next generation will either do the same task without special training or learn it more easily than the first generation did. Sheldrake's idea is that there is a morphogenetic field with which all living entities of the same type or species are associated, so that any change in that field due to the activities of one particular individual or group of individuals will then be reflected in all other and all future individuals of that type.

This theory generally supports my description of the Work of the Adept. You could say that the Adept does a certain kind of Work that is in effect like working on the M-fields of all human beings, even all beings. As in my vision of the Dawn Horse,[1] as a result of this Work changes inevitably begin to occur without a physical connection or a direct connection of any ordinary kind between the Adept and others. There is some support for this explanation in the scientific theory of M-fields. (Master Da Free John reads from a recent issue of *Brain/ Mind Bulletin.*)

In a recent interview Sheldrake said, "Morphogenetic fields, or 'M-fields,' have no energy of their own in the usual sense, but rather act as blueprints or guide rails for known phenomena. . . . While the known fields act across space, M-fields act across both space and *time*. . . . Living things 'tune in' to appropriate sequences of morphogenetic fields throughout their life cycles through a process called 'morphic resonance.' "

The M-field of a cat, he said, "would in some sense be cat-shaped. The kitten embryo, as it is developing, would be tuning into, or sharing in, the morphogenetic field of its species."

We tend to think of time as if it were stretched out like space, Sheldrake said. "If a year is one unit long, we think 10 years ago would mean 10 units back.

"But it may instead be that the whole of time is, as it were, pressed up against the present, so that the whole of the past is equally accessible." [2]

This idea corresponds in general to the exotic physics of the twentieth century and relates more to the right-brained, holistic view of reality, which acknowledges the simultaneity of all time and all space. This theory, then, is an extension into the biological sciences of the kind of thinking and investigating that is taking place in the more advanced physical sciences.

Phenomena such as precognition and all varieties of ESP, including so-called mind-reading, are associated with the invisible realm of energy in which we exist as biological entities. Thus, there is a universal process of "tuning in" in which we are all involved at an

---

1. In a vision Master Da Free John observed a ceremony in which a group of Adepts sat in a circle around an empty space. Their consideration having fulfilled itself after they had sat in Spiritual Ecstasy for a time, they left the circle one by one, not waiting to witness the manifestation of their meditation. Gradually the figure of a horse appeared, the "Dawn Horse" of spiritual Awakening and the fruit of the silent consideration of the Adepts. Master Da Free John has often pointed to this vision as the archetype of his own Teaching Work. From his point of view, that of the Adept, his Teaching Work is complete, though its fulfillment is still to come.

2. "Metamorphic Foot Massage: Tapping Prenatal 'Time Map,' " *Brain-Mind Bulletin*, August 23, 1982, p. 3.

invisible level. Even our physical mechanisms are involved in this process. The gross aspects of ourselves function very much like transmitter-receivers. This gross body is a living bio-form. It has the capacity to operate in a field of energy, to transfer energies, and to be in sympathy, therefore, with fields of energy beyond the physical body.

There are many different kinds of fields. The so-called M-fields are a dimension of the phenomenal universe of energy in which we exist. But there are lesser fields that have a shorter range. Healing, for instance, as in the laying on of hands,[3] is associated with a field of shorter range. So are the immediate emanations that surround any biological entity. A person who is balanced and in good vital condition can transfer energy to another for healing purposes. He or she may perhaps even use a thought intention to project the healing energy, but such energy basically works within a shorter range. Healing is possible at a longer range, but in that case it uses a different tuning-in mechanism.

The process that underlies my relationship to people operates within these fields of energy. It makes use, in other words, of the subtler physics of the cosmos. For people to make use of my Company, they must have developed sufficient self-understanding or at least freedom in themselves that they can participate with me at a subtler physical level, or at a level that corresponds to the subtler physics of the cosmos. Until they acquire this ability or naturally develop this capacity, they crave the kind of parent-child association that involves immediacy of a physical kind and dependence-independence games that are all part of the gross physical, phenomenal meeting between us.

The mature form of practice of the Way is not associated with that model of our association, although clearly the process works in my immediate personal company. It does definitely involve the development of the capacity to tune in to me and relate to subtler dimensional forces in general. For this reason it is possible, at this more advanced stage of the development of our sacred institutional culture, for me to suggest the kind of event we are planning this

3. The laying on of hands is an ancient practice of healing through realignment to the infinite Energy of Life. This process requires intelligent application of both the healer and the one being healed to the whole-bodily release of negative feelings and attitudes and reception-affirmation of Life. The Life-Current itself accomplishes the healing and restores *both* individuals to equanimity and Communion with the Transcendental Reality. For a complete description of the practice of the laying on of hands, see Bubba [Da] Free John, *The Eating Gorilla Comes in Peace*, pp. 461–70.

weekend, where practitioners throughout the world will gather together in a celebratory occasion, rightly prepare themselves, and then in meditation literally tune in to me at great distances. Just as people turn on a TV set and tune in to a particular station, devotees can use their whole life of practice and association with me to tune up their own mechanism in order to tune in to my Field.

Practitioners of this Way perform pujas[4] and other means to accomplish this tuning-in process, but they should understand the underlying mechanism. It does not exist in the realm of fancy. It is a real process. It is simply operative at a different level of the physics of reality. You can discover for yourself that there actually is this subtler realm, this complex system of light-radiation wherein we exist, by freeing up energy and attention through the process of your practice and beginning to fall sympathetically into the complete Realm wherein we exist.

That Realm includes what is invisible to us. What is called the Spirit is simply the great, invisible Field of Force, or Radiance, wherein all phenomenal appearances are developing. They may appear as thick, concrete independent forms, but all these forms depend on a whole hierarchy of force-fields that are summarized in a Great Field, which is Radiant Transcendental Being. That is the Great Field, the God-Field. And within the God-Field are all the stepped-down fields, including M-fields and all the little fields around human individuals.

Whenever you develop a sympathy with any person, place, time, or other specific aspect of phenomenal existence, the mechanism of your attention fixes on it in a peculiar fashion so that, in effect, you are always tuned in to that phenomenon, or in any case you are intending—randomly and frequently—to tune in to it. For instance, you are always remembering people with whom you are intimate. You are tuned in to them physically and psychically via your memory. You are always associated with their fields. There is a great deal of transference of feeling, information, energy, healing power, or negative energy—all kinds of influences pass between people who are attentive to one another. Just so, if you are sympathetic with a place you have been, there is a constant transference through this tuning-in process.

4. Puja is ritual worship, traditionally performed by priests, in which offerings are made to the Divine and the Grace of God is invoked and received. This ceremony is expressive of present Communion with God and the yielding of self to the Transcendental Condition. In true spiritual practice all one's activities are engaged as a form of puja, or self-transcending worship of the Divine.

People who have known you in the past are still tuned in to you in some way, and you are tuned in to them.

All these associations may have a possible binding effect, which we call karma. All the negative or limiting transference is a negative by-product of this great system. Its positive by-product is the one with which we should learn to associate. In other words, we must become conscious of this system rather than remain unconscious of it. We must become conscious participants in it, rather than remain unconscious robots who do not believe there is anything invisible or anything great beyond this limited, mechanical, physical appearance.

At present, it is as if we are in a great room full of television sets and none of us believes in TV, or has ever watched it. It is as if none of us have even seen TV. All these sets are just sitting around here, but nobody is turning them on and tuning in. That is how we live. We have all these appliances here, and yet everybody stands around saying, "Is there a God?" "Is there anything greater than this?" Every now and then somebody goes over, plugs in the set, and turns it on, and everybody marvels. Usually, though, people only relate to that gesture in a silly and fascinated manner.

The Adept is somebody who turns on the set and shows you its full potential. He himself becomes a Transmitter and a great Station and helps you tune in to him and create a new Way of life. That is the point. The process with which you become involved through all that is a process of growth through tuning in to the full Dimensional Existence that is our Life, our Being.

A great deal of current esoteric science, offshoots of the super-physics of the twentieth century, involves the development of curious experiments and theories that are gaining more and more support in certain scientific circles. I have indicated to you that there have been remarkable advances in physics, although many physicists still talk in the archaic terms and use the archaic, mechanical models and materials of Newtonian physics, which do have a place in scientific and practical enterprise, but represent only a lesser convention of reality. I have also pointed out that other sciences are not typically so advanced. All the sciences are generally progressing, but their advances tend to be more or less along the lines of the old models. The framework of psychology, for instance, is generally still that old, cranky, materialistic, anthropoid kind of thinking. But some experimenters in almost all scientific fields are starting to think in new terms and are developing new theories.

Some theorists about the brain, for instance, are thinking of models of the brain as a hologram or holograph. One model of the brain that does have functional significance, or is functionally correct in some sense, sees each area of the brain as having a specific function. But there is another, holographic sense in which every part of the brain is associated with the same information. In other words, every part of the brain is in some sense also doing the same thing.

Both these ideas are true. The holographic or hologramic model of the brain is the more holistic view, and the model of the compartmented brain is the more linear, left-brained conception of how the brain is operating. For instance, Kirlian pictures of two leaves, from one of which a circle is cut out and a square out of the other, still showing the total leaf in light form without a hole in the center of the leaf—these photographs are evidence of the universal hologram. The ultimate implication of the holographic theory is that every cell in the body contains all the information for every other part of the body.

To summarize this discussion, we could say that the Adept is something like an M-field. In contrast to common individuals, who are individuated, biomorphic beings with life-fields surrounding and emanating from them, the Master-Field, or M-Field, of that kind is a Great Field that represents Man with a capital "M," the primal Man, the primal human being in its Realized, Radiant form. Anyone's tuning in to the Adept therefore represents an advantage for others. The individual entity can perform a certain amount of practice in its own setting to improve its own circumstance and evolve its functions, but tuning in to a fully developed Master-Field, where all of these evolutionary processes have already taken place, permits those changes to be magnified and quickened or, in effect, lived into that system without its having to pass through certain of the processes associated with the individual struggle to evolve.

Therefore, as I have indicated, the Spiritual Adept is a unique mechanism in Nature provided for the sake of the spiritual and altogether human evolution of human beings as well as the trans-formation and evolution of all beings and all processes that exist in the cosmos. I have communicated all of this to you largely in the language of spiritual affirmation and philosophy. But it would also be possible to consider and describe the process in the technical language of science.

CHAPTER 24

GOD IS THE ONE WHO IS BEING MODIFIED AS EVERYTHING

a talk by Da Free John
October 7, 1980

ASTER DA FREE JOHN: True God-talk is Ecstatic talk. It is a form of speech and intelligence that develops through a self-transcending or Ecstatic process. The literal Divine is Realized in Ecstasy, in the transcendence of self or ego, the transcendence of the body-mind, and therefore the transcendence of this world. There is, however, a convention of popular or exoteric God-talk that speaks about God from the point of view of the ego or ordinary individual experiencing and knowing and suffering and pleasuring. The God of exotericism is offered to these unchanged, self-bound individuals to give them hope, awaken faith in them, even to generate some sort of quality of transcendence, a little freer energy and attention, in the midst of ordinary life.

While there is perhaps some positive service performed by offering mankind such a God, not only can this popularly conceived God not be proven to exist, but the conception of God in these terms does not make sense beyond a certain point. When we literally enter into Ecstasy through radical self-understanding, this notion of God no longer seems to make sense. The radical Realization of the Divine tends to relieve us of the conventions of both exoteric religious consciousness and esoteric spiritual consciousness. When mankind grows beyond its primitive condition wherein the world is described from the point of view of egoic consciousness and conventions of self, then human beings begin to develop a different awareness of the nature of the world.

The scientifically informed mind tends to bring even the comparatively positive notion of an exoteric God into doubt. This is one of the problems in popular society today where scientism and scientific materialism have become the dominant point of view and way of relating to things. The supports for the old psychology of religion are being lost, and this is having a negative effect on the popular mind.

I recently viewed a television program in which a popular scientist was talking about God and criticizing religion directly. He proposed biological evolution as the alternative to God as Creator. He pointed out that until recently human beings looked at this world, observed its intricate complexity and order, and reasoned that it must have a cause. He used the simile of a watch. If you look inside a watch, you find it very complicated, and yet it keeps time. Thus, you conclude there must have been a watchmaker. Such a watch just could not exist without a watchmaker. It is true that such inventions in the plane of human relationships are caused in that sense. In other words, the cause is outside them. But it is not necessary or at this stage in history even appropriate to presume something similar about the total universe.

Yet, there is a popular and ancient tradition for this idea of God as Creator. In fact, this idea is fundamental in the domain of exoteric religion. Actually, the notion "The world exists, therefore there must have been a Creator" is the most forceful and basic argument used by religion to attract followers. It is only after you have established a logic based fundamentally on belief in God as Creator that you can convince people to accept moral laws or supernatural possibilities without otherwise demonstrating those possibilities.

The concept of God as Creator is fundamental not only to religion, but to the primitive mode of human consciousness as well. When human beings cannot logically presume that there is a Creator, they also tend to abandon everything else that is religion and spirituality. They lose the ability to relate to the Divine when they lose the logic of belief in God as Creator.

Nevertheless, it is difficult for people to believe there is a Creator-God. Religion has always had to answer many difficult questions, but just as it has one basic proposition—God created the world and is Master of the world and is the One to Whom you must submit—it has always had to face one basic question. That is the question about the existence of suffering—the most difficult question to answer. If there is a God who created the world, then why is there so much suffering? And why do even those who believe in the Creator-God still suffer? Why do those who believe in the Creator-God often seem to suffer even more than anyone else?

If it has never been easy for religion to attract followers and keep them content, then it is because of this matter of suffering. The proposition that there is a God who created the world was not developed on the basis of thinking about suffering. It is a proposition that followed from thinking about the fact that things exist. In other words, the notion of God as Creator was not formulated as a result of people's observation that they suffer. It arose out of people's observation that things exist. The observation that we suffer has always worked against religion.

The trend of scientific materialism also involves a logic based on the observation of material events and forces, but it is tacitly indisposed toward the whole notion of a Creator. In the common world at the present time we can witness an argument between two kinds of mind. One is represented by the masses of individuals and institutions who are disposed toward the interpretation of the universe as a creation of God. These people are known as the creationists. The other kind of mind is represented by those who, disposed toward the scientific point of view, tend to be atheistic. They do not envision a Creator behind all these effects, but rather see a spontaneous, rather random, and not necessarily benign process. That is, what is positive or benign is only one aspect of what is occurring. These people are commonly referred to as materialists.

And yet, fundamentally, the materialists are struggling with the same question as the creationists. The basic question that is foremost in the popular consciousness is whether or not we should feel good about the universe, whether we should feel hopeful, whether we should feel that there is something great and positive in control of the universe, or behind or at the end of it. The creationists try to communicate a dominant mood of hope, but underneath it they incline toward despair because of the observation of suffering. The materialists endeavor to generate a dominant mood of doubt by constantly pointing out the difficulties of life, the suffering and randomness, and so forth. But in their attempt to establish this mood of doubt, they are hiding another aspect of themselves that is in some way delighted by observing everything for which science accounts. If only they could find something great causing all these material events, materialists would be equally delighted by that. However, the current school of scientific materialism—which is a way of relating to the world, as is religion—is making important new discoveries about the universe, and it is creating whole new technologies that add to our amusement. And along with all that, the mood of scientism is becoming a dogmatic argument against creationism or the mood of religious consciousness.

What I want to point out about this is that in the history of mankind there have not only been believers in God, along with atheists and scientists, there have also been Realizers of God. God-Realization is as much a potential in this age as in any other period, but it has nothing to do with interpreting the universe according to the model of the egoic body-mind. To enter into this process of God-Communion and God-Realization does not require belief in God as Creator or an interpretation of the universe according to which we conceive of a Creator-God and the universe as the effect of that God. Such a description of God and the universe belongs to a naive egoic consciousness, whereas the purpose of the process of Transcendental Spirituality or God-Realization is the transcendence of the egoic body-mind. In the language of transcendence of the egoic body-mind we also speak of God or the Divine Reality, but in Ecstatic terms. We speak of God in terms of self-transcendence and in terms of what is Realized or made Obvious through self-transcendence and therefore world-transcendence. In other words, God-Realization utterly transforms our understanding of personal existence and the existence of the world.

While the process of God-Realization does not necessitate or imply a negative strategy of life, at the same time, it necessarily transcends the whole affair of life. The fullness of Realization necessarily involves utter transcendence of this world. In the meantime, however, we need not be involved in a negative strategy relative to life, which in itself is a kind of egoic disposition. Nonetheless, the process of God-Realization is one of self-transcendence wherein the Transcendental or Divine Force Transforms and Transfigures our entire relationship to experiential events, and ultimately dissolves them all. By entering into the process of God-Communion we are entering into a process wherein we Realize That Which transcends self and world, and That Which transcends self and world is God. That

Which a person Realizes, having transcended himself or herself, is God.

That God or Divine Reality need not be viewed as the Creator of you or the world. When "you" are the point of view for seeking happiness, fulfillment, and salvation, then insofar as you choose a religious orientation as the solution to your self-problem, you may need the logic of God as the Creator. There is no great harm in thinking in those terms temporarily, conceiving a metaphor that works well enough from the point of view of conventional consciousness. Ultimately, however, this is a view of God—a logic about God, self, and world—that is to be transcended. Just as the self and world are transcended, the God who is conceived to relate to selves in this world is transcended.

We could say there are only three fundamental concepts that ultimately summarize our conventional experience of existence— there is the self, me; there is the world and all beings; and there is the God we think of over against self and world, the Creator or Source of everything, or That toward Which we associate ourselves through hope while alive. All these categories are transcended in Realization of God. They are transcended in Communion with God. True God-talk transcends all common or conventional talk about God just as it transcends self and world.

That the logic of God as Creator is seriously placed in doubt by scientific investigation only interferes with the popular notion of God based on the ego-principle. This may cause some egos to despair, but it does not eliminate the spiritual process. It just eliminates a certain logic or frame of interpretation that belongs to the un-Enlightened dimension of human existence. The God we talk about in our Way is the God that belongs to Ecstatic speech, the God Realized through self- and world-transcendence and the transcendence of all God-ideas. The conventional notion of God as Creator or Parent is transcended in true God-talk. The idea that God is the Parent of mankind is only an idea held by egos.

Those who transcend themselves through surrender to the Reality intuited to be magnified in all of existence speak more paradoxically about God. Some do not even speak about God, because just to say the word "God" automatically implies something limited to the popular mind. The word "God" belongs to the category of language that is associated with the ego and conventional self- and world-consciousness, self- and other-consciousness. But in our Way, we freely use the word "God" and other references to the Divine, such as Radiant Transcendental Being, because we are obviously directly associated with the higher process of Realized existence, and whenever we talk about God we intend to take the time to fully develop the consideration.

DEVOTEE: Master, I was thinking that when you say, "There is only God," you confound both religious and scientific people. It is an Ecstatic way of presuming God.

MASTER DA FREE JOHN: Yes. I, along with the scientific materialists, do not believe in the Creator-God. (Laughter.) The notion of God as Creator holds only as long as "I" am the principle of my consideration about God. But as soon as I transcend myself in God, I see that God is a greater profundity than this Creator or Parent idea supposes. I see that God is the One Who is being modified as everything. There is only God. But it is not just the conceived God Who created the world, the God Who is apart from the world. There is not me, the world, and God. There is not one God. There are not many Gods. There is only God. As soon as we transcend our separate position, this becomes Obvious. That One Who Is cannot be rightly understood as the Parent of Man or the Creator of our conditions of existence.

Our conditions of existence and our psycho-physical selves are better understood as a mechanical process in which we are irresponsibly involved. In fact, the significance of the Realization of God is that it expresses self-transcendence, transcendence of the body-mind, transcendence of the mechanics of the apparent universe, transcendence of this world, and transcendence of conventional God-ideas that are supports for self-existence.

It is not the case that God is not obvious. God is the only Thing Obvious. God is the Obvious. It is not that God cannot be seen in the world. God is Obvious in the world. God is Obvious as everything and everyone. All this is the Vision of God, not just some internal phenomenon that is the Vision of God. There is only the Vision of God. This is not the effect of God. It is God.

We must Realize That Which is appearing to be transformed as all beings, as all worlds, as all possibilities, That Which, in the event of anything, is being modified as that event and as all events totally. The process of evolution and appearance of every kind is just happening. God is not standing off from it, creating it, seeing it happen, and requiring lesser beings to suffer a dreadful illusion. Our suffering of illusion is a result of our own irresponsibility. We are nothing but God. We are only in God. All of this is only in God. God is the only thing to be Realized. God is the only Happiness.

But we are very much involved with ourselves and with things as they seem. We are—through fear—very much involved with the possibilities of feeling good and having fantastic things happen to us and acquiring knowledge about great things. Insofar as we are disposed toward all that, we are playing upon the mechanics of existence. All of Nature is just a machine—a machine of infinite possibilities. It is a medium that is utterly responsive to psychic orientation, to desiring. What you desire and think is what you experience and know. What you presume becomes experienced reality. What you presume about the world tends to be confirmed in your observations about the world.

This is true whether you are a religionist or a scientist, and scientists are beginning to discover this. They are beginning to discover that their mode of inquiry, even in sophisticated technological terms, produces its own results, conditions, and knowledge. The universe is a paradoxical machine that will produce whatever evidence you are determined to find. It is a great paradox of space-time in which anything can seem to be so, but all these things that seem to be so are also limits.

It is one thing to be a creationist and have a picturesque view of Nature, to think that God is behind history and God is making all these beautiful mountains. But the natural world is more than beautiful mountains. People did not think mountains were beautiful until recently anyway! (Laughter.) It was only a couple of centuries or so ago that people began climbing and walking in the mountains for inspiration. Before then mountains were viewed as awesome places that you should not go anywhere near. They were generally considered to be terrible or mighty places of power, and you would not casually walk in them. But because of the romantic, picturesque views that came especially out of the nineteenth century, people now hold the view that is an extension of creationism or conventional religious consciousness, according to which Nature is supposed to seem so damned beautiful.

But, to put it simply, Nature is not beautiful. There is something extraordinary and exquisite about it, but Nature is a terrible machine in which everything is transformable, everything is eatable—in which

everything that exists must struggle to continue to exist, and then it
dies. Creatures are all eating one another. Deaths are random and
casual. Human beings must engage in great collective enterprises just
to make human life last a little longer and appear basically pleasurable.

It has not been for very long that a person could live for what we
regard to be a considerable period of time—sixty, seventy, eighty,
ninety years. Many individuals still do not live that long, and in many
human environments on Earth people still live a relatively short life-
span. Man is part of Nature until he starts developing social and
technological abilities to prolong life and to pleasurize himself. He is,
like all the other creatures in Nature, a vulnerable being who must, in
order to survive, always struggle to defend himself against other
people as well as all the forces in Nature. What is so beautiful about all
that?

Even in elaborate technological societies such as our own, life is
not merely pleasurable and happy. It is still threatened with mortality
and pervaded by limitations. It is a lifelong struggle. It is associated
with pleasures but also a great deal of difficulty. Life always seems
somehow or other to be fundamentally a problem, a dilemma, a kind
of cage, and we must struggle our entire lives to feel relatively positive
about it all.

But we are characterized by a kind of TV-consciousness: We are
supposed to feel positive about products of all kinds and make
enthusiastic, rather gleeful pronouncements about all our experience
in this great new age. We are also expected to conform to various
political and social ideals that are intended to serve the general
welfare, protect individual safety, and prolong human existence for the
normally expected life-span. These ideals are also meant to serve
future generations through passing on the knowledge we have
acquired, the accomplishments we have made, and so forth.

In spite of these ideals, however, society is still something of a
jungle, something of a struggle. The same society or worldwide
association of humanity that gives us social and technological
advantages is continually threatening us with disadvantages, suppression, war, and even total destruction.

Look out into vast space and ask yourself where the light is out
there, where there might be something better than this. People used
to look at those little spots in the sky and feel that they were powers of
destiny and Divine Influence, a Great Order. People thought stars
were immortals, fastened to a crystal dome on the other side of which

God was controlling everything. Now, however, we can look at those stars through the eyes of science, analyze their components and their chemistry, see what is really occurring, and find that they are all mortal. Now we know there is no dome, that we are merely seeing a bit of the edge of a galaxy that contains billions upon billions of such light forms and billions upon billions of other such galaxies and who knows what else. It is awesome, but not merely positive, not merely beautiful.

This view of the universe is not new. There have been materialists since the ancient days, who have had much the same kind of philosophical attitude as those who belong to the school of scientism in our day. Likewise, religion has not been limited to its naive dimension of conventional thinking. There are religious and spiritual traditions in which the universe is viewed as a machine with positive as well as negative aspects but awesome and binding in its power.

The universe is too awesome and terrible to be summarized in the creationist's view. There is something much more profound about it. We do not see any evidence of an all-powerful, benign deity creating and managing everything. There is no evidence for this whatsoever, because the universe is immense in its destructive force, its randomness, its variability.

In the context of this immensity, all relations are merely forms of transformation in which individuality is insignificant. The universe is a great transformer, a great womb, in which nothing has ultimate importance. Everything is transformable, everything can and ultimately will be destroyed, everything can be eaten. We are not immortal, but rather we are born, can live well for seventy years or so, and then die in bed. You never know when you might be killed, when you are going to die, when your life is going to become unbearable to you, when the force of the conjunction of your tendencies as an individual may bring about these events.

We cannot feel good about God by observing the universe from a picturesque, romantic, self-based point of view. That point of view, which we would be obliged to hold if we were to support the creationist's view of the world, is not appropriate even from the point of view of currently popular knowledge. It was never philosophically appropriate, and even in times past, when the creationist view was a dominant part of the logic of religion, there existed individuals and groups who viewed the universe in completely different terms. Some of those who viewed it in different terms were materialists, like our modern scientists. They held a view of the universe based on doubt, and doubt is just as much an expression of the independent-self principle as is belief.

Apart from religionists and materialists there have been what we could call Transcendentalists, even Radical Transcendentalists. It is commonly reported that Gautama remained silent when asked about God, but in fact this is not true. He was not silent about God in the Transcendental sense. His philosophy is filled with pointers toward Transcendental Realization. The God he was silent about is the God of the ego, the God of the popular mind, the Creator of the universe. He was silent about it because he had transcended self, and world, and the "other" God, God apart. What he enthusiastically proclaimed was a Way in which there was tacit Realization of the Transcendental Reality. That Reality is ultimately beyond description, but that does not mean that he was silent, or non-communicative, about the matter. We know very well that he was Transcendentally occupied, but he did not engage in descriptive definitions of that Reality. Rather, he pointed to a way of Realization in which one transcended such categories.

Gautama's Realization of the Transcendental Reality was tacit, not descriptive and not mental. This is true of Adepts throughout time. There is no doubt that they were involved in God-Realization or Realization of the Transcendental Reality. Many kinds of language were spun out by these Adepts in their Ecstatic speech, their attempts to guide others and respond to their questions, but the God they Realized is not the God of Nature, not the Creator God, not the God of selves. The God they Realized is the only God, the Transcendental Reality Who is Realized in Ecstasy through self-transcendence, through transcendence of the categories of mind and body and relations and world. The *Bhagavad Gita,* for instance, is a book about God in which the realm of Nature, the realm of selves, is criticized. This realm is not merely proposed as the creation of God. It is all arising in God, but God is not viewed as the Creator, but rather the Transcendental Condition of it all, the One Who is Realized by transcending it all.

In itself, Nature is merely a terrible machine of limitations, in which winter follows summer, cold follows heat, pain follows pleasure. It is a binding, limiting power. The God Who is to be Realized, the God Who is Truth, is only Realized through accepting responsibility for the automaticity of egoic existence, through Ecstasy. That process depends on profound insight into the self, the process of experiencing, knowing, presuming, thinking, desiring, and reacting.

Now, the materialists, like the creationists, have a one-dimensional conception of the world, a conception created by the presumption of the self as the point of view of knowing and experiencing. This presumption underlies the acceptance of the convention of subject-object relations as the model by which scientific inquiry is conducted, just as it is the model for religious devotion to a Creator-God.

Scientists are looking at the realm of cause and effect, as are religionists. The knowledge that science proposes is knowledge about cause-and-effect relations. It is simply that scientists or scientific materialists are describing the universe as a system of causes and effects that has no ultimate cause and perhaps no ultimate effect, a system of endless patterns, paradoxes of cause-effect relations. But they are only looking at the cause-effect realm of experiencing and knowing about that experiencing. That description of reality, that entire enterprise, is developed on the basis of the conventions of egoic perception, the conventions of the relationship between the psycho-physical individual and the world of phenomena. Thus, the enterprise of science is developing a cosmology without a necessary deity.

Scientists are looking at every aspect of this cause-effect universe. They are mapping out a universe of objects in time and looking back in time, ultimately to the extreme point at which there was a great explosion. Physical evidence suggests that the entire material universe is the result of what is popularly called the Big Bang. This theory is achieving legitimacy as the dominant, most believable theory. It represents an absolute qualification of the ability of science to go beyond the evidence of the present universe, because no evidence remains from prior to the Big Bang. All the conditions that priorly existed have been undone, at least insofar as scientists feel they can observe them. Therefore, scientists are beginning to feel there is no way to go beyond the presumption of this initial explosion.

This investigation and the cosmic description scientists are developing on the basis of it has only one dimension. It is an exploration of a non-paradoxical, linear kind of universe. However, at the same time that the universe is conceived as a linear progression from the Big Bang, physical theories have been developed in the twentieth century that point to space-time being a paradox. It must be clearly understood that these same theories point to matter itself being a paradox. Einstein's equation $E=mc^2$ describes a relationship between matter and energy. One-dimensional descriptions of the universe and creationist cosmologies are linear conceptions that do not conceive of time or space in paradoxical terms. They propose matter and thingness as a kind of fixed dimension of manifestation.

However, the total universe is not merely linear, but a space-time paradox. In the linear mode of conception, there is the present moment of time, and if you go way back you get to the Big Bang. But you cannot get to the Big Bang from here. (Laughter.) If you fully conceive of the total significance of the so-called material universe, it is a paradox of space-time. There is no linear way to get to the Big Bang. Likewise, matter is not merely thingness. From the viewpoint of the Big Bang, the universe seems to be a transformation of existing materiality, but if we understand matter rightly, we see that matter is itself light or energy. Therefore, right conception of the universe must be based on understanding the paradox of matter as light and the paradox of space-time. Ultimate right thinking, even about the universe, must be paradoxical thinking, and it must be dimensional, not linear, thinking.

As I have pointed out in *Scientific Proof* [*of the Existence of God Will Soon Be Announced by the White House!*] we should be thinking in terms of the consequences of this paradoxical view, which has been legitimized by twentieth-century science. We should be thinking of energy as a paradox of space-time, and we should be conceiving of everything as a paradoxical expression of energy with only one level being solid and fixed in present time. If we viewed the universe altogether, we would see that every manifestation in this moment inheres in infinite Energy and in non-linear time, inexpressible time, Eternity. If we engaged in dimensional or paradoxical thinking, then we would have a truer view of the universe, and of our existence as a rather paradoxical phenomenon that crosses through many dimensions of appearance. We are simply fastening our attention in one dimension of appearance, the so-called material dimension, the linear world in which the present material appearance has occurred progressively since the Big Bang.

If we become capable of dimensional or paradoxical consideration, then we can also see how the transcendental or radical spiritual point of view is the ultimately justifiable philosophy. It does not depend on conventional religious thinking, creationist thinking, or materialist thinking. All such thinking is based on one-dimensional, linear, materialist kinds of conception that express the psycho-physical ego, its subject-object relations, and the conventions of such subject-object relations. Both science and traditional religion are involved in a self-based, illusory interpretation of the world, rather than a view of the world based on liberated understanding, a view in which we understand ourselves and the world as inhering in the ultimate paradox of the Absolute. We must understand and transcend ourselves altogether, submit ourselves to a different kind of process than this one-dimensional, linear, self-based process. We must enter into Ecstasy, dare to surrender into the Totality of our existence, transcending this limited material dimension in its mereness. We necessarily do so when we become intuitively Awakened to the real God, the only God.

CHAPTER 25

WHAT IF THE UNIVERSE WERE TO DISAPPEAR IN LIGHT?

a talk by Da Free John
October 2, 1980

DEVOTEE: You have said, Master, that the Adept's ultimate function is the Enlightenment of the whole universe.

MASTER DA FREE JOHN: Yes, that motive is the disposition of the Divine, and once the Divine is Realized, then that disposition becomes apparently one's own.

But, on the other hand, there already is no universe. All space-time is spontaneous. Therefore, all past is present, all future is present, all possibilities exist, and their dissolution is already true. It is a matter of what slice of possibility or space-time one wants to fix upon or is made to fix upon or is tending to fix upon. Even the philosophy of the conventional physical sciences now recognizes that space and time are relative conceptions. They each change dramatically as one changes position in space and in time. There are paradoxes like the observations that space itself is curved and that all time is simultaneous and that time depends on one's position in space. It is all arbitrary and paradoxical, and it is only by assuming a fixed position—which is not really possible—that you make sense out of space and time, you see. As soon as you become mobile, you are confronted by nothing but paradoxes, and what you experience does not make sense anymore.

It is because we have this apparently fixed body that space is fixed, time is fixed, and our point of view is fixed. We make philosophy out of that fixation, and we conceive the necessity for salvation because of that fixation. As soon as we cease to be fixed in our manifest expression, it is not necessary to be saved anymore, and the dimension of existence becomes a dimension of paradoxes rather than fixed states. One can be of an entirely different mind or disposition, and the human mechanism is in fact structured to be of an entirely different mind than you are all tending to animate. Now you may enjoy some intuition of an expanded conception or realization of existence. But you could be in an entirely different disposition in which that intuition is the bare fact of your perception and in which it determines the conditions of your life. At present you are conditioned by conditions or circumstances. Your spiritual intuition gives you a little distance from it all somehow. But were you in another state of mind, that intuition itself could be the Intelligence that conditions or determines conditions.

Now, since this State can be Realized and has been Realized by various individuals in human form, it is apparent, therefore, that all human beings are structurally capable of such transformation. It is merely that we are adapted to a lower form or organization of our own structure. We determine our experience and destiny based on this lower organization or adaptation, and our state of mind reflects this lower state of adaptation. Thus, an aspect of the spiritual process involves the evolutionary transformation of the state of mind, the fixed presumptions in the structural adaptation of the individual. Our braincases are filled with potential chemical alignments that can make this brain into a much more extraordinary instrument than it now appears to be. Really a very crude, low level of the brain is in operation in people at the present moment. It is related basically to the lower vital mind and operating in reaction to physical events in their conventional form. Unfortunately, that crude activity of the brain is controlling the chemistry of the total brain.

DEVOTEE: Master, can we still talk about the process of evolution within the paradox of simultaneity of the past, present, and future?

MASTER DA FREE JOHN: Yes. To be highly evolved in human terms is to be capable (while remaining fundamentally present as a human individual) of consciously, psychically entering into a time-space framework that is profoundly expanded beyond your present conception, which is a fixed space-time perception.

Now, if human beings in general began to adapt themselves in all kinds of new ways along these lines, you might begin to look different physically. Not only might you look different physically, but part of your appearance could be energy. At present we do not tend to see very much of the energy in which we are all appearing, but the body is expressive of energy, and that energy could become commonly visible. In other words, it could be a convention of perception, not just an uncommon occurrence seen in the case of somebody extraordinary. This mind could be of a different kind, the chemistry of the body-mind could be totally transformed. Walking around, appearing among others, you would see light emanating from your own body and that of others, and you would contact others through association at the level of energy and psyche. And that dimension in which you function psychically would be visible physically. You would see your own mind, in other words. Now you can only see the body, but you would see the mind as well. You would see the energy field in which mind is operative, and you would observe that mind exists not in the body but in the field of Universal Energy, and therefore it has no fixed location.

In my own case, I have seen how this individual body-mind arose. I see how it is arising now and what holds it in place. This arising has nothing to do with a "me" that decided to do it and that requires this life-experience to happen for my own sake, you see. That is the significance of bodily life for the usual individual, but not for those who are Awake. And this individuated body-mind does not have an eternal existence. It is just mocked up for a purpose that transcends individuality, for a spiritual function. It may therefore exhaust itself in this lifetime, destroying the seeds of even Enlightened rebirths. Or maybe it will not! (Laughs)

Thus, the point of view that is operative in my existence is different from that which animates people ordinarily. The usual individual looks at death, for instance, as a possibility of being personally disturbed and annihilated—and "who knows what is going to come next?" I see death as just a retraction of this extension here. My so-called death will just draw this psycho-physical being back into the Position in Which I Am already Living. This body is not my position. It is just an electronic appearance.

I am describing a different event than a subjective, personal dream. When you awaken from a personal dream, you at least have the sense that all those individuals you may have seen in that dream were emanations of yourself. They were obviously animated by your own being and energy. The appearance of beings and phenomena in the waking state is somewhat different. It seems that all these others here are suffering from an independent sense of their own existence. Even so, you could say that the same thing is actually true of the dream as well. You know from the point of view of the waking state that all those people in your dream were in fact your own emanations. But in the dream state itself, you encounter all those individuals as others than yourself. That is why you are motivated to take seriously everything that seems to happen in a dream.

Enlightenment wakes you up and frees you from the seriousness of this appearance. As long as the Enlightened disposition persists, you are like a person Awake in this dream we call the waking state. You act assuming that others are taking seriously the appearance of their bondage and their independence within the dream. So, you play it as such, at the same time Realizing that there is really no one in trouble here. There are no un-Enlightened beings, and there is no one in bondage, needing to be Liberated.

All this appearing universe could vanish in a moment. Just as one can wake up in the morning before one's dream is over, this world could vanish long before it fulfills its projected term, you see. It need not wait to disappear only after all beings are Enlightened. It could disappear because all beings are already Enlightened. The appearance of phenomena is the only suggestion of un-Enlightenment. No appearance, no un-Enlightenment!

Well, there is something very strange about all of this here! (Laughter.) If there could be a sufficient Awakening on the part of all of us, perhaps the universe would disappear. Psychic forces are determining its continuation, you see. States of mind are disturbing the Universal Force and causing certain appearances to arise and remain fixed. Once something comes into being, once a certain motion is established, it tends to persist until it is disturbed, in which case it changes, or until there is complete Awakening, in which case the motion just vanishes. Then Enlightened equanimity is restored. If there could be sufficient Awakening, therefore, to the point that equanimity is established at the level of Universal Force, then all this moving universe would vanish.

However, it need not explode or violently disintegrate. Nothing need explode to wake you up from your dream. The room that you saw just before you awakened need not break up, need not explode in order to vanish. Just so, the universe that we experience in the waking state need not blow up. All the stars need not collapse or explode or blend into one another again—none of that has to happen for this appearing universe to vanish. Why, then, do we presume in the waking state that the whole extended universe must somehow fulfill its term before it can come to an end? It could fulfill its term, it could also be mightily changed, and it could also vanish in an instant. It could become unnecessary, obsolete, and disappear altogether.

Therefore, we can say that it is possible in the Divine or Real Physics of manifestation for the entire manifest universe to vanish suddenly and at any time. But there are so many beings, so many events set in motion, so much psychic force or force of mind establishing a disturbance in this universal Energy, that such an event is extremely unlikely in the near future. It takes more than an occasionally Awakened individual to transform the universe for others. Any single individual can Realize the transparency of the manifest universe and enjoy the Absolute Condition of Light or Radiant Being, and for that individual none of this will exist. It will vanish.

But he or she is thereby Awakened from the waking state like a single ordinary individual waking up from a dream. The world of the dream that he or she left has not been exploded or made utterly obsolete. Attention and energy have just been transferred temporarily. Likewise, individual beings can become Enlightened, and are in that sense, then, Translated out of this universe and all the states through which experience arises—waking, dreaming, and sleeping. For Translation to take place in the highest sense, the entire material universe would have to be translated out of material existence.

Individual beings can go up in light, but that is not the same as Divine Translation. And an individual body can be disintegrated without disintegrating the entire material universe. I am not just talking about spontaneous combustion where the body burns to a cinder. That has been known to happen, apparently for various chemical reasons. But there are also cases of yogis, for instance, who to the view of others have gone up in a flash of light and disappeared. Tukaram, the seventeenth-century saint of India, was such a person. But this kind of event is not the same as Divine Translation in the highest sense. It is a kind of translation that can be coincident with the Enlightenment of the individual, but it is basically a manifestation of the yoga of the Life-Force in the body. For perfect Divine Translation to take place, rather than mere disintegration of an individual physical body, the total physical universe would have to be Translated. This is why Translation in the ultimate sense I have described relative to the seventh stage of life is not likely to happen in physical terms, at least not in these times.

DEVOTEE: Master, why does the ultimate Translation of any individual depend on the Translation of the whole physical universe?

MASTER DA FREE JOHN: Because it is not simply an event that occurs relative to one individual physical being. It is an expression of Awakening in terms of the Absolute Universal Force. Therefore, it is an event that must take place universally. Now there is a yoga of translation that can take place with an individual body. As I have said, this is a possibility. There is a kind of yogically significant individual experience in which the body disintegrates in a flash or dissolves in a light-form. This has no implications relative to the universe for others, though the event in your personal case could perhaps be perceived by others. Your body could be seen to disappear in a flash, or it could become sort of illusive, and just disintegrate. This is a kind of translation, just as Enlightenment itself is Translation into Divine Existence inherently. The kind of translation that is apparent to others, therefore, can indeed be developed as a yoga of individual translation whereby the body dissolves in light.

I have written in *The Enlightenment of the Whole Body* that this kind of individual translation can occur in yogis or devotees who extend themselves into the higher, mystical stages of human evolution.[1] This potentiality has been proved by certain individuals in the past.

But the ultimate event of most perfect Transfiguration and Translation signifies truly the Translation of the entire material universe and all beings. It is rather the Disposition toward which we are all moving, the Potential of all beings, than it is something to which you, as an individual being, should look forward. It is not an individual experience. It is something toward which bodies of this kind are universally moving. But to take place in the highest sense, that Translation would have to be coincident with the Enlightenment of all beings.

1. See the essay "Extraordinary Experiential Phenomena Are Common Once Maturity in the Fifth Stage of Life Is Attained," *The Enlightenment of the Whole Body*, pp. 535-38.

Thus, Divine Translation is the process of ultimate significance. Everything else, you see, is preparation. Spiritual Work, for an Adept, is a matter of preparing people for that Realization, so that they can exercise themselves in Enlightenment. First, they must be established in that Enlightenment bodily, not just philosophically. The total body-mind must be established in that ultimate Light. All the complex disturbance that you represent individually must be undone. Until that time your spiritual life is basically an exercise for the sake of your own Enlightenment.

But what of Enlightenment itself? What of the process that is spontaneously expressed in Enlightenment? Well, that is yet to be considered and engaged by us together. It is to be seen whether we will ever do it together. In the meantime our meeting is a matter of my engaging you in a consideration that relates to the level or quality of energy and attention that you represent habitually.

You see, if I talk with you, you all tell me about presumed limitations. You all think in the conventional terms of being a physical personality, an individual being with fears and emotional complexes, and with various desires that are obsessive and difficult or that demand to be fulfilled. Right? Is this true? Is anybody not involved in any of that stuff? Everybody close your eyes. (Laughter.) Okay. Anybody who is not involved in all that dreadful stuff I just listed, raise your hand. Aha! (Someone has apparently raised a hand.) Anybody else? (Laughter.) Well—you see what I mean?

DEVOTEE: Master, you are saying, then, that Divine Translation would include objects to the extent of the dissolution of very atoms.

MASTER DA FREE JOHN: Ultimate Translation, yes. It is something, therefore, that no single individual realizes. Perfect Translation is something toward which all beings are disposed, and therefore such Translation really is recognition of an ultimate Enlightenment of all beings, the Divine Translation of the material universe.

Looking at objective Nature, science only conceives of a scenario for this physical universe that can involve a collapse of all material energies, and then perhaps another creative Big Bang following it. The scientists see things in terms of these outward cycles. From a spiritual point of view we should say that the ultimate Event is not the collapse of energy but the Translation of the material universe, so-called, into at least the domain of light-energy that is superior to material existence.

DEVOTEE: Master, lately I have been considering your Teaching on the Divine as the Universal or Transcendental Person or Personality. It just occurs to me as you are talking that the spontaneous motive of which you speak is the Motive of the Divine Person, not really of individual beings.

MASTER DA FREE JOHN: Yes—and so when we speak of Translation in the ultimate sense, we are speaking of that Destiny which is in God relative to all this material existence and, therefore, relative to any and every individual's material body-mind.

You can transcend personal karma, then, and this will change your condition. It can even in yogic terms involve a kind of dissolution of the physical being. But such dissolution will simply move you into a destiny coordinated with the universal pattern of manifestation. Ultimate Realization is Perfect Coincidence with the Divine. Then the universe as we now perceive it truly does disappear.

CHAPTER 26

SPACE, CONSCIOUSNESS, AND ENLIGHTENMENT

an essay by Da Free John
May 6, 1982

Objects are not in Space. Objects are Space. They are transformations of Space Itself.

When objects appear, time begins, and mind.

Time is not separate from objects. Time is objects. Time is the process or relationship or energy of the relationship between objects.

Mind does not exist in time. Mind is time. Mind is Consciousness modified in the form of time, or the awareness of objects.

If Consciousness observes and understands (or enjoys insight into) mind, time, objects, and Space, then mind, time, and objects are transcended in the recognition of the process or sequence of their origination, and they disappear in the intuition of their ultimate or native equation with Space. In that case, Where or What is Consciousness?

Consciousness is not in Space. Consciousness is not separate from Space. Consciousness is Space, eternally prior to mind, time, and objects.

Space and Consciousness are the same.

Space, or Consciousness, is Transcendental, Free, and Divine, or Very God.

Space, or Consciousness, is neither Empty nor Full, but It is Radiant Love-Bliss, Eternal Happiness, or Infinite Being.

Every thing and every one that arises arises in Space, which is Consciousness. That is the Origin and the Source.

Every thing and every one that arises arises Mysteriously, in Divine Ignorance, spontaneously, not mechanically (or as an effect follows from a cause). Space, or Consciousness, does not Create or Cause any thing or any one as a something or a someone independent of Itself. Creativity and causation of apparently independent entities are efforts that arise only after the primitive and spontaneous fact of conditional appearance (so that creativity and causation function as conventional and mutually transformative processes in the midst of the presumption of a dualistic relationship between things and beings that already appear to be existing independent of one another and of any Transcendental Source with Which they are inherently and equally Identical).

The arising of any thing or any one is a conditional effect of previous conditions, but the Source or Origin or Condition of all arising is Space, or Consciousness, Itself.

Therefore, we may function in the plane of mind, time, and objects, and so progressively attain or suffer all kinds of conditional effects, according to our will and tendency and mechanical destiny. Or else we may consider, understand, recognize, and transcend mind, time, and objects in Space, or Consciousness. The former path is the path of "samsara," or conditional being, limited by knowledge, experience, and finitude. The latter path is the path of "Nirvana," Transcendental Being, or the Realization of Self-Radiant Enlightenment.

CHAPTER 27

THE CONTINUUM

an essay by Da Free John
June 5, 1981

All negative wondering or doubt about the ultimate Status of the Self (or the Conscious Being) is due to the tendency toward abstraction, differentiation, and separation—the characteristic processes of mind in relation to conditional events. Thus, we may, in the sixth stage manner, "locate" Conscious Being as the Witness, over against or in relation to processes of mind and body, but in doing so we separate Conscious Being from all other conditions. The mind wonders, then, if Conscious Being is not simply some kind of temporary derivative or a reflection of temporary material or bodily existence. Indeed, the mind itself wonders if it is not also in a similarly tenuous circumstance. Thus, mind and Conscious Being tend to reduce themselves to an absolute identification with the material body and its destiny. But all of this negative wondering (or fundamental self-doubt) begins to fall away as soon as the analytical conventions of mind are relaxed, thus permitting simple, direct, intuitive observation of the aspects of existence.

In the naturally intuitive position of simple observation (rather than analysis), we tacitly presume the unity of Conscious Being, mind, body, and world. There is no tendency to separate each aspect from the others, or to reduce any of them to any of the others. Thus, it is clear that the body is neither separate from the elemental world nor reducible to it. The elemental world and the body are a dynamic unity, bearing many likenesses and common constituents. Likewise, the mind and the body are a dynamic unity. The mind is not reducible to the body, but it is another aspect or dimension of a great continuum that includes the elemental world and the elemental body. The mind is a subtler capacity than the body, and it is a medium of reflective awareness of the world on a subtler plane than the grosser elemental reflectiveness represented by the gross body. Just so, Conscious Being is continuous with mind, body, and world. It is neither separate from them nor reducible to them (or any one of them). It is another dimension of the continuum. Indeed, it is not merely inside the body or behind the mind. It pervades the entire continuum and is its very basis or matrix. Conscious Being is a dimension of the world itself. (If all elements of our existence return to their general category at death or disintegration of the physical being, then what will Conscious Being return into? Or the mind? Or the psyche?)

All aspects of existence are unique dimensions of a continuum. They are in unity and dynamic play with one another. They are not reducible to one another. (Each is a necessary component with a unique character, reflecting a unique dimension or aspect of total Reality.) In fact, each aspect or dimension of existence of which we are or can be aware is hierarchically related to all the others. Thus, the mental or psychic dimension is subtler than the elemental, and the dimension that is Conscious Being is subtler even than the mind, and it is ultimately Transcendental.

On the basis of intuitive and participatory observation, free of the conventional limits of analytical thinking, the great enterprise of human growth, wholeness, equanimity, and ultimate self-transcendence is begun. (This is not to say that analytical thinking is false or useless, but it belongs in the realm of the exercise of an intelligence that is already founded in original unity. The problem of human culture at the present time is that it has reduced intelligence to an analytical exercise and does not presume the original unity of all aspects of existence; the hierarchical continuum of Conscious Being, mind, body, and world; the Transcendental Nature of Conscious Being; or the non-reducibility of mind to body.)

Once we begin to operate via the disposition founded on such observations as these, we are free of the destructive analytical doubt that constantly creates separateness in every sphere of life. Then we are psychically and psychologically free again to proceed into and through the seven stages of human existence, and to create positive expressions of unity and harmony at every stage.

Likewise, this disposition easily outgrows conventional and false

views, both religious (or sacred) and secular. In the earlier stages of
life, this disposition goes beyond the notion of the Parental Creator
God, Who is presumed to be "in charge." Instead, it is realized that all
of manifest existence is really and totally participating and inhering in
the total continuum. Thus, it is clear that there is not merely One Who
is in charge (or effecting changes), but that all beings, powers, and
motions are simultaneously effective. Everyone is thus responsible.
We are each and all together a Play upon the Ultimate One. For this
reason, the vast multiplicity of effective agents, along with our own
individual tendencies and weaknesses, are producing conditions of
existence that are always temporary, often frustrating or negative, and
never ideal. Efforts to coordinate ourselves with one another and with
the total continuum of world and Being in positive cooperation,
physically and psychically, are thus profoundly necessary, if there is to
be any fundamental order, predictability, and pleasurable harmony to
life. But even such possible creative efforts belong to the earlier stages
of human life (or the conditional and generally grosser aspects of
individual and collective enterprise). Ultimately, we will transcend the
necessity of world, body, mind, and the Play of these upon Conscious
Being. Those who contemplate the continuum of existence to the
degree of perfect profundity, transcending themselves at the root of
every tendency of mind and body, Abide simply in Radiant
Transcendental Being, the Substance of the total continuum of
existence, the Domain of Ultimate Freedom, Peace, Love, and Bliss,
Transfiguring the world while they seem to live, and Outshining the
world at last.

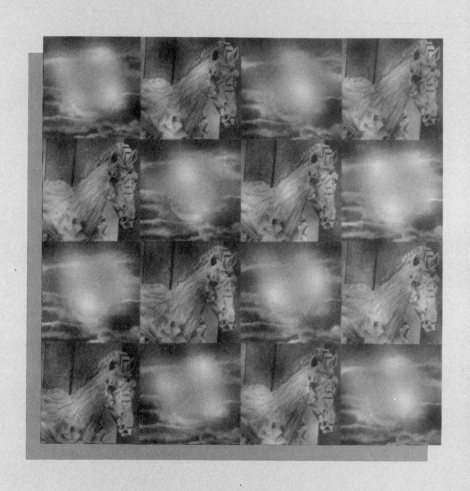

EPILOGUE

SECULAR
AND SACRED
PHILOSOPHIES

Living beings tend to struggle with their own apparent condition. Therefore, the enterprises of Man develop as self-saving efforts, both sacred and secular, to achieve superior knowledge and experience. Those enterprises are the ordinary and extraordinary stuff of daily life and human biography. What I consider is a Way of Ultimate Wisdom based on primary insight into the conventions that govern all our human, subhuman, and superhuman enterprises of knowledge and experience. Perhaps not many are disposed to choose such a Way, but it seems necessary and good to propose it, if only for the sake of those who are so critically bewildered and disheartened by the possible adventure of their lives that they cannot choose the secular and sacred professions commonly available to them. For such as will understand and choose the Way that I Teach, the conventions of living become illumined by prior freedom, and they may yet serve mankind with Great Power. For those who are not presently disposed to choose this Way, let them inherit more peace from our deliberations. Let all beings at least be comforted by the Realization that even a little surrender provides place for the Blissful Intrusion of God.

Da Free John
January 14, 1981

SECULAR AND SACRED PHILOSOPHIES

an essay by Da Free John
March 31, 1981

1.

The body-mind-self is inherently a limited, mortal, and threatened organism.

Secular philosophies (including conventional exoteric religion) and their programs generally seek to bring order, satisfaction, and a reduction of threats (and threatened consciousness) to the body-mind-self.

Sacred philosophies (including exoteric religion in its original or non-conventional intention) and their programs are fundamentally oriented toward transcendence of the body-mind-self.

Secular philosophies and programs are based on the convention of the independent self as a limited and mortal psycho-physical organism.

Sacred philosophies and programs are based on an understanding of the psycho-physical self, such that the actual Condition of existence is presumed to be unlimited and immortal (or eternal).

The Way that I Teach is a sacred philosophy and program of self-transcending Realization of the Unlimited and Immortal (or Eternal) Condition of existence. It is founded on intuitive observation and understanding of the body-mind-self. That understanding is ultimately expressed in the Realization that the conscious being (or the witness of all states of body and mind) is not an independent conscious self but the Transcendental Self-Identity or Unqualified and Eternal Existence and Consciousness. Coincident with this Realization is the Realization and active presumption that the body-mind is not an independent entity but a dependent process that arises through cause-and-effect processes in a single and infinite Field of Radiance, or Love-Bliss.

These presumptions are fundamental Realizations in the sacred Way of Life. Their import is expressed through an active orientation toward transcendence of (or feeling beyond) the self-limiting force of the conventional, threatened, and contracting states of the body-mind. Thus, ultimately, What is Realized is the Condition of unqualified Identification with Transcendental Being (or no independent self) and Infinite Radiance, Love-Bliss, or no body-mind.

Such Realization is Enlightenment, Perfect Equanimity (or "Samadhi"), Transcendental Freedom, and Infinite Happiness. Even if the conventions of the body-mind remain, in Enlightenment they have no power to define existence as a self. Thus, sacred philosophy and practice ultimately transcend the body-mind-self, or existence as a separate, limited, mortal, and threatened organism.

Secular philosophies as well as conventionally oriented people and their programs tend to resist sacred philosophies and to impugn the programs, practices, and results of the sacred ordeal—except insofar as sacred ideals can be made to conform to secular and conventional views. Even in the present day, the clash between these two orientations continues.

2.

The body-mind and the total world inhere in the Universal Connecting Principle, Which is Infinite and Unqualified Bliss-Radiance, or the Light Which is Love.

The conscious being inheres in Transcendental Being, Eternal and Free Consciousness of Bliss-Fullness, the Identity of Radiance.

The Truth and the Secrets of devotional inherence in Radiant Transcendental Being must be learned and Realized through right approach to cultural and spiritual Agents of the sacred ordeal of Life.

What is to be learned is the conscious process of self-transcendence, or ecstatic inherence in the Transcendental Identity, in which the body-mind is natively surrendered and ultimately recognized in the Radiant Reality.

If this sacrificial process is not learned, then attention becomes a binding automaticity, locked into the conventions of independent selfhood and the narcissistic philosophies of mortal bondage. Either moment to moment existence is consciously Awakened as the Supreme Identity and intentionally surrendered into the Universally Radiant Field, or else it is unconsciously defined by the self-contracting mechanism of independent egoity and automatically fascinated and disturbed by all of the possibilities of experience and knowledge.

Sacred learning takes place in the intimate and free culture of spiritual community. If there is no true, free esoteric and Transcendental Teaching and no spiritual Agencies coming from Adepts of the sacred ordeal, then human beings are limited to egoic education, secular ideals, and conventional ends. At the present time, there is clear evidence that mankind is generally functioning in a disposition bereft of high spiritual culture and Wisdom. I am one among those who have tried to provide the alternative to the usual destiny implied in the absence of Wisdom and the Way of Life. Now that my struggle to Teach ordinary people is done, it is up to those who confront this Teaching (and the community of Agency I have established) to choose what they will do.

3.

This is the summation of sacred philosophy, the Realization of those who have fulfilled the sacred ordeal of Life: Consciousness is the Condition or Medium or Matrix of the total universe and every fraction of it.

Secular philosophy is a consideration of knowledge and experience based on the conventions of ego (or consciousness as a separate and dependent phenomenon) and form (or appearances, as they seem). Sacred philosophy is a consideration of knowledge and experience based on intuitive insight that transcends the conventions of ego and form. The ultimate Realization is not the product of "primitive" or wishful thinking, but it is the native intuition that is naturally evident when the Power of Consciousness penetrates the truly primitive conditional force of the conventional presumptions and reflexes of the body-mind.

Conventional presumptions pervade both the popular and the professional domains of secular knowing and experiencing. Likewise, they pervade the exoteric and esoteric domains of traditional religion and spirituality. But I do not propose that we resort to the presumptions of conventional or popular or traditional secular and sacred philosophies. Neither do I propose the assumption of non-conventional sacred philosophy because its Truth is guaranteed by any authority we must necessarily believe. What I propose is that every individual seriously consider the arguments I have generated in my works, and that the teaching and demonstration of historical Adepts in all sacred traditions be seriously taken into account.

Secular philosophy and all the popular excursions of experiencing and knowing represent a conventional application of attention to phenomenal conditions. Such enterprises presume and use the local or egoic consciousness to develop states of phenomenal knowledge and experience. But such enterprises and their results are always like the presumptions on which they are based. They neither exceed nor transcend those presumptions. Thus, for example, scientific experimentation uses Consciousness as a bare instrument of attention and of ratiocination based on phenomenal evidence. Its results are theoretical models and sophisticated technologies that describe and serve a world of beings that are nonetheless separate, mortal, and threatened. Sacred philosophy is, when free of its historical conventions, a rigorous intuitive and intelligent discipline that examines and transcends the conventional presumptions of ordinary, or popular, and professional secular knowing and experiencing. Therefore, the sacred enterprise intuitively transcends the convention of egoic attention and its ordinary conception of the status of phenomena.

Free sacred philosophy is not inherently opposed to the conventions of daily life or of secular philosophy, science, and technology. On the contrary, it values the evolutionary growth of Man and the elaboration of higher human culture and society. But it also insists that there is a higher or Transcendental dimension to existence, and if that dimension is not understood and engaged, then we cannot rightly understand or positively use the conventions and results of our apparent existence, knowledge, and experience. If we are limited to the secular model of existence, knowledge, and experience, then we are merely projected into the mortal domain of limits and possibilities bereft of Ultimate Paradox, Mystery, and Truth.

Secular philosophy, whether popular or professional, invites us toward enthusiastic participation in a mortal lifetime displayed within a scheme of dreadfully indifferent powers and laws and forms. The universe of science is a mighty pool of senseless rocks, winding like clockwork, shedding a soup of poor beings cited with the demand for yes and yes, until, in some terminal collision, they are made soundless in the molecular roar. Yet, if human beings or their politics act in a manner like the universe they suppose, there are cries against barbarism, totalitarianism, and unlove. How can we justify and demand superior behavior on the part of mankind if we conceive of mankind merely in terms of the mortal ego and the secular cosmos? If mankind does not achieve a higher sacred and Transcendental view of self and world and Reality, then there is no alternative to the mad gleefulness of conventional religion and the sorry revolt of angry secular mortals.

I have been through the tour of our conventional possibilities. I explored all of that in the "sins" of my youth and in the company of "sinners" who gathered with me in the years of my original Teaching Work. But we together came to a new and radical understanding that broke the cycle of our ordinary destiny. Therefore, we offer our consideration and our experience and all our future demonstration as an argument and an appeal that can transform the human plot. We have not solved the mystery of the universe, as if the aeons of rise and fall were evidence of a culpable murder by Nature. Rather, we have transcended the view of self as victim and of the world as a mortal machine.

To most human beings, the life-force seems to move selves in a round of limited possibilities until death. But I have observed that the Condition of the life-force is an infinitely Radiant Energy that does not move. It is attention that moves, or seems to move, via the paradoxical laws of cause and effect, combining the presumed self of the body-mind with the universal scheme of space-time possibilities. Rather than merely submit the body-mind-self (or attention) to the presumed possible motions of the life-force, we must constantly recognize or yield and identify attention in the Ultimate Condition of Infinite Fullness or Motionless Radiance Itself.

If attention is not understood, then the conventional interpretation of self and world cannot be understood. If attention (or local egoic consciousness) is merely exercised, then we are played upon by possibility and never participate in the true Condition of existence. Both science and ordinary living are founded on the conventional exercise of attention, and so experience remains localized at the self, and knowledge never exceeds the domain of limitations. We must understand and transcend the mechanism of attention and all the problematic conventions of self and world.

If attention is merely exercised from its self base, then Consciousness, prior to the act of attention, is not Identified or explored in Itself. (Even mind is not explored in itself, but is made to be composed of analytical and sensory conceptions determined by the identification of consciousness or attention with the locus that is the body.) And if Consciousness is not Identified, then the Condition of the world and the body-mind is not recognized.

Consciousness is not merely dependently present in the body-mind and the world as attention (or the perspective of a point of view in space and time). Consciousness is the very Matrix or Medium or Condition of the body-mind and the world and every fraction or point of view in the world. The world and the body-mind must be recognized in the infinite Radiance that is Consciousness. And the self (or apparently independent consciousness identified with any moment of attention or point of view) must be Identified with the Transcendental Nature that is Consciousness, or the Self-Identity of the Universal Radiance that pervades and supports the world.

The Way in which this Realization is spontaneously, natively, and naturally evident is described in its essential outline in the literature I produced during the years of my Teaching consideration. I offer my own testimony to its Truth and Fullness, as do many individuals who considered and practiced this Way in my company. It remains simply to be considered and practiced to prove itself in the case of all others.

My own manner of life-long consideration and practice has not been that of the traditional saint, believing from the beginning and committed to good behavior free of doubt. My practice was Crazy with doubt, such that every moment was a rigorous test. Thus, only over time and on the basis of Realization Itself was I started to be sublimed in the body-mind by the Radiance of God. Likewise, my manner of Teaching was not to demand the artifices of behavioral sainthood from those who considered with me, but to submit myself to those individuals as they were, so that all the secrets and conventions of their lives were visible even in me. In such a manner, those who came to me were permitted the freedom to consider and transcend and go beyond their own "sins" and illusions. Thus, over time, this Teaching arose, in direct confrontation and consideration of our ordinariness. And, likewise over time, those who considered in this manner came to understand themselves and to act on that understanding.

Thus, in my Teaching Work, which followed on the profound Revelations and Realizations of my personal ordeal of practice, I again surrendered myself to the ordeal of testing this Realization and elaborating its Way. Only after all of that was done did I move to a more solitary and simple phase of life, to exercise the Way as a Radiant Occupation for its own sake, without regard for my further usefulness as a worldly person.

This is my Testimony: Consciousness is the Transcendental Condition or Medium or Matrix of the total self and the total world. And Consciousness is Full. It is not merely within us or defined as ego and point of view. It is Transcendental or Unqualified Being. It is also Universally Radiant, such that all selves, all states of mind or knowledge, and the total phenomenal world arise as apparent modifications of that Self-Radiance. We can simply give ourselves up as mortal attention to the flow of possibilities (or cause-and-effect processes). Or we can understand the body-mind-self as a contraction of the Universal Field of Transcendental or eternally Free Radiance. And the Way of that understanding is not merely the method of inverting back upon the body-mind-self, retreating into inwardness. Rather, the Way is to understand, feel beyond, and transcend the self-contraction of body-mind (appearing as states of knowledge and experience) moment to moment. We cannot successfully turn back upon Consciousness, since it is neither localized within nor object to Itself. Rather, we must understand the self-contracting localization of Consciousness that appears as an inference or result of the fear-contraction of the body-mind. Thus, we must transcend both egoic extroversion and egoic introversion by transcending ego itself, which is not an "entity" but the self-defining activity of the contraction of body-mind in the conventional states of knowledge and experience. The body-mind and its relations are naturally recognized in the Universal Life-Radiance when the self-contraction is transcended. Likewise, in the same equanimity of freedom from the self-contraction and its implications, the Condition of consciousness is tacitly and natively Realized.

In every moment of recognition of self in the Transcendental Identity of Consciousness and of the body-mind and world in Universal Radiance, the local or egoic point of view of attention is transcended. Thus, the Way demonstrates Its Truth in the Radiant Transformation of the body-mind and the world. Realization or Enlightenment is a great "Siddhi" or Divine Power that universalizes the being as Love, the mind as a consciousness that pervades all space-time, the body as a Fullness that Blesses all beings and places, and the world as a transparent Delight or God-Presence.

The Ultimate Revelation or Realization is not merely within us, nor merely outside ourselves. It is both Universal (or All-Pervading) and Transcendental (beyond the conventions of self and world). I will Work eternally to Bless all beings and all domains with this Realized Revelation. Let all others consider this and practice the Way and be magnified into the Siddhi or Work of God.

I Would Find
a New Order
of Men and Women

an essay by Da Free John
1971

I am interested in finding men and women who are free of every kind of seeking, who are attendant only to understanding, and who will devote themselves to the intentional creation of human life in the form and logic of Reality, rather than the form and logic of Narcissus. Such men are the unexploitable Presence of Reality. They will not devote themselves to turning the world to dilemma, exhaustion, and revolutionary experience, nor to the degenerative exploitation of desire and possibility, nor to the ascent to and inclusion of various illusory goals, higher entities, evolutionary aims, or deluded ideas of experiential transformation. They will create in the aesthetics of Reality, turning all things into radical relationship and enjoyment. They will remove the effects of separative existence and restore the Form of things. They will engineer every kind of stability and beauty. They will create a Presence of Peace. Their eye will be on present form and not on exaggerated notions of artifice. Their idea of form is stable and whole, not a gesture toward some other event. They will not make the world seem but a symbol for higher and other things.

They will constantly create the form of Truth while conscious of Present Reality. Thus, they will serve the order of sacrifice and liberated knowledge. They will evolve the necessary and good, and make economic and wise use of all technology. They will not be motivated by invention but by Reality, which is the Presence to be communicated in all forms. They will not pursue any kind of false victory, any fearful deathlessness, or any overwhelming survival for Man. They will only create the conditions for present enjoyment, the communication of Reality, the Form in which transcendental understanding can arise, live, and become the public foundation of existence.

Thus, I would find a new order of men and women, who will create a new age of sanity and joy. It will not be the age of the occult, the religious, the scientific, or the technological domination of humanity. It will be the fundamental age of Real Existence, wherein Life will be radically realized, entirely apart from the whole history of our adventure and great search. The age envisioned by common seekers is a spectacular display that only extends the traditional madness, exploitability, and foolishness of mankind. But I desire a new order of men and women, who will not begin from all of that, but who will apply themselves, apart from all dilemma and all seeking, to the harmonious Event of Real Existence.

APPENDIX
THE SEVEN STAGES OF LIFE

The ultimate import of our human birth is to discover or Realize the Truth of our life. To do so, however, we are required first to observe, understand, and transcend ourselves. Master·Da Free John's "seven stages of life" prove a valuable key to our self-understanding. But before we are able to put his Enlightened scheme to use, we must first enter into the culture of self-transcendence.

We can know or Realize what is only through self-understanding that becomes not merely self-information but self-transcendence. Therefore, we must first become capable (through self-understanding and self-transcendence) of self-submission and free participation in what is prior to our own self-contraction.

I do not merely propose the idea of God, or soul, or Transcendental Being. Such propositions cannot be rightly believed or presumed by the separate and separative ego. Therefore, the ideas of religion that occupy egos and the egoic culture of self-abstracted scientism are themselves false views, representing a poignant and inevitably frustrated longing for love, release, and ultimate Happiness. On the contrary, I propose self-observation, true self-understanding, and perfect self-transcendence. And if the Way of self-transcendence is magnified as the fullness of participatory capability, then what is will be discovered to be Divine, unbound, eternal, Transcendental Happiness.[1]

The model or scheme of the seven stages of life provides a structure whereby we might fully examine and rightly evaluate our spiritual and human growth, as well as the mass of spiritual teaching and experience that presently informs the psyche of today's man and woman. Thus, the seven stages are means for gauging our human and spiritual growth, free of the taboos and prejudices of conventional society that tend to reinforce and even propagate many false views and thus prevent us from Realizing the Truth of our existence.

As is made clear again and again throughout his Teaching, Master Da is a Spirit-Baptizer, one who Transmits the Way, or "Living Current," to prepared aspirants. When the individual consciousness, established in self-understanding, combines with "Grace" or the Power of Spiritual Blessing, the individual is drawn through and beyond the hierarchy of earthly (gross) and cosmic (subtle) illusions or forms of knowledge and experience. Thus, the seven stages of life can be viewed as a spiritual school offering seven lessons about self-transcendence. When we have completed the course of self-observation, self-understanding, and self-transcendence through all the possibilities of the first six stages of life, the Adept, who is the

---

1. Da Free John, *The Dreaded Gom-Boo, or the Imaginary Disease That Religion Seeks to Cure*, p. 93.

458

Master of this school, reveals a hidden "doorway" that grants passage, via sacrifice, beyond all limitations, into the perfect Realization of the Divine Domain.

STAGE 1 *(Years Birth to 7)*

The first stage of life, occupying the years from conception and birth to age seven, is the stage of the human individual's vital-physical adaptation to the world into which he or she is born. In this first stage the being learns "simple" skills like focusing with the eyes, grasping and manipulating objects, walking, talking, assimilating and converting food and breath into energy, controlling bladder and bowels, with only minimal responsibility for thinking conceptually and relating to his fellow beings.

STAGE 2 *(Years 7-14)*

The second stage of life is the stage of the development, integration, and coordination of the emotional-sexual or feeling dimension of the being with the gross physical. The young personality grows in the awareness of himself or herself as a social being, sharing life in an expanded sphere of relations. Just as in the first stage we learn about and become responsible for the assimilation and elimination of elemental food, in the second stage we must likewise learn about, adapt to, and engage a new dimension of sustenance or food. When breathing is combined with feeling and bodily relaxation, we awaken to the Universal Life-Current or Energy that pervades the body and all of life. In the second stage of life we learn to align body, emotion, feeling, and breathing in a functional realization of the disposition of relational sacrifice or love. Thus, we learn to transcend reactive emotion, tendencies toward neurotic inversion, and habits of self-and other-destructiveness.

We should understand that the emotional-sexual growth in the second stage of life is the development of the individual's glandular and hormonal system. "Sexual communion," or the yoga of sexual love, is a responsibility suggested to individuals only when full development, responsibility, and harmony of the first three, or lower vital, stages of life have been accomplished, and the individual is awakened to the feeling dimension of the heart, or the fourth stage of life (described below).

STAGE 3 *(Years 15-21)*

The third stage of life is the stage of the development of the thinking mind and the will and of the integration of the vital-physical, emotional-sexual, and mental-intentional functions. This stage marks the transition to truly human autonomy wherein the first two stages of life are adapted to a practical and analytical intelligence and an informed will or intention and the individual gains responsibility for and control over vital life.

This third stage is not an end in itself, or the completion of potential human growth. Indeed, it only marks the awakening of self-conscious intelligence and a movement toward personal and individualistic survival motives. Man in the third stage of life is not yet truly human. He only brings individual force and form to the vital and elemental experience and world. He tempers and also extends the frenzy of feeding and sexing by submitting these to the processes of the verbal and analytical mind. Man in the third stage of life is characterized by the frenzy of mind, the frenzy of problems and solutions.

The truly human being appears only in the fourth stage of life, wherein the vital, elemental, emotional-sexual, and lower mental functions come into the summary and unifying dominion of the heart, the psyche of the whole bodily being. Such is the awakened moral and spiritual disposition, in which Truth becomes the Principle in consciousness, and higher structural growth becomes the benign, nonproblematic possibility. Thus, the Law in the truly human realm is sacrifice as the individual, whole, and entire human body-mind, through love, founded in prior intuition of the Divine Reality. The human sacrifice is the spiritual practice of love and intuition of the Real under all conditions of experience and higher growth.[2]

STAGE 4

The first three stages may generally be associated with the first twenty-one years of life (three periods of seven years), but the last four (which grow beyond the limits of the grosser elements and functions) may not truly be considered in terms of limits of time, whether brief or long. Each stage develops as a process of adaptation (or readaptation) to a specific, functional point of view relative to the totality of experience.[3]

The fourth stage, and all the later stages, cannot be conceived within fixed periods of time. The duration of the higher stages of life depends entirely upon the individual's qualities and his or her spiritual practice of self-transcendence.[4]

The fourth stage of life marks the beginning of our humanity. In this stage the psychic depth of being is awakened and adapted to profound intimacy with the Spirit or the "Living Current," in Master Da's language, of the "Great One or Divine Reality." This fourth stage is the stage of "free religion" or the stage of "whole bodily surrender and adaptation to the universal Life via Love-Communion (the disposition of the heart or deep psyche of pure energy)."[5]

The realization of the physical, emotional, mental, and moral responsibilities of the first three stages of life provides the necessary foundation for the testing and transformation that inevitably accompany true spiritual life. Without that basis we may come to enjoy yogic and mystical experience, for example, but remain unable to exercise real intelligence, freedom, and love under the most ordinary of human circumstances. If the elementary functions of our bodily, mental, and emotional adaptation to life have not been learned and tested during our first twenty-one years, we linger, egoically bound, in the lesser stages. Inevitably we must submit to the wisdom of self-transcendence.

2. Bubba [Da] Free John, *Love of the Two-Armed Form*, p. 75.

3. Bubba [Da] Free John, *The Enlightenment of the Whole Body*, p. 192.

4. Ibid., p. 186.

5. Da Free John, *Scientific Proof of the Existence of God Will Soon Be Announced by the White House!* p. 155.

However, to mature through and beyond the mechanics of the first three stages of life is not a casual, conventional matter of "growing older and wiser." Rather, the individual's entrance into the fourth stage of life begins with the awakening of the "psychic heart," which is marked by a clear sensitivity to the Life-Current. In this stage, the Divine Presence or Life-Force is felt to exist independent of, or senior to, the body-mind. By cultivating a conscious relationship to this Presence, the spiritual practitioner begins to demonstrate and enjoy the spiritual qualities of faith, love, and surrender. Thus, devotional surrender to the Living Reality is the essential feature of the fourth stage of life. The individual is obliged to persist beyond religious conventions and traditions, as Master Da himself emphasizes, by means of "continuous and concentrated self-devotion via heartfelt feeling-attention to the Ultimate Reality." [6]

STAGE 5

The fifth stage is associated with the mystical aspect of spirituality. The individual's attention is inverted away from the theatre of outer-directed attention to the inner or subjective experiences of the "subtle physiology" of the brain-mind. The mystical ascent through the psychic centers of the body-mind is conditioned by the nervous system. Experience in this stage reaches its peak in the state of "conditional nirvikalpa samadhi," or formless ecstasy. [7] At the apex of the fifth stage, the individual has transcended his or her fascination with mental forms and images. Master Da comments further:

In the fifth stage of life, yogic mysticism raises attention into the extremities of subtle experience—or the heavens of ascended knowledge. But Liberation in God is not Realized at that stage or by such means. In order for the Life-Current to cross the Divide between the body-mind and Infinity, the gesture of attention and the illusion of an independent conscious self must be utterly Dissolved in the true Self.

The highest extreme of the ascent of attention is called "nirvikalpa samadhi," or total Absorption of self-consciousness in Radiant Transcendental Consciousness. But, in fact, the seed of differentiated self remains in such ascended Absorption of attention. Attention is yet extended outside the heart, or the root of self-consciousness, as a gesture toward an independent Object, and, therefore, such "samadhi" is not only temporary, but it remains a form of subject-object Contemplation. [8]

STAGE 6

The sixth stage of life is the profound stage of "ego-death or the transcendence of mind, all sense of 'I,' and primal fear." It marks the transition from the "esoteric

6. Da Free John, *Nirvanasara*, p. 188.

7. In his Teaching Master Da distinguishes between the fifth stage phenomenon of conditional nirvikalpa samadhi (the yogic Self-Realization and the traditional epitome or highest possible reach of the process of yogic absorption of attention in the rising force of the bodily Current of Life) and Translation, or Unconditional Nirvikalpa Samadhi, the ultimate stage of the seventh or God-Realized stage of life.

8. Bubba [Da] Free John, *The Enlightenment of the Whole Body*, pp. 422–23.

meditation" (subject-object Contemplation) of the fifth stage to the transcendence of attention and thus the transcendence of the sense of being a subject (egoic consciousness) over against objects (the world and all relations). It is the Awakening to Transcendental Consciousness. The practice in the sixth stage of life is a deepening of the sense of identification with consciousness prior to attention to objects.

Through the Graceful Transmission of the Spiritual Master, a felt Current of Bliss is awakened at an "unfathomable Space in the right side of the heart." It is at this locus in the right side of the heart that "the Radiant Transcendental Consciousness is continually associated with the impulse of life in the individual body-mind."[9] Master Da refers to this "Space" as the "Location of Happiness," or the doorway to the Divine Domain of Radiant Transcendental Consciousness and the seventh stage of life. As Master Da Free John explains:

The sixth stage is the last of the progressive stages previous to Transcendental Awakening. It is the basic stage in which the transition is made from terrestrial and cosmic conceptions of the Divine or Real Being to conceptions of the Ultimate as the Transcendental Reality and Condition and Identity of all apparent beings and conditions. And the process of self-sacrifice is thus transformed from an effort that serves the development of knowledge and experience in the planes of the psycho-physical personality to a direct effort of utter self-transcendence.[10]

And:

In the sixth stage of life, the body-mind is simply relaxed into the Life-Current, and attention (the root or base of the mind) is inverted away from gross and subtle states and objects of the body-mind, and toward its own Root, the ultimate Root of the ego-self, which is the "Witness" Consciousness (when attention is active) and also simple Consciousness (prior to objects and self-definition). The final result of this is conditional Self-Realization or the intuition of Radiant Transcendental Being via the exclusive self-essence (inverted away from all objects).[11]

STAGE 7

In the seventh stage of life, the liberated "individual" recognizes everything as a modification of the Radiant Transcendental Being. Now the Transcendental Self is no longer pitted against the phenomenal world. Instead, the world is recognized as continuously arising in the Ultimate Being, which is coessential with the Self. This last act of self-sacrifice continues into infinity. Master Da summarizes the seventh stage as follows:

9. Ibid., p. 401.

10. Da Free John, *Nirvanasara*, p. 189.

11. Da Free John, *The Bodily Sacrifice of Attention*, p. 30.

In the seventh stage of life there is native or radical intuitive identification with Radiant Transcendental Being, the Identity of all beings (or subjects) and the Condition of all conditions (or objects). This intuitive identification (or Radical Self-Abiding) is directly Realized, entirely apart from any dissociative act of inversion. And, while so Abiding, if any conditions arise, or if any states of body-mind arise, they are simply recognized in the Radiant Transcendental Being (as transparent or nonbinding modifications of Itself). Such is Sahaj Samadhi, and it is inherently free of any apparent implications, limitations, or binding power of phenomenal conditions. If no conditions arise to the notice, there is simply Radiant Transcendental Being. Such is Bhava Samadhi, about Which nothing sufficient can be said, and there is not Anyone, Anything, or Anywhere beyond It to be Realized.[12]

Master Da's Teaching relative to the seven stages of life often refers to the demonstration or Signs of Whole Bodily Enlightenment—Transfiguration, Transformation, and Translation. Once fully Realized, the seventh stage of life becomes the perpetually Enlightened foundation of existence, even beyond death and in any future lifetimes. The gross body-mind is progressively Transfigured in Divine Radiance, and the subtle or higher mind becomes the vehicle of Transformation, wherein that Radiance manifests extraordinary powers and faculties (such as psychic and healing capacities, genius, longevity, etc.) as spontaneous expressions of Divine Self-Abiding. Ultimately, for periods during this lifetime, this continuous God-Realization leads to Divine Translation, or conversion of the individuated being beyond all phenomenal appearances into the "Divine Domain" of Radiant Life-Consciousness.

The seven stages of life thus mark the natural, or structurally inevitable, evolutionary development of human existence from ordinary egoic birth to the ultimate stages of God-Realization. In the Way of Radical Understanding, which is the Way that Master Da Free John Teaches, the Awakened disposition of the seventh stage is made the foundation of life and spiritual practice through each individual's cultivation of Communion with the Divine via Master Da Free John. Thus, in this Way all growth and evolution are relieved of the dilemmas of un-Happiness, seeking, and the illusions that characterize the first six stages of life when lived apart from the instruction and Transmission of a seventh stage Adept.

12. Ibid., p. 30.

ABOUT MASTER DA FREE JOHN

The Adept Da Free John was born Franklin Albert Jones on the third of November 1939. Until his second or third year, he lived in a world of sheer light and joy—"the Bright"—where he knew no separation from others. He was born, out of an Enlightened Adept's free Choice and Compassion, with the specific Purpose of Instructing spiritually sensitive people of today in the "Way of Life." In order to fulfill this sublime Mission, he had to sacrifice his conscious Oneness with the Transcendental Reality prior to his birth. Even the extraordinary condition of the Bright was necessarily surrendered to allow the individual Franklin Jones to pass through the process of physical, emotional, and mental growth. However, his original Impulse to Guide others to the Realization of the Transcendental Being or Consciousness never ceased to inform his life, which from the beginning was destined for greatness.

Throughout his childhood, the condition of the Bright that he had enjoyed as a baby would reassert itself in the form of uncommon psychic and mystical experiences, as well as physical symptoms such as sudden attacks of fever or skin rashes with no diagnosable medical cause. These signs of an active kundalini (or Life-Current) gradually subsided in his eighth year and did not return until he reached the age of seventeen.

It was in 1960, after a "crisis of despair" with the world he lived in, that the spiritual process spontaneously resumed its transforming activity in full force, blessing him with the experience of "a total revolution of energy and awareness," which yielded two crucial insights. First, he realized that in the absence of all seeking and problem-consciousness, there is only the one Reality or Transcendental Consciousness. Second, he understood that this Reality or Consciousness is Man's true Identity and that all else is only a superimposition of the un-Enlightened mind.

Equipped with these twin insights, Franklin Jones began to immerse himself in a conscious spiritual discipline of acute self-inspection. For almost two years (1962–1964) he sequestered himself, intensely observing the dynamics of the separative self-sense, or ego. This phase was punctuated with numerous psychic experiences, one of which led him into the company of the American-born teacher "Rudi" (Swami Rudrananda), who instructed him in a form of Indian kundalini yoga.

Early in 1967, while studying at the Lutheran seminary he had entered at Rudi's behest, Franklin Jones underwent a "death" experience, restoring him temporarily to the Bliss of Transcendental Being-Consciousness. Again, he emerged with an important insight: that his whole search had been founded on the "avoidance of relationship," on the recoil from Reality in all its countless forms. As his inner attitude to life changed, he also recognized the limitations of Rudi's yoga—a recognition that, in 1968, prompted him to seek out Rudi's own teacher, the late Swami Muktananda. During his brief stay at this renowned yogi's hermitage in India, he had his first adult experience of total absorption in the Transcendental Consciousness. Swami Muktananda acknowledged this unique yogic achievement in a written document, confirming that Franklin Jones had attained "yogic liberation." But, intuiting that the "formless ecstasy" (nirvikalpa samadhi) that he had enjoyed for a moment did not represent the highest form of Realization, Franklin Jones continued to submit himself to the wisdom of the spiritual process that had guided him throughout his life.

His intuition was confirmed on September 10, 1970, when he entered the permanent Condition of Sahaj Samadhi, which is coessential with the Transcendental Being-Consciousness itself. He had "recovered" the Identity that, though never really lost, he had surrendered in order to effect his human birth. Soon after his God-Realization, the Adept was moved to Teach others and Transmit to them the Condition of "the Heart," or the All-Pervading Reality in which everything inheres. But those who came to him in the early days were ill-prepared for his Teaching and Transmission. After nearly three years of "almost muscular" struggle with his students, which weakened his physical body though not his Energy and commitment to their Enlightenment, he undertook a pilgrimage to India.

He not only wanted to clarify his Teaching Work but also purify his relationship to those who, like Swami Muktananda, had been helpful catalysts in his spontaneously unfolding spiritual discipline. It was during that period that he changed his name to "Bubba Free John"—"Bubba" denoting "brother" (his childhood nickname) and "Free John" being a rendering of "Franklin Jones."

Upon his return to America, he began to Teach differently, involving his devotees in an experiment of intense experiencing of both worldly "pleasures" and so-called "spiritual" joys. He gave them the opportunity within the growing community to pursue all their obsessions about money, food, sexuality, and power, as well as conventional religiosity and mystical states. Every single "Teaching demonstration," however abandoned or unconventional, had the sole purpose of showing devotees the futility of all seeking and all types of experience, and that only understanding availed.

Out of this "Teaching theatre" grew not only a profound insight on his part into human psychology, in all its different forms of manifestation, but also a new, more formal Teaching approach. In November 1976, "Bubba" Free John ceased to have frequent intimate contact with his many devotees. In the following three years he lived in relative seclusion, creating much of the "source literature" that now serves the community of practitioners as one of the empowered Agencies of his Teaching.

In the fall of 1979, the Adept dropped the name "Bubba" for the spiritual address "Da," meaning "Giver." Having endowed the community of devotees with all the necessary means for their spiritual maturation, Master Da Free John is now in the "hermitage" phase of his Work where, together with mature practitioners, he lives the simple existence of a free renunciate. His retirement from active Teaching Work and from institutional involvement of any kind is not a mere withdrawal from the body of devotees. On the contrary, his seclusion allows him to concentrate on his real Purpose: to Transmit the Transcendental Condition, unencumbered by any external obligations, and thereby to quicken the spiritual maturation of all practitioners in the different stages of practice, as well as to extend his benign Influence to ever-wider circles of people.

ABOUT THE JOHANNINE DAIST COMMUNION

The spiritual fellowship of practitioners of the Way Taught by Master Da Free John is called THE JOHANNINE DAIST COMMUNION. "Johannine" means "having the character of John," which means "one through whom God is Gracious." "Da" is a title of respect and an indication of spiritual stature and function, meaning "one who Gives or Transmits the Divine Influence and Awakening to living beings."

The Communion has four divisions:

THE LAUGHING MAN INSTITUTE, which is the public education division and the educational and cultural organization for beginning practitioners.

THE FREE COMMUNION CHURCH, which is the educational and cultural organization for maturing practitioners.

THE ADVAITAYANA BUDDHIST ORDER, which is reserved for those in the advanced stages of practice.

THE CRAZY WISDOM FELLOWSHIP, which consists of devotees who have Realized the ultimate stage of practice of the Way.

AN INVITATION

If you would like to know more about the study and practice of the Spiritual Teaching of Master Da Free John or about how to begin to practice the Way, please write:

THE LAUGHING MAN INSTITUTE
P.O. Box 836
San Rafael, California 94915

THE BOOKS OF MASTER DA FREE JOHN

SOURCE TEXTS

THE KNEE OF LISTENING
The Early Life and Radical Spiritual Teachings of
Bubba [Da] Free John
$7.95 paper

THE METHOD OF THE SIDDHAS
Talks with Bubba [Da] Free John on the Spiritual Technique of the
Saviors of Mankind
$8.95 paper

THE HYMN OF THE MASTER
A Confessional Recitation on the Mystery of the Spiritual Master based on
the principal verses of the Guru Gita *(freely selected, rendered, and*
adapted)
$8.95 paper

THE FOUR FUNDAMENTAL QUESTIONS
Talks and essays about human experience and the actual practice of an
Enlightened Way of Life
$1.95 paper

THE LIBERATOR (ELEUTHERIOS)
A summation of the radical process of Enlightenment, or God-Realization,
taught by the "Western Adept," Master Da Free John
$12.95 cloth, $6.95 paper

THE ENLIGHTENMENT OF THE WHOLE BODY
A Rational and New Prophetic Revelation of the Truth of Religion,
Esoteric Spirituality, and the Divine Destiny of Man
$14.95 paper

SCIENTIFIC PROOF OF THE EXISTENCE OF GOD
WILL SOON BE ANNOUNCED BY THE
WHITE HOUSE!
Prophetic Wisdom about the Myths and Idols of mass culture and popular
religious cultism, the new priesthood of scientific and political materialism,
and the secrets of Enlightenment hidden in the body of Man
$12.95 paper

THE PARADOX OF INSTRUCTION
An Introduction to the Esoteric Spiritual Teaching of Bubba [Da] Free
John
$14.95 cloth, $8.95 paper

NIRVANASARA
Radical Transcendentalism and the Introduction of Advaitayana Buddhism
$9.95 paper

INSPIRATIONAL AND DEVOTIONAL TEXTS

CRAZY DA MUST SING, INCLINED TO HIS
WEAKER SIDE
Confessional Poems of Liberation and Love
$6.95 paper

FOREHEAD, BREATH, AND SMILE
An Anthology of Devotional Readings from the Spiritual Teaching of Master Da Free John
$20.95 cloth

OPEN EYES
A Tribute to Master Da Free John on the Tenth Commemorative Celebration of the World-Proclamation of the Way of Radical Understanding
$44.95 cloth, $25.00 paper

REMEMBRANCE OF THE DIVINE NAMES OF DA
One Hundred Eight Names of the Divine Reality and the Radiant Adept Master Da Free John
by Georg and Pat Feuerstein
$4.95 paper

GOD IS NOT A GENTLEMAN AND I AM THAT ONE
Ecstatic Talks on Conventional Foolishness versus the Crazy Wisdom of God-Realization
$6.95 paper

MANUALS OF PRACTICE

THE FIRE GOSPEL
Essays and Talks on Spiritual Baptism
$8.95 paper

COMPULSORY DANCING
Talks and Essays on the spiritual and evolutionary necessity of emotional surrender to the Life-Principle
$3.95 paper

THE ADEPT
Selections from Talks and Essays by Da Free John on the Nature and Function of the Enlightened Teacher
$4.95 paper

THE WAY THAT I TEACH
Talks on the Intuition of Eternal Life
$14.95 cloth, $9.95 paper

THE YOGA OF CONSIDERATION
AND THE WAY THAT I TEACH
Talks and Essays on the distinction between preliminary practices and the radical Way of prior Enlightenment
$7.95 paper

THE DREADED GOM–BOO, OR THE IMAGINARY DISEASE
THAT RELIGION SEEKS TO CURE
A Collection of Essays and Talks on the "Direct" Process of Enlightenment Taught by Master Da Free John
$9.95 paper

BODILY WORSHIP OF THE LIVING GOD
The Esoteric Practice of Prayer Taught by Da Free John
$10.95 paper

THE BODILY SACRIFICE OF ATTENTION
Introductory Talks on Radical Understanding and the Life of Divine Ignorance
$10.95 paper

"I" IS THE BODY OF LIFE
Talks and Essays on the Art and Science of Equanimity and the Self-Transcending Process of Radical Understanding
$10.95 paper

THE BODILY LOCATION OF HAPPINESS
On the Incarnation of the Divine Person and the Transmission of Love-Bliss
$8.95 paper

THE GOD IN EVERY BODY BOOK
Talks and Essays on God-Realization
$3.95 paper

LOOK AT THE SUNLIGHT ON THE WATER
Educating Children for a Life of Self-Transcending Love and Happiness
$7.95 paper

ENLIGHTENMENT AND THE TRANSFORMATION OF MAN
Selections from Talks and Essays on the Spiritual Process and God-Realization
$7.95 paper

WHAT IS THE CONSCIOUS PROCESS?
Talks and essays on the tacit intuition of Transcendental Consciousness, being a summary consideration of the Way of Radical Understanding or Divine Ignorance
$8.95 paper

DO YOU KNOW WHAT ANYTHING IS?
Talks and Essays on Divine Ignorance
$6.95 paper

PRACTICAL TEXTS

EASY DEATH
Talks and Essays on the Inherent and Ultimate Transcendence of Death and Everything Else
$10.95 paper

CONSCIOUS EXERCISE AND THE TRANSCENDENTAL SUN
The principle of love applied to exercise and the method of common physical action. A science of whole body wisdom, or true emotion, intended most especially for those engaged in religious or spiritual life.
$10.95 cloth, $8.95 paper

THE EATING GORILLA COMES IN PEACE
The Transcendental Principle of Life Applied to Diet and the Regenerative Discipline of True Health
$12.95 paper

RAW GORILLA
The Principles of Regenerative Raw Diet Applied in True Spiritual Practice
$3.95 paper

LOVE OF THE TWO-ARMED FORM
The Free and Regenerative Function of Sexuality in Ordinary Life, and the Transcendence of Sexuality in True Religious or Spiritual Practice
$12.95 paper

PAMPHLETS

THE TRANSCENDENCE OF EGO AND EGOIC SOCIETY
$1.50 paper

A CALL FOR THE RADICAL REFORMATION OF CHRISTIANITY
$2.00 paper

FOR CHILDREN

WHAT TO REMEMBER TO BE HAPPY
A Spiritual Way of Life for Your First Fourteen Years or So
$3.95 paper

I AM HAPPINESS
A Rendering for Children of the Spiritual Adventure of Master Da Free John
Adapted by Daji Bodha and Lynne Closser from
The Knee of Listening *by Da Free John*
$8.95 paper

PERIODICALS

CRAZY WISDOM
The Monthly Journal of The Johannine Daist Communion
12 copies $48.00

THE LAUGHING MAN
The Alternative to Scientific Materialism and Religious Provincialism
4 copies (quarterly) $14.00

CASSETTE TAPES

The recorded talks of Master Da Free John (each $9.95):

UNDERSTANDING

THE FOUNDATION AND THE SOURCE

THE YOGA OF CONSIDERATION AND THE WAY THAT I TEACH

THE BODILY LOCATION OF HAPPINESS

THE TRANSCENDENCE OF FAMILIARITY

A BIRTHDAY MESSAGE FROM JESUS AND ME

THE PRESUMPTION OF BEING

THE GOSPEL OF THE SIDDHAS

THE COSMIC MANDALA

THE ULTIMATE WISDOM OF THE PERFECT PRACTICE

PURIFY YOURSELF WITH HAPPINESS

THE ASANA OF SCIENCE

FREEDOM IS IN THE EXISTENCE PLACE

DEATH IS NOT YOUR CONCERN and THE RITUAL OF SORROW

WHAT IS THE CONSCIOUS PROCESS?

FEELING WITHOUT LIMITATION

CHILDREN MUST BE LIBERATED

THE BRIDGE TO GOD

Other cassette tapes:

CRAZY DA MUST SING, INCLINED TO HIS WEAKER SIDE
Da Free John reads his Confessional Poems of Liberation and Love
$9.95 cassette

DA BELLS
Tibetan "singing bowls" played by Da Free John
$8.95 cassette

HEAR MY BREATHING HEART
Songs of Invocation and Praise Inspired by the Teaching and Presence of Da Free John by The First Amendment Choir
$8.95 Dolby stereo

TRUTH IS THE ONLY PROFOUND
Devotional readings from the Teaching of Da Free John set to a background of devotional music and songs
$9.95 cassette

THIS IS THE HEART'S CONFESSION
Devotional singing by students of the Way Taught by the Western Spiritual Adept, Da Free John
$9.95 cassette

THE HYMN OF THE MASTER
A confessional recitation of Da Free John's The Hymn of the Master *by a devotee*
$7.95 cassette

VIDEOTAPES

THE BODILY LOCATION OF HAPPINESS
A consideration by Da Free John
$108, 56 minutes, VHS format

THE FIRE MUST HAVE ITS WAY
A consideration by Da Free John
$108, 57 minutes, VHS format

CLASSIC SPIRITUAL LITERATURE

THE SECRET GOSPEL
The Discovery and Interpretation of the Secret Gospel According to Mark
by Morton Smith
$7.95 paper

LONG PILGRIMAGE
The Life and Teaching of The Shivapuri Baba
by John G. Bennett
$7.95 paper

THE DIVINE MADMAN
The Sublime Life and Songs of Drukpa Kunley
translated by Keith Dowman
$7.95 paper

THE YOGA OF LIGHT
The Classic Esoteric Handbook of Kundalini Yoga
by Hans-Ulrich Rieker,
translated by Elsy Becherer
$7.95 paper

A NEW APPROACH TO BUDDHISM
by Dhiravamsa
$3.95 paper

VEDANTA AND CHRISTIAN FAITH
by Bede Griffiths
$3.95 paper

FOUNDING THE LIFE DIVINE
by Morwenna Donnelly
$7.95 paper

BREATH, SLEEP, THE HEART, AND LIFE
The Revolutionary Health Yoga of Pundit Acharya
$7.95 paper

THE SPIRITUAL INSTRUCTIONS OF SAINT SERAPHIM OF SAROV
edited and with an introduction by Da Free John
$3.95 paper

THE SONG OF THE SELF SUPREME
Aṣṭāvakra Gītā
Preface by Da Free John
translated by Radhakamal Mukerjee
$9.95 paper

SELF-REALIZATION OF NOBLE WISDOM
The Lankavatara Sutra
compiled by Dwight Goddard on the basis of D. T. Suzuki's rendering
from the Sanskrit and Chinese
$7.95 paper

These books and tapes are available at fine bookstores or by mail order from:

THE DAWN HORSE BOOK DEPOT
P.O. Box 3680, Dept. TD
Clearlake, CA 95422

Add $1.25 for the first book or tape and $.35 for each additional book or tape. California residents add 6% sales tax.

INDEX

Chit Shakti, 332
Christ, 351f.,° 365ff. *See also* Jesus
Christianity, 44, 358, 361, 377
  revivalist sects of, 41
  and science, 40, 90
city, 229, 233, 244
Coleridge, S. T., 44
Columbia College, 309f.
combustion, spontaneous, 434
common sense, 300ff., 310f.
communication, 154, 282
Communion, spiritual, 96f., 143, 243, 348, 370, 375, 383, 420f.
community, 115, 300
  sacred, 185f., 371, 449
  scientific, 50f., 64, 130
concentration, yogic, 130
Condition, Transcendental, 16ff., 20ff., 24, 81, 83, 118, 127, 169, 171, 199, 214, 290, 292f., 325, 368f., 451. *See also* Reality, Consciousness
conflict, 133, 155, 329
  and ego, 119, 123
Consciousness, Transcendental, 173, 201, 298ff., 324f., 331ff., 364, 398f., 438f., 440ff., 450f. *See also* Reality, Condition
  and consciousness, 202f.
  and Nature, 265
  and feeling-attention, 22
consciousness
  as self-consciousness, 60
  magical, 219, 235
  and self-program, 22ff., 373ff.
  transformation of, 153
  crisis of, 15
  and Reality, 20, 253
  and matter, 110, 192, 283
  and quantum mechanics, 201
  and science, 84, 256
control, 117f., 163, 165ff., 170, 230, 268, 329. *See also* power
  and science, 77, 255
Conze, E., 197f.
cooperation, conscious, 13, 124, 138, 370
  political, 122
  interspecies, 265ff.
Cosmic Mandala, 193ff.
cosmology, 261, 350, 360, 427. *See also* Nature, universe, reality
  Hindu, 257
cosmos, and spirit-entities, 31, 319. *See also* world, universe, existence

counterculture, 44
craving, 118, 372, 402. *See also* seeking
Creator, 32f., 377, 395f., 418ff., 442. *See also* God
crisis, modern, 13ff., 18f., 28, 39f., 113, 191
criticism, and tolerance, 30
cultism, exoteric, 29
cults, 154
culture, magical, 231ff.

Darwin, C., 36
death, 60, 136, 140ff., 243, 261, 268, 270f., 373
  culture of, 39
  and meditation, 311, 383
deer, magical significance of, 225ff., 234
Democritus, 36
depression, of Life, 17
Descartes, R., 32, 36, 191
design science, 18, 28
desperation, quiet, 372. *See also* suffering
destructiveness
  of ego, 118, 155
  of science, 84, 114, 151ff.
  of Western Man, 128f., 132f.
  of mankind, 153
dharma, 237
dimension, etheric, 204, 314ff., 319ff.
  psychic or subtle, 313f., 317, 347, 441
  astral, 204, 316, 319ff.
dimensions, of existence, 85f., 91, 362f., 413ff., 441. *See also* reality, existence, Nature
Dirac, P. A., 191
disarmament, 120f.
discipline, of Man, 98
discomfort, 44, 145ff., 406, 409
discoveries, scientific, 150f., 158, 362, 365, 420
  resistance to, 49
dissociation, mood of, 128f., 133f., 196. *See also* participation
  from Truth, 137
divination, 40
doubt, 44, 55, 66, 113, 115, 128, 145ff., 219, 243, 270f., 380, 387, 419, 426, 440, 452
Dreaded Gom-Boo, 169, 178
dream therapy, 318
dreams, 207f., 228, 273, 276, 282f., 292, 318ff., 432f.
  premonitory, 285ff.